Agency
Its Role in Mental Development

James Russell
Department of Experimental Psychology
Cambridge, UK

Erlbaum (UK) Taylor & Francis

Erlbaum (UK) Taylor & Francis Ltd., Publishers
27 Church Road
Hove
East Sussex, BN3 2FA
UK

British Library Cataloguing in Publication Data

A catalogue record for this book is available from the British Library

ISBN 0-86377-228-5

Cover design by Peter Richards
Printed and bound by Redwood Books, Wiltshire

For Sally

Contents

Acknowledgements

This book has had a very long gestation. In fact it was nearly 30 years ago that I first encountered Kant's distinction between self-generated (reversible) and world-generated (irreversible) perceptual sequences— at about the same time that I was beginning to read Piaget. Despite Piaget's characterisation of Kant as a nativist, it seemed to me that this distinction was really the pivot on which the whole Piagetian system of ideas turned. What agency gives the developing individual—I thought then and more or less think now—is immediate knowledge of how his or her experiences are constrained to be. If a creature can reverse some of its perceptual sequences at will it is forced to acknowledge how the world prevents it from reversing other sequences, a process that must lie at the thin end of the wedge that splits world from self. This view made guest appearances in my previous two books and in one or two articles, but it was never examined: it just seemed such a blinding truth as to need no supporting arguments.

Two things saved me from this. The first saviour was local. In 1988 King's College inaugurated the four-year, interdisciplinary Spatial Representation Project—the brain-child of a research fellow at Kings, Naomi Eilan. The project was inspired in part by the writings of the philosopher Gareth Evans who, before his tragically early death, had been doing neo-Kantian work on the relationship between spatial concepts, referential thought, agency, and consciousness. Well, I only had to attend one or two of the King's seminars to find out that my article of faith would either have to be defended properly or abandoned; and so after the long gestation came the difficult birth. The second saviour was not remotely local: it was the fact that questions about the child's developing "theory of mind" had by this time moved to the top of the research agenda. If indeed agency has the constitutive role in the development of self-awareness that I had been assuming for it, then it was about time I spelt out the implications for "theory of mind" development.

I have been tremendously lucky in my readers. José Bermúdez's rigorous but positive report on the first complete draft was as long as an article, and he continued to save me from howlers as later drafts emerged. Jane Heal's report was similarly encouraging and helpful, and the influence of her own work will be obvious in the text. Despite the manuscript arriving when he was undergoing a move from Sussex to Salzburg, Josef Perner found time to smother the text with useful and generous-minded comments. Norman Freeman's detailed notes suggested new things to read and showed me how much harder I was going to have to work to marry the philosophical claims to the developmental ones. Suzanne Hala read most of the book as I was writing it and continued to provide advice through subsequent drafts, ranging from where to put a comma to where to restrain myself. I am grateful to her for this and for much else. Thanks are due to Al Lumb for giving a postgraduate perspective on the book and to my daughter Charlotte Russell for giving me an undergraduate perspective on it.

It would be impossible to acknowledge all those who in discussing with me the book's central thesis helped to toughen up its arguments. Certainly the most memorable encounters were with Tony Marcel and José Bermúdez.

A number of people contributed expert advice on particular sections—my wife Sally Barrett-Williams, Jon Driver, Ian McLaren, and Chris Jarrold. Thanks are due to them and additionally to Chris for three years of enjoyable research collaboration. The research reported in Part 3 was done with support from the Economic and Social Research Council, from the Grindley Fund (Faculty of Biology, Cambridge) and from the Wellcome Trust. Bill Brewer read the portions of the book dealing with his own work and took time to discuss them. It will be evident that the line is fairly thinly drawn there between my being influenced by his work and my plundering it.

The main body of this book was written in a sabbatical year. I am grateful to Usha Goswami for covering some of my teaching and to Nick Mackintosh to agreeing to the sabbatical at short notice.

J.R.

Cambridge, May, 1995

PART 1

Symbols, models, and connections

Setting the scene

While, in the last 10 years or so[1], the mainstream of cognitive developmental research has been flowing inexorably towards a sea of questions about children's "theory of mind", philosophers and developmental psychologists have often found themselves travelling in the same boat. It is fair to say though that the boat has been a narrow one—at least in philosophical terms.

We have been taken up with questions about the status of folk psychology, with the tensions between "simulation" and the "theory-theory", and we have accordingly not moved far beyond the game of "hunt the theory"—Is it like a scientific theory? Can we call it a "theory" at all? What is the One True Theory of meta-representation? And this has led us to neglect philosophical work with a different and more direct kind of relevance, where the concern is with *how it is possible at all* that we should be minds set apart from a physical world. Here questions are asked about the "pre-theoretical mind", questions that can be answered without prejudice to how development actually happens; although how we answer them will surely constrain (to put it mildly) empirical accounts of how it does actually happen. They are questions about how our cognitive capacities have to be grounded—questions about what is necessary for adequate mental development.

What I am calling "how-is-it-possible" questions require for their answers what are called (after Kant) "transcendental" arguments, and they take this form: we know X (or believe Y or have the capacity to do Z) and this would not be possible for us unless our experience had form F; therefore our experience has form F. It is the kind of a priori theorising in which the founding fathers of cognitive developmental psychology often engaged. Most notably, James Mark Baldwin drifted elegantly but confusingly between the transcendental and the empirical, and coined the phrase "genetic epistemology" to describe his programme (Russell, 1978, for a précis of his major work); and Jean Piaget borrowed Baldwin's phrase.

Although Piaget was a far more focused and scientific thinker than Baldwin, the transcendental and the empirical strands in his work are nearly as hard to disentangle. Piaget collected observations and devised tasks, but it is obvious to the reader that nothing in a child's behaviour or judgement would be allowed to undermine his fundamental assumptions—that thinking is a form of action; that thought is adaptive and adequate only insofar as it is "structured"; that learning occurs through the tension between "assimilation" and "accommodation". And lying at the heart of these assumptions was the following transcendental inference: we know X (e.g. what constitutes a rational inference) and we would not know this unless our experience were structured by our agency; therefore our experience must be structured by our agency.

My main aim in this book is to present the case for a version of Piaget's transcendental inference, and to show how this both illuminates empirical work and inspires new hypotheses. The form in which I present it—it is more Piaget-flavoured than Piagetian and so I'll write it with a small "p"—is this: "We have a conception of the external world and a conception of our own and others' minds; we would not have these conceptions unless we *experienced our own agency* and did so in a particular way; therefore adequate mental development depends on adequate, early agency." In Part 2, I discuss knowledge of objects and in Part 3 knowledge of minds; and right now I need to say a few words about how Part 1 will be located relative to these.

Part 1 is essentially an attempt at clearing away some ground in order to allow my piagetian thesis a proper run for its money, by which I mean clearing the ground of developmental meta-theories that would appear to marginalise the piagetian one. My first target will be Jerry Fodor's (1976) "language of thought" (LOT) doctrine. If Fodor's arguments about the necessity for LOT are correct, then a form of nativism is forced on us, and this would seem to foreclose options on the piagetian view. There are a number of reasons why this is so and the easiest to state concisely is that nativism of this kind would have us regard agency as an innate, formal computational module rather than as the exercise of a capacity for first-person experience. [In fact Alan Leslie (in press) has recently

LIKE AUTOMATON ?

1. NATIVISM = THE VIEW THAT PERCEPTION IS INDEPENDENT OF EXPERIENCE

2. GENETIC INHERITANCE INFLUENCES ACQUIRED (NORMAL) EXPERIENCES

gone down the Fodorian road and posited the "theory of body mechanism".] Accordingly, I spend some time presenting a case against the LOT thesis.

The second representational theory to be discussed is one that leads us to regard development as the process through which the child's thought becomes progressively more adequate as his or her mental representations become progressively more *structurally isomorphic* to that which they represent. This is "mental models" theory; and I have some sceptical remarks to make about it both as a theory of cognition and as a developmental theory.

The third kind of theory is one that *on the surface at least* looks essentially empiricist and associationist—connectionism. What I do here is to argue that, whatever shortcomings connectionism may or may not have in other areas, it is the computational theory best placed to model agency. Connectionist models will be discussed towards the end of Part 1 and they will also crop up in the final sections of Parts 2 and 3, because, in common with certain other developmental psychologists with a Piagetian cast of mind (e.g. Bates & Elman, 1993) I am an enthusiast for this approach and see connectionist models as providing existence-proofs that certain kinds of learning, and therefore certain modes of development, are possible in principle.

What is the "status" of a book like this? Surely a thesis that is neither squarely philosophical nor squarely empirical is bound to be incoherent on some level? It certainly can be, and philosophers have complained with justification about such incoherence in Piaget's own work (e.g. Hamlyn, 1978). All I will say is that I try to be clear about when my claims can be overturned by an argument or by an experiment.

Why be sceptical about "purely representational" theories?

As I said, in the main body of this book I shall be arguing that only agents can develop a conception of the external world and a conception of mind—that the exercise of agency is a *necessary condition* for what we call in developmental psychology "object permanence" and a "theory of mind". And by "agency" I shall mean *the ability to alter at will one's perceptual inputs*—motorically or attentionally. Although this claim sounds a grand one, it is almost modest; perhaps not as modest as the claim that *breathing* is a necessary condition for human cognitive development, but certainly more interesting.

Why exactly do the three metatheories of development just described (LOT, mental models, connectionism) impede such a view? They do so insofar as they all, in different ways and with different places of emphasis, take agency to be derivative of the primary mental function which is that of *representing* reality. All three assume that what must happen in mental development is the mind coming to be in the right representational state. These adequate representations will, of course, "cause" appropriate actions, and the theories will refer, in their different ways, to "operations" which have to be performed on these representations; but agency, as I have just described it, has nothing essential to do: *it is a power conferred on the organism by adequately structured representations.*

It would certainly be crazy to try to do cognitive and developmental psychology without concerning oneself with mental representation; this was the "Behaviourist" programme for cognition, and that failed entirely. *Of course* cognition involves representation and *of course* representations develop, and a theory of development that was concerned exclusively with how children come to control their behaviour and their mental states (never saying what these consisted in) would be absurd. And remember that I will be arguing that the third of these representational theories (connectionism) has the conceptual resources to model the sub-personal[2] conditions for agency; I will attempt to show how it exercises them. That said, I do have objections to make to the *imperialistic* nature of these three theories, to their assumption that cognition just is (1) the manipulation of mental symbols, or (2) the construction of mental models, or (3) the achievement of the target input–output mapping in neural networks. My arguments will be directed against these ambitions.

Before coming to the first of these representational theories—LOT—I will make a few general remarks about the role of representation in thought.

It is clear that thoughts function as a medium for representing actual and possible states of affairs. Indeed we can only understand intelligent actions on the assumption that they are driven by representations of the environment not, in a stimulus–response or "direct" fashion, by the environment itself. We behave, that is, on the basis of how we, rightly or wrongly, take reality to be—on the basis of our representations of it.

That said, it cannot be true that the representational phenomena of which we are aware when we think (phenomena such as mental images and sub-vocal sentences) actually *constitute* thinking. And so the view that, say, identifies thinking there are green apples with having a mental image of green apples, and that identifies the thought that green apples are bad for the digestion with having a sentence to that effect come into consciousness is unacceptable for at least two reasons. In the first place, thinking of this kind involves *belief*, and believing is more than representing: beliefs must involve a *commitment to the truth of one's mental representation.* And, without assuming this commitment, it is impossible to understand the link between belief and action: we act on the basis of our beliefs, even if they are false. It is not at all clear, then, how having a mental image or entertaining a mental sentence can capture the fact of commitment to truth, and attempts to explain belief in terms of the inherent character of the representational elements are doomed. David Hume, for example, who held more or less that the representational elements ("impressions") are similar to mental images, argued that a believed impression has greater "force and vivacity" than one that is not believed; but he could give no reason why the fact of a mental-image-like mental episode's being forceful and vivid should lead us to believe something (what?) about that which is being represented before the mind's eye. A Humean is even more stretched to explain the differences between the varieties of mental orientation to what is represented (e.g. hoping, expecting, desiring "that X"—see following paragraphs) in terms of degrees and kinds of "force and vivacity".

But what about the images and verbalised thoughts that pop unbidden into our minds without *any* commitment to their truth; and what about our idle fantasies? Granted, not all mental episodes are believed, but we can only make sense of such episodes insofar as they can be set against cases where the thinker is also a believer. There can only be disbelieved and unwanted thoughts against a background of thoughts that are believed and willed.

The point is, then, that, although the so-called content of a thought (i.e. the proposition "... that X") can be regarded as a representation, the attitude of belief (or disbelief or indifference) cannot plausibly be regarded in that way. Belief is called a "propositional attitude" by philosophers; and of course there are many other varieties of them. We can hope that, wish that, fear that, expect that, pretend that, have a sneaking suspicion that, and so on. In what sense are these attitudes "representations" *of* anything?

The first impediment, then, to the view that thoughts are nothing more than representations of reality or of possible realities is that it is not at all clear how one can regard the thinker's propositional attitudes—some philosophers refer to these as forms of *relation* between the thinker and the content—to these representations as themselves *being* representations.

The second problem with saying that mental images and sub-vocal sentences are equivalent to thoughts is a rather more familiar one, and one that raises what is sometimes called "the homunculus problem". If thinking of an apple is having a mental image of an apple, and if thinking that unripe apples are bad for the digestion is having the mental sentence "Apples are bad for the digestion" in our mind's ear, then what is to prevent us, in the first case from interpreting that mental picture as a picture of a smooth, green orange and, in the second case, interpreting the sentence as the first line of a joke rather than as a sincere belief? In other words, any picture, any sentence—any table, or formula, or map—indeed anything with a remotely representational status *stands in need of interpretation*[3]. How is this interpretation to be fixed as being such-and-such? You might say by some mental system further downstream which unpacks it, analyses it, and treats it as grist to some interpretative machinery. But this is no help to us if we want to be thoroughly representational about thought. The problem also occurs in theories of perception. What is seeing an apple? Is it like having a picture of an apple somewhere in the brain? If it is, then we need a little person in the brain—an homunculus—to look at this mental picture, and he will in turn need another homunculus in his brain to look at that picture, and so on and so on. The problem concerns, then, how we might give a thoroughly representational account of thinking if all we have to conjure with are representations. Doesn't the representing have to stop somewhere?

With these questions in mind, we can now turn to the LOT doctrine. As you will see, its main selling-point is that it offers a solution to the homunculus problem.

1.1: SYMBOL PROCESSING AND "THE LANGUAGE OF THOUGHT"

J. A. Fodor (1976) pointed out that there are languages that do not require further interpretation but which support processes with a mental character, namely, the languages used by digital computers. If so, we would seem to have a kind of existence-proof that the homunculus problem can be avoided; for here are systems that perform mental functions using only symbols and rules, and whose representational devices do not have to be interpreted by some homunculus-like entity downstream.

The programming languages of a computer (e.g. Lisp, Prolog, C), Fodor argued, require interpretation only in the technical sense that they have to be translated ("compiled") into another language for the computer to run the program. However the language into which they are translated—the "machine code"—does not itself require an interpretation, rather, *it causes the machine to function*. The claim is then made that any system that performs cognitive operations requires a language in which to perform them, insofar as any system must compute over representations. Fodor calls this the "language of thought" (LOT), a language, of similar status to a machine code, that causes the cognitive wheels to turn.

How does this deal with the problem, raised earlier, about the non-representational nature of the propositional attitudes? We can say that within LOT different sentences have different locations (metaphorically speaking) within the computing system; some end up in a "belief box", some in an "intention box", some in the "desire box", and so forth (Fodor, 1987). The "location" of a mental sentence will determine its causal role and thus its links to action. For example, we act on what we believe to be true and try to make our wishes come true whenever possible; and what enables us to do this is the geography of our mental sentences.

What would Fodorians reply to those who say that "causing a mental system to function" is one thing but "thinking", as we take it to be in our folk psychology, is quite another? They would say that this objection merely shows that the objector is in the grip of a dualist prejudice—a prejudice against any account of thinking "as we take it to be" being presented at a sub-personal level (at the mechanistic level of causally interacting symbols, in this case). Folk psychology cannot emerge from nowhere: there can be no folk psychology in creatures that lack the *representational format* for it. Indeed Fodor (1987) goes further and says that the categories of LOT must map onto the categories of folk psychology, taking, thereby, a "realist" view of folk-psychological notions such as "intention" and "belief", taking these to refer to *sui generis* computational states.

But, putting to one side the question of whether or not there is a close fit between LOT and everyday cognition, it is important to recognise LOT as a species of *functionalism*, with functionalism being one of the main alternatives to mind–body dualism. On functionalism, a mental state comes to be the state it is because of the three kinds of causal relation into which it enters: (1) its causation by perceptual inputs; (2) its causation of motor outputs; (3) its causal interplay with other states.

1.1(i) The slippery slope from LOT to strong nativism

Fodor (1976) was very explicit about LOT's consequences for cognitive developmental psychology. Here is the argument.

Natural language symbols are learned. But a moment's reflection tells us that symbols in LOT cannot be learned. The reason is that in the case of natural language a symbol—"dog" for example—is a sign that the developing child learns; whereas in LOT the symbol (let's call it) DOG is *the representational atom that supports the capacity to think of dogs*. Imagine somebody who was unable to think of dogs—whose mental system lacked the symbol DOG. It is clear that this person is never going to be able to acquire the dog-thinking capacity, because lacking the capacity to think X just means being unable to learn to think

X. Therefore, if there is LOT then there is a sense in which all our concepts are innate.

On the LOT thesis, then, there can be no learning in the strong sense of the acquisition of novel concepts through organism–environment interaction; there cannot be learning that is more than (a) the recombination of mental symbols which we innately possess or (b) the discovery of which sentences in the innate LOT are true and which are false of the world as it is presented to us. The pool of symbols, of sentences and of operations on them, must be finite, and so there can be no sense in which a child may lack a concept at time t_1 and possess it at time t_2. We might witness dramatic new acquisitions or even across-the-board cognitive revolutions, but these can only occur through the maturation of our innate symbolic system. At one level, this is a harmless, almost tautologous, claim: we cannot learn something without the capacity to learn it. But Fodor is saying more than this, by virtue of having a very distinctive view of what a "capacity" amounts to. He is indeed saying that all concepts are innate (Fodor, 1976, pp. 95–97); this is not just a slogan *pour épater les empiricistes*.

All learning is hypothesis-testing, argues Fodor; the only way to represent an hypothesis is in a symbolic system; therefore all hypotheses are represented as innate symbolic structures; and therefore all concepts are innate. The child eventually learns—taking Fodor's own example—that the term "chair" refers to a portable seat for one, and so the claim must be that the learning was only possible because of environmental confirmation of that hypothesis and disconfirmation of others. One of these innate hypotheses may have been that the word means "thing for wedging doors open with", and each of the symbols in this hypothesis ("thing", "wedging" ...) would itself have been acquired through similar processes of hypothesis-testing.

Fodor certainly has his supporters within the cognitive developmental community. One is Alan Leslie who refers to PRETEND as a symbol in the language of thought (Leslie, 1988), the existence of which is supposed to explain the maturation of the capacity for pretence during the second year of life. Another is Frank Keil (e.g. 1987) who argues, in effect, that the last few years of cognitive developmental research have taught us the clear lesson that development is not a matter of extracting information from the environment but of applying "proto-theories" to data. These theories are abstract and relational and can only be innate.

Now although there may be good reasons for being a nativist about human concepts, I do not think that Fodor's arguments force nativism upon us. Fodor's inference from the existence of LOT to nativism about concepts may well be secure, but if the very foundations on which the

LOT thesis rests can be shown to be shaky then we can escape commitment to this radical nativism. And recall *why* the existence of such an escape-route must comfort the supporter of my piagetian thesis. This book's thesis is that the development of our conceptions of objects and of minds depends on a certain kind of organism–environment interaction—a form of interaction in which the subject exercises agency, with "agency" meaning the ability to alter at will the perceptual inputs. If this is so then there can only be a rather weak sense in which our object- and mind-concepts are "innate", and certainly no sense at all in which these concepts depend on a symbolic representational format existing prior to experience: their development cannot be a matter of learning which sentences in our innate LOT are true. (There is, in fact, a more subtle and difficult-to-state reason why Fodor's programme would seem to undermine the piagetian thesis—it concerns the relative primacy of beliefs as against representational contents—but we shall get on to this a little later.)

Before coming to my case against LOT it is necessary to point out that the attack will be on a limited front, simply because this is all that is necessary for us to side-step the slippery slope from LOT to nativism. My case will be directed entirely against the notion of a *mental symbol* and will be agnostic about the notion of a *mental syntax*.

Let us briefly consider what mental syntax means. Thought— *mature human thought* at least—possesses something normally referred to as "systematicity", by which is intended the fact that ascribing the ability to think one kind of thought to a person must entail the ascription to that person of other, structurally related thoughts. For example, that people who can think "John likes beer" and "Mary likes whiskey" entails that they can also think "Mary likes beer" and "John likes whiskey". Thus, thinkers use combinatorial rules not unlike those that operate in natural languages; indeed it is difficult to avoid the idea that thoughts, like sentences, have an hierarchical, tree-like structure. Positing LOT explains this capacity at a stroke, and indeed supporters of LOT field the existence of systematic mental capacities as the primary reason for denying that the representational format for human thought could be sub-symbolic (Fodor & Pylyshyn, 1988). I shall have something to say about the systematicity issue in the sections of Part 1 in which I discuss connectionism, but in presenting my case against LOT I will ignore it.

But *can* one ignore the systematicity issue, when positing a mental syntax would appear to depend on positing symbols in which that syntax is expressed? One certainly can, because the representational elements of syntactic rules refer to nothing in the world and acquire their nature *entirely* from the formal roles they play in relation to other such elements. Thus a "noun" is defined in terms of the role it plays in sentences relative to other elements such as "verb", "adjective", and so forth. Nouns often refer to things and verbs often refer to actions but many nouns are *not* thing-words and many verbs are *not* action-words. This tells us that these syntactic elements are not at all like the meaning-bearing symbols in LOT which refer to items in the world (compare the example of "chair" given earlier); and because this is so we need make no inference from the fact that there is an innate mental *syntax* to the fact that "all concepts are innate". "Chair" and "dog" are concepts because they collect together groups of objects in the world; "noun" and "verb"—and thus the representational elements in a putatively innate mental syntax—on the other hand are not concepts in *this* sense.

We must now consider the notion of a mental symbol.

1.1(ii) Mental symbols, their "shapes", and holism

Mental symbols have both a semantics and an inherent or *sui generis* form, as do the symbols in natural languages such as English or Swahili. Consider the two-sided nature of the word "dog". This English word comes to be the word it is in virtue both of the class of real-world objects to which it refers (its semantics) and in virtue of its inherent phonemic (when spoken) and graphemic (when written) structure. I shall refer to the latter, interchangeably as either the "formal" character of the symbol or, following Fodor (1980), as its "shape". Mental symbols too, says Fodor, have this double-sided character. Although there are philosophers who posit an LOT without semantics (e.g. Stich, 1983; see Crane, 1990 for arguments against this view), the Fodorian, semantics-rich view is the more plausible one and it is, more importantly for us, the version that leads to nativism about concepts.

But there is another and—I shall argue—dangerous parallel which Fodor is happy to endorse between the mental symbol and the natural language symbol. Just as natural language symbols are *atomic* in the sense that each stands in isolation from its fellow constituents of the language system, so too are mental symbols (Fodor & Lepore, 1992, p.7). Thus, the fact that "dog" refers to one class of objects while "cat" refers to another class are two distinct facts that have no bearing on each other; we could change the form of "dog" to "drog" or even have it cover cats as well and there would be no implications for the meaning of "cat". There could, indeed, be a language containing only one symbol. The fact that "dog" refers to the class of canine creatures and the fact that it is said /d/ɒ/g/ and written "dog" presents no constraints on what "cat" refers to or on the word's form. Now to say that all this is also true of mental symbols is certainly an economical view of mentality; but it is economy bought at a very high price (see Clark, 1995, pp.409–410).

One reason for this is that, according to the LOT thesis, when a subject thinks about a class of objects he or she is tokening a symbol in "mentalese", a symbol with a particular shape. Thus, when Mary thinks that dogs do not belong in cities she is performing a mental version of saying to herself "Dogs do not belong in cities"; the syntax and the lexicon will not of course line up with English—she needs a "compiler"—but there is a syntax and lexicon nevertheless.

It is clear that if Mary's dog-thought is to be successful (i.e. if it is to capture the class of canine creatures and only that class) then it is going to have to make contact with an awful lot of other mental symbols and do so in just the right way. For, in tokening the mental symbol DOG she must also succeed in making the right causal liaisons with mental symbols for animal, for pet, for four-legged, indeed for three-dimensional, substantial objects that continue to exist when not being perceived; the list is seemingly endless. We can afford to be charitable because Mary may have picked up some bizarre beliefs about dogs (e.g. that they all have listening devices implanted in them by an enemy power—see later); but so long as these beliefs do not prevent her from capturing in her thought the same class of objects as do the beliefs of less eccentric people, the dog-thought is successful.

A way of saying the same thing is that if Mary can think about dogs then she must also be able to think about animals, about pets, about four-legged creatures, about meat-eaters, and so forth. This is because *it makes no sense to say that a creature might be capable of entertaining only a single thought*: ascribing one thought to a subject requires us to ascribe to her a host of others. This is "the holism of belief", and it is a doctrine accepted by nearly everybody in some form. ("Semantic" or "meaning" holism—a holism applied to mental *contents* rather than beliefs—is another matter to which I shall turn shortly.) Despite being atomists about mental symbols, LOT theorists can accept the holism of belief; indeed saying that mental capacities are "systematic" is not a million miles from saying that they are holistic.

But there is clearly a question to be answered here about the relation between the holism of belief and the purported atomism of the representational elements (i.e. the units out of which the contents are assembled and towards which beliefs are directed). What I will argue now is that this distinction is actually a fault-line in the LOT doctrine—relating the two is impossible—and accordingly I will try to establish two points. First, if the merest stain of holism is allowed to seep into the definition of an LOT symbol then its truly *symbolic* nature will evaporate. Second, the supporter of LOT must hold that an organism's having beliefs is *secondary* to its having mental representations whose elements can be characterised atomistically. Here I will suggest, without having a formal argument to the effect, that the primacy of belief is a far more plausible position than the primacy of mental representation. The belief-primacy view is, as we shall see, what is required by the piagetian thesis about the role of agency in development, given the unbreakable conceptual linkage between belief and action.

Being a symbol in LOT depends on its being atomistic

Let us turn first to the question of how we can characterise the semantic relations between LOT's symbolic atoms. The problem is this. As in a natural language, elements that are similar in shape are not similar in meaning (e.g. "cod" and "god") and elements that are similar in meaning are not similar in shape (e.g. "god" and "deity"). These facts can be captured by saying that the symbols (in natural language and in LOT) are *arbitrary*. But if they are, *what account can be given of how such arbitrary elements establish just the right kind of causal liaisons with one another so as to support adequate thinking?* One way of doing this is to move in an holistic direction.

Recall that on the doctrine of functionalism (which all supporters of LOT endorse, more or less) a mental state is individuated not only in terms of its causal links with perception and action but also in terms of its links with other mental states. If so, why not say that the causal liaisons with other mental states also serve to individuate mental *symbols*? Although an LOT symbol may be arbitrary in the sense that its non-semantic character or shape is a *sui generis* computational atom whose character is not fixed entirely by its semantic relations to other such symbols, we can still say that any shape *comes to be the shape it is* in virtue of the way in which it has to causally interact with its fellow constituents. In other words, the shape of a mental symbol is determined by its causal role in enabling the thinker to have a certain thought, in relation to the causal roles of other symbols. This position is called "functional role semantics", and expressions of it can be found in the writings of Ned Block (1987) and of Gilbert Harman (1982). Thus, Block (1987, p.164) states:

> According to functional role semantics, for me to have a thought is for something (a representation) to have a certain functional role in me, that is, for it to be inferable in certain contexts from certain other representations with their own functional roles, and for other representations with their own functional roles to be inferable from it.

Functional role semantics is a close relative of the old doctrine that meaning is use, and it is "intractably holistic" according to Fodor and Lepore (1991, p.331) because:

> ... once you start identifying the content of beliefs with its inferential role in a system of beliefs (*mutatis mutandis*, the meaning of an expression with its inferential role in language), it's hard to avoid proceeding to identify the content of a belief with its whole inferential role in the system of beliefs.

I will now try to show that this route is closed to a supporter of LOT because one cannot subscribe both to functional role semantics and to the LOT doctrine at the same time. The upshot will be that representational atomism has to be defended at all costs if the LOT thesis to be internally consistent. Later, I will argue that if it is defended at all costs then we end up with a distorted picture of the relation between beliefs and their contents.

The claim is this: if a mental symbol is to have a non-semantic character (a shape) then this character cannot be *exhausted* by its causal role in mapping inputs to outputs. Here is a fanciful illustration to explain what I mean. Imagine that the LOT symbol for dogs has a flat top and a bottom like a Maltese Cross, and imagine also that its flat top has come to be the shape it is in order that it can make the right kind of causal liaisons with mammal thoughts, and imagine that it has the Maltese Cross element in order to achieve the right causal liaisons with pet symbols. Imagine, indeed, that *every single contour* of the LOT symbol for dogs comes to be the contour it is in virtue of the causal links it has to make with certain other symbols, symbols that, in turn, have the shape they do in virtue of the shapes of the symbols with which they have to interact, and so on. This is what I mean by saying that its shape is "exhausted by its causal role". But if this is so then the way in which the shape of the symbol is determined is not unlike the way in which the shape of a cog in a machine is determined, in the sense that the density of the cog's teeth and its diameter are determined entirely by the kinds of contact it needs to make with other cogs.

In other words, if the shape of a mental element is exhausted by its causal role within the mental system (in its achievement of mappings between perception, thought, and action) then it comes to look less like a symbol with an *arbitrary* character standing for something in the world and comes to look more like a *value* for a necessary element in the mapping, a value fixed by the exigencies of successful processing. Indeed this implies that the fact that an LOT symbol has, say, a "flat top" or a "sharp edge" is no more a symbolic fact than the fact that in processing dog-thoughts within a neural network a certain unit has an activation of 0.78 and one of the connection weights has a value of +0.32. In contrast, the first letter of "dog" having the shape "d" *is* a symbolic fact.

It might be objected here that the fact that a mental symbol's shape is exhausted by its causal role does not make the symbol any less arbitrary and *sui generis* because all that is being fixed here are the *kinds* of shapes (e.g. in terms of their complexity) that all of the symbols must have. The *actual* shapes, however, may vary, depending on the way in which the system *happens* (hence the arbitrariness) to be designed; for there are very many degrees of freedom in how the initial shapes are constructed (the earliest thoughts of primitive Man?) which gradually become narrower as more and more symbols are fixed, until the shape of the *final* symbol is fully determined. This does not make these elements any less symbolic, the objector would say. But—in answer— one could make exactly the same point about a neural network. Here too the designer has many degrees of freedom (e.g. in how to configure the input units) and here too decisions about the nature of one shape (in this special sense) will determine other shapes in virtue of causal liaisons (e.g. the activation levels of hidden units), but this fact does not legitimise talk about the representational elements in a neural network having a symbolic nature. The upshot, then, is that once we allow that the shape of an LOT symbol can be exhausted by its causal role we have dissolved the distinction between computational systems that are symbolic and those that are sub-symbolic. Fodor (see Fodor, 1987, Ch. 3; Fodor & Lepore, 1992) is surely right to regard holism as the enemy.

Beliefs, not content-bearing mental representations, are primary

For the reasons just given, it is necessary that the LOT theorist should at all costs avoid being committed to the view that the content of a mental symbol is constituted by its functional role within the mental system. What is the alternative? It is to say that the holism that is true—they admit—of belief is derivative (one may even say "is an emergent feature") of the way in which symbol-strings interact, with reference being made to the metaphorical location of these sentences within the mental architecture ("belief boxes" and the like—see earlier).

What is of crucial importance here is that the LOT theorists should maintain a firm distinction between the mental character of belief and that of representation (Fodor & Lepore, 1992, p.127; original italics):

> The functional analysis of *belief* may be such as to make believing holistic [...]. But the (putative) holism of belief need not imply meaning holism [i.e. holism about mental

representations and their constituent symbols], because the notion of believing is not *primitive* in the theory of intentionality. What's primitive are mental representations with their causal relations to each other and the world; and by assumption, the semantics of mental representation is atomistic.

A little earlier, Fodor and Lepore (1992, p.124) say that a "mental representation's having the content that is does needn't be supposed to depend upon its having the functional role that it does—or, indeed, on its having any functional role at all".

Fodor and Lepore also make a point which has a rather obvious bearing on the piagetian thesis. They remind us (ibid., p.124, original italics) that "[t]okening a mental representation (informally speaking having a thought occur to one) isn't (or needn't be) an *action*, and hence need not be inextricably connected to believing in the ways that speech acts and other actions are." They do not say that beliefs (and the other propositional attitudes) are actions—they are not—but beliefs are what we act out of, and the nature of an action is determined (partly) by what is believed: there can be no action without belief while there can certainly be actions produced by creatures in which thoughts *never* simply "occur to one". Accordingly, a theorist like Piaget who makes agency a necessary condition for successful mental development will hold that belief rather than mental representation (as Fodor and many others use the term) is primary.

If Fodor is wrong and it is belief that is primary then *there is no avoiding the slippage from the holism of belief to the holism of representational content*, and this, as we saw in the previous sub-section, will tend to erode the symbolic nature of mental symbols. Given this, what the LOT theorist must do is render the idea coherent that there can be a mental life *in which there is mental representation but not belief.* For if this is not a coherent idea then theorists who hold that belief is primary may well be correct in their view that only creatures that can have beliefs can have mental states with semantic content.

Here is the argument Fodor and Lepore produce in favour of the view that there could indeed be a mental life without beliefs (1992, pp.119–120). We could imagine a creature, they say, in the explanation of whose behaviour we need make no reference to beliefs—only to desires. This is a creature that goes into state S whenever it becomes dehydrated, and in "ecologically valid" circumstances this triggers its ingestion of water. Is this good enough? Almost certainly not, because if it is legitimate to talk about the creature's behaviour being guided by a "desire" for water then it is surely legitimate to talk about the creature having "beliefs" about water and about ingestion of it (see Heal, 1993–94, p.331). The authors say (ibid., p.120) that the creature has "no beliefs about the unity of the behaviour that being in S causes it to perform; that is part of what it means to say that the behaviour is produced reflexively". So we are not talking about action at all then! The point to bear in mind here is that the very second we begin to talk about actions we begin to talk about beliefs, and so *if the LOT thesis is going to have anything at all to say about action* (more of which later) *then it is going to have to face the possibility of slippage from the holism of belief to the holism of mental content*—and thus the possibility that mental symbols are exhausted by their functional roles.

What I have just said does not establish any particular thesis about the primacy of belief over mental representation. The purpose of the last few paragraphs has been entirely negative—to attack the view that there could be a mental life with such representations but without belief; nothing positive has been said about the role of belief. I think that enough has been done, however, to show that a view of mentality, like the piagetian one, in which agency and belief are primary is plausible—*prima facie*.

We have yet to consider, however, what many would regard as the LOT theorist's trump card against holism: that there is no way of stating the doctrine that does not inevitably lapse into absurdity. Holism is a "crazy" theory (Fodor, 1987, p.59) because once you start saying that "many" of a subject's beliefs must go to make up a single belief then there is no principled way of stopping yourself from holding that *all* of the subject's beliefs must be dropped into the mixture. Apart from being implausible, this would seem to threaten the integrity of intentional or folk-psychological accounts of action; for these require transpersonal rules relating beliefs and desires to actions, and these rules, it could be said, cannot be stated if each individual's beliefs are entirely idiosyncratic and determined by his or her whole world-view. Accordingly, if holism *cannot* be acquitted of the charge of craziness then some form of representational atomism looks like a good default option.

1.1(iii) Defending holism, and the consequences for subject-hood
Three questions will be considered in this section:

A. Whether intentional explanations of action (and other everyday notions about mental content and learning) are compatible with holism;

B. Whether we can draw a line in a principled way around the set of beliefs that makes a belief the belief it is, and thus avoid slippage towards the total set of beliefs;

C. Whether there is a way of stating and defending holism about meaning that does not licence the "crazy" (all beliefs are relevant to a single belief) form.

A caveat before beginning: when I talk about "the holism of belief" I am referring to holism about the *content* of beliefs (including both the belief-attitude and the content towards which that is directed). Remember that theorists such as Fodor and Lepore are happy to allow that the properties of beliefs constrain their functional roles in relation to other mental states (although there are places where they withdraw even this concession—1992, p.134). They argue, however, that content does not depend on functional role: that the content of *what* is believed is not holistic.

Following a recent paper by Jane Heal (1993–94) I will distinguish between a modest and plausible version of holism and a radical version with which most people would be uncomfortable. The more defensible version comes in two parts. I take the definitions straight from Heal (1993–94, pp.326–327).

(1a) We cannot make sense of there being just one thought. If there is any thought then there must be quite a number of different thoughts attributable to the same thinker.

Together with the claim that:

(1b) The presence in a set of thoughts of one with a given content imposes some constraints on the contents of the rest.

As compared with:

(2) The meaning which an individual thought has depends upon the whole collection (i.e. theory or set of capacities) in which it occurs in such a way that any change in the whole collection (the addition or removal of an element or the substitution of one element for another) changes the content of every thought in it.

Turning first to question A (about intentional explanation), the representational atomist (which, remember, is what an LOT theorist must be) will say that, while (1a) is more or less acceptable, we will slide down a slippery slope from (1b) to (2) and when we have done so will find that many of our cherished folk-psychological tenets will have been rendered unintelligible—that two people can share one belief without sharing every single belief, that one can gradually come to understand something (that parts can be understood before the whole), that people can change their mind about one thing without experiencing an across-the-board intellectual revolution and, most important, that we can explain agents' behaviour in terms of rules of thumb about their beliefs and desires—these rules will generalise across people, where the holism of (2) would seem to make each person's belief an idiosyncratic affair.

Let us look at intentional explanation. If no two agents, the argument runs, ever have the same set of beliefs then no generalisations of the kind "If X believes that Y and wants K then he will do L" can be made. If we cannot fix the meaning of a belief then such generalisations cannot be made across people or even with reference to one person at different times. But we surely do want to hold on to this kind of "practical syllogism". What if we say "Okay, but the beliefs don't have to be *identical*, they can just be *similar*. That's good enough. Psychological explanation, like explanation in economics and meteorology, is approximate." Fodor and Lepore's reply to this is that the notion of similarity is meaningless without the possibility of identity—and this has been ruled out.

Must the doctrine of holism necessarily undermine intentional explanation? Khalidi (1993, pp.653–654) has suggested the following way out of the dilemma. He takes further the comparison with economics just made:

> The problem of comparing two agent's sets of beliefs is analogous to the problem of setting a 'fair' exchange rate between two economies: to achieve this, what we need is not an exact isomorphism between them but an overall fit. We might make an initial estimate based on the balance of trade between the two economies; if this comparison gives unexpected answers for the prices of too many commodities, we might revise the initial estimate, and so on.

Now take the analogous problem of trying to translate the beliefs of an alien creature (or indeed of a young child) into our own belief-system. In order to arrive at the best overall explanation of the creature's actions we do not have to assume that all of its beliefs and all of our own beliefs line up one-to-one, or even that a *specified* subset needs to be identical. It will, however, inevitably turn out that certain of our beliefs are shared (this follows from holism), although we cannot say in advance which they are. The degree of beliefs' similarity can only emerge after the processes of interpretation and translation have been continued. "Moreover," writes Khalidi (1993, p.654), "it might be a different set of beliefs for a different translation ... the question of how much congruence is required can only be answered by reference to specific cases."

To argue in this way is to assume that it is a mistake to regard the identity of beliefs and of meanings as depending on the identity of the contents of minds. Indeed it returns us to the view of meaning, and of how thoughts acquire meaning, against which Fodor was reacting when he originally developed the LOT thesis. This is the broadly Wittgensteinian (1953) view of meaning, the view that words and beliefs have a fixed meaning only to the extent that the social practices within which they are used have a fixed structure. If this is so, there can be no such thing as a "private language" (a language constructed by a solitary person), for the simple reason that although mental processes necessarily involve something going on in the head when we mean something by a word or express a belief, what a word means and what the expression of a belief means is a public fact, necessarily open to public corrigibility. Fodor's contrary view, of course, is that there is indeed a private language—the mental machine-code or LOT.

However, subscribing to a broadly Wittgensteinian view of meaning may be, for some, too high a price to pay for a defence of holism. If so, a better tactic may be to look closely at the slippage that is supposed to occur from (1b) to (2) and see whether it can be prevented. Note that (1b) states that one thought with a given content will impose "some constraints" on the contents of the rest. "But how *many*?" the sceptic about holism will rhetorically ask.

Let us return to thoughts about dogs. We are unlikely to ascribe a dog-thought to somebody who cannot think about animals; the presence of dog-thought entails an ability to hold beliefs about a certain class of living creatures. But should we not also say that the idea of dog entails beliefs about dogs having ears on either side of their heads, and that having beliefs about hearing requires the thinker to know about inaudibility and therefore to know that the farther away a sound source is the less audible its signal—and this belief must necessarily include some understanding of spatial distance. Do thoughts about dogs require adequate thoughts about space?

One way of corralling just those beliefs that are plausibly required for a successful dog-thought (e.g. animal thoughts) away from those that are not (e.g. hearing-thoughts) is by subscribing to the distinction between so-called "analytic" and "synthetic" propositions. This is a distinction between propositions true of an entity by definition (thus, "My dog is not an animal" is a contradiction) and those that are not ("My dog is deaf" is not a contradiction). We thereby end up with a rather modest form of holism in which having a dog-thought requires only that there be percolation through the set of facts about dogs that are definitional of dog-hood. The problem with doing this however, according to sceptics about holism, is that subscribing to the analytic–synthetic distinction is another high price to pay for its defence. Some philosophers are willing to pay the price and accordingly adopt a position somewhere between atomism and holism (Dummett, 1975; Peacocke, 1992); but many, especially philosophers working in North America, assume that the analytic–synthetic distinction is a dogma that was long ago disposed of in a paper by W.V. Quine (1953). Given the controversial nature of the analytic–synthetic distinction, therefore, this way of avoiding the slippage from (1b) to (2) is not highly recommended.

The solution that I think *can* be highly recommended is one developed by Jane Heal. I will present Heal's position in some detail because it will allow me to introduce a view of mentality—one standing in stark opposition to that inspired by "representational theories of mind" of the Fodorian kind—in which subject-hood rather than representation is the core feature. Subject-hood will be a central concern in Part 3, and it will emerge throughout Part 2. I will take it to mean "being a subject of experience and volition".

Let us step back a little to reconsider the Fodorian thesis that it is representations (content-bearing mental states) rather than beliefs that are the primary stuff of mentality. What makes these *mental* representations for Fodor as opposed to the non-mental species of them (e.g. rings on tree-trunks, states of a thermostat)? What makes them mental, says Heal, is that they contribute to the explanation of behaviour—that they are the states responsible for controlling behaviour, for mediating between input and output. And this, on a thoroughly representational theory of mind, is *all* they are (Heal, 1993–94, p.333): "Minds are, on this view, just black boxes containing behaviour-controlling representations and what they are like is up for empirical investigation. If [Fodor and Lepore] are right then we have no reason not to allow that any old jumble of representations occurring in a persisting structure and causing its behaviour can and does constitute the mind of that structure."

Against this, Heal then considers a conception of mentality in which one is primarily concerned not with sets of representations that cause behaviour but with a subject that is (ibid, p.333) "a unified locus of cognitive virtues, which, starting from an exiguous base, gradually builds up a more and more detailed and elaborated view of its world and of its potential for action in it, so that its interactions with that world become by degrees more effectively attuned to it." These "cognitive virtues" comprise veridical perception, memory, decision-making, and so forth; and they are unified in the sense that the exercise of any one of them can bear upon the exercise of the others (e.g. what we perceive can be remembered, and remembered facts are grist to our capacity for reasoning). The cognitive state of a subject will therefore be a joint function of how these abilities are exercised and of the kind of world in which it is situated.

Thus, if something is a subject, in this sense, then (1b) is obviously licensed: the presence of one thought is going to constrain the nature of others, insofar as its cognitive competencies are interacting across psychological domains[4]. But (2) is not licensed; nothing forces the view that each thought constrains every other. There must be constraints, and if there were not the subject's thoughts would contradict one another (e.g. thinking my dog is a mammal but not an animal); but so long as there is a mental unity of the kind described we can afford to be liberal about what beliefs have to be present for a more or less adequate thought about X. Imagine, to modify Heal's example, that a subject, perhaps through believing the wrong people, has acquired the idea that dogs are listening devices planted on us by a hostile power. We can still ascribe beliefs about dogs to this person (e.g. "She thinks the dog is flea-ridden") and in most circumstances we will be able to communicate with her about dogs perfectly well. Recall Khalidi's argument presented earlier regarding the context-sensitivity and pragmatic nature of belief ascription.

What is at stake, therefore, in assessing whether something is a mind, is not whether it has the requisite bundle of representations for controlling its behaviour and whether the beliefs that are (miraculously?) spun from these atomistic materials line up with our own sufficiently well for us to communicate with it. What is at stake is whether the entity is a unified subject, in the sense of something that normally makes rational decisions about what to do given the information variously available to it. "Mental life is active," says Heal (1993–94, p.336), "in the sense that we are constantly making choices ... and thus we launch ourselves on courses which will, we hope, result in the formation of the right beliefs and decisions. But only if I am a subject will these activities be successful." One not only needs to possess a certain range of abilities for weighing evidence and for acting on it but one must *take oneself to be* an effective subject; otherwise nothing would be attempted or achieved.

Compare this way of regarding mentality with that owing to LOT and indeed to representational theories in general. On such theories, minds are systems of interacting representations which legitimise, if these interactions control behaviour in the right kind of way, the ascription of mentality to them by observers. Mentality is a kind of third-person explanatory hypothesis—a "theory"—which allows us to predict and understand what any putatively mental system is up to. About such views, Heal makes the following remark (1993–94, p.335): "This invites the riposte 'Why should I approach any objects in the natural world with this conceptual baggage?' ". For my money, this is exactly the kind of question we should also ask in developmental psychology: Why should a child ever feel the need to ascribe thoughts, intentions and so forth to another person? Children will not do so unless they are themselves subjects in the sense sketched earlier. In the light of this, I shall be arguing in Part 3 that it is time to shift our emphasis from the developing ability to ascribe "theories of mind" towards the first-person conditions for such ascription, conditions that involve the exercise of agency by subjects.

Summary and conclusions

I have been arguing against the notion of a mental symbol on the grounds that such a notion cannot be squared with the holism of mental life. This is a conclusion that clears a passage for the piagetian thesis, because as soon as we abandon the notion of a mental symbol we are free from commitment to the strong nativism about concepts that flows from the LOT doctrine. I argued that either supporters of the LOT thesis must accept that a mental symbol is determined by its functional role—in which case the symbolic (non-semantic, arbitrary, or shape-like) aspect of the symbol evaporates—or they must insist that the content of a mental representation is independent of any belief in which it plays a role. I then argued that the latter thesis is unpersuasive because it depends on the implausible claim that there could be a mental life without belief. The piagetian thesis depends on the opposite view: that there is no mentality without beliefs and no beliefs without agency. I then defended holism against the charge that there is no way of stating the doctrine that does not license the conclusion that the meaning of an individual thought depends on the meaning of all of the thinker's other thoughts. Following Heal (1993–94), the defence involved shifting perspective from a view of the mind as a bundle of interacting, atomic, behaviour-controlling representations to that of a "subject" constituted by the coherence it achieves across its cognitive capacities and its effectiveness as an agent (together with its ability to regard itself as such). For a subject, the presence of one thought will inevitably constrain the nature of other thoughts it can have; but one can be liberal about the question of which thoughts are entailed by which other thoughts by allowing the possibility that the subject's exercise of its capacities can take place in deviant circumstances. In communicating with other minds and in the ascription of mentality to other persons we are naturally tolerant of such deviance. This focus on subjecthood will be seen to have implications for how we conceive of "theory of mind" development; and it will justify a concern with the first-person conditions for why children, as they come to ascribe mental states to others, should ever "approach any objects in the natural world with this conceptual baggage" (Heal, 1993–94, p.335).

1.2: MENTAL MODELS

Where LOT takes thinking to be a matter of tokening mental sentences, mental models theory regards it as the running of simulations of how the world would be if the thought were true. This tells us at once what the two theories have in common and how they diverge. In the first place, they share the assumption against which Part 1 is being broadly directed: that adequate thought is nothing more than the achievement of a certain kind of internal structure—and that, accordingly, mental development is the process of achieving the right kind of internal structure. And they diverge, in the second place, around the nature of this internal structure: where LOT regards it as strings of "arbitrary" (in the sense described earlier) symbols, mental models theory construes it in terms of a structure that is not remotely arbitrary—it is an analogue structure that is more or less isomorphic to an actual or possible state of the world.

What can also be said immediately about mental models theory is that, whereas LOT foundered on the holism of mental content, the notion of a mental model is not at all difficult to square with holism. Because a mental model acquires its nature in virtue of (though not necessarily *solely* in virtue of—see the "modest" version described later) its structural similarity to that which it models, we do not have to say that its inherent meaning is nothing over and above its functional role *vis-à-vis* other representational states. Let me put it this way: if we could look into the mind of a system that operated with mental models, we could make an intelligent guess about the content of its thoughts. By contrast, looking at the mental sentences churning around inside the mind of an LOT-using system would tell us nothing, because we would need a *translation*. Moreover, the notion of simulation is an inherently holistic notion in the sense that a simulation requires the simulator to represent a number of features simultaneously. Accordingly, just as one cannot picture a tree without also picturing the fact that it has a trunk and branches so we cannot model, say, a dog without also modelling an animal and a creature with four legs.

Mental models theory has a second advantage over LOT in addition to its holistic nature. One problem with the LOT thesis that I did not raise in 1.1 is that it is unclear about how mental symbols acquire their semantics (i.e. come to refer to a class of objects). We cannot "read off" the semantics from the shape of a symbol any more than somebody who does not know German can read off the reference of "*Hund*" after reading the word. "By contrast," writes Colin McGinn (1989, p.197), "mental models do incorporate the mechanism of intentionality [what the representation is about]; they do not loiter impotently waiting for a jolt of semantic life to be delivered to them."

Why piagetians should reject the mental models theory

The main progenitor of the idea that thinking requires the construction of mental models was the pioneering Cambridge psychologist Kenneth Craik (1943). Craik drew an analogy between thinking and the processes by which a scientist might try to predict and explain a physical phenomenon by literally making a model of that phenomenon, a model that physically instantiates the relevant variables. Craik wrote (1943, p.50):

> By a model, I mean any physical or chemical system which has a *similar relation-structure* to that of the process it imitates. By 'relation-structure' I do not mean some obscure non-physical entity which attends the model, but the fact that it is a physical working model which works in the same way as the process it parallels ... Kelvin's tide-predictor, which consists of pulleys and levers, does not resemble a tide in appearance [my italics].

A little later I shall be distinguishing between ambitious and modest versions of mental models theory; but both versions would endorse what Craik says. However, what I have to do before describing these two versions is to say why mental models theory is in tension with the piagetian thesis that I shall be supporting.

In Part 2 we shall be concerned with how infants acquire the knowledge that objects exist independently of their perceptual experience of them, and in Part 3 we shall be concerned with how young children acquire a concept of mind. To anticipate: my argument will be, in the first place, that to know there are physical objects is to know something about the way objects resist the will, and, in the second place, that the experience of controlling the content of our experiences is necessary for the development of first-person thoughts. In both these cases—it will be evident—the acquisition of a concept is taken to depend on the exercise of agency.

Now consider what a species of mental models theory might say about the acquisition a concept of an object and a concept of a mind. To acquire a concept of an object (as something existing in the external world when I am not perceiving it) is to acquire the ability to simulate what an experience of that object would be like if I were, for example, to remove an occluder or change my spatial location. Relatedly, acquiring the concept of mind is a matter of learning to run simulations of what beliefs and desires I would have in given situations and run simulations of what beliefs and desires other people are having and might come to have. What would piagetians say to this? They would say "Yes that is indeed what creatures with object concepts and mental concepts can do: these are the kinds of representational capacities they possess. But in no sense does saying this amount to a theory of *how these representations come to have the requisite content*. It is just a statement of what is achieved—of the developmental *terminus* of the exercise of these concepts. What is required for possessing these contents, however, is (a) experiencing how the exercise of our agency is constrained by the refractory nature of physical objects and (b) experiencing, conversely, how we are able, within limits, to control the contents of our experience from time to time. If there were a reason to believe that the content of object concepts and mental concepts could be accounted for purely in terms of mental modelling then the thunder of the piagetian thesis would have been stolen; but there is no such reason." What I shall be arguing in the next section is that mental models theory does *not* provide an adequate account of mental content in general, and, accordingly, that it cannot provide an account of how these two fundamental concepts are acquired. After this will come a section discussing a development theory couched in terms of mental modelling.

1.2(i) The "ambitious" and the "modest" versions of mental models theory

Here are the two versions of mental models theory. The second version is certainly owing to Colin McGinn (1989). The provenance of the first, stronger version is, however, rather less clear. There are passages in Johnson-Laird's book *Mental models* (1983) that are consistent with it—I shall quote some of them—but Johnson-Laird's main aim is to present an empirical theory of cognition rather than a philosophical account of mental content, so it is perhaps unfair to saddle him with it squarely; although for expository purposes saddling is just what I shall be doing. There are passages in Craik's book *The nature of explanation* that endorse the stronger version (they are discussed in McGinn, 1989). I shall present each in two parts.

The ambitious version

(1a) A mental model is the content of a thought. Accordingly, the construction (possibly following recursive revision) of a mental model is the *terminus* of successful cognition, whereas the tokening of mental sentences (insofar as we token them at all) is a transitional process towards the model which can be seen as the "translation" of these propositional representations.

(1b) To describe how mental models are constructed and manipulated by the thinker is to give an account of rationality. The systematicity and inferential structure of human thought can be explained entirely in terms of how mental models are constructed, recursively embedded, and revised.

My task now is to do two things. First, I have to show why the ambitious version is incorrect and then show why a more modest version is not strong enough to threaten the piagetian thesis.

Turning first to (1a), Johnson-Laird (1983, p.156, original italics) is clear about the relation between LOT-like representations and the model: "A principal assumption of the theory which I am developing is that the semantics of the mental language maps propositional representations into mental models of real or imaginary worlds: *propositional representations are interpreted with respect to mental models.*"[5] Elsewhere he writes that a propositional attitude is "a relation between an individual and that individual's mental model of the relevant state of affairs. To represent a propositional attitude, it is *merely necessary* to allow recursive embedding of mental models" (ibid, p.433, my italics). Second, Johnson-Laird says that what makes a mental model true is the structural similarity between it and a bit of reality (ibid, p.441, my italics): "In principle, we can assume that a discourse is true *if and only if* there is at least one mental model of it that can be mapped into the real world model in a way that preserves the content of the mental model—i.e. the individuals represented in the mental model occur in the real world with the same properties and the same relations holding between them.". His "principle of structural identity" runs: "The structures of mental models are identical to the structures of states of affairs, whether perceived or conceived, that models represent." (ibid, p.419). Finally, when discussing sentences that invite a number of different models (e.g. "Every man owns a car") Johnson-Laird says that "a mental model represents the *extension* of an assertion, i.e. the situation it describes, and the recursive machinery for revising the model represents the intension of the assertion, i.e. the set of all possible situations it describes" (ibid, p.440, original italics).

With regard to (1b) let us look at Johnson-Laird's well-known work on deductive reasoning. What happens in syllogistic reasoning, according to the theory, is that we represent the classes referred to in the problem (e.g. "all A") by particular exemplars (e.g. a row of three As) and we represent the relations between the classes by some convention (e.g. if all As are B we have may have equals-signs between three As and three Bs; if no As are B we may have a dashed line running between three As and three Bs). (The equals-signs and the other conventions are just for the convenience of Johnson-Laird's readers. I assume that reasoners are supposed to have a set of more or less idiosyncratic devices to represent the concrete facts of equality, distinctness, and so forth—there will be more on the status of these conventions later.) What is happening, then, is that the thinker is arranging an "inner" version of what could equally well be arranged in the physical world, a process that Johnson-Laird compares to having a troupe of actors setting up an "internal tableau" (ibid, p.95) to represent how the classes in the premises relate to one another. Deciding what follows from the premises is then achieved in the following way. Situations are envisaged—"mental models are constructed"—in which the premises can both be true. Sometimes there will be only one such case (e.g. all A are B, all B are C, therefore all A are C), but for some of the 64 syllogisms the reasoner will need to construct two or three models; while the theory successfully predicts that the difficult syllogisms are those that require the greater number of models (Johnson-Laird & Bara, 1984). When the reasoner is satisfied that he or she has constructed all models in which both premises can be true he or she reads off the one fact that is represented in all premises. For example, when given the premises "No A are B" and "Some C are B" we have to construct three models and the only situation that holds in all three is: "Some C are not A". My example has been of syllogistic reasoning, but Johnson-Laird sees mental models theory as explaining all kinds of rational thought, from problems in formal logic, through the drawing of spatial inferences, to comprehending a piece of text. But syllogistic reasoning is the theory's flagship.

Problems for the ambitious version. To say that propositional representations are interpreted with respect to mental models and that a propositional attitude is a relation between an individual and his or her mental model is certainly to invite the interpretation that what a mental model does is to provide a thought with content. This is the claim derivable from (1a), and it runs us flat against the homunculus problem. Why? Because a straight-ahead correspondence theory of content in which (a) the truth of a discourse is entirely a function of whether the structure of its mental model corresponds with the structure of a piece of reality and (b) the meaning of a discourse is explained in terms of correspondences between the structure of its mental model and the structure of a possible world[6], will necessarily require some mental entity "higher up" to assess the degree and adequacy of that correspondence. Notions such as "similarity", "mapping", and "correspondence" are psychological notions in the sense that whether A is similar to, maps onto or corresponds with B is something to be decided in relation to a standard—a standard "in the mind of the homunculus".

Let us look at correspondence theories of truth. There are problems with these theories, and we shall see that these exist whether it is a proposition or a model that is supposed to be true (or to mean something in a possible world) in virtue of what it corresponds to.

Despite its intuitive appeal, a correspondence theory of the truth of a proposition requires us to ask: What is the proposition meant to "correspond" to in the world? A "fact"? Well, facts do not lie around in the world, neatly packaged and waiting to be picked up. Facts, like propositions, are mental constructs. So is it concrete situations (such as a real cat being on a real mat) to which the proposition is supposed to correspond? But how do we achieve the trick of mapping an abstract entity—a proposition—onto a slice of concrete reality?

Mental models theory (the ambitious version) appears to promise a way out of this dilemma. This is because, in the theory, it is not propositions that are supposed to map onto reality, but the representations we construct to infuse these propositions with content. It is the models that are supposed to correspond to states of affairs not the propositions that "travel" towards them. So, superficially, it would seem that a mental model, simply because it is a little slice of life, is exactly the right kind of entity to succeed or not to succeed in corresponding to how things really are. But in fact the correspondence problem remains.

The theory can go in two opposite directions to explain correspondence, and it fails in each. First, if understanding the proposition expressed by a sentence is a matter of constructing a tableau that is just like a real situation except that it happens to be a mental situation, then the theory is now telling us nothing about *how the gap is bridged* between hearing the sentence and constructing the tableau. The mental tableau will fit or fail to fit the world so that problem has, in a sense, been solved; but this is done at the expense of pushing the problem upstairs into the mental realm. Now what is obscure is how the proposition is supposed to map to the mental model, so that what used to be a problem of mind→world mapping in now a problem of mind(proposition)→mind(model) mapping. What was a problem for outer mapping has now become a problem for inner mapping.

Second (moving in the opposite direction), if mental modelling is regarded in a more abstract light, as a matter of constructing a representation that is concrete only insofar as it has spatial properties (e.g. As and Bs are lined up together) but which is otherwise essentially formal, then the mind→world mapping problem looms nearly as large as it did when we were worrying about how propositions are supposed to map onto facts in the world. Models may have spatial properties, but if they also have formal elements then we encounter the problem of how such formal elements map onto the world. (This point will be extended when we come to discuss the mental models account of syllogistic reasoning.)

So, in summary, the more infused with real life these models are taken to be, on the one hand, the greater the problem we have in explaining how they come to be constructed from sentences. On the other hand, the more abstract we take them to be the greater the problem of representation→world correspondence.

But surely—you may think—*any* ambitious theory in cognitive science must inevitably rest on *some* philosophical presupposition or another, and it just so happens that mental models theory rests on this one—on a correspondence theory of truth. Maybe. But remember that the theory also has the ambition of explaining reasoning in terms of structural analogues to states of affairs, which amounts to a correspondence theory of *validity*. For validity is nothing, on such a view, beyond the construction of inner versions of notional outer realities.[7] We have just seen that the correspondence theory of truth has difficulty in saying what it is in the world that corresponds to a proposition, but at least it makes sense to say that *something* can.

When we come to validity however, the correspondence has to be with *all possible worlds*: an inference is valid if in all possible worlds these models and these alone can be constructed from the premisses. But here one would ask *how the model-constructor is supposed to gain a grasp of validity*, how, that is, he or she is able to appreciate that the (say) three models he or she has constructed to fit the two premises are true in all possible worlds, not just true in the notional world he or she has just constructed. Perhaps one would say that a conception of necessary truth is grounded in the experience of finding certain model constructions possible and the experience of necessary falseness in that of finding others impossible. People of a broadly Wittgensteinian persuasion, however, would reject that idea on the grounds that it reduces concepts such as necessity to "inner" mental events, when they are in reality concepts grounded in public practice. "Necessity" is a concept with public criteria in whose use one gains expertise as one develops; it is not a private feeling one undergoes in finding some kinds of model construction satisfying. In other words, mental models theory shares the fundamental error of all purely representational theories of the mind in placing meanings "inside the head" (Russell, 1987a).

This is not to deny that some kinds of thinking can be described in terms of the construction of mental models. People—*some* people[8]—do set up mental models when tackling problems in logic (others use formal rules, Galotti, Baron, & Sabini, 1986). And sometimes the best way to analyse peoples' interpretation of a problem or of a piece of information is to try to reconstruct their model of it. But my target is the view that once we have described the models constructed when having a certain thought or series of thoughts then we have explained *what it is to have thoughts with that content*. My target is the (1a) claim that adequate thought just *is* the construction of a mental model that corresponds to reality, that understanding a concept, an argument, a sentence, a principle just *is* to have an "inner" representation that lines up with an "outer" reality; that there is a terminus of understanding, and mental modelling is it.

I now come to (1b)—to the claim that the kind of machinery Johnson-Laird describes is capable of accounting for logical reasoning. We have just been discussing difficulties with the view that correspondences between something mental and something in the physical (or in a possible) world could capture our conception of logical necessity; but now I am concerned with the status of the theory in relation to symbol-processing theories. We need to ask, in fact, whether the theory is successful on its own terms and whether it really escapes commitment to formal (*à la* LOT) symbols and rules.

Does this theory succeed in weaving logical structure from materials which lack formal structure—from the modelling of possible situations? It is not surprising that many have been unconvinced (e.g. Rips, 1986; Russell, 1987a; Stenning, 1991; Stenning & Oberlander, 1995). Let us first consider problems with Johnson-Laird's specific proposals about syllogistic reasoning.

Lance Rips (1986) has identified the following problems:

(i) Mental models theory, far from being an alternative to the view (compatible with the LOT thesis) that we employ formal rules of inference, *posits* a set of formal rules, albeit a rather eccentric set;

(ii) Given the interpretative devices that Johnson-Laird allows himself (parentheses to represent optional elements, for example) the number of models it takes to solve a syllogism can be relative to the *first* model that the reasoner constructs;

(iii) The theory cannot explain the well-known "content" effects (roughly: reasoning about concrete, plausible, and familiar situations is easier than reasoning about abstract contents) because it *deals* in formal principles [see (i)] and uninterpreted symbols, not in real-world knowledge. That is to say, the theory does not have the resources to explain why mental tableaux with concrete referents—such as artists, beekeepers, and chemists rather than As, Bs, and Cs—make problems easier to solve.

To make these criticisms is to resurrect the homunculus problem. The theory naturally invites the caricature that cognition must involve an homunculus manipulating mental entities according to its self-chosen (and, as Rips and as Stenning point out, essentially formal) principles and then looking at and interpreting the result of these manipulations. Indeed, the process of sequentially testing mental models is constrained only by decisions made by the homunculus—by decisions about which rule to apply when and about how to interpret what Johnson-Laird calls the "directorial devices".

However, I should say, by way of anticipating what I will call "the modest version", that none of these critical remarks is supposed to undermine the mental models thesis as a "performance" account of what can go on in the mind's eye when we reason and comprehend texts—as an empirical theory. But as a theory of what *constitutes* thinking—as a competence theory—it should be called into question (Russell, 1987a). I will return to the competence–performance distinction shortly.

The modest version
This version says the following:

(2a) The construction of a mental model is *necessary* for a thought to have content, but it is *not sufficient*. What is required in addition is that models should be embedded within a teleological background and that they should be causally related to other models in a certain way (cf LOT). The construction of a mental model is not the terminus of successful cognition because models have no propositional structure; they only *ground* a propositional ascription in a similar way to that in which the analogue structure of a map grounds judgements about the relation between places.

(2b) Mental models theory can make empirical claims about what goes on in the mind in real time when we reason (e.g. solve syllogisms) but it has nothing to say about validity. The grounding of rationality is the construction of mental models, but because models are not related to one another logically they cannot in themselves explain our facility for reasoning. The relationship between models is *causal* not *inferential*.

The best way of filling out (2a) is by reference to a distinction McGinn (1989) draws between the *ground* and the *object* of a propositional attitude. He gives the following analogy and also introduces a third term—*indexing*. In measuring the temperature of water we "index" the physical state of something (its ground) with abstract entities (its object)—with numbers—and there is no temptation to confuse the two because we do not think that water contains anything numerical. Moving to the mental realm, in indexing "states of a subject's head with propositions we are not thereby committed to inserting logical structures *into* the subject's head [...]. Rather, the modelling theory will maintain, we simply need some systematic rule for selecting an appropriate item from logical space as the index to be assigned to a given model—a *rule or function that takes us from models to propositions*" (McGinn, 1989, p.183, second italics mine). The way in which a mental model relates to propositional content, McGinn says, is similar to the way in which an analogue representation such as a map relates to the propositions that describe what the features model.

This is clearly *not* the view that constructing a mental model is the "terminus" of a thought, and it is the symmetrical opposite of the Johnson-Lairdian view, in the following respect. Recall that for Johnson-Laird the "semantics of mental language" was seen as mapping propositional representations onto mental models: the sequence was from primary representation (e.g. a phonological representation of a sentence), to mentalese, to mental model. On the McGinn view, however, the sequence is—primary representation, followed by the construction of an analogue representation (a mental model) which only has propositional content insofar as it is indexed with an appropriate propositional item from "logical space". The model is necessary for content but by no means sufficient; and far from being the terminus of the thought it is something standing in need of propositional indexing.

On this view, the construction of models is a way of solving "an engineering problem" (McGinn, 1989, p.189), meaning the evolutionary problem of how organisms' mental states can be made to accord with reality. In other words, we are designed as reality simulators because that is a good solution to a biological problem.

One possible objection to this view is that although it explains how we and other animals generally survive in a world in which we need to seek correspondence with reality and shun mismatches to it, it has no resources to explain the *normativity* of truth, and that if it tries to do so it will inevitably inherit all the problems of a naive correspondence theory which were rehearsed a couple of pages ago. How can such a thesis, in other words, account for the fact that we *believe* what we take to be true and disbelieve what we take to be false: why do we think that truth is a Good Thing? McGinn's reply illustrates very clearly my reasons for calling this a modest version. "This complaint would be justified," he writes, "if our project was to account for all aspects of content in terms of mental models, but that is not our project." (ibid, p.189). He then points out—it is the *motif* of his book in fact—that a model, indeed any kind of mental representation, must be viewed in the light of the subject's "teleological background"—in the light of the fact that one of our main cognitive *goals* is to have our thoughts line up with reality. The whole point of a mental model is to achieve isomorphism to the world or to a possible world, and its success in doing so can only be assessed in the light of the goals the thinker has in launching that particular thought. Moreover, this background is nothing if not complex because it must encompass not only what we want to achieve cognitively but the way we live and are socially located—what Wittgenstein famously called our "forms of life". (There are many reasons for the complexity and one is that truth-seeking is only one of our cognitive goals; there are many "language games".) So McGinn's point is essentially Wittgensteinian (ibid, fn p.189): that the content of a mental representation cannot be captured through reference to its inherent structure, rather, it can only be understood in relation to the subject's aims and capacities and relative to the way he or she lives. The view is holistic, although in a deeper sense than that in which the model itself is holistic, and it is generally held by sceptics about "the representational theory of the mind" such as John Searle (1984).

But surely the homunculus problem does not just shrink back into its coffin when the "forms of life" talisman is brandished at it. A mental model of the premiss in a syllogism, for example, is still going to require interpretation by some higher-order entity, by the *inhabitant* of this "teleological background". Models do not have goals, only their users have goals; and why should we not view the model-user as an homunculus? In answer to this charge McGinn writes (1989, p.200):

> There is no need for internal gazing at mental models. Rather, the organism's cognitive (and conative) system is simply wired up in such a way that the models operate according to certain laws and principles. What breathes semantic life into the models is not some cranial incubus squatting up there thinking its own dubious thoughts, but rather the pattern of causal–teleological relations by which the models are surrounded. […] Mental models do not need to be interpreted—they need to be used.

This is certainly an answer, but in giving it, the modesty of the theory is revealed rather starkly. What is being referred to here is any form of analogue representation, something that is far removed from the content-bearing representations of the ambitious version. What is being referred to is, in fact, something much closer to a mental *map*. To illustrate: studies of migrating birds and homing pigeons tell us that the mature animals make use of the sun's azimuth as a compass, in addition to utilising information from their diurnal clocks and ultimately from local landmarks. More important, they also appear to have a map that tells them the direction in which to fly when information from these other sources is artificially distorted; for a compass without some representation of the direction you are from home is no use to you. This map, it has been conjectured, is constructed in terms of two intersecting gradients (see Keeton, 1981 for discussion). Bees also use the sun's azimuth as a compass and take short-cuts—suggesting that they have map-like representations (Gould, 1984).

Now the birds and the bees are not noted for their reflective capacities, and it would be absurd to suggest that they use mental maps as mental models in the way in which, say, a syllogism-solver is supposed to do. But what McGinn says would seem to capture just what is going on in their case. The "laws and principles" could be taken to refer to the kind of laws and principles manifested in the causal interactions between values of the sun's azimuth, readings from the diurnal clock, and map-like representation in terms of intersecting gradients. But it is a mistake to believe that these laws and principles have the same status as the constructions and recursive revisions that are supposed to ground human rationality in the ambitious theory. The pigeon uses a mental map to get from A to B, whereas we (on Johnson-Laird's theory at least) construct models to get from premisses to conclusions or from a discourse to an interpretation. The fact that we can explain what the pigeon does in terms of the "causal–teleological relations by which the models are surrounded" and do not have to refer thereby to a homuncular interpreter does not legitimise an account of human mental model construction in just the same terms. Indeed, the admission that the syllogism-solving organism, or indeed any language-comprehending organism, achieves what it achieves by virtue of being "wired up" in a certain way runs flat against the claims of the ambitious version. It is the use of exemplars in models and the sequential testing of model after model that makes us rational, on Johnson-Laird's account, not being wired up in a certain way. (Try to solve one of Johnson-Laird's 3-model syllogisms and notice how little "wiring" you appear to have to do it!)

Indeed McGinn revealingly says (1989, fn p.200) that "[i]t might be easier to rest easy on this point [i.e. his defence against the homunculus charge] if one thinks first of lowly intentional system such as frogs or bats or rhinoceri. For they seem sufficiently tightly wired (or highly strung) to render an homunculus redundant."

This brings us naturally to (2b)—to the modest version's disclaimer about having anything to say about logic and mental syntax. It can say, of course, that there is an analogue grounding to deductive reasoning, for example, but it must stay silent on questions about validity and about how models relate to one another—except by saying the relation is "causal". Again, McGinn is explicit: the theory "will not seek to explain the validity or otherwise of such reasoning; for considered merely as a causal theory of mental transitions, it will simply not have the resources to answer such questions of logic." (ibid, p.190). This allows him to highlight its status as an empirical theory about what goes on in real time when we make certain logical moves. Indeed he suggests an experiment (on p.206) which could compare the theory's predictions against those of the rival view that logical tasks are performed by a formal system of "mental logic"—an experiment that, it turns out, Johnson-Laird's group has run (Byrne & Johnson-Laird, 1989). This reinforces my previous conclusion that the mental models theory of reasoning is a performance theory not a competence theory. Obviously, that's not a bad thing; but it shows us how the thesis stands in relation to the LOT thesis. The latter is more of a philosophical doctrine than an empirical hypothesis.

"Plenty to be modest about."[9]   What the modest version boils down to is a case for analogue mental representations—such as mental maps. Unlike the LOT doctrine, it does not attempt to give an account of the content to which propositional attitudes are directed: they are grounded in analogue representations and these representations "causally" interact with their fellow constituents; but otherwise propositional content is the business of something like an LOT.

Moreover, although it may look as if the modest version is being pitched at the same philosophical level as the LOT thesis, in fact it is not. Both may appear to be species of what McGinn calls "internal structure theories" and symmetrically conflict about the nature of these internal structures, but to the extent that the modest version talks of "teleological backgrounds" and nods towards Wittgensteinian forms of life it is not an internal structure theory at all. Of course, it says that certain kinds of internal structures are *necessary* (analogue for the ground and propositional for the object) but there is not a theory of mentality on earth (Behaviorism has gone elsewhere) that does not claim that mental representations with some kind of structure are necessary for adequate thought—as I said at the beginning.

So just as the true worth of the ambitious version is as a performance theory of cognition—a theory of what *can* go on in the mind's eye when we make logical moves and understand discourses—so the worth of the modest version is not as advertised. Mental models theory, as it is eloquently presented by McGinn, is best read as a sceptical position *vis-à-vis* the LOT thesis: it is a theory whose point is to show the insufficiency of LOT. One can be chary of its positive claims while recognising its power as a sceptical case.

Conclusion about mental models

I hope to have shown, in the first place, that any theory which would say that having conceptions of objects and minds is nothing more than the successful construction of analogue representations of unexperienced objects and of possible mental lives must fail. It must fail because the "terminus" of successful cognition is not the construction of a mental model: mental content is not reducible to the possession of a model with an identical "relation-structure" to a bit of reality. In the second place, I hope to have shown that a more modest version of the theory which would say that construction of a mental model is not the terminus of an adequate thought and accepts that models lack truth and meaning without a teleological background is, by virtue of not being a thoroughly representational theory at all, no threat to the piagetian thesis that successful agency is necessary for the possession of these concepts. Indeed, far from being a threat to the piagetian thesis the modest version accords with it well. For only agents can possess a teleological background.

1.2(ii)   Mental models and development:
"Understanding" as competence not performance

In this briefer section I want to look at the kind of use to which the notion of a mental model has recently been put within developmental psychology. This will give me the opportunity to show the empirical cash-value of my sceptical remarks.

Some developmental psychologists employ the notion of embedding one model within another as a way of capturing the difference between what a younger child and an older child can understand within a certain domain (e.g. Perner, 1991, p.32). Others subscribe to the view that children's third-person understanding of mental categories is achieved by mentally simulating another's mental state on the model of one's own (e.g. Harris, 1991). But what these writers are doing is helping themselves to a useful metaphor: they are not committed to the claims of what I have been calling "the ambitious version". Johnson-Laird

(1988) himself limits his discussion of developmental issues to the topic of reasoning.

However, at least one leading developmental psychologist has a fundamental commitment to the ambitious position—to the position that the growth of understanding is a matter of progressive model-construction and that understanding has been achieved insofar as a model is structurally isomorphic to reality or to the problem space. That person is Graeme Halford.

It has to be said, first of all, that Halford is very liberal in his use of the term "mental model", being happy to accept, for instance, that models can have propositional components (1993, p.23). But this does not mean that his commitment is really to the modest version: his commitment to the view that understanding means having a mental representation structurally isomorphic to concepts and states of affairs is as strong as Johnson-Laird's and even pre-dates Johnson-Laird's classic statement of the view (Halford, 1982). For Halford (1993, pp.7–8), "To understand a concept entails having an internal, cognitive representation or mental model that reflects the structure of that concept.[...]The important thing is that the structure of the mental model must correspond to the structure of the concept, phenomenon, or task that is represented." There is no reference to anything like teleological backgrounds. Sometimes Halford's use of "mental model" is in the "useful metaphor" style mentioned earlier. In saying (ibid, p.2), for example, that physics students fail to predict how a bomb will fall from a travelling aircraft (McCloskey, 1983) because they construct mental models with vertical and diagonal rather parabolic trajectories, the term "mental model" is doing no work: it is equivalent to saying that the students think the wrong thought. But in other cases the notion of understanding and mental modelling produces a very distinctive view of what develops, best seen in Halford's influential work on transitive reasoning.

According to Halford, explaining how a child develops the capacity to reason transitively (e.g. A > B; B > C; therefore A > C) is a matter of explaining how the child comes to map the problem domain (the premisses as they are presented to him or her) onto a model with spatial properties. He calls this "structure mapping". For example the transitive relation may be "happier than", while in the model the "happier" the element the farther to the left it is placed. "We know all this," Halford writes (ibid, p.10), "because we 'understand' both the concepts of transitivity and what it means to place people in order with respect to happiness." There is, however, something odd here because an account of mental development in terms of mental modelling must really say that the "understanding" to which Halford refers just *is* the construction of a mental model, rather than saying that the understanding of a principle is one thing and the ability to order elements another.

There certainly *is* a distinction to be drawn between understanding a principle and constructing a model. For example, you are given the following problem: Peter is happier than Tom, Bill is happier than Peter, who is the happiest? As Halford says, you will experience a "slight feeling of effort" in solving the problem. What does this consist in? It consists in the mental work that has to be done to put the elements into an order, that will allow the right answer to be read off—Bill>Peter>Tom. Nobody has any quarrel with calling this "constructing a mental model". But before you did this you understood that what you were faced with was a transitive problem and you did this with some appreciation that transitivity is a logical principle; and you certainly had the "concept of validity" (discussed at the end of the previous sub-section).

To be a sceptic about a thoroughly representational theory of understanding boils down to denying that this understanding is a matter of having a representation of *any* determinate kind—and certainly not one that has to line up with reality. It is no good saying that the understanding consists in tokening a prototypical transitive relation (such as three sticks graded in height), because the same problem remains: How is this representation understood *as* a transitive one? All that has happened is that we have moved the problem of explaining how transitivity is understood from the physical realm to the mental realm.

There is a collateral problem. Because of Halford's highly ecumenical reading of the term "mental model" mentioned earlier, he is happy to say that, rather than being a model with spatial properties, the model may be in the form of a rule (a "known rule" as he calls it: ibid, p.14). In this case the difference between a mental model and symbols in a language of thought appears to have dissolved. But more important, this implies that the reasoner has, in theory, some degree of choice about how the problem is modelled (by spatial model or by known rule); and *this*, it would seem, must drive the wedge still further between our "understanding" of the transitive principle and the mental work we carry out in solving a particular problem.

No doubt some readers have difficulty catching their breath at this point: "You surely don't mean that this kind of work is based on a mistake—that it's all just a waste of time!" Of course I don't mean that. But psychological theories normally have two faces: face one is what they advertise themselves as explaining and face two is what they actually explain. My target is face one—the view that a theory of this kind can explain the development of understanding. The best way to describe the difference between the two faces is by referring again to Chomsky's distinction between competence and performance. With this distinction in mind we can see that Halford purports to explain competence (understanding *per se*, paralleling what Chomsky called our "linguistic intuitions") while actually presenting a processing theory of the mental operations we may perform when solving problems; this is not a theory of what it takes to understand the transitive principle but a theory of the kinds of spatial representation that we utilise when solving transitive problems and of how capacity limitations constrain their use.

Face two of Halford's theory is a very sophisticated stage-wise theory of mental development. It is a theory that seeks to explain logico-mathematical development in terms of resource limitations (basically in the working-memory system) and models these processes in a connectionist style (Halford, 1993). Far from regarding this as a mistake, I would say that this is exactly the way forward. I would argue, however, that although the structure-mapping principle may enable Halford to think more clearly about the rule structure and the processing constraints within a given cognitive task, it misrepresents the nature of understanding.

By way of illustration, I will briefly mention how this way of thinking was manifested in some earlier work by Halford. Halford and Wilson (1980) presented a formal theory of cognitive development in which the structure-mapping principle was worked out with impressive thoroughness. The thoroughness was mathematical; which is to say that they took a technical definition of what it means for one system to be mathematically "represented" by another system (Suppes & Zinnes, 1963) and then applied this to the mind–environment relationship. One was just a mirror image of the other, except that their symbols had different subscripts. Now, although this way of proceeding can pay dividends through making the theorist think hard about task structure and about how new tasks measure stage-wise changes, the view of understanding that it advertises may still be mistaken.

Let us return, finally, to the competence–performance distinction. My criticisms are levelled entirely at mental-modelling theories of development as *competence* theories, in the sense that such theories are presented as if they were capturing what it means to understand and know something. This leaves an awful lot untouched. It leaves untouched the performance theory that the timing and nature of certain stage-wise developments is determined by resource growth, which in turn determines the complexity of the models the child can construct. But we do not want to say that the development of knowledge—of *competence*—is a matter of resource growth alone.

It is worth noting that Halford regards his developmental theory as "neo-Piagetian" in the sense of positing stage-wise developments specified by their logical structure. Other neo-Piagetians of this stamp are Robbie Case (1985) and Robert Siegler (1989). But, although there is certainly a Piagetian flavour to this way of thinking, the notion that resource limitations set the timetable for development is not in the Piagetian spirit, as Annette Karmiloff-Smith (1993) has pointed out. Karmiloff-Smith emphasises Piaget's concern with fundamental restructuring and qualitative representational change; and I emphasise his concern with agency.

1.3: CONNECTIONISM

A good way to begin is by thinking about what the distinction between connectionist theories and LOT theories turns on. It turns on the fact that connectionism posits sub-symbolic representations while LOT posits symbolic ones. A related difference is that in connectionist networks representational elements that are similar in their contents are similar in their values: elements with similar functional roles have similar activation vectors. Accordingly, not even in the weakest and most metaphorical sense do the elements in neural networks have a "shape" (i.e. have non-semantic or arbitrary properties)—as compared to linguistic symbols in which similarity of meaning almost never guarantees similarity of graphemic or phonological structure. This means the representational elements in neural networks must be regarded *non-atomistically*, in the sense that the value of any such element is a direct function of its causal liaisons with its surrounding milieu. It also means that problems which exist for LOT cannot exist for connectionism; there is nothing mysterious, for example, about how representations are causally related to one another in connectionism and so there is no problem with marrying the nature of these representational elements with the holism of the mental.

It is clear, then, that an holistic theory of how concepts are represented emerges naturally from connectionism. In such models, representation is achieved by patterns of activity distributed across units whose nature is mathematical rather than symbolic. As we have seen, these are *values*—activation vectors—not formal entities. This also makes for a highly context-dependent view of concept representation such that, for example, the representation "dog" in "Jack walked his dog" and in "The dog chased the leaves" will be achieved by different sub-patterns of activation. And although one can talk metaphorically about connectionist systems having "sub-symbols", this is only by way of stressing that, unlike true symbols, they have no fixed, atomic, *sui generis* character. As Smolensky (1988, p.17, original italics) puts it, "the context alters the internal structure of the symbol: the activities of the sub-conceptual units that comprise the symbol—its sub-symbols— change across contexts [...]. In the symbolic paradigm the context of a symbol is manifest *around* it and consists of *other symbols*; in the subsymbolic paradigm the context of a symbol is manifest *inside* it, and consists of sub-symbols". In this way then, connectionist models can capture the fact, stressed by holists about mental content, that representations of concepts and thoughts are relative to the patterning of the total representational system: what is "inside" a symbol is determined by the wider processing context.

The difference between connectionism and mental models theory is nearly as stark. Neural networks do not represent states of affairs in terms of models that are more or less isomorphic to states of affairs, and so their representations do not require interpretation by centres further downstream in the processing system. Because connectionism is closer to the neural level than to the conscious level, it is not, unlike mental models theory, saddled with the idea that what makes a representation true of something is its structural similarity to its referent. We do not find isomorphic structures in the brain.

To the eyes of developmental psychologists, connectionist models have, moreover, a third advantage: they *learn*. Remember that symbolic theories disallow genuine learning (i.e. via organism–environment interaction which causes the acquisition of new concepts) because, by definition, a mental symbol cannot be learned. The only kinds of learning they can allow, remember, is learning in the sense of recombining innately represented symbols and of coming to know which sentences in LOT are true of the world as it is presented to the developing mind. Against this view, enthusiasts for the connectionist approach will say such things as "the Tabula Rasa case provides a genuine proof of the ability of some systems to engage in rational knowledge acquisition without an innate representational base ... The connectionist is able to offer a genuinely *empiricist* vision of learning ..." (Clark, 1993, p.593; original italics). The point is debatable of course (no doubt Fodor would question whether acquiring an input–output mapping for a specific task is "learning" anything about the world); but this is certainly the *prima facie* attraction of such a sub-symbolic approach and the reason why developmental psychologists often take to it so warmly. So does connectionism give us what we want?

Yes and (maybe) no. The negative face of this section will consist of some broadly sceptical remarks about whether connectionism is able to capture the so-called *systematic* nature of mature cognition (see p.9). In the next section, however, I will argue that connectionism is certainly the best-placed of the three representational theories to describe the kind of sub-symbolic processing that underlies the exercise of agency. This will be a rather paradoxical conclusion because it is generally regarded as a thoroughly bottom-up account of cognition, and nothing could be more top-down than action.

Let us begin by considering two common criticisms of connectionism. The first is based on a misconception, but the second is a harder nut to crack—if it can be cracked at all. The first is that the essentially *associationist* nature of connectionist models ensures that they are little more than machines for doing lots of correlational statistics at the same time. To this extent they do not really have representations at all: they simply record stochastic regularities and contiguities. Here I will do little more than précis James McClelland's (1992) answer to this criticism.

It is true, McClelland points out, that connectionist models bear similarities to associationist models and true that both of them employ statistical techniques; but connectionist models go beyond this. These models do not merely strengthen some connections by contiguity between bits of information and weaken others, rather, it is a matter (McClelland, 1992, p.12, original italics) of:

> *totally recoding each input so as to map it into a similarity space whose structure depends*, not on the surface properties of the inputs, but *on the demands that are made by the task of predicting outputs from inputs*. This sensitivity of the internal representations to the task they are required to perform dramatically increases the range of what such models are able to achieve compared to associationist models or standard statistical techniques.

The model McClelland uses to illustrate this fact is Hinton's (1986) kinship task; and kinship knowledge is, by a nice irony, just what nativists such Keil (1987) often cite to illustrate the importance of innate structure over learned regularities. The network was given information about two families, an English and an Italian family. It was then trained to answer questions of the following kind: "Who is Alfonso's/Colin's Uncle?". When the net had learned the task (which involved generalising to cases on which it had *not* been trained) it was possible to examine how the representation had been achieved in n-dimensional state space[10] by examining the similarity structure (roughly, items with similar roles cluster together in state space) in the hidden-unit representations. "Slices" through this space were taken, one plane for

English and another for Italian. The result was that each had a hierarchy-like structure and one structure paralleled the other. In both cases, the older generations were at the top of the plane, the younger generation at the bottom, and the middle generations in between, while individuals on the left/right of the tree were on the left/right of the plane, for both families. What was responsible for the fact that individuals at similar locations on the tree had similar representations was that this enabled the network to solve the problem. So clearly we are not dealing with simple associations between inputs and outputs; and the resulting representations have "structure"—in *some* sense.

Some recent work of Jeffrey Elman (1993) reinforces this point. Here, the network's task was to learn number agreement across the clause boundaries of sentences. Elman trained a network to be sensitive to the presence of a relative clause. For example, the verb "see" in the following sentence has to agree in number with "boys" not with "girl" although it is nearer the latter: "The boys who the girl chases see the dog". Analysis of the state space[11] of the successful networks showed that structured representations existed in which dimensions such as grammatical category, number, grammatical role, and so forth were located in different areas of the space; and these were represented on different planes—as were the families in the previous example. It was possible to understand the representations of different sentences as "movements" through this space.

Having discussed the charge that connectionist models are associationist, we come to a second and more serious criticism. It is that these models cannot capture the systematicity of thought.

A warning before I proceed: things may begin to seem a little paradoxical at this point because the argument from systematicity is *a kind of argument from holism*; it may feel strange to find LOT theorists recruiting a kind of holistic argument. But recall that LOT theories can accept the holism of *belief* while strongly rejecting the holism of content—or "meaning holism" (recall the discussion of Fodor & Lepore, 1992). Well, arguments that stress the systematicity of cognitive capacity look rather like arguments from the holism of belief. In order to make things appear as unparadoxical as possible we need, then, to bear in mind the difference between the holism of mental *content* (anathema to LOT theorists) and the holism of mental *capacity* (equivalent to systematicity). The former, recall, refers to the content of what we represent when we mean things by words and to propositional contents. Connectionism is holistic, as I said just now, in *this* sense.

In the holism of *mental capacity*, by contrast, what is asserted is that it makes no sense to say that a person can think one kind of thought (e.g. John loves Mary; 2 + 2 = 4) if he or she cannot think other kinds of thought (e.g. Mary loves John; $1 + 1 = 2$). Far from undermining the LOT thesis, the holism of mental capacity bolsters it, because structured representations give one holism of capacity for free. Accordingly, Fodor and Pylyshyn (1988) insist that connectionist models do not display a holism of capacity (*not* their term) because connectionist representations can be "punctate" (their term): a connectionist simulation may indeed by able to represent A's loving B but not be able to represent B's loving A.

The best way to understand the intimate linkage between the holism of mental capacity and the LOT thesis is in terms of Chomsky's famous claim that the human language capacity is "creative". Language is creative because we are constantly framing sentences we have never framed before; and this is possible, according to Chomksy, because we have a set of formal rules (a linguistic competence) which "generates" a potentially infinite number of sentences—rather as πr^2 "generates" an infinite number of circles. Well, what goes for language also goes for thinking, argues Fodor.

It would be a good idea to take Fodor's argument a little slowly at this point. What grounds the systematicity of our language competence, he argues, is the fact that sentences have *combinatorial semantics*. This term refers to the fact that, in thinking, arguments and predicates are freely combinable. For instance, the predicate "white" can be attached to the argument "car" just as well as to the argument "house", while the argument "car" can be attached just as well to the predicate "red". But some further capacity grounds combinatorial semantics, namely, the *constituent structure* of language. The reason why language-users can combine arguments and predicates in this way is that the system they are using consists of embedded, hierarchical elements. If I can think "The car is white" I am not merely uttering a string of symbols in which a predicate is *associated* with an argument. Indeed, for the sentence to have meaning it must have a structure in which the noun-phrase, the verb-phrase, and the qualifier are constituent elements with specified roles; the predicate qualifies the argument within the sentence and thereby expresses a proposition. The LOT theorist can now say, in effect, that if you accept this about language why do you not accept it about thinking—given that much of human thought has a linguistic character? Or in Fodor's words (1987, pp.150–151): "OK, so here is the argument: Linguistic capacities are systematic, and that's because sentences have constituent structure. But cognitive capacities are systematic too, and that must be because thoughts have constituent structure. But if thoughts have constituent structure, then LOT is true."

Before getting back to connectionism I need to make one comment, a necessary one given my earlier negative remarks about the LOT thesis.

We can agree with all Fodor says in that passage except the final sentence—the conclusion that the truth of the LOT thesis follows from these facts. The reason is simple: the LOT thesis *is not supposed to restrict itself to mature, human, verbal thought*, and yet it is only of such forms of cognition that we can unequivocally say "thoughts have constituent structure". Remember that the LOT thesis—as originally proposed by Fodor—concerned itself with the representational format that must underlie any adequate thought and *make language acquisition possible*. Fodor was clear, indeed, that he intended the thesis to apply to animal as well as to human cognition. He argued, for example, that the reason both humans and rats find disjunctive rules harder to learn than conjunctive ones is that we share with rats a representational format (Fodor, 1976, p.57). But do rats have thoughts with constituent structure? If there is a sense in which they do, then I am sure it will be a very different sense from that in which human thought has a constituent structure. Accordingly, one can be sceptical about the view that our possession of an innate pool of atomic mental symbols underlies our capacity to acquire language while agreeing that mature, human thought has a systematic character.

We now return to connectionist theories of representation. Fodor and Pylyshyn (1988) argue that if thought is systematic then internal representations must be structured; connectionist models posit unstructured representations, so these models fail as models of cognition.

Andy Clark (1989, pp.146–150) has defended connectionist theories against this charge in the following way. It does not follow, he argues, from the fact that our thought *ascriptions* (i.e. the criteria we use to judge whether somebody is a thinker) are systematic that the underlying representational system of a thinker should itself be systematic. (His position is similar to that of Dennett, 1981, who denies that we should expect sub-personal, "in-the-head" processing to line up neatly with folk psychology.) There are two things, he insists, which should not be confused: the systematicity of the thought-ascribing sentences (a *conceptual* requirement on being judged rational) and the systematicity of behaviour (an *empirical* matter); and connectionist models do behave systematically, as most would agree. "The upshot of this position," writes Clark (1989, p.150, original italics), "is that as a holist (and, indeed, a kind of behaviourist) about thought ascription, I would deny that *any* systematic description of a thought as picked out by our daily talk of thoughts is likely to be a good guide to actual in-the-head processing."

I think it is easy to agree with Clark that the systematicity of our conceptual system should not be confused with the systematicity or otherwise of the sub-personal machinery that enables us to be users of this system. But I am not sure that Clark's defence meets the full force of the challenge from systematicity. The Chomskian argument from the creativity of language, borrowed by Fodor to apply to thought, is that if there is to be a capacity for comprehending *and producing* an infinity of sentences then the generative system must have rules for generating. If we accept that this is true of thinking, then we have a reason to believe that rules are needed to generate thoughts; and this is not just a matter of how our conceptual system functions as a criterion-setter for whether or not somebody is "a thinker". Imagine Clark's argument being applied to the language capacity. In this case the concept of "a well-formed sentence" would reduce to a matter of the *structure of our public judgements* about whether somebody is speaking grammatically. There must be more to it than this. In order to make judgements of grammaticality—in order for us to have the right kind of linguistic intuitions, as Chomsky calls them—we must (tacitly or otherwise) be following complex rules similar to the ones that the speaker, whose utterances we are assessing, is following when generating his or her sentences.

These remarks depend, of course, on taking a broadly Chomskian view of language; and so to that extent they have a limited force. So let us consider another kind of defence against the claim that connectionism fails to accommodate the systematicity of thought in virtue of lacking structured representations. In this case, the defence is not that the sub-personal mechanisms of creatures that have systematic thoughts ascribed to them do not themselves have to be systematic, it is that the representations within connectionist models *are* systematic: "*Of course* connectionism posits structured representations. You have just given us two examples of them—hierarchical representations in kinship and syntax."

The problem with this reply, however, is that there can be structured representations that *lack the resources to support systematicity in production*. These representations, recall, were structured in the sense that elements that played similar roles in the input–output mapping task were located in roughly the same areas of state-space. But there is more to systematicity than this. Being located in the same area in the network's state-space is not the same as that network's using rules in which there are *recombinable abstract elements and the recursive embedding of elements within others*. As McClelland made clear, locating elements with similar roles in similar regions of state-space is done in the service of solving a particular task. But linguistic competence is something that exists over-and-above the processing of any particular sentence or set of sentences; it is not something that emerges from the process of finding a sounding–meaning mapping for individual sentences.

Consider an analogy between a connectionist language-learner and people learning a language with a phrase-book. The phrase-book users are solving lots of "particular tasks" too. They can comprehend a large number of sentences and may even make intelligent inferences to the correct meaning of sentences they have never heard (like a network generalising to new cases), but could be doing all this while being unable to produce their own sentences (sentences that are not merely re-arranged versions of ones whose meaning they already know) *because these "creative" sentences must be generated by rules, not by local analogies from sentence to sentence*[12]. There may come a time when the phrase-book users have constructed a grammar for the language and can therefore be linguistically creative. But once this has happened they have moved beyond the phrase-book and the solving of local problems about sound-to-meaning mappings and are using rules productively.

What this boils down to is the familiar claim that the ability to comprehend an infinity of sentences is conceptually related to the ability to produce an infinity of sentences. As Fodor says (1987, p.150), "Productivity and systematicity run together; if you postulate mechanisms adequate to account for one, then—assuming you're prepared to idealise—you get the other automatically."

It may look as if I am having my cake and eating it here. In the section on LOT I argued against the notion of a mental symbol on the grounds that it cannot be squared with the holism of mental content. (As we have seen, connectionism naturally accommodates the holism of mental content.) And yet here I am siding with the view that the productivity of rational thought must depend on the possession of language-like rule systems. Isn't there a contradiction? No, because one can deny the existence of mental symbols that ground thoughts about dogs, cats, and ice-skating while still believing (1) that there are abstract rule-systems in the language user, (2) that the mature thinker uses these, and even (3) that language learners must innately possess them.

What this view hinges on is the fact that the elements of syntax (in natural language: noun, verb, etc.) and their inter-relations (e.g. agreement and embedding rules) do not mean what they mean in virtue of what they refer to in the world. As I stressed earlier a noun is not a term that refers to objects and a verb is not a term that refers to actions, because there are many nouns that do not refer to objects and plenty of verbs that do not refer to actions. To say that a word is a noun or a verb is to say that it plays a particular role in a sentence in relation to the roles of other kinds of term: there is a holism *without semantics*, without a meaning determined by the kinds of objects picked out by the word.

Thus, language-users mentally manipulate symbols for "noun phrase", "verb phrase", and so forth and perform operations on these symbols; but, because these symbols stand for nothing outside language itself, the holism or otherwise of mental *content* is beside the point. One is therefore free to be a nativist or an empiricist about how symbols (in this special sense) such as "noun phrase" come to be "in the head". For the nativist, one of the major tasks of language development is to give them a semantics (the "semantic bootstrapping" of Pinker, 1987)[13]. Or one can be an empiricist and say that "noun phrases" are emergent properties of language acquisition and that once they have "emerged" the thinker is using mental symbols that stand for abstract linguistic entities.

What is the worst one can say about connectionism as a meta-theory? Connectionist models achieve mappings between input and output without using symbols and rules, and one may see them as existence-proofs against the view that learning is impossible without innate, atomic mental symbols. But to the extent that they limit themselves to this role they may not turn out to be adequate models of rational thought. The reason is that the systematicity of rational thought is inextricably bound up with its productivity, with the capacity of the thinker to generate thoughts that cannot be characterised as mappings from inputs to outputs.

1.4: WHY CONNECTIONISM IS THE REPRESENTATIONAL THEORY BEST PLACED TO MODEL ACTION

In this section, I will put to one side the question of whether a sub-symbolic system can model the systematicity of mature cognition and consider what these three representational theories can say about action. Note that I am referring to "action" rather than to "agency" because, as I said right at the start, I shall be going on to mean something particular by "agency" in Parts 2 and 3, namely, "the ability to alter at will one's perceptual inputs". For the time being, I just want to talk about the "output" side of things—the organism's ability to act on the basis of its representations (whether we think of these as mental sentences, mental models, or patterns of activation across units). In a nutshell, I will argue that the first two representational theories are debarred from saying anything informative about action, whereas the third, although more naturally adapted to modelling data-driven, bottom-up processes, is adaptable to modelling the sub-personal conditions for activity.

Our folk psychology is sometimes referred to as "belief-desire psychology", and this fact alone is sufficient to show us the insufficiency of a *thoroughly* representational theory of mind: desires are not representations, and without desires we would never act. To desire a certain outcome is, of course, to represent an outcome, but to represent it as desirable is not just to "add something to the representation". This is because there is nothing in either the concrete or the abstract world that the mental orientation of feeling desire *represents*.

The LOT doctrine, as we have seen, proposes a kind of solution to this problem, a solution in terms of "boxes" into which mental sentences can be put depending on the propositional attitude of which they are the object (e.g. belief that-, hope that-). The box a sentence is in will determine the way in which it relates to inputs, to other sentences, and to output. As we shall discuss much later, desire does not function as an attitude in the way in which, say, belief does (it can govern objects rather than propositions—we can desire a cheeseburger but we cannot believe one); but we could say that if a sentence is in our desire-box then it will cause us to make that sentence (e.g. "There is a cheeseburger in my hand") come true.

However, this is not just a fanciful metaphor: it is an inadequate one. For how is it that a given location of a sentence within the mental architecture makes just those causal links with output that we need it to make? There is a whiff of the magical in all this. Moreover, do we seriously want to explain, say, *thirst* in terms of putting the sentence "I drink fluid" in my desire-box and keeping it there until it has been made true?[14] Are there better metaphors? Another metaphor used by Fodor and others to talk about the attitudes—and thus, by extension, the desire for objects—is that of the subject or agent being in a "relation" to the content expressed by a mental sentence. So can we think of desires as being "relations" between ourselves and our mental sentences? But "relation" is a spatial metaphor equally as obscure as the spatial metaphor of being at a "location" (in a box). At this point, one is tempted simply to reprise the late Alan Newell's statement that "The more the metaphor the less the science"[15].

We have already encountered another, deeper reason why the LOT thesis is ill-adapted to explaining action. Recall that towards the end of 1.1(ii) we encountered Fodor and Lepore's claim that it is contentful mental representations, not beliefs, that are primary—"primary" in the sense that there can be a mental life without beliefs but that there cannot be a mental life without representations. What I argued was, roughly, that the idea of there being a mental life without beliefs is only coherent if organisms enjoying such a mental life never act; they may have desires and react to the presence and recoil from the absence of "desired" stimulation but insofar as they have no beliefs about the world they will never act on it. This theme was taken up again in 1.1(iii)—with full orchestration—in my discussion of Heal's argument that in making atomistic mental representations the primary mental stuff, we render ourselves incapable of giving a plausible account of rational action, whereas a view of mental life centred on a unified subject is well placed to provide such an account.

In sum, I do not think David Hamlyn (1990, Ch.7) is overstating matters by saying that symbol-processing theories of mind have nothing plausible to say about action. When, he says, the LOT-subscribers who are enemies of folk psychology (e.g. Stich, 1983) explain action by appeal to "representations" it is "something of a fraud: the appeal is made simply to provide an otherwise missing connection between the central processes and behaviour". And when it is the friends of folk psychology, such as Jerry Fodor, who are making this appeal then they should "make it clear exactly what they see folk psychology as explaining on the output side" (p.129).

In fact *any* thoroughly representational theory of the mind—to bring the ambitious version of the mental models thesis within the ambit—looks unconvincing when it has to explain action. I will have a lot more to say in Parts 2 and 3 about the respects in which agency does not reduce to representations, so I will leave things here for now.

But does connectionism fare any better?

1.4(i) Connectionism's difficulties with action
The case that connectionism cannot model action would go something like this.

The previous section ended by asking whether connectionism has the resources for explaining the productivity of structured thought. Well, one could say that the difficulty of conceiving how connectionist models might generate original sentences is just a special case of the problem of how they might generate *any* kind of intentional behaviour[16]. We produce sentences for all kinds of reasons and we do things for all kinds of reasons. To do things for reasons means that *we*, as it were, set the agenda: the world is not evoking behaviour from us. Action is top-down; reaction is bottom-up. And any system whose primary function is to "predict outputs from inputs", in McClelland's words, is reactive: it lacks the resources to model action.

This is not to deny, the argument runs, that there might be connectionist models in which "framing an intention" is a *variable*. For example, a subject's attempt to name the colour or name the word in a Stroop[17] test is coded on "task-demand" units (Cohen & Servan-Schreiber, 1992). Something similar occurs in a model of the

Wisconsin Card-Sorting Test[18] (Dehaene & Changeux, 1991), where "current intention units" represent strategies such as "sort by number" or "sort by shape". But such models say nothing, the objector claims, about how these intentions are *generated*. The modeller can, of course, bracket off questions about the source of intentions; but he or she will do so at the cost of representing that intention *as being informationally equivalent to an environmental input*. That is to say, an intention within the network will be a variable that directs the network towards a certain class of input (e.g. the colour rather than the shape of a card), but that is simply equivalent to being *presented* with that class of information.

Suppose—this objector is warming to his theme—that I give you the instruction to do a dance of your own invention for one minute. What you will be doing here is manifesting the ability to perform meaningless actions at will: you will not be generating "information" that serves as input to a learning system. And what, to reiterate, is *generating* the information? *However* we conceptualise the generator, it can surely not be as just "more information". Moreover, dancing is not goal-directed in any obvious way (there is no distal goal, just the movement of one's limbs for its own sake) and so it is difficult to imagine what role can be given to such things as "strategy units" that code the kind of goal that limb movements are meant to achieve.

What the objector is worried about here is the fact that networks model how information flows between input and output, whereas active mental systems set about collecting the input for themselves, and that it is unsatisfactory to model this "setting about" collecting new input as just *more input* to the network. It is, in fact, a version of the general complaint that neural networks model cognition in a bottom-up fashion and so they cannot capture the fact that minds frame intentions when the environmental input to them is *unchanging*.

Finally—the objector says—although the content of an intention can be something in the world (e.g. my intention to eat *that* cheeseburger over there) the fact that it is an intention not, say, a hope or a fear in relation to the object, refers to nothing in the world. In other words, insofar as connectionism is a species of representational theory, it is saddled with the view that a propositional attitude is a representation. Accordingly, a network can be given intention-units or strategy-units but, unlike units that represent features of the environment (e.g. verb-stems or right-angles), they have no referents: they are just postulations. So the situation is not very different from that identified in the LOT thesis, in which a representational (spatial) metaphor is used to capture something that is not representational.

And yet and yet ... although there are grains of truth in what the objector says, it reduces to little more than the plaint that no simulation (sub-symbolic or symbolic) can model *free will*; or at least that we lack the imagination to see how this might be done. (It is a version of the so-called "Leonardo–Shakespeare gambit" used by opponents of the whole AI enterprise.) How we should even frame questions about the "source" of our intentions presents us with a conundrum, and it is surely unfair to expect neural networks to unravel it for us. Regarding an intention as a pattern of activation flowing from one part of a network to another may be misconceived in some degree but it looks like the best we can do for now.

We clearly need to ask a more modest question: Can connectionist systems (systems whose only resources are units and connections-weights with modifiable values) model the sub-personal flow of information in an organism that acts rather than reacts?

1.4(ii) Connectionism's successes with action

In this section I will describe two examples of recent connectionist research which can be read as success stories, or at least as unfinished but upbeat narratives. Although the first deals with goal-directed motor control and the second with sequencing and attention, both fall under the heading of *"dynamic"* modelling, whose broad aim is to model the transitions between states in the system which are unprompted by changes in the environment. This falls well short of "framing intentions", but it is a condition for it.

Example 1: The "forward" model
It is clearly a *sine qua non* for successful action that one be able to predict the phenomenal outcomes of one's movements, because if we had no advance notion of how actions can affect our experience we would have no reason to do anything. I now describe a model whose distinctive feature is that it predicts the sensations that will result from muscle movements. It was developed originally by Michael Jordan (1990).

Jordan and Rumelhart (1992) explain the necessity for their model with the following example. What a basketball player must learn is the appropriate muscle commands for propelling the ball towards the basket, with different commands being needed for different locations of the goal relative to his body. It is clear, however, that the classical "supervised" algorithm (coding the difference between the output produced and the "teaching" signal and then adjusting the weights by back propagation) will not be sufficient here. This is because certain muscle commands must *themselves* be targets for the learner's intentions—the muscle commands that map to the desired outcome. In this case, however, the only information the player receives is in terms of the outcome of his movements—in terms of what it looks like for the ball to travel in a certain way towards the goal, missing it or hitting it. But knowing that our intentions do not map to the desired outcome *does not tell us the actions we have to take to improve the mapping*. In other words, we require a mapping between visual experience and muscle commands.

One may add that the problem being identified here is just a special case of the general problem with all purely S–R (and thus essentially reactive) theories of learning. It is all very well for the environment to give an error-signal or a hit-signal after movements have been produced, but this is useless to an organism that does not know the kinds of movements that will pull it away from error and towards success.

Jordan and Rumelhart draw a distinction between *proximal* variables (the actions the learner controls) and *distal* variables (the environmental outcomes he witnesses). The learner's problem is, therefore, to find a mapping from his intention (to get the ball into the net from a certain angle) to his muscle movements to yield the correct distal outcome, something he must do by discovering "how to vary the components of the proximal action vector so as to minimise the components of the distal error" (Jordan & Rumelhart, 1992, p.309). This is achieved by having an initial phase of learning in which the learner forms "an internal predictive model" (the "forward model") of the mapping from actions to distal outcomes. It begins randomly with a kind of manual babbling but eventually a predictive system emerges. When this set of predictions has been at least partially achieved, it can be used indirectly to map intentions to outcomes. In other words, a predictive model of which muscle movements lead to which kinds of exteroceptive outcome can be used in order to learn what must be done to realise certain intentions.

There are, then, two components of the network (see Fig. 1). There is the part that feeds information from input units for the current state of the environment and current intentions (variously dubbed by Jordan "the inverse model" or "the controller"—the latter in the diagram) up to action units. Then there is the part (the forward model) that feeds information, via banks of hidden units, from these action units to the output units *specifying predicted environmental outcomes and sensations*. Then, in order that intentions can map to outcomes, the output of the forward model feeds back to the state-of-environment (or "context") units. Such a model has been used to simulate the movement of a jointed arm in both static and dynamic (tracking a moving object) environments.

I am not saying that models of this kind magically resolve the kind of problems raised in the previous sub-section—that intentions can never be informationally equivalent to inputs and that much of our

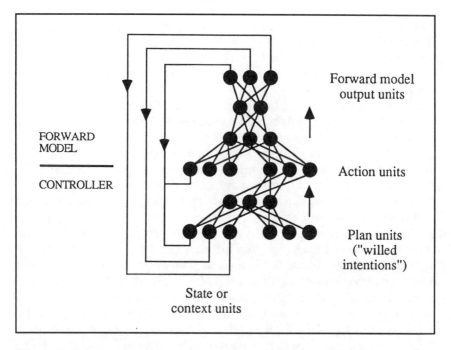

FIG. 1. Jordan's forward model. Redrawn from Brown, Britain, Elvenåg, and Mitchell (1994), with permission from Academic Press.

behaviour does not have a distal goal (recall the dancing example). In their discussion, Jordan and Rumelhart (1992, p.346) deal with this latter issue, using (by chance) the same example of behaviour.

> In a complex task such as dance, it is presumably not easy to determine the choice of sensory data to be used as distal targets for the learning procedure. Indeed the learner may alter the choice of targets once he or she has achieved a modicum of skill ... We suspect that the role of external "teachers" is to help with these representational issues rather than to provide proximal targets directly to the learner.

There is a dilemma looming here. In one sense, as we have just seen, goal-directed behaviour is ideally suited to connectionist modelling because a distal goal can serve as a teaching input in a fairly straightforward way; and so it is behaviour *without* a distal goal that provides a challenge: how does one model the meaningless actions done at will for no reason? But, on the other hand, it is goal-directed behaviour that is sometimes seen as being the significant challenge, because the model must make a principled distinction between responses to input and actions taken in order to realise a goal. As we shall see later, some would argue that data from animal learning experiments (and from everyday experience) suggest that responses and actions are mediated by different systems and that, as yet, no connectionist model has succeeded in distinguishing them in a principled manner (Dickinson & Balleine, 1993). In this spirit, one would say that the Jordan and Rumelhart simulation *is* really an S–R system not an intentional system: the intentions are stipulated as inputs, the movement–outcome mappings are learned by blind trial-and-error as are the intention–action mappings, and that embedding one S–R system inside another does not make the whole system intentional.

I am going to leave the issue of goal-directedness here, and return it to it towards the end of Part 2.

Example 2: Sequencing, selective attention, and opponent processing
One of the consequences of connectionism's having (at least *prima facie*) an essentially data-driven, bottom-up character is that it seems ill-adapted both to modelling sequences of actions that are not mere responses to sequences of stimuli and to modelling selective attention. In both cases the model has to do something that is the opposite of "parallel" and "distributed": it has to be serial and it has to focus on one datum rather than distribute itself among an array of data. There have been a number of attempted solutions to this problem (e.g. Rumelhart & Norman, 1982), but the most successful to date has been produced by George Houghton (1994).

Houghton makes use of a notion that has previously been applied at many psycho-physiological levels—"*opponent processing*". Opponent processing requires two excitable processes—the "primary" or alpha-process and an "opponent" or beta-process, with the latter inhibiting the former. It is also assumed that there is a lag between the onset of the primary and the opponent process, and that when the former is de-activated the latter is "unmasked" in its pure form. A second assumption Houghton makes, but one not common to all forms of opponent-processing models, is that activation of the primary processes leads to activation of the opponent process. Opponent processing concepts have been applied to processes ranging from the synaptic firing (the principle of lateral inhibition), to colour vision (Mollon, 1982), to high-level hedonic processes such as drug addiction (Soloman & Corbit, 1974).

Turning first to action-sequencing, when applied to neural network accounts of phoneme sequencing in speech and to serial recall, opponent processing is manifested in a so-called "competitive queuing" model

(Houghton, 1990). This is a "parallel" rather than a "serial" queue, in the sense that people lined up at a crowded bar trying to get the bartender's attention are in a parallel queue (people lining up behind one another to buy a ticket are in a serial queue). The basic assumptions here are that a sequence node feeds information down via weighted connections to the item nodes which differ in activation levels, and that the higher the activation level (the louder the would-be drinker's voice) the sooner it will trigger its associated output. Second, there are inhibitory processes that both suppress the activation of elements after they have fired (and thereby enable the next item to be selected) and that, in speech production, take the form of the mutual inhibition of the item nodes through a process reminiscent of lateral inhibition.

The problem in selective attention is clearly reminiscent of the problem of sequencing, in the sense that in both cases we have to explain how one item is selected from many, whereas this time it is a component of a perceived array selected in preparation for action rather than one motor output among others. One aim of the model that Houghton has developed with Stephen Tipper (Houghton & Tipper, in press) is to reproduce the "negative priming" (Tipper, 1985) effect in visual selective attention. On the basis of a number of experiments, Tipper and others have proposed that an organism's selective attention to one element of a scene results in the inhibition of other elements—a kind of opponent processing. The evidence for this proposal comes mainly from reaction-time studies with a prime→probe sequence of the following kind. In the prime phase subjects respond to one of (say) two stimuli on the basis a selected feature (e.g. colour), after which, in the probe phase, they have either to respond to (1) the same stimulus as before; or to (2) the prime distractor stimulus which had previously appeared with the target, is similar to the target on some dimensions, but differs in colour; or to (3) a control stimulus which is different from both target and distractor. Reaction times are slowest in (2).

In a nutshell, the Houghton-Tipper model has the following four, functionally-separate systems (see Fig. 2). There are two forms of input—external, bottom-up information from the visual world (the "object field") and top-down internally-generated goals and plans (the "target field"). The third system is a match/mismatch detector which takes these two as inputs; objects matching the target become thereby selectively enhanced and those mismatching have their activation levels suppressed. Then, according to Houghton (1994, p.144), the "opening up of this activation gap between targets and distractors allows task-relevant information from target inputs to coherently bind the parameters of the currently active action schema." This is the fourth system—the "variable binding system".

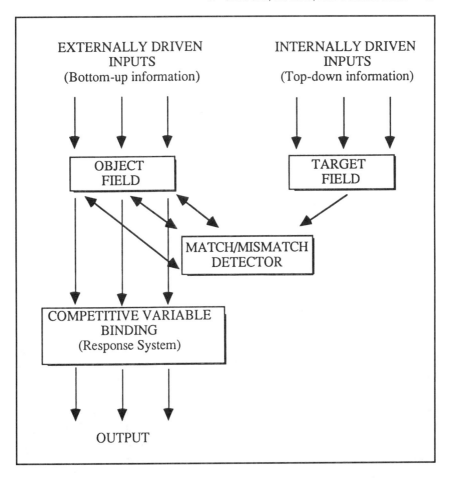

FIG. 2. The Houghton-Tipper model of selective attention. Redrawn from Houghton (1994), with permission from Academic Press.

To say, like the objector in 1.4(i), that intentions are simply being treated here as being "informationally equivalent to environmental inputs" and that we see nothing about the "source" of these intentions is, as I said, little more than the complaint that these models do not solve the deep conundrum about the source of intentions—and that is to ask too much. We shall see right at the end of the book that connectionist models that share the basic assumptions of Jordan's and Houghton's help us to understand volitional impairments in mental illness and—by extension—the development of those aspects of mentality that are dependent on adequate volitional control. It is to developmental matters, in fact, that we now turn.

1.4(iii) Modelling development in a connectionist style

There are two things needing to be discussed here. First, I must point up some parallels between the way in which Jean Piaget conceived of development by organism–environment interaction and some basic ideas in connectionism. Next, some (inevitably speculative) things need to be said about the necessity for positing innate activity.

Learning via organism–environment interaction

There is a learning principle which McClelland (1989, p.20) states thus:

> Adjust the parameters of the mind in proportion to the extent to which their adjustment can produce a reduction in the discrepancy between expected and observed events.

This principle is manifestly at work, McClelland says, in the back-propagation algorithm for multi-layer networks, in the Rescorla-Wagner (1972) theory of classical conditioning—and in Piaget's principle of "*accommodation*".

Development, according to Piaget, is primarily a matter of adaptation to an environment via "equilibration"—the process of adjusting the contours of one's actions or one's thoughts (these being mental actions) to data. Learning is successful, he said, when equilibrium is achieved between "assimilation" and "accommodation". The former is a conservative form of activity—the attempt to assimilate new data to pre-existing behavioural "schemes" (e.g. sucking, grasping, tracking); the latter is the modification of these schemes in the service of successful action—accommodation. The contours of the old scheme have to be changed in such a way that the greater the novelty (e.g. applying a rattle-grasping scheme to a pillow) the greater the degree of accommodation acquired. This principle is supposed to be applicable throughout development, right from the infant's first actions on objects to the adolescent's logical constructions. Although, as Jerome Bruner (1959) among others has observed, by the time we arrive at adolescence this learning principle has become somewhat turgid and overblown, it is plausible and powerful when applied to infancy; and infancy was supposed, by Piaget, to be the period during which the fundamental cognitive structures developed, the base of the "spiral" for later developments on higher representational planes.

It does not take much imagination to apply Jordan's forward model here in order to account for forms of assimilation–accommodation in which there are distal goals. One might say, for example, that although a simple back-propagation algorithm may account adequately for what Piaget called "primary circular reactions" (in which activity has no effect on the external world, e.g. thumb-sucking), for "secondary circular reactions" (in which there is an external effect, e.g. pulling a cord attached to a mobile) the forward model is more appropriate.

A further parallel between Piagetian theory and connectionism is historical; and history can sometimes tell us who one's true allies are. One of the earliest attempts to simulate psychological processes in neural networks was a model of assimilation–accommodation in the liquid conservation task. In the early 1960s Symour Papert (Papert, 1963) worked in Geneva towards a connectionist model of the equilibration process, although the resulting "Genetron" model failed for the (by now) familiar reason that it used a single-layer network. More recent work by Mareschal (1991) along similar lines (using a procedure called "Cascade correlation") has been more successful.

There is, finally, a higher-level parallel between connectionism and Piagetian psychology. As Bates and Elman (1993) and McClelland (1992) have recently argued, Piagetians and connectionists share a common concern with explaining development by organism–environment interaction; they both, in contrast to enthusiasts for LOT, believe in concept acquisition. And they both hold that the organism/network undergoes structural change as it interacts with the environment. Consequently, they share a lack of sympathy with nativism; not because they deny that innate mental capacities exist but because they adopt the opposite of the classical nativist tenet called by Steven Pinker the "continuity assumption". This states that "the null hypothesis in developmental psychology is that the cognitive mechanisms of children and adults are identical; hence it is an hypothesis that should not be rejected until the data leave us no other choice" (Pinker, 1984, p.7). Piagetians and connectionists, by contrast, are happy to accept that the structure of the naive organism/network can be *discontinuous* with that of the mature system, that the structure of the system can change as it interacts with the environment.

However, it could be objected that if both approaches have this broadly empiricist character then they must lack plausibility, given what we have learned in the past 30 or so years about the richly innate endowment of human beings. If Piagetians and connectionists wish to account for mental development purely by assimilation and accommodation, it might be said, then they are flying in the face of the evidence. Some recent proposals of Andy Clark might lay this worry to rest.

Clark (1993, p.597) argues that connectionism should adopt the position of, what he calls, Minimal Rationalism, characterised as follows: "Instead of building in large amounts of innate knowledge and structure, build in whatever minimal biases and structure will ensure the emergence, under realistic environmental conditions, of the basic knowledge necessary for early successes and subsequent learning." The simplest examples of this involve pre-setting initial weights to ensure that the developing network converges on the solution. This is best achieved (for technical reasons) not by "hand-crafting" particular weights but by having small initial weights with small variances and constraining some to be positive and some to be negative. How small may these initial biases be? As small, he says, as the bias that very young infants appear to have towards attending to "three high-contrast blobs in the position of the eyes and mouth" (Karmiloff-Smith, 1992, p.256). This filtering bias will ensure that centres further downstream in the brain will become specialised for face perception. Another example is provided by Elman's syntax-learning model which I described earlier. Elman (1993) found that the network was unable to learn the task (of number agreement across clause boundaries) if it had been initially presented with the *complete* sentences. However if the network was given a short-term memory limitation or attentional window (it amounts to the same thing) of three words, which gradually increased to four, five, and so on the task became learnable. Taking small, bite-sized chunks of information prevents the network from converging on a solution too early and forces it to decompose the mapping task into sub-problems. So it may be, as Elman himself argues, that evolution has seen to it that children have limited memorial/attentional capacities because this forces them to learn complex tasks in a step-by-step fashion. This rather neatly explains Elisa Newport's (1991) finding that immigrants to the USA who arrived as small children turned out to be more competent at English than those who arrived later.

Kick-starting development: innate activity

Arthur Schopenhauer (1844/1966, p.24) (of whom more later) observed that neonates "who exhibit hardly the first faint trace of intelligence, are already full of their own will: in unbounded, aimless raging and crying they exhibit the urge of the will, with which they are teeming, while their will has yet no object, i.e. they will without knowing they will." Freud, on whom Schopenhauer was a major influence, held, of course, a similar view. This way of regarding the primordial state of the infant mind seems quaint in this era of cognitive science; but I would argue that it is a view that is forced on developmentalists who would take a broadly connectionist-cum-Piagetian line. That is to say, it is not sufficient to posit innate accommodatory capacities and a Minimal Rationalism unless one is prepared to ascribe to the infant innate assimilatory drives—innate desires. I will call this "Minimal Vitalism", and describing it will involve a brief and feverish dash into the realms of science fiction.

We might think of the neonatal network as having "drive units" with activation levels that vary, within limits. These will, additionally, compete with one another in competitive queuing fashion and, when one of them reaches its threshold, it will drive a motor output and *thereby determine what the perceptual input will be to the organism from a range of possible inputs*. (For example, there may be competition between units that drive fixation on mother's face and units that drive fixation on father—a novel stimulus—who has just entered the room.) It can only do so, however, indirectly. That is to say, drive units will only determine behaviour relative to what is being attended to. Imagine that these units feed down to the "internally driven units" and thus to the "target field" of Houghton and Tipper's model of selective attention (see Fig. 2), and that, in addition to determining what the organism will attend to, the model determines which actions it will take—what assimilatory attempts are made—and thus the next set of environmental data to be fed to the model's "externally driven" inputs. The sequence is "desire selected via competitive queuing→firing of particular drive units→target field→comparison with object field→motor output→new object field".

Could a network such as this generate appropriate behaviour, given a certain motivational state and a new state of perceptual input? Such an ability is certainly not unique to humans. For example, Anthony Dickinson and colleagues (see Dickinson, 1988) have shown that rats will utilise their past experience that sucrose is thirst-quenching when presented with a lever that they had earlier learned *under the previous motivational state of hunger* produced sucrose when pressed. They perform a kind of practical inference: pressing this lever gave me sucrose when I was hungry; sucrose is thirst-quenching; so to earn sucrose now I am thirsty I should press this lever. Could, in other words, such a network learn what to do in a *new* stimulus environment in the light of its needs? As it stands, almost certainly not. This is because it would need the additional capacity for representing the consequences of past behaviour in an hedonically-neutral fashion. But my only concern here is with the *necessity* for Minimal Vitalism not its sufficiency!

Although these proposals are sketchy in the extreme, they make a point. Minimal Vitalism models the contribution of an organism's endogenous activity by units whose spontaneous activity generates behaviour, and thus new inputs. It is minimal in much the same sense that Minimal Rationalism is minimal: it does not provide the organism with plans, strategies, or potential decisions any more than Minimal Rationalism provides it with knowledge. But it could, in principle, canalise learning in such a way that the motor outputs come to be produced which are directed towards elements of the environment in the service of desires. Minimal Rationalism may kick-start networks into concept acquisition; Minimal Vitalism could kick-start them into doing things for reasons.

What I will *not* do now—I will take all of Part 2 to do it—is to spell out why it is important for organisms spontaneously to change their perceptual inputs in this way.

1.5: "WORKING FROM THE OUTSIDE IN"

Representational theories work "from the inside out". That is to say, they line up behind a particular philosophical view of representation (sentential and nativist for LOT, a correspondence theory of truth and meaning for mental models, a broadly empiricist view for connectionism) and then set about explaining how these representations have to be configured if they are to provide the subject with objective knowledge.

In contrast to this, the approach to mental development I shall be presenting in the rest of the book is one that travels in the opposite direction: it works "from the outside in". That is to say, one begins, not with a representational theory, but with an active organism, enjoying sensory inputs, and located in an environment. The task is broadly to say how this organism must interact with its environment if it is to gain knowledge both of that environment and of itself as a knower of the environment.

What I do *not* intend to imply here is that developmental psychologists must plump for either one of these two approaches—inside→out or outside→in. Indeed, although I think it is fair to say that the outside→in approach has been neglected recently and that one can make out a case for pursuing it, the absolute necessity for the inside→out approach has to be acknowledged at the same time. How, for example, could one explain the acquisition of language in an outside→in fashion? The more sensible option would seem to be working from a competence model—structuralist for Chomsky (1980); functionalist for, say, Van Valin (1991)—of what has to be computed, that is, from a model of the formal rules and representations (on structuralism) and of the pragmatic regularities (on functionalism) that underlie grammar, and then moving towards an empirical account of how these are computed by the mind[19]. One may even say that it is difficult to take outside→in theories of language acquisition seriously nowadays; at the very least, the prospects do not look very bright for explaining, say, the ability to use clausal constructions in terms of organism–environment interaction[20]. On the other hand, if the aim is to give an account of how we come to the view that the external world and our mind exist, an approach couched in terms of the representations that underlie skilled performances (e.g. seeing in depth; parsing a sentence) begins to look less fruitful. For here one has to make an enormous assumption: that such fundamental forms of knowledge *are* explicable purely in terms of computing the right kind of representations. What I have been doing in Part 1 is arguing that attempts to explain cognition in purely representational terms are not successful, and although use of the term "cognition" has been a broad one, I have tried to keep an eye on these two fundamental forms of human knowledge—of the external world and of the mind.

One implication of the previous paragraph is that the outside→in approach is well placed to explain what Fodor (1983) calls "central systems" of the mind, whereas the inside→out approach is well placed to explain its "input-systems". In other words, if we are interested in mental faculties that are, in Fodor's expression, "global" (I have been calling them "holistic")—the systems spreading "horizontally" across all domains of information—then we should look at a whole organism acting within an environment. If, on the other hand, our interest is in the organism's ability to pick up information, to parcel it, and to send it "vertically" towards these higher systems, then the kinds of questions about agency and mental unity ("subject-hood" I called it earlier) with which we will be concerned in the rest of the book can be shelved.

Fodor famously said that the more "central" a cognitive function is the less we understand it; and this was "Fodor's First Law of the Non-Existence of the Cognitive Sciences" (1983, p.107). But perhaps this failure is a self-inflicted one—caused by our trying to explain central capacities in inside→out, thoroughly representational, terms. I will return to this question in my summing-up; but before moving to Part 2 here are some further points to be borne in mind about these two ways of doing developmental psychology.

- The two approaches view "the problem of consciousness" in quite different ways. On the inside→out view, consciousness can be seen as an emergent property of a form of processing; whereas on the outside→in view consciousness is a matter of gaining access to reality by establishing a division, via action, between oneself as a representer and that which is represented. The first view is essentially solipsistic and idealist, the second essentially vitalist and realist.
- It goes without saying that on the outside→in view the organism must begin with representations of *some* kind and that its representational capacity will develop in various ways. But the

hallmark of this approach is that it takes a relaxed and ecumenical view of mental representation and then works towards empirical accounts of the form these mental representations take in different domains and at different ages.

- One can accept, on the outside→in view, that much of (at least, mature) cognition has a syntactic nature, that what children and adults achieve in certain domains can best be explained on the "high" level of mental modelling, and that much of what they can understand and do must be modelled at the "low" level of neural networks. But there is no commitment to a particular theory of representation or to any particular theory of the representational end-state of development. Instead there is a commitment to "transcendental" arguments. Recall that these take the following form: we could not know (or believe or have the capacity to ...) X unless we had Y experiences; we do know (etc.) X; therefore we must have had Y experiences. Note that these arguments are about modes of experience not forms of representation: these are arguments about the form experiences necessarily have to take if there is to be objective knowledge.

- There must be a lingering question in some readers' minds about how one is supposed to draw the line between a priori proposals of the above kind and the developmental facts of the case. Unfortunately, no crisp answer can be given to this question any more than one can stipulate where, say, Fodorian arguments about LOT end and empirical proposals about sentence parsing begin (on which see Fodor, 1983, pp.75–81). However, readers may justifiably be worried in case I move from the a priori to the empirical when their attention is distracted elsewhere. Well, how one moves from one to the other is a second issue that will be re-encountered at the end of the book, but for now I can say that what an transcendental argument can give to developmental psychologists is the advice about where to direct their attention. Having looked in that direction, nothing is thereby revealed, of course, about the truth of the transcendental argument.

- As I have been saying throughout, my general thesis is that "the ability to alter at will one's perceptual inputs" is a necessary condition for developing a conception of the external world (Part 2) and of mind (Part 3). It will soon emerge, however, that these are not distinct topics; they are, rather, the two faces of the growth of self–world dualism, and this is the primary concern of the outside→in approach.

NOTES

1. 1983 was probably the *annus mirabilis*. This was the year when Alan Leslie presented his poster on the relation between pretend play, logical opacity, and theory of mind at the annual conference of the British Psychological Society's Developmental Section meeting at Oxford, and the year when Heinz Wimmer and Josef Perner published their false belief study (Wimmer & Perner, 1983).

2. This is a term coined by Daniel Dennett, originally in Chapter 4 of his *Content and consciousness*. The personal level is the level on which we talk about acts, intentions, beliefs, thoughts, reasons, feelings, and the like (the so-called "folkpsychological" level); while the sub-personal level, as Dennett put it elsewhere, is the "behind-the-scenes *machinery* that governs speech dispositions, motor sub-routines, information storage and retrieval, and the like" (Dennett, 1978a, p.216, italics mine). Obviously, when we are talking about neural processes we are at the sub-personal level.

3. Wittgenstein (1953) considers the view that understanding what it means to climb a hill is a matter of having a mental picture of a person climbing a hill coming into the mind's eye. "I see a picture; it represents an old man walking up a steep path leaning on a stick. How? Might it not have looked just the same if he had been sliding downhill in that position? Perhaps a Martian would describe the picture so. I do not need to explain why we do not describe it so" (1953, p. 54; § 139).

4. It is interesting that Fodor certainly seems to be endorsing a form of holism in his description of "the central systems" (Fodor, 1983). Perhaps he thinks that these systems only involve a holism of belief rather than of content.

5. Indeed at some points in his book Johnson-Laird says that constructing a mental model is not even necessary for understanding a discourse. For example, we cannot construct of model of a sentence like "Two hundred men driving cars"; but we clearly understand it. What happens here is that in the representation of the sentence "a propositional representation is set up but never actually used in a procedure to construct a model. It is a cheque that is not presented for payment, but which, if presented, would be honoured" (Johnson-Laird, 1983, p.443).

6. This is in the spirt of so-called "Montague Semantics". The basic idea behind this semantic theory is that meaning is accounted for in terms of denotation alone. For example the meaning of a predicate is taken to be a function from an argument to a truth value—using the terms "argument" and "function" as they are used in mathematics. For example, squaring a number is a function, the number is the argument, and the square is the value (parallelling semantic value). Montague semantics is, needless to say, highly congenial to mental models theory.

7. As McGinn points out, the early Wittgenstein (of the *Tractatus*) was highly sympathetic to this kind of view. Later it became anathema to him.

8. A collegue of mine says that his ability to solve syllogisms improved after reading Johnson-Laird's book. But, of course, if the book's thesis is correct, he should have been doing what the book describes before he ever read it.

9. "A modest man with plenty to be modest about". . . an unwise wisecrack by Churchill about Attlee.

10. The number of dimensions in the state space represented in the hidden units of the network is equal to the number of input units; 20 input units, 20-dimensional space.

11. This was achieved by a using a statistical technique called "principal component analysis"—similar in some ways to the cluster analysis familiar to psychologists. The idea is to look at the components that are principally responsible, within the n-dimensional space of the hidden units, for the network's success in learning a certain training set.

12. As psycholinguists of a nativist persuasion often remind us, making analogies is as likely to lead to error as to success. For example, analogy-using would lead the learner to think that if he or she can go from "John drove the car into the garage" to "John drove the car" then he or she can go from "John put the car into the garage" to *"John put the car".

13. Pinker makes the point that innate knowledge of (say) the noun class is no use to the language learner unless he or she is able to learn what are the nouns in the language he or she is learning. He proposes that the learner begins with rules of thumb of a semantic nature (e.g. "nouns refer to agents and objects") to kick-start the process. These generalisations are strictly false (many nouns are neither agents nor objects), but this is sufficient, according to Pinker, to allow the learner to map rough knowledge of the noun class for a language onto his or her innate knowledge of grammatical structure.

14. I am not saying, of course, that an "agent" of *some* kind could not be controlled by symbol strings. Some robots work on just this principle. For example "Sam" was controlled by a problem-solving system called STRIPS (Fikes & Nilsson, 1971). Sam moves around among three rooms containing items of furniture and is able to transfer things from room to room. Sam represents the problem situation as a data-structure made up of strings of predicate calculus symbols. The initial data structure (the situation at the outset) is treated as analogous to the initial object in Newell and Simon's General Problem Solver, which has to be transformed in a step-by-step manner until the goal is attained. What STRIPS does to achieve this is to perform the "operation" on the "object" (problem) situation as if it were a problem in predicate calculus. How one proceeds in predicate calculus is to begin with a well-formed formula and a fixed set of axioms and then see whether the formula is provable. What STRIPS does is the opposite: it erects a goal (e.g. Sam by the window, table in alcove) as a false formula (i.e. yet to be achieved) and then attempts to make the formula true by *changing the axioms* (i.e. the sequence of situations mentioned in the data structures). These changes are the movements the robot makes. This is "agency" by pure syntax; and I will spend a good deal of time in Part 2 saying that this is not agency at all. All I am saying for now is that nothing warrants the ascription of desires and beliefs to Sam.

15. Newell was one of the founding fathers of cognitive science—see my reference to him in note 14. This remark of his was quoted in Richard Young's obituary of Newell in *The Psychologist*, 1991.

16. To my knowledge, there are no connectionist robots. However, Brooks (1991, p.139) has constructed "an intelligent system ... decomposed into

independent and parallel activity producers which all interface directly to the world through perception and action, rather than interface to each other particularly much ... everything is both central and peripheral". He claims provocatively that "representations are not necessary and appear only in the eye or mind of the beholder" (p.154).

17. For example, the subject is faced with the word RED written in green ink and told to name the colour of the ink. It is very difficult to stop oneself reading the word instead.

18. This is a task in which the subject has to shift his or her criterion of sorting cards, from sorting by (say) colour to sorting by shape. The experimenter gives negative feedback about when the criterion should be changed. As we shall see in Part 3, this is a task that patients with frontal lesions—and other clinical groups—find especially difficult.

19. I am referring here to David Marr's (1982) famous distinction between three levels of explanation in psychology. This is Level 1.

20. In a sense, Piaget himself attempted to do just this: he tried to explain the development of syntax in terms of structured actions and extra-linguistic forms of understanding (Piaget, 1972). This was a doomed enterprise (see Karmiloff-Smith, 1992).

PART 2

Knowledge of objects

The development of self–world dualism is a fairly traditional concern in psychology, and in fact my conclusion about how it develops will be a somewhat time-honoured one. For I shall argue that the child's experience of the world as being *resistant to his or her will* plays the central role in this development; and this is theme is naturally associated with major developmental theorists such as James Mark Baldwin[21] and Sigmund Freud.

Readers may recall from the beginning of Part 1 that my position will be called "piagetian"—spelt with a small "p"—because it is more "Piaget-flavoured" than Piagetian. It is now time to say why.

Piaget was the developmental psychologist of agency *par excellence*. As we saw earlier, he regarded mental development as a process of progressive self-regulation (as well as representational change), arguing that children gain a more adequate grasp of reality as they regulate and organise their representations of it. Although he had rather little to say specifically about "the will", every aspect of his theory is infused with the notion of regulation, and this is one of the core features of agency. That is why Piaget himself is needed.

But the small "p" is equally essential because I want a theory far weaker and a framework far looser than Piaget's. For Piaget was notoriously reluctant to acknowledge the role of innate structures in mental development: agency was the engine of development for him, driving along everything from vision to syntax to reasoning. In other words, we need a theory in which agency is a *necessary* component, but we do not want a theory in which adequate agency is more or less sufficient for adequate mental development. So I have opted for the term "piagetian", given that "executive" has a more technical reading (to be discussed) and coinings like "action-based" are a little awkward.

Before proceeding though, I need to hammer home the point about the inadequacy of a traditional Piagetian theory as a theory of self–world dualism. Doing this will help me set up the issues to be addressed in the rest of Part 2.

2.1: SELF–WORLD DUALISM AND THE WATERED-DOWN PIAGET

Piaget was concerned with the preverbal roots of the distinction we naturally make between our experience of how things appear at particular times and a world of enduring, mind-independent objects. And this led him, as every student of psychology knows, to study infants' developing knowledge that objects continue to exist when not being perceived—"object permanence" or "the object concept". Infants' senses may tell them, for example, that all that exists within reaching space right now on the carpet is a cushion, while, in reality, there is both a rattle and a cushion, the former occluded by the latter because of the infants' position in space. What they will eventually gain is the conception that their current field of visual (in this case) experience can only reveal a sliver of reality, and that how much and what it reveals is, in part, a function of where they are located—as experiencing bodies—in three-dimensional space.

However, in common with many developmentalists of his own and of the preceding generation—Baldwin and Freud again—Piaget assumed that the infant's psychological starting-point was a state of *adualism* in which no distinction is drawn between how things appear to him or her and how things are in fact. Moreover, Piaget had a very strong and distinctive answer to the question of how infants develop from adualism towards self–world dualism: they do so through exercising agency, through their actions on the world becoming progressively more spontaneous, differentiated, and integrated. He opposed nativist accounts of this and, in his writings on infancy in particular, he strenuously rejected nativism about spatial, causal, temporal, and object concepts, a nativism that he ascribed (wrongly)[22] to Kant.

Contemporary developmental psychologists are generally, and with justification, dissatisfied with this answer. This is not simply because we have uncovered so much innate structure in the past 30 or so years, but because the claim itself seems conceptually ill-founded. Take the case of spatial concepts—the fundamental concepts for Piaget. Piaget's view was that through exercising progressively greater control over what they experience infants are able to bootstrap themselves towards an allocentric[23] from a purely egocentric conception of space. That is to say, by forging links between their actions and the perceptual outcomes of these actions, they develop a conception of the spatial world that is perspective-independent, environment-centred, and map-like (Piaget, 1955, pp.198–218).

Some philosophers have rightly dismissed the very possibility that development could occur this way. James Hopkins (1987, pp.153–54) has argued that if the primordial state of infants' minds is adualistic then no amount of activity will provide them with the experience of an objective spatial world. For there is nothing on which to build, given that it is in the nature of purely egocentric experiences that they can never yield an objective content. The neonate must, at the very least, be able to achieve some primitive coding of certain experiences as having a bodily origin (e.g. hunger, kinaesthesis) and certain others as having an origin in the world (e.g. looming objects).

In a different vein, John Campbell (1993) has argued that our self-conscious grasp of how we are located within the spatial world must be grounded in *allocentric* representations of space in which we ourselves are represented as objects, and that, although grasping the *causal significance* of our actions within this allocentric framework is necessary for successful spatial thinking and for our thinking about objects, this grasp can only emerge in creatures that possess a prior capacity for allocentric coding. As we shall see later, the kind of allocentric coding system that Campbell has in mind here is that investigated by John O'Keefe and Lynne Nadel (1978) in their work on the functioning of the rat hippocampus as a mental map. Indeed O'Keefe (1993), in turn, says that his neuropsychological research provides evidence for the "Kantian" position that allocentric spatial coding is innate—that it is a system applied in experience rather than developing out of it.

But if we agree that Piaget's bootstrapping-from-egocentric-to-allocentric view is wrong, there still remains a very substantial role for action—for two reasons. First, as I briefly said *a propos* Campbell's views, a creature must come to know about the causal significance of its own actions. It must come to know, for instance, that the fact that one thing is closer to it than another or behind another has implications for what it can do. And indeed some minimal capacity for navigation may be necessary if a creature is to come to appreciate how one location is related to others. Second, and more to the present point, there is an important distinction to be drawn—one drawn by Campbell himself—between *practical capacities* and *theory-like conceptions*. Let us consider the spatial behaviour of animals. Here is the kind of fact that renders implausible Piaget's claim that activity alone provides creatures with an allocentric spatial understanding: three-week-old rats are able to swim through opaque liquid straight to a platform hidden under the surface from a *novel* starting point (Nadel, 1990). Do we really want to say that this animal has in its early weeks heroically "constructed" its spatial knowledge through the differentiation and integration of its own actions? Do we want to say that this capacity demonstrates "self–world dualism" in the rat? No, but then the piagetian concern is not with this kind of practical capacity: it is with the origins of the *conception* of self–world dualism. Obviously, conceptions and practical capacities are related; but there is a clear sense in which a conception need not be fully manifested in behavioural skills—although it must result in awareness. An awareness of one's place in the physical universe as at once an object within it and an experiencer of it is one that is not "exhausted in action":[24] it does not just line up neatly with facts about what we can do. It is in *this* sense then, that self–world dualism is a "theoretical" notion. The piagetian says that agency is *necessary* to the acquisition of this theoretical notion.

But for the purposes of later exposition—and to make some links between Parts 1 and 2—it would be well to flesh out this distinction with another distinction—that between *non-conceptual* and *conceptual content* (Crane, 1992; Peacocke, 1992). One way to approach this distinction is through thinking about what it takes for us to have a verbal concept. As we saw in our discussion of mental symbols in Part 1, to have a successful thought about, say, a dog requires the capacity to think about animals, three-dimensional objects, creatures that breathe, and so forth: having the thought implies a capacity at once holistic and systematic. Much the same goes for thoughts about objects and about space. In this case, one may ascribe to an animal, say, the ability to represent the world in certain ways (e.g. representing something as red or as a threat) while withholding from it the possession of the concepts that would enable it to specify how it is representing the world. Thus, an animal may be able to represent something as red and generally discriminate between objects on the basis of their colours without understanding the conceptual linkages between being coloured and being red—that being red implies being coloured, for example. If a representational content is non-conceptual then representing something as red does not imply the capacity to represent it as coloured.

For Piaget, our understanding of objects has conceptual content—he coined the term "object *concept*" after all—because such understanding requires the holistic and "structured" (more of this notion later) capacity to think about any given object under any description—a capacity that I shall later describe as meeting The Generality Constraint (after Evans, 1982). A non-conceptual capacity in relation to objects, on the other hand, is a capacity that can only be manifested in certain ways or in certain domains. Thus, the spatial capacities of homing pigeons and migrating birds, which we considered in Part 1, would appear to be non-conceptual in the sense that their dependency on given kinds of sensory input (e.g. from the sun or from geomagnetic fields) ensures that they do not generalise to spatial coding tasks at which, say, rats excel. Readers may want to think of this in terms of conceptual capacities being "central system" capacities and non-conceptual ones being "input system" or modular (Fodor, 1983). The piagetian claim is that the transition from non-conceptual to conceptual content in the object domain occurs through the exercise of agency.

I think it is also useful to think of a form of *appearance–reality distinction* as being integral to these "theoretical" and "conceptual" capacities. As we move about and as we attend to different things, the world always appears to us to be a certain way; while all the time we believe that a perspective-neutral and mind-independent reality *causes* these appearances to be the way they are. The development of this distinction was one of Piaget's central concerns, and the claim that it was achieved through the progressive structuring of actions was his most distinctive claim. The piagetian tempers this view with nativism about allocentric-coding capacities.

But before presenting the case for the piagetian view I need to say something about its *status*. Is the piagetian position a kind of abstract psychology or a kind of empirically-minded philosophy? Like the "genetic epistemology" of Baldwin and Piaget, it is a bit of both. As I said earlier, this can lead to incoherence (e.g. Hamlyn, 1978); but it need not do so long as one is clear about whether it is the empirical or the conceptual face of the thesis that is currently being defended (Russell, 1979a). I shall try to keep clear about this. There will be claims made about how object permanence should properly be assessed and about how it develops; but the case for the piagetian view will depend principally on the kind of claims that philosophers call "transcendental"—after Kant. Kant sometimes used the term "transcendental" when referring to what it takes for us to come to know objects, specifically with regard to the non-empirical conditions for this knowledge (Kitcher, 1990); but, more generally, a transcendental *argument* refers to an argument with this form: "We know X (or believe Y or have the capacity Z) and this would not be possible unless our experience had form F; therefore our experience has form F".

Readers will also encounter some material on agency that is not directly relevant to the development of the object concept; but this material will be needed in Part 3 when we discuss self-hood.

2.1(i) Intentionality and agency

To be conscious is to be conscious *of* something. We cannot, for example, just "think" or just "believe" or just "hope" without thinking, believing and hoping *that* something. This is the famous "intentionality of the mental", a term introduced by Franz Brentano in the 1870s. It does not matter whether there is something actually being picked out in reality by our thought, just as long as there is a mental something that serves as the object of our mental orientations or "propositional attitudes". (Brentano called this "intentional inexistence".) In reality—to field a well-known thought-experiment in philosophy—you may just be a brain in a vat on Alfa Centauri wired up to a machine which causes you to believe you are reading a book right now on planet Earth; but you are conscious *of* something nonetheless.

Now imagine a creature that does not achieve this three-term relation between (1) itself, (2) propositional attitudes, and (3) contentful thoughts. It is not, consequently, in a position to think *that* something is the case. It may, nevertheless, have a form of consciousness. It is conscious to the extent that it makes a division between objects in the world and its experience of them. Like us, it is "at two with Nature" (to borrow a Woody Allen quip): it has only the briefest of short-term memories, no language, and a minimal attention span, but it experiences objects as being distinct from itself, it locates itself in the world as one of these objects in so doing, and it has a conception of "here" versus "there".

The piagetian claims that being conscious in the first, full, propositional-attitude-adopting sense is grounded in a conception of the external world of just this kind. That is to say, *to be able to take up different mental orientations towards intentional objects one must first have the experience of taking up different physical orientations towards real objects* (Russell, 1988, 1989). Note how different this starting point is from that of the representational theorist. For the representational theorist, as I noted in 1.5, the starting point is "inside" the mind—Fodor (1980) calls his position *"methodological solipsism"*—and the question is "What kind of representational medium or content must be innately present or must develop if this is to become the mind of a successful thinker and agent?". As I said, the representational theorist works "from the inside out". For the piagetian, on the other hand, the theoretical starting-point is not a mind requiring representations to have access to an "out there", but an acting, sensing organism within a world of objects. The question then becomes: "What does this organism have to be able to *do* in relation to objects if it is to develop an adequate representational system?". The piagetian works "from the outside in", and can afford, as I said, to be ecumenical about the representational medium.

But does the direction not *have* to be from the inside outwards—from representation to successful interactions with objects? How can an organism act at all if it has no representational capacities to speak of, if representational capacities are instead supposed to be the *explicanda*? Answer: the piagetian does not claim that the developing organism begins as a pure agent—like an existentialist hero. Rather, the claim is that interaction with objects is a necessary feature of mental development. It is, as I said at the very beginning, an almost modest proposal.

We can now begin to consider *why* piagetians think that activity is necessary to establishing self–world dualism. The answer I shall be giving in Part 2 is that only through the exercise of agency—by which the piagetian means recall, *changing the nature of perceptual inputs at will*—can subjects come to experience the "refractoriness" of reality, experience the constraints that reality sets on what they can experience. This will enable them to regard objects as the external *causes* of their experiences. Moreover—I shall have more to say about this in Part 3—only through the exercise of agency are subjects able to gain a conception of themselves as being in some degree "responsible for" some of their experience, as having experiences that belong to them. Only through "making a contribution" to what they experience can organisms construct a subjective mental life set off from an objective reality. The expressions "responsible for", "making a contribution", and "belonging" are, of course, mere metaphors; but they can be explicated.

I also need to highlight the difference between the piagetian notion of agency italicised earlier and motor behaviour. The piagetian claim is not that successful *movement* is necessary for mental development; and it is emphatically not that only the motorically skilled can achieve normal cognitive development. Of course, through moving one does alter one's perceptual inputs dramatically; but movement is not necessary. Any kind of selective attention falls within the ambit of piagetian "agency"—visual, auditory, or motoric. It is not even helpful, as work undermining "spotlight" theories of visual selective attention has shown (Driver & Baylis, 1989), to think of visual attention on the model of a metaphorical eye-movement. Being an agent, in this sense, means being something that has a degree of control over what, from the manifold sensory input, one centres upon.

2.2: THE FOUR FEATURES—
AND THE EXPERIENCE OF AGENCY

In this section we will consider four integral features of agency and the role that each plays in self–world dualism. Each feature, predictably enough, takes the form of a distinction. The first two describe kinds of information-processing and control that the agent must achieve, whereas the other two describe the kind of self-knowledge that is available to agents and to agents alone.

Feature (A): Locating the cause of altered inputs in one's body rather than in the world—"action-monitoring"
Our perceptual input is in a constant state of flux. Some phenomenal changes are caused by the world (e.g. when a car drives past me or it starts to rain) and some are caused by our own movements (e.g. in moving my head to the right I fill my visual field with bookshelves rather than a window). But how can I tell whether it is I or the world that caused the change? You may say that this is specified by the *content* of the change (e.g. rain cannot be caused by a bodily movement, and rooms do not shift themselves laterally); but we can only make content-based judgements about whether we or the world caused a change once we already have a secure grasp of the difference between self-caused and world-caused changes. The distinction is unlikely to be based on relative *plausibility*. Moreover, plausibility can sometimes not be called upon. I am looking, for example, at a feather and the feather moves from the left to the right of my visual field. How do I decide whether the feather has been blown to one side or the movement was apparent—having been caused by my moving my eyes a little to my left. Or, I am an animal watching my prey; did the prey jump to the left just then or did my eyes move? In practice, of course, we don't have to agonise about such questions because we know when we have moved "immediately". But how is this possible?

The evolutionary advantage of distinguishing between self-caused and world-caused changes in experience is obvious, and it is a distinction drawn by creatures at least as primitive as insects. Fruit flies, for example, produce an "optokinetic reaction", meaning that they turn in the direction of world movements: if a stimulus moves to their left they produce a leftward movement. Now consider the consequence of the animal's being unable to distinguish between self-caused and world-caused changes in the visual input. A stimulus moves leftwards across the animal's visual field, the fly moves its head to the left, the visual field appears to move to the animal's *right*, so the fly moves to the right, causing the visual field to appear to move to the left ... Clearly, if the fly were treating the apparent, self-caused movements of the visual field as real movements it would become as paralysed as Buridan's ass each time it made the optokinetic reaction. It must, therefore, be capable of coding self-generated changes in visual input *as* such.

This was the reasoning of von Holst and Mittelstaedt (see Gallistel, 1980) who carried out the classical work in this area. They claimed that the fly produces a copy of the motor command to make the bodily movement—it is called an *efference copy*—and that this solves the problem of self-ascription versus world-ascription in the following manner. If the motor signal is "+4" (with "+" meaning rightwards and "4" being a unit of extent) then the efference copy is also "+4". The phenomenal outcome of this action will be a so-called "reafferent signal" which is the symmetrical opposite of this, i.e. "−4": the world appears to move to the left. These positive and negative values cancel, so the animal's nervous system records the fact that the altered visual input was caused by self-movement rather than by world-movement. Of course, if no efference copy had been made and there was only an afferent signal of "−4" then a world-movement would be recorded and an optokinetic reaction triggered.

What we have here then is a sub-personal mechanism that enables the animal to make a very primitive form of *appearance–reality distinction*, in the sense that a distinction is drawn between changes in the appearances of objects to the animal and actual changes in objects' location relative to the animal. Moreover the animal's nervous system is able to, as it were, "claim responsibility" for some phenomenal changes and not for others. For if an organism cannot determine whether it is it or the world that is responsible for a change in perceptual input it cannot take the first step towards achieving self–world dualism. *Action-monitoring*, as I shall call it, is one way of ensuring that this distinction is made.

However, although copying a motor command constitutes a feedforward mechanism, it does not involve *predicting* the phenomenal outcome of making a certain movement. Recall that, in Part 1, I illustrated why such a predictive mechanism is necessary with reference to Jordan's forward model: the organism must be able to predict the phenomenal outcomes of certain muscle movements, because, unless it could do that, the information that it has failed by a certain degree to attain its target would be of no use to it—it will not know how to change the muscle movement so as move away from error and towards success. Accordingly, I need to make some remarks about why prediction—this is a second feature of action-monitoring—is integral to successful action.

Action must involve more than responding to external stimuli and more than a susceptibility to random internal triggerings. Acting must be something the organism does for a reason—there must be an answer to the question of why it was done even if the organism itself cannot answer it—and if this is so then it must know something about the phenomenal outcome of its actions *before* launching them. For if the organism has no idea what the effect of doing X would be it will never have a reason for doing it. This, then, is another aspect of action-monitoring. It will be recalled from the discussion of the forward model that there is a distinction to be made between actions done for the sake of distal goals and actions that involve proximal (of the body) control. Although the latter, as we saw, may not be done for a reason, in the usual sense, they certainly involve prediction. What about actions done out of curiosity whose prime motivation is to see what the result of this action (say a glance around an unfamiliar room) will be? There is still prediction here but it is of a coarser grain. In glancing around an unfamiliar room we will predict seeing another wall when we turn through 90 degrees: we won't predict seeing a blasted heath.

Like efference-copying, predicting the phenomenal outcomes of action educates the subject in the distinction between appearance and reality and in having responsibility for his or her experiences. This is because predictions are about changes in appearance. Thus, if there is red on the left and green on the right the subject makes predictions about the consequences of turning in either direction, predictions that are not about the way the world can be *changed* but about the way the world can *appear* to him or her, predictions about changes in input for which the subject is responsible.

Broadly speaking, efference-copying and predicting the phenomenal outcome of actions enable the subject to locate the cause of altered inputs in his or her own body. It could be said, however, that purely *exteroceptive* information could have the same effect. For example, in what J.J. Gibson called "visual kinaesthesis" the visual input alone can tell us that we are moving (e.g. we feel we are moving when an adjacent railway carriage moves). But in this case the subject's nervous system is inferring that the subject is moving on the basis of visual data. Gibson may be right to refer to this "egoreception" as being direct (see Bermúdez, 1995, on this) in the sense of being perceived rather than known by reflection, but when we know through efference copying that we have moved we are not even knowing something *through perception*.

Agents know they have acted when there is no exteroceptive information. For example, in a pitch-black room wearing a suit to insulate you from all tactile inputs you will know you have raised your arm or stood up without needing to look at your body and without feeling it brush against something: kinaesthetic feedback will be sufficient. But my point is not merely about kinaesthesia. You will know that you have acted because you will have launched the motor command and because you will have made predictions about the phenomenal outcome of your launched movement. In that sense you know "immediately" that you have acted; you do not have to wait for the world to tell you whether you have done so. It is important, however, not to confuse two things here: (a) knowing that one has acted, in the sense of having launched an action, and (b) knowing whether that action was successful or not. In the latter case, we may need to be informed by exteroceptive feedback; but in the former case—where what is at issue is whether we have launched an action *at all*—we do not need the world to inform us.

I will have much more to say about this under feature (C), but, for now, I will just say that knowledge of our agency is not knowledge gleaned by observation: if we have to find out whether we have caused a movement by coding the structure of our perceptual input, then what we are coding is whether something *was caused by our moving body* or by the world moving relative to our body. It is irrelevant to agency, *which is not a fact about our body's moving but a fact about our moving our body*. What's more, the notion of acting for a reason has no foothold when the question of whether a bodily movement has taken place is something that is decided—something that the subject is, as it were, *told*—exteroceptively: actions are what we know we have taken before we observe their results.

I hope I will be allowed to be a bit cryptic at this point because more will be said on this important matter later.

Feature (B): The perceptual sequences brought about by acting are reversible; but those experienced in perceiving are irreversible

The next feature is best understood as the step beyond prediction. The ability to predict the phenomenal outcome of acting does not of itself make that action *self-determined*, and the self-determined nature of action is my topic in feature (B).

Action-monitoring ensures that the agent knows that a change in input was generated by itself. It is entirely possible, however, that although subjects know this they do not actually *select and generate* the action: they may find themselves doing things without being in *control* of themselves. They know, by action-monitoring, whether their movements have caused a change in perceptual input, and predict the movements' phenomenal outcomes when they are launched, but they do not control the nature of these actions. In other words, although it is a *necessary* component of doing something for a reason that subjects be in a position to predict the outcome, this is not sufficient; because they may not be determining what they do from moment to moment—their behaviour may not be self-controlled.

One hallmark of self-determined actions is that the agent has the power to decide the *order* in which percepts arrive. Subjects can, for example, visually examine an object and in so doing see different parts of it in any order they like and return to re-experience any portion they wish. In contrast to this, there are the cases where subjects have no power at all over the order in which percepts arrive—when they observe an event unfolding. But how can we characterise this power to determine the order of self-determined perceptual sequences? The proposal here is that a hallmark of self-determined sequences is the ability of the subject to *reverse* their order; whereas the hallmark of world-determined perceptual sequences is that their order cannot be reversed.

The following definitional remark is needed before I pass on. What is being intended here by the "reversibility" of action is something very close to the reversal of an attentional shift. Thus, I can glance from A to B and back again to A; and I can attend to A's colour or to A's shape without moving. Sometimes it is not physically possible to reverse the sequences of percepts; for example, few of us are agile enough to reverse the sequences of percepts enjoyed in jumping down from a wall by jumping back up on it again. But the nature of the constraint here is not conceptual: it is physical. By contrast, the fact that a sequence of events in the world (e.g. a cat walking past from left to right, or a car skidding then crashing) cannot be reversed by one's moving one's body in relation to objects is not a fact about our lack of control over our bodies, it is a conceptual fact—a fact that is definitional of what it means for something to be independent of our control.

Self-determined versus world-determined perceptual sequences

The distinction between self-determined and world-determined perceptual sequences was one drawn by Kant in the Second Analogy section of the *Critique of pure reason*. Although Kant's concern in that section was not with agency but rather with the so-called causal "necessity" that the ordering of world-determined sequences possesses[25], this distinction has major implications for how agency contributes to objectivity.

The example that Kant gave of self-determined—and therefore reversible—sequences of perception was that of scanning the front elevation of a house. In this case, the subject is free to look at the roof, then at the front door, then back to the roof—and so on. Kant's example of a world-determined sequence was that of watching a ship sail downstream, where the viewer must see the ship on his or her (say) left before seeing it on his or her right and has no power to repeat the sequence left→right: it is "irreversible". As we have seen, perceptual exploration of stationary objects can be reversible whereas the perception of events must be irreversible.

Only agents can draw the distinction between reversible and irreversible perceptual sequences, because only agents can reverse perceptual sequences. A puppet-like system, by contrast, can *experience* the two kinds of sequence without being *responsible* for them; and I will have more to say about this in 2.3(ii). How does drawing this distinction contribute to self–world dualism?

Paradoxically, the reversibility of self-determined perceptual sequences can reveal to us how the scope of our experience is *constrained*. For it is difficult to imagine how a conception of the irreversible, world-dependent nature of some modes of experience could arise if we never experienced the reversible, action-dependent nature of others. Moreover, the freer we are to determine the nature and order of our inputs (i.e. the less our behaviour is called out by stimuli and the less our attention is captured rather than directed), *the more possibilities for resistance to our will we encounter*. The more we can do, that is, the wider the variety of ways in which the will can be resisted and its experiential outcomes limited. The freer we are to alter our perceptual inputs the more we learn of the *refractory* nature of the world, and, correlatively, the richer the conception we gain of ourselves as determiners of our immediate mental life. This refractoriness, therefore, sets the limits on what our agency can achieve in the determination of our experiences, thereby engendering in us a conception of something as setting these limits, as *causing* them to be set. [The term "refractory", by the way, is borrowed from J.M. Baldwin (1906), who used it in much the same way as I am using it to describe how objectivity in the child's experiences emerges partly as a function of the world's resisting the child's will (see Russell, 1978, Part 1.2, for a summary of Baldwin's "genetic epistemology").]

Recall that many kinds of actions, and therefore many kinds of action-generated perceptual sequences, are not reversible (e.g. diving into a pool) because we lack the requisite control over our bodies. And recall also that these are actions that do not have an *attentional* character. Attention-shifts, however, are inevitably reversible (at least in normal adults). For the class of reversible actions contains all those actions that change the subject's perspective on the environment, taking these perspectival changes to encompass everything from moving around the world, to changing visual fixations, to shiftings of auditory attention. Recall that the piagetian interprets "action" in a very broad sense to refer to the changing of perceptual inputs at will, and that this must include attentional changes.

Reversibility inevitably plays a role in establishing the appearance–reality distinction integral to the development of self–world dualism. On the present view, it is the experience of achieving reversibility, the experience of changing our inputs by changing our physical or mental (attentional) relation to objects, that affords us changes of appearance; while the manifest constraints on how appearances can be altered (e.g. by moving round an object) show us the limits that are set on *how one appearance can follow from another*.

It is not only a matter of changing *how* things are perceived; it is also a matter of changing *which* physical objects become perceptible as we change perspective. And it is in this latter sense that the notion of refractoriness has the clearest application, simply because the term "will" has such a clear application when we are dealing with which objects can be experienced. A baby desperately desiring the nipple and turning to its left when the nipple is on its right provides a potent example of refractoriness.

I will also briefly (and more speculatively) explore the role that reversibility might play in a developing conception of temporal duration. One may see the exercise of reversibility as affording the subject (a developing human infant, say) an escape from the continuous present. (I am building here on a recent discussion by Bermúdez, 1995, of the relation between returning to locations and escape from the continuous present; although he does not argue that reversibility plays the role that I claim it might.)

The conception of an enduring cause of past and future experiences would seem to depend on the ability actively to recall experiences rather than merely to enjoy feelings of familiarity when certain perceptual inputs recur. I have no argument to show that only agents are able to recollect previous experiences. However, I think it is natural to believe that a creature all of whose experiences are irreversible, for whom the flow of percepts is in a single, fixed direction, would indeed live in a continuous present. It is difficult to imagine, that is, something that has never been capable of "casting its attention back" (e.g. by reversing an eye movement) to the cause of a prior experience and is nevertheless able to "cast its mind back" to a previous event. As I said, such a creature might feel some inputs to be familiar; but that capacity could exist *without a conception of the duration of the causes of these inputs through time*. However, a creature who has the ability to return to a location at will (e.g. glancing from A to B to C and then back to A) is at least manifesting the ability to code A as a location that causes experiences to which it is possible to return. I am not, however, in a position to claim that reversibility is *necessary* for grasping the fact that what is being experienced at the moment existed in the past and will continue to exist in the future; this is why I say that my remarks on this are "speculative".

I should finally say a few words about how the term "reversibility" is used by Piaget himself. Many readers will be familiar with the distinction Piaget drew between perception, which is irreversible, and intelligence which is reversible (e.g. Piaget, 1950). Trains of rational thought ("intelligence"), Piaget said, are like actions in the sense that they can be reversed. It is also worth pointing out that reversibility is only one of the characteristics of self-determined perceptual sequences, and reminding the reader with some knowledge of Piaget's theory that reversibility was, for him, one of the *set* of properties belonging to "structured" actions. Borrowing the formalisms of mathematical group theory (Piaget, 1950) Piaget added "identity" (doing nothing should result in no phenomenal change—unless the world changes); "combination" (actions can be combined into complex sequences); "associativity" (the way in which actions are subsetted—e.g. "AB then C" or "A then BC" has no effect on the final outcome). The term reversibility may also recall Piaget's use of the term "circular reaction" (after J.M. Baldwin, 1906) to describe the essential element in an action absent from a reflex: a reflex is called out by a stimulus, whereas an action can be repeated at will. I will, therefore, use the term "reversibility" as the synecdoche for all the forms of input-ordering that the self-determination of perceptual inputs gives us.

To sum up this sub-section: my claim is that unless subjects can reverse the sequence of their perceptual inputs they will be unable to achieve a conception of the world as being something that sets limits on what they can experience, as the refractory cause of their experiences. I will return to this central claim in the next full section, and I will there describe another route towards it. It is the pivotal claim of this book.

Feature (C): Our actions are known non-observationally whereas the world is known by observation

Where features (A) and (B) point up links between agency and our conception of physical objects, the next two features are ones with clearer implications for the "self" side of "self–world dualism". They are about modes of first-person experience that are only available to agents (when they are acting).

Imagine subjects who have to watch themselves to find out what they are doing. When they are not attentive they have no idea what they are up to[26]. I think the natural reaction here would be to say that these subjects are not really in control of themselves at all; for there would seem to be a division between their inner, homuncular eye and their acting body of such a kind that their body was "in the world" just like any other objective phenomenon of which the subjects could gain knowledge through observation.

This highlights the fact that we know what we are doing in a special way—*without self-observation*. Brian O'Shaughnessy (1980, pp.31–32) makes the point elegantly, so I will quote him in full:

> If one is to relate as observer to anything then one has be "without" it, whereas if one is intentionally to do anything then one has to be "within" the action we are attempting to observe, in which case we have an entirely empty and self-delusive experience of observation—comparable to Wittgenstein's example of the right hand attempting to pay the left hand money—or else we remain "without" in some less serious sense and genuinely seem to observe the action. But remaining "without", we lose the action as ours in gaining the observation: we lose any "withinness". The action becomes for us a mere event in the world, and we ourselves become dispersed and lost among the bric-a-brac of the world: we become of the world in our own eyes; we suffer the experience of loss of identity.

The relationship between being an agent and having a sense of one's identity is an intimate one in the sense that through acting we gain a kind of immediate knowledge which is not available when we do not act and which cannot be available to non-agents. As O'Shaughnessy says a little earlier in his book (*The will*, Vol. II, pp.3–4):

> So at the risk of uttering a tautology, I shall say that what at any moment I am doing is, from my point of view, not a part of *the world* (which we all inhabit), but of *my world* (wherein are exclusively set those internally intelligible linked items which unburden their heart exclusively to me) ... [W]ere I *per impossibile* to relate to my actions in the observational mode that I use in the case of others, then this would succeed in removing the relation between the world and my world which is the very foundation upon which rests the identity both of my world and of my actions.

This kind of view—as we shall see—is also to be found in Schopenhauer.

Before I pass on, I need to re-emphasise the distinction between the role of observation in (a) intending to do something, and the role of observation in (b) knowing about the intention's motor outcome. In the latter case, it certainly makes sense to say that I may sometimes observe my body to see if an attempt to move it in a certain way has succeeded—particularly if I suffer from brain-damage or if I am a subject in a psychological experiment. There can be such cases. However the following kind of situation cannot obtain: I routinely intend certain actions and routinely watch my body to find out whether or not these intentions have been successful. Agents do not relate to their bodies in this way, for if they did then there would be a *gap* between their intending and their acting such that they would never have the experience of being in control of themselves. The subject would intend something and then, as Bill Brewer puts it (1993, p.305, original italics; I will later describe his position in detail) "things are in the lap of the gods ... When she is successful it is just a happy accident. So the idea of her being an *agent* is completely out of place."

In the first case [(a)] however—when we focus on the intention—there can be no cases in which I observe myself to find out *what I am intending*. G.E.M. Anscombe (1957) coined the phrase "knowledge without observation" to refer to the kind of knowledge we have of our intentions; and Stuart Hampshire's (1959) name is also associated with the thesis. Anscombe argued that, insofar as intended actions are done for a reason, we do not have to reflect on what that reason was to know why we did the action. The *reason's being immediately manifest to us is what made the action intentional in the first place*[27]. This matter will see taken up again when I describe feature (D).

I also need to clear up a possible confusion about the relation between action-monitoring by efference copying and the prediction of phenomenal outcomes—discussed under feature (A)—and our non-observational knowledge of our actions. Does not the term "action-monitoring" immediately suggest self-observation? It does not, for two reasons. First, it is obvious that the mechanisms described do not require an inner eye to observe the fact that a motor command has been launched and that a prediction has matched the received input. Second, action-monitoring is something done by the nervous system: it is a sub-personal mechanism. In this section, however, we are located squarely at the personal level, at the level of "what it is like to be an agent", at the level of beliefs, intentions, and knowledge.

Before closing this section I will say something about a much stronger form of the view that actions are known non-observationally—one lying at the core of Schopenhauer's philosophical system. I am not doing this simply to make an historical point; although the historical relation between the Kantian distinction discussed under feature (B) and Schopenhauer's position is an interesting one[28]. Rather, Schopenhauer's views are relevant to us because they provide a classic statement of the view, touched on briefly in Part 1, that knowledge of our agency is knowledge without a *representational* character.

Schopenhauer's claim is that we know everything representationally except facts about our willing; our epistemic relation to volitional states is not a representational one. This view is tendentious in a way in which the views just described are not. For what these authors are saying is not that knowledge of action contains no representational element but that these representations (e.g. I am doing X) are not gleaned from self-observation: they are known immediately, in the sense of "without inference". On the surface, Schopenhauer's position seems on odd one because acting is often goal-directed and our epistemic relation to goals must surely be a representational one. But "having a represented goal" is clearly not all there is to goal-directed behaviour. All I will say on this topic for now is that, although goals are representations, the existence of agency does not appear to be something about which one can tell a purely representational story—as I argued towards the end of Part 1. The capacity for free action does not seem to be reducible to the possession of the requisite representations and attitudes towards them.

Feature (C) bears on self–world dualism in the following way. What we know about ourselves as agents and what we know about the world are different modes of knowledge, gleaned in different ways. What is "in the world" is that which we observe; what is not "in the world" are our own volitions, and these are not known by observation.

Feature (D): Agents have a privileged knowledge of their own "tryings" which they lack when observing the "tryings" of others

This final feature is again about the mode of knowing involved in agency by contrast with knowing something about the world, although we are concerned here with the *status* of what is known rather than with how it is known. The claim is that our knowledge of what we are trying to do in acting is—or can be—a form of privileged, incorrigible knowledge, unlike knowledge about events in the world. I will again draw heavily on O'Shaughnessy.

One of the things O'Shaughnessy attempts to establish in Volume II of *The will* is what he calls "Principle A"; and the following is what he calls the "slogan-like" version of it (1980, p.88):

> Given C1: trying guarantees awareness of and strong knowledge of itself; and seeming trying guarantees trying.

Let us unpack this "slogan". C1 stands for a set (impossible to define exhaustively) of conditions for saying that one has "strong knowledge" of mental events. These are defined in terms of (1) their "psychological setting" and (2) their "psychological type" (e.g. bodily sensations). The settings for C1 might be: "sanity, wakefulness, relative mental normality, attention not grossly overwhelmed, subject actively searching for an item of the type in question" (1980 p.78). An example of the psychological type might be pain. Thus, given C1, when we are experiencing a searing pain in the jaw in the dentist's chair we strongly know that we are in pain in a sense in which the dentist does not strongly know this from observing our writhings. Why "strong" knowledge as opposed to any other kind? Strong knowledge is supposed to obtain "when it is impossible even to *imagine* what, *if* it happened, would falsify the claim" (1980, p.79; original italics); whereas I can only weakly know facts such as that my petrol tank is full or that the stuff that comes out of the tap is water. Thus, to add a little to this example, if it should turn out that the drill had not really touched a nerve at all and that, accordingly, we had only imagined the pain, *then the imagined pain was no less a mental event to which we had a kind of privileged access*. It would be impossible for us to imagine that we had not really had the illusory pain; for in the case of certain kinds of mental event the difference between the real and the illusory event dissolves: pain that was not caused in the normal way is still pain.

O'Shaughnessy says that taking such a view involves "*conditional Cartesianism*". It is conditional because of the existence of the two stipulations of psychological setting and psychological type I have just mentioned. These conditions ensure that this makes it fall a long way short of full-blown Cartesianism, which states that privileged access is *true of our epistemological relation to all our mental phenomena*.

It is important, before passing on, to say that O'Shaughnessy is not committing himself to the view that the meanings of terms like "pain" and "hurts" and so forth are grounded in the experience of turning our inner eye upon our 'private sensations'—the view that Wittgenstein famously attacked in his "private language argument"[29]. There is no implication here that the *meaning* of the term "pain" is a sensation to which nobody else can have access. But it does imply that the patient has a special kind of knowledge of his or her sensation which the dentist lacks. In fact it is fair to say that somebody who had no conception of how these kinds of access differed would not understand the concept of pain.

We now turn to the parallel between the having of certain bodily sensations, such as pains, and the fact of trying to do something. (In non-instrumental, "basic" actions such as lifting one's arm one does not naturally speak of "trying to do X": in lifting my arm I'm not trying to lift it, although in some circumstances, such as your preventing me, I would be said to be trying. But we will concentrate on goal-directed actions for the sake of exposition.) O'Shaughnessy's claim is that the agent's knowledge of what he or she is trying to do is strong knowledge, that is, knowledge whose falseness it is impossible to imagine.

There is an obvious sense in which we *can* indeed be mistaken about what we are trying to do: when the action is being described from a third-person perspective. For example, in returning to my office late one night I climb to the second rather than the third floor and try to unlock the door at the end of the corridor. According to me, I am "trying to get into my office"; but in reality I am "trying to get into the office of Dr. X in Biochemistry". But this fact about the logical behaviour of terms like "trying", "striving", and so forth merely illustrates that they share features with mental verbs such as "think", "hope", and so on: the truth of a sentence containing them is relative to the informational state of the person referred to in the sentence[30]. It remains the case that *what I take myself to be trying to do* at the time is not something about which I can imagine myself being mistaken. This is not to say that if I am trying to do something then I necessarily *know* that I am trying to do it; rather the claim is that whatever I take myself to be trying to do I am indeed trying to. This is, in part, a consequence of feature (C)—the fact that the nature of my actions is non-observationally known to me.

Let us take another example to reinforce the generality of this principle. I am watching you talking to Jenny. You think that what you are trying to do is put her at her ease, whereas according to me you are being patronising. Putting to one side the question of whether there is really any fact of the matter here, even if 20 other observers agreed with me this would not alter the fact that if you thought you were trying to put Jenny at her ease then that is what you were in fact trying to do—your behavioural leakage notwithstanding.

The point we have established, then, is that the agent's knowledge of what he or she is trying to do in goal-directed action has a degree of first-person authority similar to the first-person authority of an experiencer of a sensation. It follows from this that knowing what it is to act on the world cannot be given a purely third-person treatment any more than knowing what it is like to be in pain or to taste a kumquat can be grounded in our observations of others' behaviour.

What are the implications of this final feature of action for the development of self–world dualism? First, and more important for our purposes, one may know that some observations of other people are observations of their agency, but observations of others' agency have a fallibility that immediate knowledge of our own agency does not.

Accordingly, one's knowledge of agency is missing a vital ingredient if it is only third-person knowledge; a creature that never acted but could parse the intentional behaviours of others would not know what it is to be an agent. I shall argue in Part 3 that this implies that the development of agency cannot be explained in terms of an innate input system that parses behavioural events, with "self" and "other" being epistemically equivalent subjects within this parsing.

Second, if a first-person and a third-person experience of agency differ in the way I have been describing, then agency may also be seen to be necessary for an adequate division between *self and other*. Although the child may observe agency in others, the knowledge of his or her own agency has a privileged status.

More generally, features (C) and (D) point us towards the respect in which agency and our ability to regard experiences as being "owned" by us are conceptually linked: they point up the relation between agency and subjecthood. One does not, on this view, gain a general conception of "what it is to have an experience" which one can apply to oneself or others; rather, through the exercise of agency, one gains the conception that agents have immediate and incorrigible knowledge of some aspects of their mental life.

The "experience of agency" and willing

I hope it has emerged from the last few pages that there is something one can call "the experience of agency", and that this has an essentially first-person character. Its ingredients do not fall out in four neat packages from the features, but some of them are more naturally related to one of the features than to others. In the first place, the experience of agency will involve the immediate knowledge that one has acted (an action has been launched) and will involve, as it were, the ability to predict future events (e.g. I can predict that I will stand up soon because I have just decided to do so) and future experiences (in standing up, the floor will look farther away).

In the second place, agents are in control of their experiences in a way in which they are not in control of how events unfold in the world: agents are able to impose a self-chosen order on these experiences and can reverse and re-experience certain orders at will. Third, the fact that agents are in control provides them with a special kind of knowledge of what they are doing: they do not know what they are doing by observing themselves. This is because there is an intimate linkage between the way in which intentions flow into bodily movements and the fact of being in control of what one is doing in the instant of doing it. Subjects who invariably have to watch themselves to see what they are doing would not be in control. Fourth, the experience of agency involves the experience of trying to bring about certain ends, and the kind of knowledge that agents have of what they are trying to do is incorrigible. There is always, of course, the possibility of failing to act as we wish and always the possibility that we have mischaracterised what we are trying to do, but what we take ourselves to be trying to do is what we *are* trying to do. This fact captures something important about what it means to have a mental life: the fact that one can conceive of oneself as "owning" certain experiences—one conceives oneself as both determining them and being the unique subject of them. I know what I am trying to do because it is *I* who am trying to do it. Thus, the experience of agency is something that can be seen to ground first-person thoughts—an idea that will be explored at length in Part 3.

Terms like "the will" and "willing" sound somewhat quaint to the psychologist's ear; but if we remind ourselves that the "agent" or the "subject" to which I have been referring in 2.2 will be people with *desires*, then the fact of willing is exactly what has been described. Could not the four features characterise a cognitive system *without* desires? Am I helping myself to too much by simply stating their presence? It is certainly possible to imagine creatures that desire nothing, that merely react to the presence of what they need when not glancing idly about, their passionless movements determined perhaps by a random-number generator. But because such creatures would never prefer one course of action over another, because they would never make choices, the idea of their being "in control of themselves" seems to make no sense; for being in control implies being able to do what one chooses to do. [Would such creatures have a mental life? Even Fodor & Lepore (1992, and see p. 15 earlier) in their thought-experiment about the belief-less but mentally representing creature credit that creature with desires.]

In short, if you add the fact of desiring to the capacities conferred by the four features (being in control and so forth) then one can talk without embarrassment about "willing". Perhaps one can also say that what the four features describe is not only a competence which may or may not be exercised (e.g. like Chomsky's LAD); it *is* a competence, but it is also a disposition. Agents are not just mental systems that *can* self-monitor, that *can* reverse experiences and that *are* in control of themselves: they are mental systems that are *disposed* to exercise these powers because they desire certain outcomes. Indeed, as I said earlier, unless agents had desires then they could not experience the physical world as refractory; and one may add to this that they would never have the experience of knowing incorrigibly what they are attempting, because there would be no attempts.

2.3: WHAT THE FOUR FEATURES GIVE US

I have described four ways in which agency is integral to the distinction we draw between ourselves and the external world. What I do not have, however, is a single decisive argument to show that this is the *only* way in which such a conception could develop. I suspect that no such argument will ever be forthcoming. This is not because the claim is too weak, but because it is in the nature of this kind of enterprise that one gradually accumulates material in favour of a certain picture of development rather than—as in Fodor's nativism for example— producing a knock-down argument which tells us "*This* is how develop- ment must happen". Accordingly, in this section I will fill out the picture; and I will try to consolidate the claims made in the previous section by doing two things. First, I need to say more about how objectivity emerges from reversible actions through making the agent aware of the refractory nature of his or her experience. Then I will contrast the present view with a possible view in which it is argued that self–world dualism could emerge in a creature whose information-processing system lacked features (A) and (B).

2.3(i) Refractoriness and reversibility revisited

As I said at the beginning of Part 2, the thesis that objectivity develops through subjects experiencing the resistance of the world to their will was a familiar one in developmental psychology about a century ago. It enters Piaget's theory by way of his notion of accommodation, discussed in Part 1, insofar as failures to assimilate data to action-schemes force the child to modify these schemes. But the position also has a clear philosophical ancestry. It can be found in Locke and runs through much of Schopenhauer's work. More recently, it has been developed by David Hamlyn (1990, pp.105–6) and by Thomas Baldwin (1995), who argue, with some reference to Schopenhauer, that experiencing the resistance of *substantial objects* to the willed movements of our bodies (when we touch things, lie on them, push against them, and so forth) is necessary if we are to regard objects as mind-independent[31]. My position, by contrast, implies that this requirement may be too strong: *visual* experience of the kind described earlier may be sufficient for us to experience data as refractory. (I doubt that auditory experience is sufficient[32].)

Baldwin (1995) begins his argument from a point different to that from which I began mine. Rather than arguing from a form of experience that agency affords us, he starts from the position that if we are to view ourselves as perceivers of an objective world then we must regard objects as the causes of our experience. This in turn requires us to acknowledge the *modal* nature of causality (i.e. that causes *necessarily* precede effects, while it is *possible* that events could have unfolded differently). He then argues that if we adopt a view of volition in which voluntary action is taken to be the exercise of a bodily power, we can explain how this modal conception can arise: when substantial objects impede the exercise of the will we experience the *impossibility* of certain bodily attempts[33], we encounter "forces acting upon us to place limits on our bodily power" (Baldwin, 1995, p.113).

The position I outlined earlier under feature (B) implies, of course, that felt resistance is *not* necessary for this modal conception to emerge; although it obviously implies that it is sufficient for it. That is to say, out of *non*-physical interaction between one's body and the world (such as moving the eyes across scenes, or moving the body in relation to objects without ever making bodily contact with them) the modal conception (on which the notion of objects causing experiences depends) will emerge. It will emerge, I argue, from the tension that will be experienced between how and what things *must* appear to us and how and what things *may* appear to us.

That said, the similarities between Baldwin's position and mine are far more notable than their differences: they are both arguments for objectivity from refractoriness via agency. Indeed, towards the end of his paper Baldwin opens the door to a thesis not unlike the present one in which (1995, p.121; my italics):

> it is by finding that the content of visual experience, *unlike its direction*, is not subject to the will that such a subject encounters a kind of impossibility within visual experience (a visual analogue of tactile resistance), and is thus led to the thought that the content concerns objects whose existence is independent of the experience and can therefore be employed to explain the experience.

2.3(ii) Activity and subjectivity: The case of "The Receiver"

With the aid of a thought-experiment, let us consider the anti-piagetian view that self–world dualism could emerge in a system incapable of action-monitoring and reversible activity.

Imagine something called "The Receiver". The big difference between us and it is that The Receiver has no mechanisms for monitoring its movements (within which I include shifts of attention) and it cannot reverse them at will. We can allow that it acts in a reflexive manner, e.g. grabbing items that appear in its visual field or turning its head towards stimuli[34]; but its actions cannot be characterised by the four features.

The Receiver is moved around on a trolley so that it is subject to what Gibson called *visual kinaesthesis* (discussed earlier)—the flow of visual input accompanying self-movement has a different character to that caused when objects move towards it, past it, or away from it. When it is moved directly forward, for example, the visual world flows towards and past it, expanding from the point towards which its eyes are directed; whereas when it is stationary visual data do not expand or flow past in this way. For this reason, one might want to say that the exteroceptive input is telling The Receiver when it is moving and when it is not moving in relation to the world; so why deny that it could develop a theory-like grasp of the dualism between its body and the environment? In one case the input tells The Receiver that the world is stationary while it is moving and in the other case it tells The Receiver that it is stationary while the world is moving: why could this not be the thin end of the self–world wedge?

The answer is that all that visual kinaesthesis (making this the test case) can give The Receiver is a distinction between two kinds of exteroceptive input, and this distinction is not sufficient to ground a division between the subjective and the objective character of experience. There is nothing in the information generated when The Receiver's body moves (e.g. when its head moves reflexively or when its minder moves it on the trolley) that specifies it as a *subject* of experience. Why not?

The first reason emerges straight from what was said before under feature B (reversibility). The Receiver will be subject to two kinds of visual input, but because it is not an agent it cannot have the experience of its perceptual inputs being *constrained* by the way the physical world happens to be. Recall that in discussing feature B I concluded, in agreement with T. Baldwin, that only agency can provide an experience of refractoriness and that the experience of refractoriness is necessary if the subject is to gain any conception that its experiences are caused by something. Well, if there is no objectivity in experience—no conception of the objective causes of what one perceives—then neither is there subjectivity. Accordingly, The Receiver could never come to the view that it is the subject of objective experiences.

The second reason for saying that The Receiver could gain no conception of itself as a subject of experiences is more difficult to state. Also, in order to state it I have to rely on a distinction between events in the external world and events that are in the subject's "inner world". Under the first heading we have to put the kind of events that cause The Receiver to experience visual kinaesthesis, such as its minder moving it on the trolley, its head turning reflexively when a flashing light appears at the edge of its visual field, its hand reflexively grasping a bite-sized green object. In these cases The Receiver will be subject to distinctive forms of visual input to which it is not subject when objects move while it remains stationary. However in every case *the cause of the movement is an event in the external world*: The Receiver is in the position of a puppet, and the causes of its movement may indeed be photographed. Intentions, by contrast, and thus their character (the non-observational knowledge the subject has of them and the incorrigibility of the "tryings" they involve) do not have world-located causes; and this is what is meant by saying that actions (*qua* intentional movements) are top-down rather than bottom-up. Needless to say, brains too are "in the external world", and indeed one might observe neurones firing in the cortex to bring about the launching of purposive movements; but if intentions have a mental character (eliminatively reducible to neuronal events or otherwise) then they are not in the external world. I am talking, needless to say, at the personal level, and at this level intentions are not events in the physical world. They are acts of will generated in the agent's "own world". Accordingly, systems like The Receiver that never intend, but are merely subject to the distinction between the kind of optic flow caused by their bodily movements and the kind of optic flow not so caused can never be in a position to conceive of experiences being generated within their internal world.

Recall, in this context, what was said earlier about the way in which intentional actions are not part of *the* world but occur, rather in *my* world: "... what I am at any moment *doing* is for me at the juncture of my world and the world; and at that point 'inner' meets 'outer', whereupon 'inner' becomes objectified and 'shed' into the world as a thing"[35] (O'Shaughnessy, 1980, p.3). If actions are neither monitored nor self-determined—and thus not known non-observationally and in a privileged manner—then they are phenomena in the world, phenomena that The Receiver would observe just like any other phenomena, though with a distinctive point-of-view.

A caveat here: by saying that intentions have a "mental character" I do not mean that intended actions (unlike The Receiver's) are bodily movements plus a mental cause—a Humean view[36]. This implies that the mental event of intending something is independent of its physical effects—as if the intention and the action were only *contingently* related, as if it were just our good fortune that when we intend, say, to raise an arm it rises. This is not the way things are. Thomas Baldwin expresses the situation this way (1995, p.114): "The experience of agency is not one of acts of will regularly conjoined with bodily movements; it is one of acts of will that extend themselves to those parts of the body that are under the direct control of the agent". When somebody acts, we see the will "coming to fruition" (O'Shaughnessy, 1980, p.214); the event is psychological in the sense that it involves a subject's control over his or her body, but not in the sense of a mental cause having physical effects. Accordingly, it is one thing to argue, as I am arguing here, that intended actions have a mental character insofar as they belong to the agent's world rather than to the external world, and quite another to say that intentions are mental events that cause bodily events just as a physical event causes another physical event.

Next, even if visual kinaesthesis does not provide a wedge sufficient to split inner from outer, are there not other forms of experience—available to non-agents like The Receiver—that could do the job just as well as those provided through agency? What if we allowed the possibility, for example, that The Receiver feels sensations such as thirst (imagine that it is like the creature described in the Fodor and Lepore thought-experiment)—sensations whose *origin* is its own body? In this case the sensation would be emanating from its "internal world"; and if it experienced the tension between sensations of this kind and exteroceptive sensations of *any* kind (caused by self-movement or world-movement) then would this not be just the kind of distinction upon which a developing self–world dualism might pivot? Yes, it would certainly be a distinction between inner and outer origin—and indeed this was admitted earlier in the context of Hopkins' (1987) denial that neonatal experience might be entirely adualistic. But to say that this is the distinction we need would mean equating something coded as having its origin in one's body with the notion of an event's being in one's mental world rather than in the external world. In other words, the fact that a sensation has a bodily origin does mean that it has any more mental a character than a sensation caused exteroceptively. This serves to remind us that what makes intentions a species of mental events is not their "location in the body"—if they have a physical "location" at all—but the fact that there is a clear sense in which their cause is not something in the external world. Water depletion is an event in the external world—in the world of tissue and H_2O—in the sense that it is a physical change that happens to us; intentions, on the other hand, cannot be regarded as physical changes that happen to us.

There are, then, two reasons for saying that The Receiver could not come to regard itself as a subject of objective experience. The first reason is rooted in what I have already said under feature B about reversibility: because The Receiver experiences no refractoriness it can gain no conception of something as causing its experiences to be the way they are, and thus can gain no conception of itself as their subject. Part 2 pivots on this claim. The second reason is being offered more tentatively because, not being fully spelt out, it has a somewhat intuition-heavy character; and for this reason I will not build on it. It is that, insofar as The Receiver never intends anything, there is nothing in its life with an inner mental character: all of its sensory phenomena are caused by events in the physical world whereas intentions (talking at the personal level) are not caused by physical events. If no phenomena have this inner character there can be no scope for the development of subjectivity.

Finally, would one be conceding too much to The Receiver's champions by saying that it has a "point-of-view"? Would this not be tantamount to an admission that it has at least an "ecological self" (Neisser, 1991). In a weak sense The Receiver obviously *does* have a point-of-view and indeed this will be specified—remaining with the visual modality—by the structure of the optic flow (e.g. how its head frames the input, how the input converges to a point). And of course the character of this point-of-view will be different for self-movement and for world-movement: the optic flow will have a different character when, say, trolley-movement causes changes in the flow than when world-movement causes it. But if I am admitting *this*, have I not admitted that The Receiver possesses the much-vaunted subjectivity? What more is there to being a subject of experience than having a point-of-view in this ecological sense? The reply must be that it is one thing to possess a "point of view" in the sense in which I have admitted The Receiver possesses one, and another for a creature to locate itself within the world as an experiencer through utilising only the fact that it is *a point at which perceptual inputs converge* (The Receiver's situation).

What I have just said clearly needs to be defended. However, its defence properly belongs in the next section, in which I discuss the relation between agency and self-locating thoughts.

Perhaps I should say at this point that even if these are not decisive arguments against the anti-piagetian position, the perspective on mental development that I will defend in the remainder of this book will still be worth defending. All the reader needs to agree is that the form that self–world dualism takes in human mental life *comes to be the form it is because of what we possess and The Receiver lacks*.

2.4: SELF-LOCATING THOUGHTS AND "EXTERNALITY"

In the first part of this section I will take up the question that was left dangling just now: How does agency contribute to the *spatiality* of experience? How, that is, can agency enable a subject to locate itself? In the second part of the section I will discuss spatial thoughts about physical objects rather than about locations; and this will predictably involve drawing again on what has already been established about the role of refractoriness in the conception of physical objects. It will be a bringing-together of conclusions about refractoriness and about self-location in order to say what it means for a subject (a human infant in particular) to have a conception of objects existing in the external world independently from his or her experience of them. I call this "*externality*".

Let us return to The Receiver. I hope I have already established that the system could not regard objects as the causes of its experiences; if it can do nothing at will then there can be no refractoriness. But somebody might concede this and yet say that, although The Receiver has no conception of physical objects, it does have a conception of a space in which it is located as an experiencing point: it has a conception of *places*, which might be marked by colours or sounds. The objector could then say that I have done nothing to substantiate my denial that The Receiver could locate itself relative to such places. Could The Receiver develop a sense of so-called "egocentric" spatial location, meaning "self-locating spatial percepts", perceiving itself as being here in relation to objects over *there*. [Note that "egocentric" is now being used in a sense entirely different from Piaget's; more of this later.]

Drawing on some recent work by Bill Brewer (1992), one could imagine objectors making two kinds of argument in favour of their position.

(1) A system can *infer* its location in the world from the way in which perceptual inputs converge on it. It has wired-in inferential mechanisms that derive egocentric position on the basis of exteroceptive information—as if solving lots of simultaneous equations.

(2) A system's coding of its location in space and its perceptions form a *simple psychological unity*. Perceptual experience itself "displays the double aspect definitive of its both building up a picture of an independent spatial world and constituting its subject's particular experiental route through the world" (Brewer, 1992; p.23). [This view is one proposed by philosophers (e.g. Campbell, 1984; Strawson, 1966); but it also echoes the Gibsonian idea of the "co-perception" of self and world.]

Here is one of Brewer's arguments against (1). It is difficult to see how a system could infer its place in the world from afferent information alone unless it had some preliminary awareness of itself as a subject of experience. Without this, there could be no "grasp of the contingent dependence of the course and nature of his experience on the way the world is in itself and his continuous spatio-temporal route through it" (Brewer, 1992, p.20).

On the first argument, a system could infer its position in space purely on the basis of its sensory inputs—and this is supposed to ground its first-person thoughts about itself as a spatially-located entity. But how could it infer, from the fact that (say) the Albert Hall is filling its visual field right now, that "I am near Hyde Park" unless it already knows that *it* is the subject of the visual experience and not somebody else? All it possesses is visual input from the Albert Hall, information that may just as well have been caused by a video link-up as by its own orientation to the building. In other words, any sensory input that such a system receives must *exhaust* its conception of itself: there is nothing over-and-above what it experiences. Accordingly, it is in no position to appreciate that what is being experienced now is *contingent on* where it is. And this will inevitably be beyond its grasp just as long as it has no prior conception of itself as an element in the spatial world whose experience is contingent on the way things objectively are and on its passage through the environment. In short, inferences from *this* experience to *my* location are only possible for creatures that *already possess* some conception of themselves as spatially located within an objective world.

It is important to be clear, at this point, exactly what the idea of contingency amounts to. On Brewer's view, simply being the subject of perceptual experience is not sufficient for individuals to know that what they experience is contingent on—as meaning "being a function of"—where they are located in space. But grasping this contingency is integral to grasping the distinction between what is contingent to my experience at this time versus what is *necessary* to it—a rather *different* sense of contingency. Thus, if I know that what I am experiencing now is contingent on where I am presently located, then I will also grasp that if I am, say, seeing a person's face right now then I necessarily cannot see the back of her head (assuming the absence of mirrors) at the same time; that if I move to the left of the face it will move to the right of my visual field; that certain objects will be occluded by certain others by virtue of where I am located. I will know, then, that my experiences are *necessarily* dictated and constrained by where I am physically located relative to other objects. In short, what Brewer is alluding to[37] is the fact that grasping the relation between visual experience and the subject's spatial location involves a *modal* conception. In this respect, then, there are parallels to be drawn between this view and Baldwin's thesis that experiencing felt-resistance brings a modal conception in its wake; but there are differences too, on which there is no need to dwell.

Let us now—moving beyond Brewer's position—make explicit the role that agency plays in supporting the inferences from "what is being experienced" to "where I am". Because a system like The Receiver is not an agent, the movements it is caused to make by its minder or by the world (reflexes) cannot discriminate between cases in which its own eyes record the Albert Hall by virtue of being in front of it and cases where, say, a video camera projects images to it when it is located elsewhere. But in systems capable of action-monitoring and reversibility—systems that knowingly determine their own input—this distinction can be made. The agent is, as it were, its own cameraman and knows immediately that it is. This is sufficient for the subject to claim responsibility for its experiences, and this is a *necessary* condition, I am arguing, for experiences to be located spatially.

We now turn to (2), to the view that self-locating and perceptual inputs form a primitive psychological unity. The problem here is that although there may be some kind of supra-modal (neither visual nor spatial) structuring of the input, this fact does not help us to explain how an eventual *division* between egocentric spatial judgements and judgements about the appearance of places comes about *at the conceptual level*. (Recall the distinction between non-conceptual and conceptual content made earlier.) At some point we have to drive a wedge between the two faces of this primitive psychological unity if we are to have these kinds of thoughts. (This is a very broad paraphrase of Brewer.) In other words, a primary, supra-modal unity of visual and spatial information must contain within it the seeds of a distinction that will enable the subject to develop thoughts about his or her location that are not visually grounded, as well as thoughts about how things appear that are not also thoughts of his or her spatial location. It is not, therefore, sufficient for the objector to posit this simple psychological unity without saying something about these "seeds".

These are reasons, then, for saying that a mental system that is no more than the point at which perceptual inputs converge will lack the resources to enjoy spatially egocentric or "self-locating" thoughts. I need to say more, however, about how the exercise of agency comes to be a necessary condition for the having of such thoughts. As a route towards this, let us think a little more about what has to be achieved for a judgement to be spatially egocentric—bearing in mind that "egocentric" is being used to mean "self-locating", not what Piaget meant by the term.

Egocentric spatial judgements are those in which subjects locate themselves relative to other places. Thus, to think of something as "on my left" or "above me" is to have an egocentric spatial thought. It is certainly possible to imagine a form of spatial coding that, in contrast to this, is entirely allocentric, in which the subjects code whether a datum is, say, resting on another or between two points without at the same time locating their body within the framework. Self–world dualism clearly depends on the ability to make both kinds of judgement—judgements about objects *vis-à-vis* one's body and judgements that are entirely object-centred. Next, an essential ingredient of egocentric spatial judgements is that they require the subject to distinguish between a *here* and a *there*, between the place at which one is located and the place at which the object being experienced is located. Terms like "here" and "there" are called spatially *indexical* terms, with "now" and "then" being temporally indexical terms. Indexical terms are terms that, as it were, point to particular places and times and whose reference is determined entirely by the spatial or the temporal context or the communicative act—as it is in pointing.

The view I need to explore is that such judgements are impossible without the ability to act in relation to places. Let us consider what philosophers have said on this question.

Janaway (1983, taken from Brewer, 1992, p.18, original italics) attributes the following two theses to Schopenhauer:

(i) *qua* subject of representation (thought and experience) *alone*, I can have no sense of myself as an item in the world; but (ii) *qua* subject of will, I do have a sense of myself as an item in the world. Therefore any subject whose perceptual experience displays the egocentric spatiality we are interested in must be a subject of will.

The idea is that the contents of the subject's perceptions guide his or her actions in space and locate the subject in the perceived world in virtue of doing this. One might say percepts "advise" subjects about how to act (e.g. they tell one to reach there for the apple) and because they do this, and irrespective of whether the subjects actually *succeed* in the attempt, they enable the subjects to locate themselves in the spatial world.

This is not a million miles from Piaget's notion of *assimilation*: the primary role of percepts in the developing child, according to Piaget, is to determine assimilatory actions—reaching, tracking etc. Certain percepts determine certain action-schemes. It also bears an interesting relation to Gibson's (1979) notion of "affordances". We perceive locations not contemplatively, said Gibson, but as having implications for action; we see, for example, this water in a cup as affording drinking and that water in the pool as affording diving. And it also bears comparison with the view that selective attention should be regarded as the perceptual preparation for action (Allport, 1987). Objects play a role, then, in determining purposive actions, or, as Brewer puts it in the same paper, "objects are the focus of perceptually controlled behaviour". (Brewer, 1992, p.26).

Remember that our immediate concern here is not with what might be called, "object-hood" (by which I mean the conception of things as being the substantial causes of our experience of them) but with *locations* affording certain sensations or as enabling certain kinds of action—a move *here* will give me a cool, blue sensation and a step *there* will raise me up. In this restricted sense one may say that locations are understood by us in terms of what we would do to have the experiences they afford; insofar as we experience the locations relative to ourselves we know what actions we would need to take to enjoy these experiences. Or one might put it in the following terms: these three are not separately known, (1) the place's location relative to us, (2) what we can do in relation to the place, and (3) our purposes. Rather, these three form a unity, in the sense that we conceive of places in terms of the actions we could take towards them to realise our actual or potential purposes.

What it takes, then, for an organism to have an "egocentric space"—a space organised around its own body and serving as the informational underpinning of "here"-thoughts—is that, in Gareth Evans' words, there should be "a complex network of connections [which] exists between perceptual input and behavioural output. A perceptual input [...] cannot have a spatial significance for an organism except in so far as it has a place in such a complex network of input–output connections." (Evans, 1982, p.154; see also Peacocke, 1983).

Consider, in illustration, how terms like "up", "down", "left", "right", "in front", and "behind" get their meaning. These meanings are not derived from *proximal* bodily cues (e.g. my feet are "down", my head is "up") because I might be bending over or upside down. Neither are these directions defined by objects, such that "down" is the earth and "up" is the sky—because the earth might be sloping. "Rather, up and down are related to how one would move and act in the field" (Taylor, 1978–79, quoted in Evans, 1982). Imagine, in illustration, a creature that, unlike The Receiver, is capable of making intentional movements: it can move forwards, backwards, up, down, and so on. It makes no sense to say that this creature possesses the information that a sound, say, is in front of it yet has, at the same time, *no idea how it should move in order to approach the sound*. If this is so, we can say that the question of whether The Receiver has a conception of egocentric space does not even *arise*.

Evans (1982, p.158) points out that we are talking here not about perceptual *experiences*, not about a subject's conscious states, but rather about states of his or her information-processing system—"in terms of computing the solution to simultaneous equations". But he goes on to say that conscious, concept-applying, rational *thoughts* about the world and our location in it "should depend systematically upon the informational properties of the input" (p.159; cf the earlier comments about the "primitive psychological unity" view). And moreover (ibid pp.161–162), "[i]t is difficult to see how we would credit a subject with a thought about *here* if he did not appreciate the relevance of any perceptions he might have to the truth-value of the thought, and did not realise its implications for action (consider, for instance, a thought like 'There's a fire here')".

If these claims are correct, they show that unless our behaviour were determined, in some sense, by our perception of objects, unless we were disposed to behave towards percepts in certain ways in order to satisfy our desires, we would be unable to locate ourselves egocentrically in relation to data. This is not of course equivalent to stimuli *evoking* behaviours (which is the opposite of willing); it means rather that what we do is relative to what we want and what we experience as fulfilling our purposes. We want to swim, for example, so we dive *there* where we see water, not *there* where we see gravel: percepts control behaviour in this sense.

This aspect of the percept–behaviour relation was not properly covered in my presentation of the four features. For example, features (A) and (B) could be true of somebody who had no real purposes—who was indifferent to objects and who simply glanced idly about or flexed his or her limbs. But when we put desire—and thus the fact of willing—at the centre of the picture we have the following view: the agent must be, as it were, "connected" to percepts because of what he or she wants to bring about. This inevitably leads to an enrichment of the thesis that percepts of objects will tend to resist the will: that they will be refractory.

2.4(i) Externality

I now want to consider thoughts that are not merely self-locating in relation to places, but in which thinkers locate themselves in relation to physical objects—externality. Agency is necessary, we seem to have established, for both the self-locating aspect and the objectivity aspect.

The argument from refractoriness established—whether expressed in terms of reversibility or in the felt-resistance form of Thomas Baldwin—that no conception of objects as the causes of our perceptions is available to non-agents. Furthermore, the view developed over the past few pages is that subjects' ability to locate themselves in relation to places depends on agency in a different sense: that indexical thoughts are grounded on our ability to perceive places as having implications for what we can do in relation to them towards the fulfilment of our purposes.

Let us consider what it means, on this view, to perceive an object as being *external* to the self—as something *over there* and *causing* me to have the experiences I am now having. By the way, in what immediately follows my use of the term "know" and its cognates is only for ease of exposition: what I am referring to are sets of structured expectations, not fully conceptual, propositional knowledge. And I will refer only to the visual modality.

(1) I know that if the object does not itself move then my eye and head movements will cause certain, very tightly specified, kinds of change in the input. For example, if I glance upwards, the image of the object will move downwards in my visual field. This emerges from action-monitoring.

(2) I know that unless the object moves it can be re-experienced after I have looked away from it. It is "available" to cause the same experiences when I reverse glances away from it. This emerges from reversibility.

(3) I know that there are very strict limits on how I can change my experience of the object. I cannot change its colour by blinking, I cannot make it larger by staring at it, and so forth; but I can affect many other kinds of change in the input it causes. This is refractoriness.

(4) I know that if, for example, I want to bring the object closer to me I must move towards it, that if it is on my left and I want to distance myself from it I must move to the right. I know, more generally, how my purposes in relation to the object can be fulfilled by actions relative to it; and in knowing this I have indexical thoughts about the object. This is the thesis, just discussed, about the dependency of indexical thoughts on purposes in relation to objects.

The claim I shall now make is that one cannot reasonably say of subjects that they know an object is in a certain place relative to their own position and is the physical cause of the (say) visual inputs they are receiving unless they know these four things. In other words, for subjects to experience an object as external to the self—externality—they require more than a "representation" of it. What is required is knowledge of *how* their *actions can affect their experience of the object* as well as knowledge of how the object's movement will affect their experiences. There is a conceptual linkage, in other words, between externality and agency. To put it in a rather pat form, externality is part and parcel of self–world dualism while the exercise of agency is necessary for this dualism.

What is true of the experience of currently visible objects ("visible" will equal "perceptible" here) applies equally well to the experience of objects that are occluded by other objects; although the situation is obviously more complicated. This time, what subjects have to know is not merely how their experience of the object will be affected by their own actions and by movements of the object; the subjects must also know about how moving relative to the occluder will reveal the object. Let us consider occlusion in terms of the four kinds of knowledge listed earlier.

(1) I know that if the object remains behind the occluder and if the occluder does not move then (say) lateral movements will eventually cause the object to become visible again so long as the occluder is flat. If a lateral movement does not cause re-appearance then the object has moved.

(2) I know that the kinds of re-appearances described in (1) can be reversed: that I can always re-experience occlusion by reversing my action. Repeating the same actions will result in the same experiences unless object or occluder have moved.

(3) I know that the kinds of action that can cause re-appearance are very tightly specified. For example, moving towards the occluder can never cause re-appearance; moving away from the occluder can sometimes cause re-appearance; movements of the self relative to the occluder will eventually cause re-appearance unless the occluder covers the object; if the occluder covers the object then its removal will necessarily cause the object to re-appear.

(4) I know that if I wish to see or grasp the object again there are certain things I have to do. And in knowing the necessity for them I know about the relation between me here, the occluder $there_1$ and the object $there_2$ and about the relation between the latter two. What constrains the fulfilment of my desires is the spatial relation between the three of us.

Perhaps one way of expressing the conceptual link between understanding occlusion and being an agent is in terms of the impossibility of the following three statements all being true at once.

• "She knows where the occluded object is in relation to her and in relation to the occluder."
• "She is able to move about at will."
• "She has no idea what to do to re-experience the object."

(Note here that I am talking about knowing where something is *in the relation to one's own body*. Also note that the claim is not that "knowing where an occluded object is in relation to oneself" implies the *ability* to make the movements necessary to re-experience it; my point is about the impossibility of at once having that ability and not knowing how to exercise it in cases where one knows where the object is in relation to one's body.)

This does not imply that there cannot be cases of neurological impairment in which all three statements are true of a patient. Indeed the cognitive neuropsychological literature contains many examples of patients' holding logically contradicting views. For example a patient may say that it is 1994, and that he has just returned from the Second World War which finished in 1945 (Hodges & McCarthy, 1993). Stroke patients often claim both that they have lost the use of their limbs and that one needs working limbs to drive a car, but insist nonetheless that they can drive. My point is simply that these three statements *do* mutually contradict—no less than the claims that it is 1993 and that it is 1945 or that I lack the capacity necessary for doing X and I can do X.

2.5: SEARCH, DISHABITUATION, AND "REPRESENTATION PERMANENCE" IN INFANCY

In developmental psychology "object permanence" or "the object concept" is taken to refer to the pre-verbal child's knowledge that objects continue to exist when they are occluded from view. *If* "object permanence" is taken to mean "externality"—it was by Piaget—and *if* what I have just said about the conceptual linkage between occlusion, externality, and agency is valid then it follows that one should assess what infants know about the external world in terms of what they do in relation to objects, not in terms of how they react to events.

This is a very controversial and unfashionable claim and I will spend most of this section showing how it contrasts with the opposing position currently dominant in psychology. In the next section I will defend objections to this piagetian view.

Broadly speaking, there are two ways of assessing what infants know about the physical world. One is in terms of how they act towards objects—searching, for example—and the other is in terms of how they *re*act when witnessing anomalous or "impossible" physical events. The fact that the latter seems to allow us to ascribe object permanence to infants well *before they are successful agents*, before they are even able to co-ordinate what they can see with where they reach (at about 4.5 months), seems to pose a very strong challenge to the thesis that infants' knowledge of the external world is conceptually linked to the control they can exercise over their experiences of objects.

Before proceeding, however, we need to be clear about the status of the piagetian claim. It is difficult to imagine *data* that could undermine the position I developed in the previous section; for that position is conceptual not empirical and is vulnerable, therefore, to arguments not to experiments. My arguments about refractoriness and so forth have implications for how we *assess* permanence because they concern what "object permanence" should be taken to mean. They do not, however, directly generate empirical predictions. On the other hand, to say that object permanence is *developmentally correlative* to the degree of executive control[38] that infants can impose on their experiences *is* vulnerable to empirical refutation. We might find, for example, that infants have superb means–end skills, motor co-ordination, behavioural inhibition, attention-shifting capacities, working-memory, and so forth, *well before* they can manifest these in searching for currently occluded objects. The first is a claim about what is conceptually necessary for what, and the second a claim about what develops before and alongside what. I will, then, deal with some purely empirical issues, and sometimes empirical and conceptual issues will be difficult to discriminate; but most of the time I will be concerned with the question of assessment—of what we should take object permanence *to mean*.

[As will gradually become evident, the distinction between conceptual and empirical claims about object permanence parallels the difference between the "piagetian" and the "Piagetian" views of its development. The arguments reviewed in the previous section are what I call "piagetian"; but the views about the actual course of object permanence development (the empirical theory) are those of Jean Piaget: they are Piagetian. Sometimes, of course, piagetians and Piagetians say the same thing.]

According to piagetians, then, object permanence should be taken to mean externality. This is in stark contrast to those who (usually implicitly) take it to mean *maintaining a representation of a currently unperceived object sufficiently well to drive some kind of behaviour*. I call this "*representation permanence*" and will be arguing that representation permanence is a phenomenon different from and more primitive than externality. Let us look first at the development of searching.

As Piaget (1955) showed—it has been massively confirmed since—the broad facts about the development of search are these:

- Before about 8 months of age infants show a variety of behaviours towards objects, such as anticipating the trajectory of falling objects and retrieving partially occluded objects (e.g. a rattle peeping out from behind a cushion). But they do not search for *completely* occluded objects. It needs stressing here that failure to search is *not caused by a simple motor incapacity*—otherwise this fact would be trivial. Babies of 5 or 6 months are perfectly capable of (say) lifting cups and cloths, parting curtains, and pushing cushions out of the way and, as I have just said, they can perform the retrieval act when the object is only partially occluded. So it is as if "out of sight" equals "out of existence" for them.

- After about 8 months of age infants do search for completely occluded objects but they do not search after the *visible displacement* of the object to an adjacent occluder. For example, if they retrieve, or see an object retrieved, from behind occluder A and then see the object transferred to occluder B they will tend to return to A. This is known as the "A-not-B" or "perseveration" error.

- Around 12 months of age, the A-not-B error ceases to be made; but infants will generally be unable to search correctly when the displacement of a target object is *invisible* to them. For example, if A and B are spatially transposed after the object has been hidden at A (e.g. A is now on their right rather than their left) the infants will tend to search at B—on their left, as before. This error ceases to be made after about 18 months of age.

Taking the first kind of search failure (with a single occluder) as our test case, we can now ask why infants younger than 8 months do not search although they are motorically capable of doing so. The piagetian answer is, broadly, "Because self–world dualism is incomplete". Piaget used the term "egocentrism" to describe this state of affairs. And note that this term is not to be confused with the term "egocentric" as philosophers use it to mean "self-locating" (see p. 99): in this sense a capacity for "egocentric" thoughts is just what *has* to develop! From now on I will use "egocentrism" and "egocentric" in Piaget's sense.

Egocentrism takes many forms throughout mental development, according to Piaget, but in this case we can think of it as equivalent to the belief that "what I currently experience is all there is". Obviously, there is nothing that literally corresponds to this belief in the baby's mind because, on this view, there is nothing that corresponds to what we refer to as "I"—but what I say has the accuracy of a caricature.

The situation of the infant who does not search for completely occluded objects while being motorically capable of the action is the following (at least as far as the visual modality is concerned). Because they have *relatively* little control over what they visually attend to—because, that is, their exploration of the visible world is a good deal less planful and co-ordinated than that of older infants—*they have a correspondingly poor grasp of the distinction between the changes in their visual experience that they have brought about and those that the world has brought about.* They have only a weak capacity for reversibility.

One of the things these infants will inevitably be bad at is intentionally altering their visual perspectives. And if they are bad at doing this, they will be correlatively unaware that they *possess* a visual perspective. They will fail to appreciate that the current invisibility of the object is a function of their present spatial location—it is a function of the fact that there is an occluder between them and it—and that this is a relation alterable by their actions. So to be egocentric in this situation means to lack the conception that one's perspective on the world is a *contingent fact* (see pp. 98–99) alterable by action on the occluder or by changing one's position. In creatures who only weakly know what it is to alter their visual experience at will there will be a correspondingly weak grasp of the fact that what they can see is a function of where they are. All this follows from the arguments in the previous section.

Piaget's claim that failure to search is caused by egocentrism is then, a hybrid of the conceptual and the empirical. But the insistence that object permanence should be assessed in terms of infants' actions on objects rather than in terms of their reactions to physical events is entirely conceptual. For if, as I said, you believe that object permanence equals externality and if you believe that externality is something that only an agent can possess then you must also believe that externality can only be manifested through action (in non-verbal creatures).

This is not to say, of course, that we only manifest externality at the time of acting: we can obviously just *think* about objects. According to Piaget, children above 18 months or so have developed a conception of the external world sufficient to allow them to think about objects in their absence, which he called *représentation mentale*. (I use the French to distinguish this from the usual contemporary meaning of "mental representation".) But, he insisted, they have only been able to win through to the *représentation mentale* of objects because they are agents, because they have established self–world division through their actions. It is meaningless, a piagetian would say, to ascribe thoughts about objects—Piaget's *représentation mentale*[39]—to an infant who is not even able to engage in visually-guided reaching (younger than about 4.5 months).

2.5(i) Assessing object permanence by reactions

I now turn to the case against the piagetian account of object permanence—against the view that (a) adequate agency is necessary for its development and (b) that it should be assessed in terms of what infants can do in relation to objects.

The contrasting view rests on the following methodological point: one has no warrant for assuming that if a baby cannot achieve the retrieval of an object then he or she does not know it is there. Talk about the dependency of knowledge upon agency—and about what metaphysicians like Schopenhauer may have thought—is neither here nor there; for there is nothing illogical or incoherent in the view that preverbal children's knowledge of object permanence should be *assessed* separately from their motor development and their means–end skills. What we require is a set of experimental techniques—these were unavailable in Piaget's household when he was studying his three children—for tapping the child's knowledge without requiring him or her to do anything.

No doubt psychologists were making this kind of objection as soon as Piaget's infancy trilogy appeared; but it was first made forcefully and with supporting data by T.G.R. Bower. Bower wanted to show that when new assessment procedures are used, perceptual and cognitive skills can be revealed which Piaget's informal procedures had missed. For example, operant conditioning procedures seemed to reveal shape constancy at 6 weeks (Bower, 1966; and see Slater & Morison, 1985), something that Piaget (1955) claimed must be dependent on manual exploration. But, crucially, Bower argued that we should study the infants' reactions to anomalous events involving occlusion, because if infants are surprised by the anomaly then we can infer that they are perceiving it *as* an anomaly, and to do *this* implies that they have expectations about permanence similar to our own. For example, if we take decrease in heart rate as a measure of surprise (or at least "orientation to an interesting event") then we can ask how surprised young infants are when removal of an occluder fails to reveal an object that has just travelled behind it (Bower, 1974).

However, the problem with this work was that heart-rate decrease is not a very sensitive measure of surprise and, to a lesser degree, neither is the cessation of sucking (another technique Bower used). Attempts to replicate Bower's results were, accordingly, often unsuccessful. Operant measures too (e.g. reinforced head-turning and non-nutritive, rewarded sucking) have their problems. Accordingly, in recent years, infancy researchers have come to rely instead on a different technique for gauging discrimination and surprise: the technique of *dishabituation*. This exploits the fact that when infants are presented with a novel stimulus or event then, provided it is neither too simple nor too complex, they will attend to it. The measure of attention is looking. After a while however, they will habituate to this stimulus and begin to look away from it for progressively longer periods as if getting bored. The question can then be asked: How do we need to change the display so that the infant will treat it as something new and therefore recover his or her interest in it? Under what circumstances will infants *dis*habituate? Although dishabituation involves the baby in doing something—in looking back at the array for longer periods—the *fact* of dishabituation is not in any sense a fact about an action. This is because *a recovery of interest is something that happens to an organism: it is not something it does*; and for this reason I refer to dishabituation as a "reaction"[40]. Of course the head movements in dishabituation will inevitably *result* in altered visual inputs, but these altered inputs are caused by a reaction to anomaly; they are not altered inputs produced at will of the kind enjoyed when, say, glancing around a room.

Since Bower's pioneering work, researchers armed with the dishabituation technique have begun to apply a similar logic to questions about infant cognition, and even to apply similar stimulus arrays to those originally used by Bower. For example, when a partially-occluded stick is removed from behind a block will infants be surprised if it is revealed to be in two halves instead of being a unitary object (Bower, 1966; Kellman & Spelke, 1983)? Elizabeth Spelke (1991, Spelke & de Walle, 1993) has gathered a substantial body of evidence from dishabituation studies in favour of the view that infants as young as 6 months expect the laws of "naive physics" (such as gravity and inertia) to hold: they are surprised by their violation. But more to the present point are the dishabituation studies that bear *directly* on the issue of object permanence. Here the work of Renée Baillargeon is the most impressive and the most widely discussed.

Baillargeon's best-known study was based on the assumption that if very young infants expect currently invisible objects to resist the movement of other objects then they should be surprised at the violation of this expectation (Baillargeon, 1987). The infants were only 3.5 to 4.5 months old, which is younger than the age at which visually guided reaching normally appears. The experimental and the control group were habituated to a silver, cardboard screen swinging towards and away from them through 180°—imagine looking at a drawbridge—and before this, they had all been allowed to manipulate a yellow wooden box. After habituation, this box was placed, clearly visible, just behind the screen as it lay flat against the floor of the apparatus face forwards—imagine somebody standing at the entrance to the castle when the drawbridge is down. Clearly, this would prevent the screen from moving backwards through its 180° arc. Accordingly, the experimental group witnessed a violation of this assumption: the screen moved backwards and *completed* its arc (the experimenters having surreptitiously removed the box in the meantime). The control group, on the other hand, witnessed an event that did not violate the permanence assumption: the box impeded the motion of the screen, stopping it at 112°. Note that the box impedes the screen *while it is invisible*.

The result was that there was a significantly greater degree of dishabituation in the experimental group than in the control group. And note also that what makes this demonstration so impressive is that, if we subtract the fact that the box had been placed behind the screen in the interim, the control event was actually *more dissimilar* to the habituation event than was the experimental event. For the arc was different (shorter) in the control event than in the experimental event, so what surely made the experimental event special was that it was, given the permanence assumption, "impossible".

It is worth mentioning, before passing on, that infants of about this age dishabituate to kinds of permanence-violating sequence other than ones in which an invisible object impedes movement. Baillargeon (Baillargeon & Graber, 1987) has also shown, for example, that infants as young as 5 months are more likely to dishabituate when a tall object (a cardboard carrot, for example) does not reappear in the window of a screen behind which it is passing than when a short object (another carrot) does not reappear—implying some expectation that objects retain their *properties* when occluded. Moreover, babies as young as this have expectations about the impedance of moving objects by currently invisible objects even when the moving object is itself currently invisible. They expect, on the dishabituation criterion, that a Mickey Mouse doll will impede a moving truck *behind a screen* when it is in the truck's path but not when it is out of that path (Baillargeon, 1986).

To many, studies of this kind provide decisive evidence against the piagetian account of object permanence. They argue that babies between 3 and 4 months of age are not motorically skilled nor skilled at attention-shifting and yet they tacitly judge invisible objects to resist the movement of other objects; and how could they do this unless they also judge that the resisting object is *still there*?

Obviously, a different sense of "object permanence" is in play here from the piagetian one: it certainly does not mean "externality". What this conception of object permanence seems to amount to here is the maintenance of a representation of an occluded object during the period of its occlusion, a representation that drives the reaction of surprise. As I said at the start of this section, I will refer to this sense of object permanence as *"representation permanence"*. And I will refer to those who hold that "object permanence = representation permanence" as "informational theorists" because the implication from their view is that knowing an object exists is equivalent to retaining information about it.

It is fair to say that informational theorists—they are in the majority—are not united behind any theory of what develops, because their motivation is essentially to show that when we use the "appropriate" procedures competence appears earlier. One can detect, in fact, at least three forms of informational theory. One form is direct realist or Gibsonian, and relies on the claims that object permanence is something that is perceived rather than conceived, and that there are invariants in the optic flow which define an occluding event. This way of thinking is evident in some of Bower's early work (e.g. Bower, 1967) and in the current theoretical position of Eleanor Gibson (Gibson, 1987). Another way of being a informational theorist is by being a nativist. Here one would say that there are innate rules and representations—perhaps inscribed in the language of thought— which ensure that certain judgements are made when occlusion is witnessed (see Leslie & Keeble, 1987, on causality perception). Direct realists and nativists share the view, then, that object permanence is not something that infants "acquire"; although they have very different reasons for that view. A possible empiricist view, by contrast, would be that object permanence does indeed develop; and it develops from experiencing "what leads to what"—what kinds of situations precede resistance events, for example. And, in classical empiricist style, it could be assumed that passively enjoyed experiences are sufficient for this. Such a theorist might cite the fact that infants of 3.5 months of age have experienced, on average, around 800 hours of alert wakefulness (Parmelee, Wenner, & Schulz, 1964), and say that this is sufficient to train up their expectations. This way of thinking would be sympathetic to some workers in connectionism; and I will have something to say about connectionist modelling of object permanence in section 2.8.

What we need to do at this point is to stand back and consider just how this divergence between informational theorists and piagetians highlights the deeper divergence between those who are happy with an essentially representational theory of the mind and those who are not. The assumption behind the informational account is that maintaining a representation of an object when it is currently occluded is equivalent to knowing that the object continues to exist. The piagetian denies this. Unless we mean by "representation" just what Piaget meant by *représentation mentale*—and clearly informational theorists do *not* mean this—it is simply false that maintaining "a representation" of an object when it is invisible is the same as knowing that the object exists. This view falls out naturally from what I argued in section 2.4(ii) with regard to externality. If we take object permanence to mean externality, then to know that an object exists at a certain place (as opposed to knowing that there is a certain object somewhere unknown[41]) is to know something about the relation between oneself as a spatially located experiencer and the object as the cause or possible cause of one's experiences: this does not reduce to "having a representation" of it. Even those who do not accept the claim that agency is necessary to the development of this knowledge can accept that this is what object permanence amounts to. Moreover, it would surely be a very badly designed nervous system that routinely extinguished representations of objects as soon as the objects were lost from sight. At time t_1 there is a representation of an object with the causal powers to impede other objects; at time t_2 this representation has ceased to exist; at time t_3 it pops up again ... . This would be the nervous system as *mirror*!

I should also stress that the piagetian resistance to the claim that dishabituation studies demonstrate object permanence is a million miles from the claim that young infants are just like The Receiver. The claim is not that infants of 3 or 4 months are so executively incompetent as to have *no* conception of an external world. Rather, the claim is that in *experiments* on how subjects react to events stage-managed to be unusual the question of what they know about the external world—in Piaget's strong sense—*does not even arise*. Because the subjects have to do nothing, they cannot manifest knowledge about the relation between themselves and objects; they can only manifest expectations about which inputs should follow from which. For, on the definition of externality given earlier, this can only be manifested (nonverbally) through what we do. Subjects who wish to retrieve or regain sight of an object will, all things being equal, act on that knowledge if they are able to organise the actions. If subjects' knowing that an object exists amounts to their knowing about the relation between themselves and it, and if the subjects want that object, then they will alter the relation between themselves and it—by searching behind the occluder for example. We know that infants of under 8 months *can* alter the relation between themselves and objects (e.g. they retrieve partially occluded objects) so why do they not do so? Because, says the piagetian, they cannot grasp the relation between their experiences of objects and what they have to do to enjoy this experience again. The fact that they dishabituate when a currently invisible object fails to impede a moving occluder *does not tell us that they have knowledge on which (for some reason or other) they do not know how to act*.

Remember that to be a piagetian means believing that there is a conceptual link between having spatial knowledge and knowing what to do.

2.6: ANSWERING SOME OBJECTIONS

In this section I will attempt to answer three substantial objections to the thesis being developed here. But before I do, I want to reply briefly to the most common objection, one that is based on a simple misunderstanding. (The others are based on sophisticated misunderstandings.) The common objection is that the piagetian view is "circular"—"object permanence is externality and externality requires agency; therefore object permanence develops via agency". That is to say, one is defining a competence in terms of agency and then concluding that it must develop via agency, so we have moved no farther than our own front door.

To say this is circular, however, is to deny the possibility of there being conceptual arguments in developmental psychology. That claim is, first, that if we take object permanence to be equivalent to externality then, (a) adequate agency is necessary for its development and (b) the criteria on which it should be assessed must involve taking action. This is not circularity: it is a conceptual claim. Second, there is the empirical claim, associated with Jean Piaget himself, that the development of externality is *correlative* to the development of agency. As I said earlier, this is an empirical claim that can be—and to some degree has been—overturned by data, as we shall see.

Objection 1: The representation in "representation permanence" has content

This objection states that there is no warrant for, as it were, downgrading the status of the representation in representation permanence. Piagetians have to accept that this representation has what philosophers call "content": it has meaning for the infant. For if it did not have meaning for the infant it would not generate the appropriate kinds of surprise reaction. It is not as if—the objection continues— there are only two kinds of cognitive state at issue here: there are (1) contentless representations in the nervous system, two-a-penny, and telling us nothing about knowledge, in contrast to (2) full-blown externality, richly expressive of beliefs and intentions. Between these two extremes there are representations whose content is what the subject currently knows about physical reality, but on which the subject is not in a position to act; and perhaps dishabituation studies reveal this kind of representation.

This is the piagetian reply. The kind of content we are ascribing to the young infant's representation is a content in which the content-holder's perspective (e.g. occluder between me and target) is not included; and this is the reason why the infant cannot act on that representation. "Occluded" does not have to mean "occluded *to me*"; for we can understand what it means for something to be occluded without needing to ask "From whose point of view?". In the present case the "to me" provides a link to behaviour: there is an occluder between me and the screen and they are in my reaching space.

The piagetian is denying that the contentful representation of an occluded object revealed in dishabituation experiments has the status of "knowledge that cannot be acted on". If "cannot be acted on" just refers to motor incapacity then obviously there can be knowledge that cannot be acted on; but infants of, say, 6 months clearly are motorically capable of retrieving objects. What seems to be the case is that they *do not know what to do* to retrieve the object and, to labour the point, if they do not know this then it makes no sense to say they know where the object is in relation to them—given the arguments in section 2.4(ii). So, ascribing "knowledge that cannot be acted on" is not justified. And more generally, as Hamlyn (1990) has pointed out, knowledge is always knowledge *for somebody*: the putative "knowledge" revealed in dishabituation experiments is "knowledge for nobody" insofar as it has no implications for what the knower does.

What *kind* of content do such representations have? Ron Chrisley (1993) has argued that the kind of content possessed by infants' pre-objective representations of objects is *non-conceptual* content (Crane, 1992). The content is non-conceptual because it fails to achieve the systematicity of objective thought. Recall that we have already encountered the notion of systematicity in Part 1 in the discussion of connectionist modelling of language competence; but it is important to recognise that this notion can also be applied to non-linguistic competences. Consider, in illustration, two ways of representing objects—*F* and *G*—and also consider two objects *a* and *b*. If the subject's thoughts about objects are systematic then she should be able to think *Fa*, as well as *Ga*, *Fb* as well as *Gb*. If objects are objective to the thinker then there should be, in Chrisley's phrase, a "united framework" within which properties (e.g. *F*) and particulars (e.g. *a*) can be freely related. The cognition of young infants does not meet this condition for systematicity insofar as they can represent, say, the particular occluded block as "resisting movement" but not as "reachable"—as if being able to think *Fa* but not *Ga*. This condition on systematicity is commonly known as the Generality Constraint after Evans (1982, pp.100–104) and I shall have more to say about it later on.

I now consider a related objection. What is being assumed in the present thesis is that human infants develop from a situation in which their experiences have non-conceptual representational content (as evinced by their dishabituation performance, for example) and in which they have no concepts of objects and space at all, to a position in which they exercise concepts. So the assumption seems to be being made that there *can* be non-conceptual contents in the absence of any concepts at all. This assumption is called by Christopher Peacocke (1992) the "Autonomy Thesis"—the thesis that non-conceptual content can exist autonomously from the possession of any concepts. Peacocke argues against the thesis, so it would be well to say something about his views—at least in passing.

We need first to be clear about the nature of non-conceptual content. It is a fair assumption to make that our experiences have a finer grain than our concepts—that more delineations are made between perceptual experiences than between concepts. For we want to be able to say that the perceptual experiences that a creature enjoys may be enjoyed without the exercise of the relevant concepts. For example, we want to be able to say that somebody is seeing magenta or seeing a rhombus without being committed to the view that he or she is capable of exercising either concept (e.g. knowing that if something is magenta then it is coloured). We also want to be able to say that there is a sense in which observers with quite different conceptual capacities (e.g. a chimp, a human baby, and a Nobel Prize winner) have the same raw perceptual experiences when they look at a lampshade. Peacocke has no quarrel with this: his quarrel is with the view that such non-conceptual contents can exist in creatures *with no concepts at all*.

The main strand of Peacocke's argument against the Autonomy Thesis involves a demonstration that when we examine a form of non-conceptual content called "scenario content" we find that such contents cannot be enjoyed without some basic concepts being in play. Very roughly, he argues that a creature whose experiences have scenario content is capable of reidentifying places over time, and that this must require both (a) the ability to identify its own current location with a location previously visited and (b) its building up over time an integrated spatial representation of its environment. But (a) and (b) together require that this creature possess some form of first-person concept; so there can be no scenario content without the possession of concepts. This argument has been disputed by José Bermúdez (1994) on the grounds that the way Peacocke sets up scenario content guarantees that only a concept user can be the subject of it, indeed that the argument "places such strong conditions of possibility upon scenario content that it *effectively transforms scenario content into conceptual content*" (Bermúdez, 1994, p. 416, my italics). Peacocke (1994), argues in turn (among other things) that the fact that scenario content has to be *specified* in such a way as to require the possession of concepts does not show that scenario content just *is* conceptual content.

The developmental implication of Peacocke's view would appear to be that one cannot describe conceptual development and the development of non-conceptual experiences separately: they must be elucidated together (1994, footnote 4). [Perhaps this is a position that Fodorian nativists about concepts—see 1.1(i)—would find sympathetic.] But maybe this is no great threat to the present view, in the sense that what is being argued is that infants in dishabituation experiments may be evincing representational capacities without possessing the concept *of an object*; and this may leave room for the view that infants do possess innate concepts that are not object concepts but which make certain non-conceptual experiences possible. What sort of concepts would these be? Perhaps some would want to call the innate capacities for allocentric coding described at the beginning of Part 2 examples of "the exercise of spatial concepts".

But a response to the Peacocke position that fits more naturally with the present thesis is one that says there is nothing about dishabituation performances to legitimise the ascription of concepts to the infant, and that just as long as this is so Peacocke's claims about scenario content are beside the point. In a later paper Bermúdez (submitted) expresses his support for the Autonomy Thesis with specific reference to the literature on dishabituation studies of object permanence. He says that for us to regard the infant as possessing the concept of an object we need to ascribe to the infant the ability to identify something for a *reason*: "An individual identifies something as an object if he knows what criteria for objecthood are, and can recognise that they are by and large satisfied … The subject is making a judgement which can be justified or unjustified, rational or irrational" (p.74). This would not appear to be what is taking place in dishabituation studies where, although we see manifestations of the ability to parse the visual array into "bounded segments that (more or less) correspond to objects" (p.7), we see nothing that we could count as the infant making judgements that may or may not be justified[42]. In the first part of my reply to "Objection 3" (to follow) I will try to say why infant *actions* count as forms of judgement—roughly because an intentional action is something taken on the basis of a belief, whereas a surprise reaction need not be described in terms of the subject's beliefs.

Objection 2: The objectivity and the primitive self-awareness that co-exist in externality cannot emerge from action alone

This objection is something of a straw figure; but only in the sense that answering it will require me to discuss more thoroughly the points I made briefly at the beginning of Part 2 when distinguishing between the Piagetian and the piagetian positions. It was stressed then, recall, that the present claim is not that externality can emerge from agency alone—this seemed to have been Piaget's view. But more needs to be said on the matter—for two reasons. First, because doing so will force us to think harder about how the notion of externality bears on spatial concepts and, second, because we need to get clearer about the distinction between egocentric and allocentric spatial coding.

The objector might put it this way[43]. "You are arguing that the ability to act on an object is *constitutive* of what subjects grasp about objectivity and about their own relation to that object—their primitive self-awareness *vis-à-vis* objects. But these constitutive links with action can never yield more than *egocentric* representations and egocentric representations are generally taken to yield only non-detached, and in this sense non-objective, representations of space—in particular representations that do not exploit the representation of oneself as one object amongst others. You miss the dependency of these things on allocentric, perspective-neutral, 'absolute' representations. There is important empirical work in animal spatial cognition and its computational modelling, as well as work by philosophers, which shows that, despite the dependency of spatial concepts and object concepts on the organism's own capacities for action, these capacities *must build on an action-independent and perspective-independent conception of space and of the causal powers of physical objects*. Dishabituation experiments demonstrate the primitiveness of these representations, and it is entirely unwarranted to say that they are constituted instead by the later-emerging ability to act upon objects."

This objection is a serious one but it is really, as I say, directed against the view that I explicitly rejected at the start of Part 2—that an allocentric conception of space and a realist conception of objects can emerge from agency *alone*. The piagetian view is *not* the view that infants begin with entirely egocentric representations of space and that as their actions become more spontaneous, differentiated, and integrated they are able to bootstrap themselves up to an allocentric, perspective-neutral conception.

As noted at the start of Part 2, it is research in animal learning rather than in infant development that has provided us with the substantial evidence for there being innate neural structures in mammals dedicated to computing allocentric spatial relations. Let us return to O'Keefe and Nadel's (1978) work on the hippocampus as a cognitive map—as a "plausible Kantian a priori spatial system" as O'Keefe puts it (1993, p.51). As I mentioned before, a rat of 3 weeks of age is able to swim through opaque water to find a platform that it had previously visited but which is now occluded (Nadel, 1990). Because the rat begins its second swim from a different point at the edge of the pool it obviously cannot be relying on egocentric cues (on the movements it made previously and their perceptual effects) to achieve this. O'Keefe's claim is that there are two kinds of allocentric information enabling the animal to compute measures both of the direction in which it is pointing and of its own distance from cues in the environment. In the first place the animal computes the "slope"[44] of the environment—a measure of deviation from symmetry of all the visible cues. If the animal keeps pointing in the same direction the slope does not change, but if it rotates then the slope changes. In the second place, the animal computes the "centroid"[45] of the environment, meaning the environment's spatial "centre of gravity" (if each cue were one unit of mass and rigid rods connected the centroid to each then the cues would balance on the centroid). The animal computes vectors from the centroid to a cue and stores the cue's location in these terms; and, given the slope too, it can compute routes from where it is to a location after its spatial position has changed (when performing, for example, in the "water maze" just described).

The basic claim, then, is that the rat hippocampus is dedicated to computing allocentric, perspective-neutral or "absolute" maps of the environment. Well, rats are not the only creatures with a hippocampus. It is entirely possible that the same is true of us. And when we couple these facts with more theoretical considerations, mentioned by the objector, against grounding an eventual allocentric spatial system in the organisation of actions alone, it might *appear* as if the piagetian is left with rather little to say. I shall answer this question by reprising John Campbell's (1993) views.

Campbell argued that a purely geometric, environment-centred representation of space of the kind just outlined leaves something out of the picture. For a creature must gain a conception of the bearing that certain kinds of input have on its action (e.g. whether a thing is closer than another, behind another, within reach) and this can only be achieved by reference to *its own capacities to act and perceive*. Campbell calls these "causally indexical" notions. Moreover, a representational system of the kind described by O'Keefe will not by itself enable the creature to register the spatial connectedness of its environment (the fact that every location is related to every other) unless it can appreciate the causal significance of its own actions and perceptions in relation to places (e.g. by navigating). And more still is required if this creature is to represent objects as internally causally connected physical entities whose interactions with one another are independent of itself—a "*non*-indexical" conception. This is a *truly* allocentric conception of space, argues Campbell, insofar as it involves a "theoretical" (Campbell's term) grasp of interactions with the physical world as contrasted with the mere practical ability to find one's way around. To gain this theoretical conception it would seem to be necessary for the creature to reflect on its own actions and reactions to objects. It is at *this* level that we can talk about "self–world dualism", a conception that is theory-like in the sense that it is a state of consciousness rather than the form of information processing necessary for successful interaction with the world. (The 3-week-old rats in Nadel's experiment surely did not *utilise* a self–world dualism to find their way back to the concealed platform!) In the gaining of this theory-like conception, facts about the way in which a creature's location affects its experiences are of crucial importance. Campbell writes (1993, p.88):

> The most striking causally significant aspects of location are their implications for whether and how the place can be perceived by the subject, and for whether and how it is possible for the creature to act with respect to the place, to avoid it or reach for it, for instance. There are also, of course, the opportunities for mechanical interaction with whatever is at the place, which the creature shares with any other physical thing. This provides a reflective counterpart to the animal's causally indexical thinking; a 'theory' of the animal's own interactions with the environment.

It is at just this point that the piagetian tries to provide an account of how is it possible for such a theory-like conception to emerge—the conception that one is an experiencing object within a mind-independent spatial universe of other objects. The claim is that the ability to change one's perceptual inputs at will is necessary if we are to draw the form of appearance–reality distinction that is integral to self–world dualism.

So as a piagetian I am accepting (as if one had any choice in the matter!) that there is a great deal of innate apparatus which enables us to compute environment-centred representations of space; while at the same time insisting that self–world dualism—a theoretical conception that exists over-and-above these computational successes—is not possible without the kinds of exercise of agency that I have been describing.

This final statement leads naturally on to the third and final objection, insofar as it implies a division between the *sub-personal* facts about allocentric coding and the *personal*-level notion of self–world dualism.

Objection 3: Representation permanence and externality are equally sub-personal and accordingly require the same kind of explanation

The kernel of the third objection is this: Whatever distinctions one wishes to draw between object permanence as assessed by dishabituation and object permanence as assessed by reaching, in both cases we are dealing with behaviour generated by representations. Surely, the brain of the successful reacher has to be in the right configuration (or "representational state") if reaching is to occur; and talk about "externality" does not alter this fact. What I have done, according to the objector, is to perform a kind of sleight of hand: I have used a sub-personal style of language to talk about representation permanence (representations being described as "causing" surprise reactions) and the personal-level language of intentions, desires, and beliefs to talk about externality—when *both* require a sub-personal explanation.

Viewed sub-personally, the objection continues, representations cause behaviour; they cause both reactions *and* actions, both dishabituations and reachings. So what we should do is to abandon all the personal-level considerations in favour of taking object permanence to mean externality and look simply at (what J.B. Watson called) "colourless movements" and their causation. Personal-level accounts only buy us a set of prejudices about what object permanence should mean. An obvious first step is to look at the *relative causal powers* of the different kinds of object representations that organisms can enjoy. In this light, the dissociations infants show between what they seem to know on the basis of dishabituation and what they seem to know on the basis of reaching make better sense. In younger infants the *causal power* of their representations of occluded objects is relatively weak—strong enough to drive dishabituation because it is a more 'primitive' behavioural system, but too weak to drive intentional behaviours. With experience, these representations become strengthened to the extent that they can drive reaching[46].

I will answer this important objection in two parts. First, I will argue (a) that although successful action must be understood as the manifestation of a "structured" capacity, showing appropriate surprise-reactions need not be understood in that way; and (b) that this kind of structured capacity justifies the ascription of beliefs to the subject. Second, I will say something about how, if this is so, one should regard the relation between the sub-personal and the personal levels of explanation for infants' behaviour towards objects.

We can approach the first argument by asking first why it is supposed to be appropriate, on the present view, to talk of representations "causing" behaviour in the case of dishabituation but not in the case of searching.

What occurs in dishabituation experiments is the violation of an expectation; a certain kind of visual input at time t_2 is predicted by the nervous system, but not received. In Baillargeon's drawbridge experiment, for example, the expectation is that the block will impede the movement of the screen, and, because the representation of the block is not obliterated in the instant it ceases to be visible, this expectation carries forward to cases where the block is temporarily invisible. There is a mismatch between expected and received input that drives a surprise reaction, and so in this sense the behaviour is "caused by" a representation—strictly, by the failure of predicted representation to match received input.

It may be tempting to say that if the subject "expected" or "predicted" a certain outcome then there is nothing to stop us saying that he or she *believed* that something would happen at time t_2. Let us call these "expectancy-beliefs". Well, it is clear that these expectancy-beliefs are not what the infant acts out of. What happens is that the infant reacts to their violation; and that is why the notion of "cause" has a foothold in this case but not in the active case. So where does this leave the notion of an "expectancy-belief"? If these are mental states whose nature is exhausted by their predictive function, and if they are states that only generate behaviour when their predictions are violated, then the "belief" component is doing no work at all: "expectancy" by itself or "prediction" will do just as well. By contrast, when we lift a cloth to retrieve a bunch of keys from under it we are acting out of the belief that there are keys there; people do not act *because they expect keys to appear* but because they believe them to be there before they instigate the action. Moreover, we do not say we were "caused" to lift it, because we assume that we chose to do so. In this case the role of the relevant mental state is a "positive" one insofar as its presence contributes to the behaviour— rather than the violation of its prediction. When we are surprised by the violation of expectancy-beliefs, by contrast, the notion of "cause" is clearly doing some work: we do not choose to be surprised.

In other words, retrieving an occluded object is not behaviour "caused by" the subject's representational state: it is an action taken on the basis of a belief about where the object is located relative to the self[47]. And if we want to use the language of causes here we can only do so in a folk-psychological style, in terms of desires and beliefs coming together to "cause" actions. But the folk-psychological "cause" is a different creature from the sub-personal "cause"; for in the former case one means, in effect, "is sufficient for (in normal circumstances)"[48] rather than "drives" or "triggers"; and one takes the behaviour in that case, as we have just seen, to be something done at will rather than something evoked by anomalous input. Having desire X and belief Y is in normal circumstances sufficient for action A to occur; and we can say this while also saying that A was done at will. We are not, however, surprised "at will".

One natural objection to this line of thought must be that it is only our folk-psychological prejudices that prevent us from talking about "beliefs" in the dishabituation case. Surely the infant "believes" that the block will impede the screen and he or she believes this because of what he or she "knows" about the causal powers of solid objects. To say this, however, is to ignore the fact that for something to be done "out of a belief" entails the ascription to the subject of a network of further beliefs: beliefs are ascribed *holistically* [see 1.1(i)]. This is to assert that the beliefs we have about objects and their existence relative to us form part of a system, they are part of a structured and global competence. I will argue that actions on objects must have this structured character whereas reactions to anomalous inputs need not, and that only the former allow the ascription of beliefs to the subject. But first, in what sense is action structured?

It is the spatially structured character of the knowledge underlying successful actions that gives these actions an holistic character. We cannot imagine, for example, what it would be for a creature to understand the spatial relation of "on my left" and *no other* spatial relation. Moreover, to say that our understanding of the spatial world in which we act has a structured nature is to say that this understanding is general and supports an infinite capacity for spatial analogy-making. To reprise Evans' example (1982, p.163), "The subject must be able to think of the relation in which he stands to a tree that he can see as an instance of the relation in which (say) the Albert Hall stands to the Albert Memorial." This will, I hope, recall the Generality Constraint, the meeting of which is a condition on representations of objects having conceptual content. And for readers who know something of Piaget's theory it will recall his claims that successful actions in space have a logico-mathematical structure, describable by the mathematics of groups (Piaget, 1950), and that both spatial action and rationality express "*structures d'ensemble*". Accordingly, when an infant manifests through action knowledge of the relations between objects and between these objects and itself this can be seen as the exercise of a capacity that is structured and holistic in a way that parallels the exercise of a system of verbal concepts[49]. But why should such a capacity not be exercised through *re*actions rather than through action?

I have done nothing so far to justify the denial that reactions to anomalous perceptual inputs can be regarded as evidence of a structured competence. Why could a subject who lacked the capacity to alter his or her perceptual inputs at will not manifest through reactions exactly the same kind of spatial understanding as a subject who was an agent? This non-agent would have families of reactions, each of which was applicable in different circumstances. So why could the two sets of behavioural competencies (the families of reactions and the network of active capacities) not be seen to mirror each other except insofar as one set is manifested passively and the other is manifested actively?

There is nothing impossible or contradictory about such a situation. But the present claim is not that competencies manifested through reactions could never have the kind of complexity that we might want to call "structured"; it is, rather, the claim that only in the active case is one justified *on the basis of that structuring* in ascribing beliefs to the creature; only in the structured-action case do the folk-psychological modes of explanation naturally apply. This claim depends, in part, on there being a conceptual link between a subject's being a believer and being able to do things at will; beliefs are what we act out of—they are dispositions to intentional action—and if a creature can do nothing at will (only reacting to inputs) then reference to its "beliefs" is otiose. By a similar token, reference to the beliefs that a subject in a dishabituation experiment may or may not have is beside the point; the term "predicted representation" will do just as well. This claim is in need of some spelling out.

The thought is that if we can be confident that a creature has the capacity to act at will towards an object on, say, its left-hand side then we must also be confident that it can act at will towards objects on its right-hand side, below it, above it, and so forth. And one is, of course, not referring here to mere motor capacity but rather to the ability to guide behaviour intentionally in certain ways—choosing to do one thing rather than another. What is at issue here is the ability to launch intentions that guide certain actions—those that "come to fruition" as actions of the left-hand side in this case. In other words, the criteria for the ascription to a subject of the ability to do X at will are holistic, as are the criteria for ascribing beliefs about X. Furthermore, as soon as we say that the subject did X at will—as soon as we say that the subject exercised one of his or her structured capacities—we are implying that the subject had a belief about the result of taking a particular action. Of course the appearance of a stimulus in the left visual field can evoke a leftward reaction, but if we deny that the behaviour was merely evoked and assert that it was indeed an action we have to assume that the subject did it in order to bring about a particular experience; and this is tantamount to saying that the subject believed that such a performance would bring about that experience. Viewed in this light, therefore, it is no accident that the criteria for the ascription of beliefs and the criteria for the ascription of abilities for acting at will are both holistic. For when a subject chooses to act on an object he or she exercises one of a set of capacities based on structured knowledge of space, and once we ascribe the ability to do something *at will* we imply that the subject had a belief about the results that his or her action would bring about, and so the ascription of these beliefs must be similarly holistic[50].

The same cannot be said of reactions to anomalous events. To say that a subject was surprised at the non-resistance of a currently invisible object to a backwards-moving screen implies nothing about what other kinds of anomalous input would or would not be similarly surprising. It is unlikely but possible, for example, that young infants are surprised at the non-resistance of objects behind screens that swing backwards but are not surprised by the non-resistance of objects behind screens that recede vertically into the distance. It is not merely "unlikely", however, that a subject should be able to choose to act on his or her left-hand side but not be able to choose to act on the right: to choose to go to the left at will implies not making other choices, such as going to the right. These choices must be available for taking as well as available for not taking.

Another way of appreciating how expectancies need not be structured is by taking the example of classical conditioning. A subject in a laboratory can be led to expect stimulus B immediately after stimulus A. After many A–B pairings we present a trial in which A occurs without B or with stimulus C instead—and the subject demonstrates surprise. In theory, there is no constraint on the nature of these stimuli. They are arbitrary, and because of this we cannot describe the expectancies that we set up in the subject as being structured: being surprised at A occurring with C instead of B *implies nothing about what other expectancies the subject may have*. This leads naturally to the thought that the subject in such an experiment is surprised because the A–C pair is *unusual* not because it is *anomalous*, not because the subject has some conception of the way the world is which renders A–C unlawful or impossible. Can we not say the same thing about infants in dishabituation experiments? We need only say that they are suprised at the, say, non-resistance of the screen because it is unusual—a point made by Bermúdez (submitted)—not because they have some modal conception of what is possible and what is impossible in a world of impenetrable objects. Recall that Baldwin (1995) argued that this modal conception requires the experience resistance and I argued that it requires experiencing how one's actions cannot determine one's (perhaps visual) experiences.

Before passing on, it is worth driving home the point that what I have said does not merely add up to the folk-psychological stipulation that intenders (e.g. reaching infants) have beliefs whereas reactors (e.g. surprised infants) do not. One is not just resting on the claim that ascribing intentions to a subject *requires* ascribing beliefs and desires to that subject (an agent will not do action A unless he or she believes A will have the desired outcome) whereas, by contrast, ascribing surprise at anomalous inputs to someone may *allow* belief ascription without *requiring* it (coding something as anomalous can just mean that it is coded as unusual). The idea is, rather, to say why the spatially structured nature of action grounds talk about beliefs in one case and not in the other. To act towards location A on the left implies the ability to choose to take this action rather than B-directed or C-directed etc. actions. Moreover, the very fact of making such a choice implies some structured understanding of how these different locations relate to one another. In other words, a subject is not *choosing* to look to his or her left or choosing to lift a cup unless the ability to look to his or her right or to act on the cup in another way or not at all is part of his or her background competence. This implies that what makes behaviour like reaching "intentional" and behaviour like the recovery of visual attention "non-intentional" is not their different *morphologies*; it is that in the first place a movement is selected from a range of potential movements in such a way as to imply a grasp of how their outcomes are related to one another. Reactions do not have this holistic quality and we accordingly do not have to say they are generated by beliefs.

Moving to the second part of my reply (about how the sub-personal and the personal levels of explanation are related), the onus is clearly on me to say something about how the personal level—the talk about beliefs, desires, and knowledge of the external world—is supposed to be related to sub-personal talk about the how the brain must be processing information if the owner of that brain is to act on objects at will.

First, there is no denial being made here that a sub-personal story must be told about how externality is possible; indeed I shall discuss the connectionist modelling of externality towards the end of Part 2. What one can deny, however, is that talk about acting at will on objects that one takes to exist in an external world simply reduces to talk about sub-personal processes. In other words, I will follow those who argue that the personal level is an *autonomous* causal-explanatory theory that explains an agent's behaviour on the basis of his or her perceptions and needs (e.g. Hornsby, 1985).

If one does not believe that the personal level is autonomous then there are two main options open to us: (1) to say that personal-level processes constitute a stage in successful action between input and output and (2) to say that there is no personal level, because it is just a folk-psychological story we tell to ourselves about ourselves.

Let us look first at (1). Consider the following picture of visually guiding action (see Fig. 3). Brewer (1993) calls this the "super-imposition" view—personal-level processes being superimposed on sub-personal ones. But in such a picture visually-guided behaviour (Brewer, 1993, p.305, original italics) is little more than:

> ... a mentally induced reflex. For little sense can be made of the subject's being in control of what is going on, of its being something she is doing. She looks around, thinking what would be desirable, useful, worthwhile and so on. She immediately perceives what should be done, intends (and wills) it to happen. Then things are in the lap of the gods ...

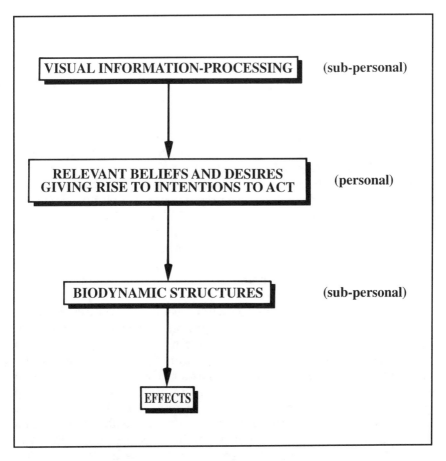

FIG. 3. The "superimposition" view rejected by Brewer (1993).

When she is successful, this just seems a happy accident. So
the idea of her being an *agent* is completely out of place.

In other words, if we regard the personal level as part of a chain of
events then we must inevitably fail to account for the fact that an agent
is in control of his or her behaviour. Moreover, we give a distorted picture
of the respect in which action is a *mental* event (see p.94). It is not a
mental event in the sense that some inner event of striving makes
mysterious contact with the triggers for physical movement; it is a
mental event in the sense that it is in the agent's "world" not in the
external world, it is an event that the agent is "within".

The second option is to say that the personal level reflects no more
than our way of talking about actions on objects as compared to our
reactions to them. This implies that in becoming language users, infants
join us in subscribing to folk-psychological assumptions about intention,
belief, and knowledge of the external world, assumptions that are no
more than aids to behavioural explanation and prediction. In other
words, the personal level is equivalent to our pre-scientific "theory of
mind" which could, in theory, be replaced by a "computational",
sub-personal account delivered to us by cognitive science (Stich, 1983).

In Part 3—and at the very end of the book—I shall argue that there
is indeed a sense in which a "theory of belief" is not something that can
plausibly be said to exist before a child acquires language; but this is a
million miles from saying that beliefs about objects cannot be *ascribed*
to children before they are language users. One can say that a creature
with a conception of the external world possesses something that should
be characterised within the language of folk psychology, while at the
same time maintaining that folk-psychological categories such as
"belief" will not figure in the creature's mental life if it is not a language
user.

Moreover, if we insist that the sub-personal story about actions on
objects is not only necessary but sufficient, then we are faced with the
awkward question of whence the adult's personal-level experience of
externality and of acting at will *originates*. Nobody can deny that,
moments of terror, ecstasy, and intense concentration apart, we do in
fact experience ourselves as agents set apart from the external world.
Well, if we deny even a version of this experience to preverbal children
then what sort of account will be open to us for the developmental
grounding of *our* experience? Could this be grounded in language? There
are severe difficulties here. First, it would be no mean feat to explain
how linguistic symbols can find a purchase in preverbal children's
experience and "bootstrap" them towards externality when the
structure of their experience has no such feature—when it is adualistic.

Second, we may want instead to regard symbolic thinking as something that emerges out of early interpersonal experience—doing this perhaps in the style of Werner and Kaplan (1963), rather than from an innate language-acquisition device. But, if so, we have no choice but to regard the fact of externality as a social construction. Any theory that says that it is only through our dealings with other people that we come to believe that there is a mind-independent reality is not worthy of consideration. How can social interaction get off the ground in the absence of *some* prior conception that the participants in this interaction inhabit a potentially shareable reality?

Piaget's (1955) central empirical claim about the relation between externality and language acquisition was that the full object permanence that is supposed to be achieved at around 18 months and that is a marker of *représentation mentale* provides the child with the representational format for the acquisition of symbols, for the insight that objects, actions, and so forth have public names. There is some evidence for this proposal—see Gopnik and Meltzoff (e.g. 1987) and Tomasello and Farrar (1986). In fact it is to empirical questions that we turn next.

2.7: SOME EMPIRICAL ISSUES

In one of her novels, George Eliot satirised a certain kind of intellectual enterprise. Here was a theory, she wrote, "not likely to bruise itself unawares against discoveries: it floated among flexible conjectures ... it was as free from interruption as a plan for threading the stars together"[51]. I am sure a few readers will think this a fine description of the preceding sections. But if they do, it will be in spite of my insistence that I have been talking about *conceptual* not empirical issues. Moreover, although a conceptual claim *need* not be refuted empirically, facts—perhaps ones collected by experimentation—can reveal that it was unsound in the first place. In any event, I will turn to the area where it is possible to sustain a few "bruises". This is the point at which my proposals shade into Jean Piaget's actual theory of sensorimotor development.

While the conceptual claim is that only agents can develop externality, the empirical claim is that we can explain the development of object permanence in terms of *particular developments in executive skill*, that the developing ability to cognise objects is *correlative* to a developing agency whose features we can specify. It may seem, of course, as if the theory is "not likely to bruise itself unawares against discoveries" because piagetians wish to *assess* permanence in terms of actions, but that is not so—for the following reasons. First, we may find that the executive abilities (e.g. means–end behaviour) that Piaget proposed in order to explain search for occluded objects cannot in fact explain this development, because infants who have been separately assessed as *possessing* these abilities nevertheless fail to search. Second, the way in which infants fail to search (e.g. when making the A-not-B error) may indeed be explicable in executive terms but in such a way as to show that the failure was a *performance* error: their true representational capacities are being masked by poor executive control. We will see examples of both kinds of phenomenon in this section.

I will discuss two of Piaget's empirical claims: (i) that the ability to retrieve completely occluded objects at 8 months emerges through the development of means–end skills and (ii) that older infants' failures at visible-displacement and invisible-displacement tasks is caused by egocentrism not by "performance limitations" such as weak short-term memory or the inability to inhibit the repetition of an action.

2.7(i) Means–end skill and "stage 4 search"

Piaget proposed a 6-stage sequence of sensorimotor development in infancy, "stage 4" of which begins around 8 months of age. At this age, as we know, infants begin to search for completely occluded objects; and so I will sometimes refer to this as "stage 4 search". In one book in his infancy trilogy (*The child's construction of reality*) Piaget described these stage-wise changes in terms of their *content*—objects, space, time, and causality. In another (*The origin of intelligence in the child*) he set himself the more ambitious task of explaining these stage-wise changes in terms of what one might call the underlying executive developments. The basic executive units, for Piaget, were J.M. Baldwin's "circular reactions". "Circular" because they can be repeated at will—because they have a degree of reversibility. Primary circular reactions are roughly equivalent to what philosophers call "basic" actions (non-instrumental movements of the body); secondary circular reactions are actions that have effects on the world (e.g. pulling a string to activate a mobile); and tertiary circular reactions are procedures the child invents "off the cuff" to solve a novel problem. These were his *only* explanatory tools.

Stage 4 was supposed to mark the onset of the "co-ordination of secondary circular reactions", the clearest example of which is means–end behaviour. For example, an infant wants to retrieve a toy which is out of reach and which rests on a towel *within* reach. If the infant is able to co-ordinate secondary circular reactions he or she will be able to pull the towel in order to bring the toy into his or her reaching space; the circular reaction of toy-lifting is "embedded" within the broader circular reaction of towel-pulling. Infants begin to be able to do this at about 8 months of age. Now Piaget's entirely *empirical* claim was that it is the acquisition of means–end skills of this kind that underpins the ability to perform stage 4 search. Accordingly, what occurs at stage 4 is not regarded as a *representational* change in the sense that the infant is now able to mentally represent the occluded object; rather, he or she has acquired a procedure for retrieving things; that it *is* just a procedure, Piaget believed, was revealed by the fact that these infants will make the A-not-B error, to which I will turn in the next sub-section.

We immediately encounter a paradox. The emphasis on means–end difficulties is superficially similar to the kind of claim that *informational* theorists make about stage 4 search. Baillargeon, Graber, de Vos, and Black (1990), for example, argue that infants under 8 months have the following executive difficulty that prevents them from acting on their knowledge of object permanence. They are unable to perform a means act *when this is in apparent conflict with the achievement of their goal.* Thus, in retrieving objects, they have to perform an action other than one directed straight at the object, such as a detour reach or the removal of an occluder.

In fact the paradox can be easily resolved. Two entirely different senses must be given to the term "executive failure". Baillargeon et al. (1990) are explaining failure to search as an executive *performance* failure, as a failure that *masks knowledge.* The infant knows the object is still there but is unable to perform the means act in that context due to competition between two actions. Piaget never referred to "executive failures", but I hope it is clear from what has gone before that piagetians would give an entirely different sense to the phrase. In this case the failure is to *understand* what has to be done: it is a *competence* failure. That is to say, infants before stage 4 are taken to lack adequate ideas of how two actions can be related as means and end, and lack this conception because of "egocentrism", because they cannot conceive of how, in a retrieval situation, *their visual experiences are a function of what they can do.*

However, the difference between Piaget's and Baillargeon et al.'s (1990) claims about what develops is entirely empirical; and so I will now consider the relevant evidence. First, there is evidence in favour of their *shared* view that the stage 3 infant's difficulty is indeed with the co-ordination of two actions—whether we take this as a performance or as a competence difficulty. Following an earlier study by Bower (1974), Hood and Willats (1986) demonstrated that infants of 5 months of age (i.e. in stage 3) will reach appropriately for objects that they cannot see after the room has been plunged into darkness. In this case, when there is no problem with the co-ordination of actions, they succeed.

Next, is the inability to co-ordinate actions a performance or a competence failure? One way of asking this question would be by looking for cases where stage 3 infants are able to perform the means act but where their subsequent behaviour reveals that they have not *understood* what they have just done. In this case we will have witnessed executive-performance success and executive-competence failure, and therefore gathered some support for the piagetian view that stage 3 infants lack a competence (a grasp of action→experience relations) that stage 4 infants possess. There is a phenomenon, observed originally by Piaget and since named by Peter Willats "transitional search", that seems to fit this description. Piaget noted that infants much younger than 8 months will sometimes remove an occluder (e.g. lift a cloth) under which their toy has just been placed but then, having done so, ignore the toy and perhaps play with the cloth instead. What seems to have happened is that hiding the toy under the cloth calls out the familiar procedure of lifting; but the infants do not understand the relation between what they did and what their actions brought about. Accordingly, we can witness what appears to be retrieval behaviour in stage 3 children without a retrieval intention: the infants lifted an inverted polystyrene cup because it was associated with the trinket, without seeming to realise the relation between doing this and seeing the trinket again. Transitional search was present in the vast majority of the infants Willats studied and often lasted for one or two months (Willats, 1984).

Does this show that stage 3 infants are able to perform the means act in an occlusion context without understanding what they are doing? This is certainly not the only reading of the evidence. Baillargeon et al. (1990) can say that it is only when retrieval and occluder-removal *are seen by the infants as conflicting* that executive-performance failure comes about. Moreover, they can argue that in transitional search the lifting of the occluder is invariably a chance event: it is not caused by the occlusion event. Indeed Willats' report that 6-month-olds were equally as likely to pick up the cup when there was nothing under it as when there was something under it is consistent with this claim. (Between 6 and 8 months they become more likely to lift the cup when there is something under it.) But *if* it turned out that hiding a toy under the cup was more likely to trigger transitional search (i.e. where the trinket is ignored after lifting) than simply acting on the cup in a neutral way then this would favour the competence-failure view. For this would show that the "search" was being triggered by an occlusion event rather than just being triggered by any action on the cup, showing that infants were "searching" without understanding what outcome would result from this. The correct action was evoked but it was not understood. In any event, the question can be decided empirically—which is the main point I wish to make right now.

However, a more serious challenge to Piaget's account would be posed by evidence that stage 3 infants are able to perform means–end acts adequately but are nevertheless unable to search for completely occluded objects. Indeed if these means acts involved a clear conflict between the two requisite actions then this would additionally be evidence against the Baillargeon et al. view. We do not have evidence that means–end behaviour *developmentally precedes* stage 4, but we do have evidence that infants can perform means–end routines more successfully when the goal object has a *transparent* screen in front of it than when the goal object has an opaque screen in front of it. This suggests that invisibility *per se* is posing a challenge when the means–end skills exist. This study was performed by Yuko Munakata (reported in Munakata, McClelland, Johnson, & Siegler, 1994). Munakata trained 7-month-old infants to retrieve a toy telephone, which was lying out of reach on the far end of a towel, by pulling the towel towards them. She then introduced two further conditions: there was a condition in which a flexible opaque screen was interposed across the towel between the baby and the telephone, and one where the flexible screen was transparent. In the control conditions there was no toy present and the screen was either opaque or transparent. In the cases where there was no toy and the screen was transparent the babies pulled the towel towards themselves an average of just over twice in a session, and when the screen was opaque this figure rose to an average of just over three occasions (a nonsignificant difference). But when there was a toy present and the screen was transparent the average was just over five pulls per trial—a significantly greater number than in the opaque+toy case. Munakata points out, however, that this difference may have been due to the positive visual feedback that the infants were receiving after each tug on the towel in the transparent+toy condition— a case of what she calls 'hill-climbing' rather than means–end search. Accordingly, she ran a second experiment in which the babies had to press a button to raise either a transparent or an opaque screen and bring the toy telephone sliding down a slope towards them. There could be no hill-climbing strategies in this case, and the data were very similar to those in the first study.

These data speak against both Baillargeon et al.'s (1990) and Piaget's version of the means–end-failure view. But Munakata notes that the way in which the infants behaved in the transparent screen versus the opaque screen experimental conditions was particularly difficult to explain in Baillargeon's terms. When the toy was visible they showed *frustration* because it was out of reach. Sometimes this was accompanied by successful retrieval and sometimes not. When the toy was not visible—because it was behind an opaque screen—they showed no frustration; they behaved just as they did when the screen was opaque and there was no toy. These are qualitative rather than quantitative data but they are no less persuasive for being so. If Baillargeon is correct that 7-month-olds know the object is still there in the opaque+toy case but are simply unable to perform the means–end act then they should have shown a *similar* degree of frustration.

But this is also—as I said—a bad result for Piaget insofar as the data suggest that the stage 3 infant's problem is not solely with means–end behaviour but also with performing the means that will return an object *to view*. They appear to have a fundamental failure to grasp how their motor acts relate to what they see; and we shall later see that they continue to have this problem long after 8 months of age. This is not decisive evidence against Piaget's claim about the developmental role of "the co-ordination of secondary circular reactions" because Munakata did not actually show that means–end skills precede stage 4 search "across the board". But it is not at all clear how Piaget would explain these data; and this is partly because the explanatory apparatus he built for himself in terms of different kinds of circular reactions and their stage-wise evolution was too coarse-grained. One can say this, however, while retaining the view that the transition from stage 3 to stage 4 is essentially one of executive *competence*—of appreciating how actions taken relate to changes in visual experience. Executive competence may be what the infants lacked, but Piaget's account of this in terms of the co-ordination of circular reactions seems inadequate.

Part and parcel of Piaget's claim that the stage 3→4 transition is essentially a transition in understanding the co-ordination of actions was his further claim that within stage 4 there exists no capacity for representing the occluded object as independent of one's own actions. But if Piaget was wrong about the nature of the transition, what prevents us from saying that infants over 8 months do indeed mentally represent the occluded object, having made a giant step in understanding how their actions relate to their visual experience? What prevents us is the existence of the A-not-B error and the later inability (during stage 5 between 12 and 18 months) to record invisible displacements.

2.7.(ii) Failure to search after visible and invisible object displacements: An executive performance or an executive competence problem?

Piaget denied that stage 4 infants search because they believe the occluded object is presently existing behind the occluder, and he interpreted the A-not-B error as evidence for this view. If it could be shown, however, that the A-not-B error is a *performance* error then Piaget's claim could not be sustained. As we shall see, this would amount to showing that the error is not caused by the fact that babies between 8 and 12 months have a continuing difficulty with understanding the relation between what they can do and what they can experience, but is caused by their inability to manifest in their behaviour what they actually know.

What does it mean to give a "performance" account of the A-not-B error? I will describe the two most popular performance-failure accounts. One is that infants return to search at A because they have weak short-term memories, and the other is that they are unable to inhibit the incorrect search act—an executive *performance* error, as it was defined in the previous section.

First, it is widely reported (e.g. Diamond, 1991) that (i) if the stage 4 infant is allowed to search immediately after the object has been concealed at B, search is successful, and (ii) as we increase the time-lag between hiding at B and allowing the baby to search we increase the probability of a return to A. Could failure at A-not-B simply be caused by poor short-term memory?

Piaget was alive to this possibility and argued against it in definitional terms, as if retreating to what I have called the "conceptual" face of the account. He said (Piaget, 1955, pp.64–65) that if the infant has a memory so poor that it cannot even retain information for a second or so then, by definition, he or she cannot have object permanence. But this reply only works if the memory-failure hypothesis is that stage 4 babies' memories are this bad in *all* situations. That is to say, although an infant with a short-term memory of one second in every situation surely cannot "have" object permanence, it is perfectly possible that stage 4 infants' short-term memories are only this bad when presented with tasks like the A-not-B; and Piaget would have to say *why* this occurs. In fact, we know that 8-month-old babies have memories for events that happened 30 seconds ago (Baillargeon, De Vos, & Graber, 1989), so Piaget's argument cannot be sustained. But this result is, of course, also bad for the memory failure hypothesis itself. For any account in terms of memory failure has to explain why memory is so poor in the A-not-B situation as compared to other situations. Moreover, it must explain why the infant is worse than chance—why he or she is actually more likely to return to A rather than searching randomly—if he or she has merely forgotten behind which occluder the object has been placed.

An account in terms of so-called "proactive interference" can explain both why memory is especially bad in the A-not-B task and why it is worse than chance. It says that search at A is caused by the information that the object is at A proactively (i.e. before the event) interfering with the new information that the object has been placed at B: an old, strong trace prevents a new weaker trace being laid down (Harris, 1973).

But there is a piece of evidence that speaks against the proactive-interference version of the memory-failure hypothesis. Bjork and Cummings (1984) showed that, when an additional three containers are placed between A and B, infants do not return to A to search after the object has been moved from A to B, as the proactive interference hypothesis must predict. What they do instead is to search under the additional container *nearest* to B. This was the most common form of error. What seems to he happening, then, is that infants are unable to retain information about the place to which the object has been moved with sufficient accuracy: they know it has moved to a container on the (say) right of A but are not sure which one it is. This is obviously a *performance* failure. However the Bjork and Cummings data yield to another explanation, namely, that these performance errors were caused by the fact that errors are more infrequent on the A-not-B task when there are multiple B-locations (Wellman, Cross, & Bartsch, 1987) and because increasing the spatial separation between A and B also improves performance (Horobin & Acredolo, 1986). In other words many of Bjork and Cummings' subjects were indeed making performance errors because the experimenters' manipulation made the task *easier*. Accordingly, the possibility remains that infants who fail on the more difficult versions of the task (and of course those who still fail on the easier versions) do so because they make competence errors—because they believe the object is behind A , not simply because they have forgotten.

There are two further sets of data that should undermine faith in a simple memory-failure explanation for the A-not-B error. First, why is the A-not-B task easier with multiple B-locations? Diamond, Cruttenden, and Neiderman (1994) argued that this was because when moving an object from A to another location it is not possible—as we only have two hands—simultaneously to cover the A well and all the other four, five, or six wells at the same time. So what happens is that experimenters have left the covers on all the incorrect wells, hidden the toy, and then covered the correct well. But if the last event before search begins happens at the correct well then this will help the infant keep his or her attention focused on where to search. In fact, in his proactive interference study with two hiding locations Paul Harris (1973, Experiment 3) had already shown that if the correct location is the last to be concealed, the search is more successful.

Diamond et al. then went on to compare the predictions of the memory-failure hypothesis to those of the hypothesis that the infant also has difficulty *inhibiting* search at A. The memory-failure hypothesis should predict that when there are multiple hiding locations, errors should generally be distributed around the correct well, as we have seen. A memory+inhibition hypothesis, on the other hand, predicts that more errors should occur near the A location. This was what Diamond et al. found.

The final piece of evidence against the memory-failure view is stronger still. Harris (1974) found that not only will 10-month-olds search at A when the object is still visible at B, but they will even do so when they can *see* that A is empty. In this study, the target object was a toy car and the locations were transparent, lockable "garages". Having retrieved the car a few times at A the infants saw it placed at B, after which event both garages were locked. A minority of the subjects went straight back to A and tried unsuccessfully to gain entry to the visibly empty compartment. The majority of the subjects went to B first, where they could see the car, failed to gain entry, and then returned to A, with the result that all the subjects ended up at A stubbornly trying to force an entry; indeed the older they were the more strongly they persevered.

What bearing do these studies have on the executive competence versus executive performance question? Not only do the Diamond et al. (1994) study and the Harris (1974) study bolster Piaget's denial that the A-not-B error is caused by memory failure, they make the claim that infants' essential difficulty is with understanding how their actions relate to their visual experiences look rather plausible. In short, it supports the hypothesis that the A-not-B error is an executive-competence error.

But these data can also be lined up behind the view that search at A is an executive-*performance* error. And this brings us to our second kind of performance-failure account; we have already had a hint of it from the Diamond et al. (1994) experiment. The claim here is that the infants know perfectly well that the object is now at B, but that they cannot inhibit searching at A; their problem is simply one of *controlling* their actions, not the executive competence problem of *understanding* the relation between what they do and what they experience. Transparency is a good test case and, certainly, the difficulties that infants experience with transparent barriers do have a performance-error flavour. Studies by Lockman (1984) and by Diamond (1991) have shown that infants between 8 and 15 or so months of age have great difficulty with performing so-called 'detour-reaches' (reaching round a barrier) when the barrier is transparent. When the barrier is opaque, however, there is no problem. Thus, it appears that what is difficult for them is inhibiting the habitual act of reaching along their line of sight.

How do these data bear on the results of Harris's transparent garages study? Although the barriers in Harris's experiment were transparent, just about everything else in the experiment differed from a detour-reaching task. In the transparent garages case the infants were not searching inappropriately (along the line of sight) for something that they could see: they were trying to search for something that they could *not* see.

But let us keep running with the executive-performance-error view for the time being and consider a group of subjects who make errors on tasks that require the inhibition of prepotent responses which *do* seem to have a performance character—adults with damage to the pre-frontal cortex. According to Luria (Luria, 1966; although see Drew, 1975, for contrasting data) there is a dissociation in these patients between what they fail to do and what they can verbally report: they tell the experimenter that they *know* this is the wrong thing to do but they just cannot help doing it. When we add the evidence (i) that lesioning the dorsolateral prefrontal cortex in monkeys causes failure on A-not-B and detour-reaching tasks (Diamond & Goldman-Rakic, 1986), (ii) the fact that infants sometimes remove the occluder at A while *looking* at B (Diamond, 1991), and (iii) the long-standing assumption that one of the principal functions of the prefrontal cortex is that of behavioural inhibition, many are led inevitably to the view that if only our 10-month-olds could speak they would say things like "I just can't help looking for the toy here though I know really it's over there".

There are two directions for the supporter of the competence-error view to travel in at this point. One is towards the conceptual argument that in children as young as this the distinction between an executive competence and an executive performance error breaks down: that the distinction only really makes sense when subjects are *in a position to distinguish between what they know and what they find themselves doing* (as are frontal patients). This would be a little like Piaget's answer to the memory-failure hypothesis (see earlier)—the argument being that if the stage 4 infants' executive capacities are in *this* bad a shape in all situations, then they must lack any conception of how their (visual) experiences of objects relate to their actions on them; the performance error collapses into a competence error, in other words. In the case of the frontal patients, by contrast, we *may* (see Drew, 1975, for negative data) have independent evidence (from what they say to us) that they know the object is at B; but in the case of infants we have no such evidence.

I find this argument plausible; but only because I am already committed to the broadly piagetian view of object permanence on which it depends. So it is probably better to stick with the competence-versus-performance-error distinction until it gives out for some empirical reason, and look for evidence that speaks to one view or the other. Certainly, the transparent-garages data—as I say—yields more easily to a competence-failure than a performance-failure view.

I will briefly mention another phenomenon which has not, to my knowledge, received attention in the literature; although it is certainly commonly observed[52]. Elizabeth Meins (Meins & Russell, in press) and I ran a study in which one of our questions was about the relation between infants' ability to search for toys and for their mothers (as it happened, they were generally better at searching for toys). The behaviour of some of the infants in the A-not-B and the invisible displacement (transposition) tasks was intriguing. Mothers sat in what looked like confessional boxes on wheels, and search consisted of the infant pulling back the curtain to reveal her. (The toys could be placed on a removable shelf in these boxes.) In both the A-not-B task and the transposition task (in which the concealed mother would be wheeled from one side of the infant to another, swapping places with the empty box), when the infants had pulled back the wrong curtain they would often fail to search in the other box right next to it. For instance, a toddler of about 17 months had failed to find his mother after transposition of the boxes and obviously wanted to have her back immediately, but despite encouragement from the experimenter and despite very heavy hints he never looked in the other box.

It is useful to compare this kind of phenomenon with those that Diamond cites in favour of her claim that the A-not-B error is an executive *performance* error—that infants will sometimes return to A, remove the occluder and, not even bothering to look in, go to B. These behaviours do indeed have all the character of performance errors, and it is not surprising that infants make them. Indeed, adults make such performance errors—looking for keys in places where we looked just a few minutes ago, for example. But normal adults do *not* make errors of the kind I just described in the mother-hiding experiment. Such errors have all the appearance of *competence* errors—errors caused by an inadequate grasp of how one's actions can effect what one can experience.

I should mention in passing a piece of evidence about A-not-B performance that is highly consistent with the piagetian position. Any theory that grounds the development of object permanence in activity should predict that performance on search tasks will be better in infants who have had rich experience of how their actions can affect their perceptual experiences than in infants who have relatively poor experience. In support of this is the fact that the longer an infant has been crawling the less likely he or she is to make the A-not-B error

(Horobin & Acredolo, 1986); although this may be due to the fact that infants who crawl early are generally more advanced—cognitively as well as motorically. A study by Kermoian and Campos (1988) was able to avoid this confounding of locomotor experience and rate of development. They looked at the performance of three groups of same-aged infants—(a) pre-crawlers, (b) crawlers, and (c) pre-crawlers who had spent time in baby-walkers so they could enjoy about the same amount of experience of the effects of self-generated movement as the crawlers. They were given three kinds of search task—under a single occluder, under one of two occluders, and the A-not-B task. The data were very clear. The pre-crawlers—group (a)—were by far the least advanced group, while the performance of groups (b) and (c) was very similar. Moving around the world in a baby-walker can be said to discourage the infant from coding places relative to his or her own body and encourage allocentric coding. We also know that performance on A-not-B is better in infants who crawl round a transparent barrier toward the two locations than in infants who (although being able to crawl) are carried round the barrier by their mothers (Acredolo, Adams, & Goodwyn, 1984).

Before rounding off this section I need to say a few words about what Piaget took to be the developmental terminus of "the object concept"—searching after invisible displacements. This, as we have seen, was supposed to occur because the 18-month-old is capable of *représentation mentale*—the ability to evoke a representation of an absent object. This is the object concept as it exists in adulthood, where representations of absent objects are, what one might call, "contemplative" in the sense that they are representations we can evoke without entertaining goals in relation to their referents. But despite their being contemplative, they are, as I insisted earlier, conceptually linked with our knowledge of what we would *do* to experience again what they represent. Of course, we can have thoughts about objects of whose location we have no idea (Prince Charles's stolen cufflinks) or a future object (the first galley-proof of the next Labour Party Manifesto) and an imaginary object (Madame Bovary's new black dress). But if we were told where these objects were in relation to us *we would know what to do to experience them*.

Piaget's actual account of how *représentation mentale* developed (in terms of "internalised imitation") was a rather implausible one which will not detain us; but it is worth reflecting on the qualitative distinction Piaget drew between this kind of knowledge and it predecessors. Up until this point in development, he was claiming, search is a more or less *instrumental* achievement, a matter of what needs to be done to experience what one wants to experience. We do not, as I say, have to accept Piaget's account of *représentation mentale* in terms of internalised imitation; but the piagetian *has* to say that no contemplative form of object permanence can be possible unless the developing infant has come to understand how his or her experiences depend on his or her actions. What is being "contemplated", after all, is a possible cause of our experiences and for such a conception to emerge, it has been argued here, the experience of refractoriness is necessary.

Of course, the piagetian—like Piaget himself and like all other developmental theorists—has no convincing account of how this transition to contemplative object permanence becomes possible. A pure maturationism is of little help to us, because what would it be for the 18-month-old to become suddenly capable of contemplating absent objects if he or she has no prior grasp (perhaps a non-conceptual grasp) of the division between himself or herself as an experiencing agent and a world of physical objects? We certainly need, however, to posit such a capacity as *représentation mentale*, whether or not we are piagetians. David Olson (1993), for one, has recently outlined a theory of early development in terms of "holding in mind", by which he means the ability to evoke a representation of one thing while experiencing another. Give or take a bit, this is *représentation mentale*—as well as an early form of working memory (Russell, 1996).

But the point I wish to make here is an entirely empirical one. It is that if Piaget is correct in saying that at 18 months, and not before that, children become capable of *thinking about* objects that are no longer present, then this new acquisition must reverberate throughout the child's mental life; it will not only have implications for object permanence. As I mentioned earlier, there do appear to be such reverberations: there are, at least, a "naming explosion" (Bloom, 1973; Nelson, 1975), the appearance of symbolic play (McCune-Nicholich, 1981), and the categorisation of objects by touching and sorting (Gopnik & Meltzoff, 1987). The last-mentioned study, in fact, produced impressive correlations between search skills, categorisation, and the onset of the naming explosion.

2.8: COMPUTATIONAL MODELLING OF OBJECT PERMANENCE

In this final section I will be able to bring together the major positive conclusion of Part 1 with that of Part 2. It may be recalled that, towards the end of Part 1, I argued that developmental change is best modelled in a sub-symbolic style. This is because the connectionist meta-theory does not commit one to a language of thought (putting to one side the question of whether thought in *language-users* can be modelled sub-symbolically); it does justice to the holistic nature of mentality; it avoids the homuncular difficulties of mental models theory; it is well adapted to the modelling of learning and of motor control; and it has commonalities with Piaget's theory of learning. In Part 2, my major positive conclusion is that object permanence—"externality"— develops through infants coming to understand how their actions affect their perceptual experiences—that this is a necessary condition for them to come to regard objects as the external causes of their experiences.

I will try to bring these two conclusions together by arguing that externality can, in principle, be modelled in neural networks, and that there are unmistakable parallels between how Piaget regarded sensorimotor development and how one committed to the connectionist metatheory would regard it. I shall make this case with three things in mind. First, there is a sense in which the Piagetian view of object permanence lends itself to connectionist metaphors. I will spend a little time defending this position against those who would argue that object permanence—that any cognitive achievement—must be modelled symbolically. Second, this will make it necessary to square up to the challenge made by Fodor—and discussed in 1.1(i)—against any sub-symbolic account of the structure of the child's pre-linguistic knowledge: How can a child come to talk about what he or she knows (knows about objects in this case) if this knowledge lacks a protolinguistic structure? Finally, because there is at least one connectionist model of representation permanence (Munakata, McClelland, Johnson, & Siegler, 1994) it is necessary to consider what we would need to add to such a model to make it a model of externality.

2.8(i) The connectionist metaphor

As we have seen, the piagetian insists that for subjects to regard something as external to themselves they must not merely possess "a representation" of it in their nervous system. It is necessary also that they should know how their experiences of the object will be affected when they act in relation to it [see 2.4(ii)].

For the knowledge just described to be present there must exist sub-personal mechanisms whose purpose is to make predictions (recall Jordan's forward model discussed towards the end of Part 1) that are sufficiently systematic for the infant to have the right kind of expectations. There must be a *system* of such predictions about what can happen to percepts and what cannot happen to them when the subject acts. For example, an eye movement to the left will be accompanied by the prediction that the percept will move to the right. Also, these mechanisms must predict that reversibility will be achievable in some cases but not in others; achievable, for example, for stationary objects (e.g. scanning their portions) but not achievable in tracking a moving object. They must also be able to code the different ways in which action–outcome pairings are predictable, discriminating between the tight predictability possible in scanning stationary objects and the looser kind of predictability possible when tracking moving objects. What we are dealing with here, of course, are expectations that are *egocentric* insofar as they concern what will happen and what cannot happen to percepts of objects when the subject moves. In tension with these will be sets of *allocentric* (or "environment-centred") expectations; expectations about how objects can and cannot interact with one another—exactly the kind of naive-physics expectations, in fact, that dishabituation experiments exploit (see Spelke, 1991).

On the present view, externality is only possible when the nervous system encodes the distinction between two kinds of prediction—about self-generated and world-generated experiences. This is required, on the present view, if the subject is to experience the world as refractory.

Now this kind of claim may seem offensive to common sense on a number of grounds. For one thing it would appear to lead to a hideous combinatorial explosion. Surely *all* possible actions and their phenomenal outcomes are not encoded when I look at a coffee cup. Not all, but many—something that is more offensive to common sense than to neuroscience. We know, for example, that cell groupings in the cortex code a multiplicity of possible movements. David Sparks and his colleagues have shown in their work on the ocular-motor system in the monkey that any eye-movement the animal makes is encoded in terms of the activities of a whole population of cells, and that each of these cells carries a representation of a slightly different movement. The action taken corresponds to the average of all these active cells (cited by Hinton, 1992). What I am adding to this picture is the claim that when an object is experienced as external to the self there are connections between cells encoding a multiplicity of possible movements in relation to that object and constellations of cells encoding the *phenomenal outcomes* of these movements.

A second way in which the present view may offend common sense is through the assumption that the experience of externality does not exist, as it were, at a point in time, but is, rather, emergent *through time* as computations are made about the relation between past and future action–outcome relations. This is indeed the claim; and it is the kind of claim that piagetians share with J.J. Gibson. For, in a rather similar spirit to that in which Gibson insists that perceiving a scene is nothing like taking a snapshot of it and that perception occurs through time as the organism interacts with its environment, the piagetian proposes that the experience of an object as external to the self is a *process* rather than an event. Representation permanence, by contrast, does have a "snapshot" character; and we will shortly encounter an example of such a snapshot.

The connectionist flavour of all this is not difficult to discern. What is supposed to constitute externality, on this view, is the existence of connections between possible transformations and their phenomenal outcomes, some transformations having to be egocentrically generated (the claim distinctive to the piagetian view) and some having to be allocentrically generated. Then, to push the metaphor a little harder, we can think of different connections being either exhibitory or inhibitory, and this to differing degrees. For example, the connection between "egocentric movement west" (e.g. I move my head in that direction) and "datum moves east" (i.e. the object I am looking at phenomenally moves to the right) will be strongly positive, that between "egocentric movement west" and "datum move north-east" weakly positive, while that between "egocentric movement south" and "datum moves south" will be strongly negative. And, in all this, the central fact of *refractoriness* finds a sub-personal foothold in the strongly negative connections encoding *im*possible egocentric transformations— encodings of how experience *cannot* be altered by action.

The core of the metaphor, then, is that externality is knowledge distributed across a multiplicity of connections. On this view, a subject's experiencing something as external to him or herself cannot be described in terms of sets of "rules and representations" in the subject's central processor; it must instead be described in terms of sets of relations, simultaneously computed, between possible actions and their phenomenal outcomes. This requires processing that is both "parallel" and "distributed".

The somewhat fanciful nature of this metaphor is, perhaps, an easy target. But someone may be happy to accept that externality can be regarded in this manner while denying that there is anything particularly *connectionist* about the metaphor. That is to say, why should a symbol-processing system not handle the task equally well? Why might each action and each phenomenal outcome not be represented by a symbol rather than by units and weights, and why might the relations between these not be represented by causal links based on the symbols' "shapes" [i.e. their non-semantic properties; see 1.1(i)] rather than by weighted connections? There are three answers to be given.

My first answer is essentially a reprise of what I argued in 1.1(ii). It is that the kind of system I have just described is *holistic* in the sense that each action and each outcome is individuated by its relations to many (if not all) others. Next, if a system is both holistic and symbolic then the symbolic nature of the representations is doing no essential work (see p.81).

Although there are those, as we saw in Part 1, who subscribe to "functional role semantics", which is at once holistic and symbolic, the question we need to ask again is: Just how much holism can a symbolic theorist afford to accept without jettisoning the non-semantic character of the symbols? Nodes and connections have values, but these values are meaningless when set apart from the values of all other nodes and connections in the system: they have no inherent character. A symbol, by contrast, no matter how much its individuation is dependent on other symbols, must have a *sui generis* character—a "shape"—if it is to be taken to stand for something. Its nature, as I put it in 1.1(ii), *cannot be exhausted by its causal role*. For if all that fixes the character of a symbol is its relations to other symbols which themselves are fixed in terms of *their* relations to others, and so forth, then we have an holistic system, all of whose elements have their character exhausted by their causal roles. Consider, in illustration, how representations in connectionist models come to have "content". Regions of state-space may be said to refer to elements in the domain of data, and one can say that this content is fixed holistically; fixed, that is to say, in terms of the way the total system has to configure itself to solve the problem of mapping inputs to outputs. But in a symbolic system content is not fixed in this way because symbols also have a "shape"—a non-semantic character; and if a representational unit is to have a non-semantic character its content *cannot* be exhausted by its causal role in mapping from inputs to outputs.

I am not arguing here that non-connectionist, thoroughly symbolic systems must fail to model externality. But if externality requires an holistic form of representation—in which each possible action and each possible phenomenal outcome is constituted by its relations to every other—then computational systems that are *inherently* holistic are well placed to model it. It is knowledge that can be represented without recourse to non-semantic, "shape"-like elements, and connectionist models do not have such elements.

I now turn to a second respect in which externality invites a connectionist rather than a symbolic treatment. Despite the fact that spatial concepts would seem to be grounded in innate capacities for environment-centred coding (see pp.71–72) we can certainly regard the "connections" that I described earlier between, say, "egocentric movement west" and "datum move east" as *learned* connections. Roughly speaking, the assumption is that the infant's nervous system begins by making more or less inadequate predictions about the phenomenal consequences of action which are corrected by the neural network—perhaps by difference-rules. [Recall the parallel that McClelland (1989) draws between Piaget's accommodation principle and learning by back-propagation, mentioned in Part 1.] Mental symbols, by contrast, are not learned. Indeed this is what constitutes symbols in LOT (as opposed to public symbols), and it is something that makes a symbolic system ill-adapted to the modelling of externality.

Third, even at the most metaphorical level one cannot say that the computations underpinning externality have a syntax. Symbol-processing, however, *is* a syntactic process for the simple reason that it requires the application of formal rules, with "formal" here meaning rules defined in terms of operations internal to the computing system, rather than in terms of causal interactions between the system and the world. For example, the rule that I must move forward to grasp something in front of me and to the left to grasp something on my left is not a formal rule; whereas a rule for transforming an active sentence into a passive one in English is formal. Formal rules are fundamentally arbitrary and *sui generis*; and in this sense they, like their constituent symbols, have "shapes".

However, denying that externality requires syntactic rules is not the same as denying that the computational system that underlies it must be *structured*; for structure and syntax are not the same notion. By way of answering Objection 3 in section 2.6, I discussed what it means to say that actions on objects are structured, and it may be recalled that an analogy with language was hinted at (see note 49). But this analogy was not based on the claim that we use formal rules when we act on objects; it was drawn in terms of the fact that both actions in space and language-use manifest a generalisable, holistic competence rather than a set of atomistic procedures. In fact it is to parallels between language use and externality that I now turn.

2.8(ii) Externality: Without symbols but with "combinatorial semantics"

If one argues that externality can be computed by a sub-symbolic system, argues indeed that such a system is better suited to the task than a symbolic one, then one would appear to be setting oneself a problem in explaining how a child comes to acquire language. Recall Fodor's argument that acquiring linguistic terms requires the learner to possess a representational format in LOT capable of mapping onto terms in the natural language. If one does not possess, for example, the representational format for the predicate {is a portable seat for one} then one is hardly likely to learn to apply the English predicate "is a chair".

So the question is: How could the mapping between the non-symbolic and the symbolic be achieved unless there were some commonality of format? The answer I shall give is that there is indeed some commonality: that there is at least one property of symbolic systems shared by non-symbolic ones, and that this property enables externality to function as the semantic underpinning of verbalisable representations of objects.

The property I shall consider is that of *combinatorial semantics*—the fact that arguments and predicates are freely combinable, that if we ascribe to somebody the capacity to think "white car" and "red shirt", for example, then we must also ascribe to them the capacity to think "white shirt" and "red car" (see 1.3). As Fodor and Pylyshyn (1988) argued, it is possible for a connectionist network to *lack* combinatorial semantics—to be "punctate"; possible, for example, that it should be able to represent cars as being white but not shirts as being white. This is true, but one of the things it means for a network successfully to model externality is that it possesses combinatorial semantics. My subsequent argument will draw heavily on Evans' work on referential thought (Evans, 1982; pp.100–105).

In the first place, a language user cannot be said to be making a judgement about an object unless he or she can identify the object that the judgement is about (Evans, 1982, Ch.4). This is because the capacity to think certain thoughts rests on the capacity to re-identify enduring objects over time. This bears directly on our current interests because the capacity to re-identify objects over time can be said to depend on externality: it is *objects* that are being re-identified rather than sensations (e.g. "there's that twinge again") and the ability to re-identify something as that which endured during the time we were not perceiving is to conceive of the object as external to the self. This is obviously not *sufficient*, however, to serve as a cognitive underpinning for verbalised thoughts about objects.

Evans' next step was to argue for the necessity of combinatorial semantics, for a certain kind of structuring of the cognitive capacities. "The thought that John is happy," he writes (1982, p.100), "has something in common with the thought that Harry is happy, and the thought that Harry is happy has something in common with the thought that John is sad". To be able to think Fa and Gb entails the ability to think Ga and Fb. This is the "The Generality Constraint" which I have already discussed.

If we set this beside Fodor and Pylyshyn's (1988) claim that a subject cannot be credited with the thought that "John loves Mary" unless he or she can also think that "Mary loves John", and beside their insistence that connectionist models, by virtue of being sub-symbolic, may be able to "think" one but not the other (and consequently are not computing the structured, "systematic" property of thought), it would *appear* that

Evans is arguing for a symbolic underpinning. In fact this is not so—as we shall see.

I will come to Evans' placement of his own claim relative to the LOT doctrine very shortly. But before I do I must make the point on which this sub-section depends: that the actions on objects that manifest externality meet the Generality Constraint (see Chrisley, 1993; Russell, 1988; and see my answer to Objection 1 in 2.6). It is an argument based on an analogy.

The analogy is between an object and the argument of a sentence, on the one hand, and between an action on that object and a predicator in a sentence, on the other. A pre-linguistic child who grasps the relation between him or herself as an embodied, experiencing agent and a world of substantial, mind-independent objects will be likely to conceive of an object ("argument") as capable of being acted on in an infinity of ways and of a single action ("predicate") as being applicable to an infinity of objects. Objects and actions are freely combinable in this sense. Moreover, an *appearance* of an object to the subject can also be analogised as a predicate because actions on objects alter how they will appear to us. Accordingly, an action-generated experience of an object (e.g. shifting one's visual perspective on it) is analogous to a predicate in the sense that the subject will have, for each imagined action, an imagined appearance of the object. For this reason, to the extent that the child's conception of this combinativity between objects/arguments and actions/predicates is *limited*, so will his or her conception of the mind-independence of objects be limited. Thus, there must be some conception of the free combinativity between the object/argument rattle and the appearance/predicate *visible to me* if the infant is successfully to retrieve hidden objects; for he or she must also be able to apply the experience/predicate *invisible to me* to that object/argument.

We are, then, re-encountering the reasons that lead piagetians to insist that externality is achieved through the subject's representing a multiplicity of relations between possible actions and their phenomenal outcomes. Externality can only emerge when the agent is free to "predicate" a range of actions to a single object, and free, conversely, to substitute different objects as the "arguments" of single actions.

Does this boil down to an admission that externality requires computations in LOT? Martin Braine (1992), for one, would argue that it does. His claim is that a number of basic ontological categories—he refers to these as Kantian "forms of thought"—ground semantic categories which ground, in turn, syntactic categories. For example, the subject–predicate distinction is grounded in the distinction a child makes between an object and its (temporary and permanent) properties. But this then leads to the claim (Braine, 1992, p.80) that "If one accepts

Fodor's arguments for a 'language of thought', then predicate and argument would be syntactic categories of the language of thought, aspects of an innate format for recording information." But one can equally well argue the other way round: that a language learner acquires semantic categories (such as subject-predicate and agent-action) partly by virtue of having available the kind of objective knowledge described earlier; knowledge that, as I have argued, does *not* have to be computed symbolically. That is to say, these "forms of thought" make possible the exercise of whatever (innate or otherwise) syntactic knowledge we possess, rather than being grounded in syntactic categories.

The fact that the Generality Constraint is met by language users does not tell us that the representational format—this term is Braine's—underlying this fact must be language-like, or at least it only does so if we are *already* subscribers to the LOT doctrine; I spent some time in Part 1 arguing that this subscription is not mandatory. Evans writes (1982, pp.100–102, original italics) that it may *appear* that the kind of thought-structuring described under the Generality Constraint:

> ... might lead immediately to the idea of a language of thought, and it may be that some of the proponents of that idea intend no more by it than I do. However I certainly do not wish to be committed to the idea that having thoughts involves the subject's using, manipulating, or apprehending *symbols*—which would be entities with non-semantic as well as semantic properties, so that the idea that I am trying to explain would amount to the idea that different episodes of thinking can involve the same symbols identified by their semantic and non-semantic properties. I should prefer to explain the sense in which thoughts are structured, not in terms of their being composed of several distinct *elements*, but in terms of their being a complex of the exercise of distinct conceptual *abilities*.

In other words, there is no reason to insist that the exercise of a network of abilities (for object retrieval or for sentence comprehension) forces us to explain that exercise in terms of symbols with "shapes"—with non-semantic properties. Meeting the conditions on adequate thinking made by the Generality Constraint is a manifestation of combinatorial semantics; but this does not necessarily require computational elements with a non-semantic as well as semantic character. So, when Piaget himself (1955, Ch. 2, § 4) described the "structuring" of actions he was not unknowingly committing himself to LOT.

Finally, an important caveat. It may seem as if what I have argued in this sub-section conflicts squarely with what I said towards the end of Part 1.3 about the possible inadequacies of connectionist accounts of language production. By apparent contrast, in this passage I have just said that connectionist systems may manifest a form of combinatorial semantics; and is this not tantamount to saying that there are no impediments to connectionism modelling linguistic capacities? No. My claims in this section are about externality and about the form of "combinatorial semantics" that this involves. One is not forced to assume that a sub-symbolic system that can achieve this can also achieve the production of sentences in a natural language. [This is, however, a claim that Piaget himself made (Piaget, 1972).] What is being argued here, remember, is that there is a commonality of format between representations of objects (about which we speak) and the grammar of natural languages—not that there is strict equivalence between their representational systems and their productivity. The obvious difference between the rather metaphorical "combinatorial semantics" manifested in externality and the combinatorial semantics manifested in natural language use is that in the latter case the elements involved must have a non-semantic as well as a semantic character.

2.8(iii) From modelling representation permanence to modelling externality

One way of approaching the question of how externality might be modelled in a connectionist style is by thinking first of how representation permanence might be modelled and then of what one might add to made it a model of externality. The first step is easily taken. Yuko Munakata (Munakata et al., 1994) has recently reported a connectionist model of Baillargeon's (1987) "drawbridge" experiment[53].

In the first phase of modelling, the notional eye of Munakata's network faced an X-Y grid on which there was a travelling "ball", or this plus a "block". These could be at different points on the grid, across which the notional eye "sees" the ball rolling in each episode. If there was a block present, the ball would either pass behind the block, or in front of it, or it would collide with it. What the network had to do initially was to predict where the ball would end up at t_2 given information about where it had been on the previous time-step t_1. A recurrent network (Elman, 1990) was used for this purpose.

In the next phase, the network was presented with some anomalous events (i.e. which would have this character by virtue of the training) and its "surprise-reactions" recorded. An anomalous event might be the non-reappearance of the ball from behind the block. The degree of the network's surprise reaction was measured as the amount of discrepancy between its prediction of what would occur (e.g. "ball visible at t_2") and the observed event (coded as "ball invisible at t_2")—a difference in the activation the net gave for the ball at the place where it should be and the activation of zero at that location. Munakata's assumption was that this is the signal which, in an infant, would cause an increase in looking time. The more experience with the three kinds of interaction between the block and the ball that the network had, the greater was its degree of surprise at these anomalous events.

Munakata then modelled a situation similar to that used in Baillargeon's (1987) drawbridge experiment. The same network (i.e. with weights trained by the original experience) watched a different event on the grid. This time a screen swept laterally across the display, the front part of it occluding a stationary block and then being impeded as its back collided with the block (possible) or not being impeded (impossible). Testing took place after 1000 epochs (i.e. the number of runs through the training patterns) of exposure to the two kinds of event. There was indeed an early preference for the impossible event (i.e. greater prediction–event discrepancy). Moreover, the degree of the discrepancy ("looking time") remained unchanged at 16,000 epochs for the impossible event, whereas the looking time to the possible event had smoothly decreased to zero by this time.

Munakata carried out a further simulation to see how robust the network's knowledge was. She did this by trying to habituate the network to the *impossible* event on the assumption that, if the knowledge was robust, the net would have difficulty in habituating, but that if the knowledge was labile there would be habituation. The result was that only networks that had received at least 5000 epochs of training could resist habituation to the impossible event through 30 epochs of exposure to it. "Mature" networks, in other words, continue to be surprised. (And this raises the interesting questions of how rapidly infants will habituate to impossible versus possible events, and of how old they have to be to resist this habituation.)

This original and provocative work is, in the present terms, a simulation of what I have been calling "representation permanence"; and indeed Munakata and her colleagues were able literally to observe the permanence of the object representations. When photographic images were made of the activation levels in the hidden units of the network it was evident that in situations when the ball was behind the block the units *maintained a representation* of the ball while correctly outputting "not visible".

So we are now in a position to ask what has to be added to make this a simulation of externality. Would it be sufficient to make the response one of reaching rather than of looking? We might do this in order to study the conditions under which the net learned to reach (rather, predicted the result of occluder-removal) for objects when they were occluded behind blocks, while learning *not* to reach when there was only a block present. Would the network develop like infants of between 6 and 8 months who begin by being equally likely to lift a cup that occludes a trinket as one that does not until they are more likely to lift the former (Willats, 1984)? This would certainly be worth attempting; but what would be the status of the "reach"? Crucially, if the network is learning to predict the result of removal of an occluder then *this prediction has the same status as a reaction*; no distinction has been made in the network between a reaction to a situation and an action taken on the basis of representations of the spatial location of an object relative to oneself. In other words, making the network respond by reaching rather than by looking does not make the simulation one of externality.

In saying this, I am not implying that we should regard the difference between representation permanence and externality as absolute and unbridgeable—that we should think of the non-conceptual, non-objective content in representation permanence as a kind of mental stratum discontinuous with the conceptual and objective mental content achieved in externality. Was it not Piaget himself who tried to explain how non-objective contents develop gradually into object contents? (What he called *représentation mentale* in older infants was supposed to be the terminus of object-concept development, not a *deus ex machina*.)

So what might be added to a model of this kind to make it one of externality? It goes without saying that modelling externality is a goal towards which one travels hopefully rather than something one sets out like a grant proposal. But here are some things that would have to be included in the simulation:

- The distinction between the phenomenal structure of world-caused and self-caused changes in input;
- Coding when a change in input has been self-caused without needing exteroceptive information;
- Goal-directedness;
- Returning to and re-identifying locations.

These requirements will be more difficult to meet the further down the list we travel.

In the first place, we have to ensure that the notional agent has grounds for distinguishing between changes in its visual input caused by its own movements and changes caused by movements of the ball or screen. One way of creating this distinction would be by tailoring the exteroceptive input. If the occlusion event is caused allocentrically, the exteroceptive information could be identical to that in Munakata's first ("ball and block") network. However, if the occlusion was caused by the, say, leftwards movement of the agent then the background would shift to the right, the occluding screen would shift to the right also, and the ball would shift to the *left* until it disappeared on encountering the screen; and these events would all take the same time.

Coming to the second *desideratum*, we recognise that this exteroceptive information must be insufficient, essentially for reasons I gave when outlining action feature A (2.2). For the notional agent must know *immediately*, rather than by drawing inferences from exteroception, that it has moved, for the simple reason that it is going to have to act *in order to regain sight of* the target. An action must be something that the notional agent takes, rather than something that it infers that it has taken by observing exteroceptive changes *post hoc* (action feature C, 2.2). It must, therefore, (a) know that it is *responsible* for the subsequent exteroceptive changes by monitoring its actions; and (b) be able to predict the phenomenal outcome of its actions.

To meet the first of these requirements the network could be trained to produce efference copies of it motor commands—see action feature A (2.2). It would appear indeed that this is something to which neural networks are ideally adapted, given that the inferences drawn about real (allocentrically generated) versus apparent (egocentrically generated) movements of the world are drawn in terms of *difference rules*—the kind of rules that also drive the back-propagation algorithm. The network would learn to construct efference copies of its launched actions and would thereby develop rules of the following kind: "efference copy is the symmetrical opposite of reafferent signal = self movement but no world movement"; "no efference copy plus a change in exteroceptive input = world movement and no self movement"; "efference copy is not the symmetrical opposite of reafferent signal = world movement *plus* self movement".

But—moving to (b)—in addition to recording a perceptual change as apparent or real, the network must also predict what the phenomenal outcome of an action will be before taking it. That is to say, it must know what the effect of self-movement will be, not merely whether a change in the input was egocentrically or allocentrically generated; and without this capacity, the network would have no reason to act. Moreover, it will be recalled that the core of the metaphorical parallel between externality and connectionism was a system of such predictions in relation to an object. In fact, the development of neural network models that can achieve this is well underway, as we saw in the discussion—in both Part 1.4(ii) and in 2.2—of Jordan's forward models (Jordan & Rumelhart, 1992). Recall that these are models that predict the effect on the world of carrying out particular actions, taking as their input a specification of a planned or recently executed action (e.g. a motor command) plus a representation of the current world-state. The output is a prediction of what the new world-state will be when the action has been carried out.

We come now to goal-directedness. One might think that we already have goal-directedness in the network. If we have succeeded in training a network to (say) reach and if the network distinguishes between world-generated and self-generated inputs and predicts the results of action then do we not have goal-directed behaviour for free? No. We have no warrant for saying that it reaches *in order to* retrieve the target; for sight of the target (e.g. in the forward model) may simply be *eliciting a reaching response*. This may be turn out to be a significant hurdle for the externality simulation; and some intimations of this could be seen in my discussion in 1.4(ii).

It is generally accepted that for a creature to evince goal-directed behaviour two things must be true of it, namely (1) it must be capable of representing the goal before taking the action and (2) the act must be done for the sake of the goal (see Taylor, 1964). These conditions are not met in a creature that merely associates a stimulus S with a reward R and in which presentation of S routinely calls out R-directed behaviour—and this is the situation of the network as it stands. However, if we accept that instrumental conditioning is not associative behaviour and that it involves an action being taken for the sake of a reward, then a broadly connectionist model of instrumental conditioning would serve as an existence-proof that the modelling of goal-directed behaviour is possible. There is at least one sub-symbolic model of instrumental conditioning, owing to Sutton and Barto (1981).

However, Dickinson and Balleine (1993) have recently presented a sceptical view of whether models of the kind described by Sutton and Barto —they dub them "associative-cybernetic" models—are simulating genuine goal-directed behaviour. They argue, broadly, that certain phenomena in animal learning and their human analogues—such as the effect of goal "devaluation" on subsequent behaviour[54]—show us that there is a dissociation between "responses" (e.g. a rat's failure to approach the food magazine to gain the worked-for but nausea-producing reward; a human's feelings of nausea at the sight of a novel food which had been ingested shortly before nausea) and "actions" (e.g. a rat's bar-pressings; a human's initial searching for food). This, they argue, suggests that these behaviours are "mediated by different goal 'representations' " (Dickinson & Balleine, 1993, p.288). They further argue that any "associative-cybernetic" model must make a *principled* distinction between these two kinds of representation, and that the Sutton and Barto model does not achieve this because, in that model, responses that the animal is caused to make are *equivalent* to actions the animal takes on the basis of a representation of a goal. However, although the authors hint that this *desideratum* may set a limit on what connectionist models of learning can achieve, they present no argument against the possibility that connectionist systems—in which no representations are individuated non-semantically—should fulfil it[55]. Their case is against one particular model, not against the whole enterprise.

It must be said, however, that the externality-simulating enterprise stands or falls by its success at modelling goal-directed behaviour. This is because the goal-directedness of an action is integral to the agent's experience of refractoriness—the world's resistance to our will. Although some of the behaviour we perform at will is not goal-directed in any obvious sense (twiddling our thumbs or dancing) it involves the wilful control of the body and this experience of control would seem to require some conception of what we want the body to do—a proximal goal.

A further question is whether we can speak of "goal-directedness" in relation to the role of percepts in directing the fulfilment of our purposes—discussed in 2.4. I argued there, following Schopenhauer and a number of contemporary philosophers, that for a creature to develop "self-locating" spatial concepts (without which there can be no externality) the contents of its percepts must guide its actions relative to its purposes. Note that we are not talking here about what students of animal learning such as Dickinson and Balleine refer to as "responses" (for the "contents of its percepts" are not merely calling out responses); the parallel is, as I said in 2.4, with the Piagetian notion of assimilation and Gibson's notion of affordance. But, whether or not we mark it as full-blown goal-directedness, the guidance of behaviour by percepts relative to purposes obviously implies that the organism or computational system *possesses* purposes. Perhaps our imaginary network could be provided with these through the expedient of giving it "drive units" of the kind described in my discussion of "Minimal Vitalism" [Part 1.4(iii)].

Turning to the final *desideratum*, what are the prospects for modelling the organism's ability to return to and re-identify locations? The first of these would clearly require a sophisticated model of the executive and motivational systems, a simulation of the notional agent's ability to select its own goals in the light of its background desires. This is indeed a tall order, but there have been some encouraging movements in the right direction, as we saw in Part 1.4(ii). So-called "neurodynamic" models have recently emerged (i.e. models that determine their own sequence of functioning rather than having it determined by the environment) of the attention-directing mechanisms within the frontal-limbic system (Jackson & Houghton, 1992) and of the executive dysfunctions of this system (Brown, Britain, Elvevåg, & Mitchell, 1994), in addition to modelling of the so-called "supervisory" (Norman & Shallice, 1986) function of the executive system by "dynamic schemata" (Oaksford & Malloch, 1994). This is not the place to review such work; though the Brown et al. model will be discussed at the end of Part 3.

What I will do instead is make some final remarks about the *representational consequences* of a network's notional agent returning to one place from different routes—something that is of course integral to reversibility.

A subject possessing externality must be able to re-identify objects, and this would not be possible unless it were able to re-identify places. Next, the representation of places must be context-sensitive in the following sense. A place is represented as being the place it is, not simply because of its perceptual features (otherwise similar-looking places would be represented as being the same place), but also because of the other places that have to be traversed to get to it. A place is the point at which different routes from different directions converge. Thus, although place X is the same place whether approached from the north or the south, we can reasonably say that *somewhat different though overlapping* representations of it need to be constructed for it in the different cases. This kind of many-to-one context sensitivity (i.e. many representations to one referent) is a natural feature of connectionist but not of symbolic systems (Smolensky, 1988).

What bearing does this have on the role of reversibility in constructing adequate representations of places? Chrisley (1993) has recently argued that this many-to-one context sensitivity, when manifested by a network that routinely returns to starting points, will result in the construction of the kind of adequate representations of places described earlier—similar and overlapping but not identical. He calls this "objective content".

Chrisley carried out a simulation in which a notional agent learns to find its way around a grid world. (The reader may want to hang on to the relevance of this to reaching simulations by taking the movements through the grid world as analogous to eye movements or to movements of the agent's arm.) What happened was that when the agent had to *double back* to a cell it had visited before, the network's coding for that cell turned out to be *different but similar* to that assigned on an earlier occasion. Thus, the network (Chrisley, 1993, p.349) had "through learning forced these two representations together to such an extent that they are functional equivalents in the local context". And out of this functional equivalence emerged the following kind of generalisation.

Imagine three cells with A at north, B in the centre, and C at the south, and a fourth cell D to the east of B. B has received two different but similar and functionally equivalent codings in the following way. The coding produced when travelling south from A to B is similar but not identical to that produced when the agent has travelled from B to D and then doubled back to B. The generalisation happens like this. The code produced for cell C when the agent travels south towards it directly from A→B for the first time is similar but not identical to that usually produced when the agent has doubled back to B from D and then gone south to C. Chrisley argues that this increase in the systematicity of the representations (i.e. generalising "similar but non-identical" from one context to another on the first trial) is made possible by neural networks' many-to-one representational system.

This exercise in speculation can, perhaps, be seen to illustrate what I meant at the end of Part 1 when I said that the approach to development being adopted here is an approach working "outside in" rather than "inside out". In this case one views a system—whether this is a developing child or a neural network—as something with pre-configured representations (Clark's "Minimal Rationalism"), and the capacity for altering its sensory inputs at will, embedded in a physical environment. The task is then to say how this system has to interact with its physical environment (both what has to *happen* and what forms of agency have to be *present*) to gain the conception that this environment is the external cause of its experiences. Questions about the kind of innate representations that have to exist for this to happen and about the nature of the sub-personal processes necessary for this (broadly, either sub-symbolic or symbolic) are decided pragmatically. As I put it earlier one has a "relaxed and ecumenical" view of these.

The approach is also outside-in in the sense that one seeks to model conceptions of the external world in terms of a theory about the role of agency in the development of spatial and object concepts—a theory applied from "the outside". The inside-out equivalent would be to begin with a theory of *mental representation* and then work outwards towards the point at which one would say that these representations (e.g. the syntax of the mental sentences or the embeddings of the mental models) are configured so as to represent an external world.

NOTES

21. Baldwin was an American philosopher-psychologist who produced his major work around the turn of the century. He clearly had some influence on Piaget, but the differences between the two theorists are more

interesting than their similarities. For instance, Baldwin placed greater emphasis on social learning than did Jean Piaget. See my *The acquisition of knowledge* (1978) for a summary of his three-volume work *Thought and things* and for a comparison with Piaget's theory.

22. One can read Kant as producing a "crude, innatist psychology" in Strawson's (1966) words. But his concern was with the forms of experience that are necessary for objective knowledge, not with which mental structures have to be innate. He never explicitly argued for nativism.

23. To code spatial relations allocentrically is to code them without regard to one's point of view. Some relations are allocentric *per se*, such as place B lying *between place* A and place C. An "allocentric representation" is a rather loaded term (Brewer & Pears, 1993). However, in experiments with animals and human infants the term "allocentric coding" simply means coding in terms of the relation between two points without regard to where the subject is placed.

24. The phrase is borrowed from Brian O'Shaughnessy's *The will*.

25. Strawson (1966, pp.135–9), among others, has argued that the attempt was not successful, essentially because Kant makes a conclusion about a causal necessity from what is a conceptual necessity—i.e. moving from the fact that if A takes place before B we perceive A before B to the claim that B follows from A by a kind of causal necessity.

26. This is not the same as "keeping your mind on what you are doing". What this means is keeping one's immediate goals in mind; it does not mean watching oneself to *find out* what one is doing. Failure to do the former might result in, say, putting porridge in the washing machine. See James Reason's (1979) work on "slips of action".

27. Anscombe writes (1957, p.24, original italics): "Intentional actions, then, are the ones to which the question 'Why' is given an application, in a special sense which is so far explained as follows: [...] the answer may (a) simply mention past history, (b) give an interpretation of the action, (c) mention something future. In cases (b) and (c) the answer is already characterised as a reason for acting ..."

28. Schopenhauer believed there were shortcomings in the way in which Kant drew this distinction. He argued that Kant's examples did not make the contrast between self-caused and world-caused sequences adequately, claiming that in the house-scanning example the viewer is still perceiving the movements of two bodies (as he is in the ship-sailing example)— eye movements in relation to a house. He also said that the ship movement would indeed be reversible if we had the strength (see Hamlyn, 1980, p.48). In the first place, however, one is clearly not *perceiving* one's eye movements, and in the second, one could easily produce examples of events that are not empirically reversible—e.g. a car crashing and catching fire. Of course if we take care to treat reversible actions as similar to attention-shifts, Schopenhauer's criticisms are beside the point.

29. I discuss this later in the context of theory of mind development (pp.185–186). The essential point is that if one is the sole arbiter of the correctness of one's application of a word to an experience, then there is no possibility of being incorrect about the application—and accordingly no possibility of being *correct* about it either.

30. Philosophers distinguish between the *"de re"* (in fact) and the *"de dicto"* (as expressed in words) truth of a sentence. When sentences are framed with mental-state terms such as "think that " or "hope that", the two can diverge. For example if Suzanne does not know that Kevin is the head of the maths department then the sentence "Suzanne thinks that the head of the maths department is a Mormon" is true *de re* but false *de dicto*. "Suzanne thinks that Kevin is a Mormon", however, is true in both senses. This is sometimes called "logical opacity" and sometimes called "intensionality". My point is that verbs like "trying" share these logical properties.

31. Somewhat similar views have also been expressed by Peacocke (1993) who argues for a conceptual linkage between conceiving of a material world and having some grasp of "intuitive mechanics". For a different view see Cummins (1989, Chs 4–6)—the view that seeing objects as material objects is a matter only of the causal covariance between the object's being present and our experience of it.

32. On the possibility of purely auditory experience being sufficent see Gareth Evans' (1985) thought-experiment about an abstract subject of purely auditory experience called "Hero". My reason for thinking that purely auditory experience would not be sufficient is that although, given a number of sounds, one can attend to sound A, then to sound B, then back to A, one cannot obliterate a sound from one's experience in the way that one can remove a sight from view by changing perspective or shutting one's eyes.

33. Hume would have opposed this view because he believed that in acting voluntarily we experience only the conjunction of occurrences of willing and bodily movements. On this view, no modal conception could arise. This view will be confronted a few pages later.

34. I am leaving out a lot of detail that is relevant but which complicates the picture. It could be said, for example, that if The Receiver experienced vestibular feedback when its head moved reflexively or when it moved around on the trolley, this would provide it with the crucial information about self-located sources of experience. I would argue, however, that if there were no action monitoring then information emanating from the inner ear would be merely *correlated* with forms of exteroceptive input; nothing would mark it out as having an inner source. I discuss a similar question a few pages later in relation to bodily located experiences such as thirst.

35. O'Shaughnessy does not seem to be claiming that we can draw this distinction simply by virtue of being agents: more is required.

36. See note 33.

37. Personal communication.

38. I will have much more to say about the executive functions in Part 3, but, for now, they encompass the subject's ability to initiate, inhibit, monitor, and plan actions—both physical and mental actions. One can distinguish executive from representational capacities in the following way: a subject may have all the relevant representations available to him or her (e.g. of the variables in a task) but be unable to control himself or herself sufficiently well to produce an action or judgement based on the correct one. Executive problems are particularly common in patients with lesions

of the pre-frontal cortex and in disorders in which frontal damage is implicated, such as schizophrenia and autism.

39. In an influential paper Jean Mandler (1988) pointed out that if we consider infants' memory performance (as well as other kinds of skill) we can see that they are clearly utilising mental representations of states of reality in addition to Piagetian action-based schemes. Certainly Piaget tended to play down the kind of phenomena to which Mandler refers. But his *représentation mentale* (arriving at about 18 months) is a clearly different sense of the term to that of "mental representation" as used in cognitive psychology, which is how Mandler uses the term. As I said, the French is being used here in order to distinguish the two senses.

40. Another popular technique is that of forced-choice preferential looking where a baby is presented with two visual stimuli. If the baby prefers to look at one rather than the other, then we can conclude that he or she has discriminated them. But this too is "reaction", because what we are observing here is the capture of attention not the free decision to look at this rather than that.

41. All object permanence experiments employ situations in which the subject is in a position to know where the unperceived object is currently located. There would appear to be no logical barrier against running experiments with infants where the question is about whether the subject knows the object is *somewhere* but does not know where. I assume Piaget would regard this as a case of *représentation mentale*.

42. Bermúdez also makes the point that dishabituation studies of object permanence can more parsimoniously be regarded as tests of the infants' reactions to *unusual* events rather than to *impossible* events. Recall that Thomas Baldwin (1995)—in line with the present thesis—argues this modal conception can only be gained through action.

43. The objection was put to me in almost exactly this form by Naomi Eilan and Tony Marcel.

44. Imagine two landmarks in the animal's environment and imagine a line connecting them which has, of course, a particular gradient in egocentric space. One can then take the average of all the gradients of all the lines connecting pairs of landmarks. This is the "slope". As the animal rotates the slope changes, although the slope is constant through sideways translations of the animal.

45. One way to find the centroid is to take the average of all the egocentric vectors to landmarks around the subject. Given values for both the slope and the centroid the position of a particular landmark can be worked out in terms of its distance and its direction from the centroid. This is an allocentric coding of places.

46. This point was put to me by Kim Plunkett, and it can also be found in Munakata et al., 1994.

47. I am talking about mature reaching here. I am not assuming that all search in infancy has this status. Indeed Piaget seemed to regard the successful search for occluded objects at around 8 months of age as essentially an instrumental act. The point is that one acts out of beliefs whereas one does not "react out of beliefs".

48. There is not a strictly *logical* link between belief, desire, and action because we need to leave open the possibility of weakness of will.

49. Peacocke (1983), for one, draws an analogy between the structured nature of spatial actions and the structured nature of language understanding, in the sense that understanding one sentence implies the capacity to understand a host of other sentences. In acting on objects at will, the subject manifests a system of beliefs about his or her spatial relation to these objects—as I say in the text—and in understanding one sentence he or she manifests a structured competence in something like Chomsky's sense. Just as language users do not learn sentence–meaning mappings one by one (recall my parallel with language learning in a phrase-book fashion in Part 1) so there is nothing atomistic about how we relate percepts to what we do: we do not learn the correct actions in space one by one.

50. This implies that the holism of belief is grounded in the holism of action. I am not arguing explicitly for this bold view, but it is implicit in what I have said.

51. This is a reference to Casubon's theorising in *Middlemarch*.

52. Personal communication from Gavin Bremner.

53. Yuko Munakata herself rejects this distinction between "representation permanence" and "externality". Personal communication.

54. In goal devaluation experiments the animal is made ill (usually by an injection of a mild toxin) after the ingestion of food. In one of the studies described in the paper under discussion illness was induced after lever-pressing for food. At extinction the rats pressed the lever as much as controls, but they approached the food magazine less often than controls. Their actions (i.e. the bar pressings) were controlled in a different way to their reactions (i.e. failures to approach the food magazine). Dickinson gives an autobiographical anecdote to illustrate this disjunction between actions and responses in humans. When on holiday in Sicily he ate water melons for the first time and had a nausea-provoking hangover the next day. He set out in search of more water melons (an action) but on seeing them felt nauseous (a reaction).

55. Perhaps such an argument would go something like this. To perform action *a* for the sake of goal *G* requires *G* to be represented not solely as positive or negative. If it were represented solely as one or the other then *a* could be regarded merely as a *response* made in the context of desirable or undesirable circumstances. *G* must therefore be capable of changing its value from positive to negative *while remaining itself*. Next step: the purpose of a neural network is to map inputs onto outputs; therefore every representation constructed in state space is nothing over-and-above its role in achieving this function (i.e. the representations are semantic and individuated purely by their causal roles—see p.81). But if *G* is to be able to remain itself while changing its value from positive to negative then it must acquire a *sui generis* nature, a nature that remains the same whatever its causal liaisons. Does this suggest individuation by "shape"? I have no idea whether or not this argument is successful.

PART THREE

Action and our knowledge of minds

I said at the start of Part 2 that self–world dualism is a "theoretical" notion, using the term to distinguish it from the practical capacities that we and other animals exercise when acting on objects and making our way around the world. Our conception of a mind-independent reality and the correlative view of ourselves as experiencers is "theoretical" in the somewhat technical sense of being reflective rather than practical, something that, though *grounded* in action, is not *exhausted* in action.

First, I should stress that this is not at all the same sense of "theory" as that employed by psychologists who work on the development of children's "theory of mind". In contrast to this usage, this present sense of "theory" is intended to capture what it takes to have a mind at all; what it takes to be the "self" referred to in "self–world dualism". I will have a lot to say about theory of mind development (in the usual sense) later in Part 3; but what I will say will be constrained by views that I shall present about what it takes to have a mind at all—and about the role of agency in this.

Developmental psychologists normally pay rather little attention to questions about what it takes to have a mind "at all" because these would seem to demand metaphysical answers; and questions about theory of mind development feel almost homely by comparison. In the latter case we ask how children come to "subscribe" to what is variously called "commonsense", "belief–desire", "folk psychology" or "propositional-attitude psychology"; and of course the idea of subscribing to something naturally inspires experimental tests for whether children of a certain age are yet subscribers. But the position I will try to justify in Part 3 is that one cannot construct an adequate account of how children (at age 18 months or 4 years, or whenever) come to subscribe to a theory of mind unless we are armed with some theory of—what one might call—their "pre-theoretical" mentality. In fact, this is more or less the kind of question we were tackling in Part 2, insofar as studying the conditions for knowing objects is studying the conditions for being a knowing mind. Predictably enough, my main claim is that one must be an agent to have a mind and thus to possess "a theory of mind"—as the term is currently used.

Obviously, an answer to the question of "what it takes to have a mind at all" will be, to a large extent, philosophical; and, accordingly, the earlier sections of Part 3 will involve some borrowing from and tailoring of philosophers' views. But ultimately I will climb down from the "platforms of empirical consensus"[55] on which philosophy is done and hack through wilder territories inhabited by warring tribes of experimental psychologists. There was an element of this towards the end of Part 2; but in Part 3 I shall be more directly concerned with constructing testable claims about development and psychopathology. Part 3 will proceed in three phases:

First, what does a subject's possession of externality imply about the subject's mind? Kant will be our guide here, and particularly Kant-the-psychologist as recently resurrected by Patricia Kitcher (1990). A conception of objects as causally coherent within themselves and in relation to other objects, as existing in space and through time is only possible for a unitary consciousness that *synthesises* its experiences. I call this a "synthetic" mind ("mind$_s$"). I then argue for the role of agency in the achievement of this unity. In the next section I consider the role of agency within a reflective experience of self-hood—one in which one takes oneself to be an "owner" of experiences ("mind$_o$"). Here the guide will be Schopenhauer, as mediated through some contemporary commentators. What lies at the heart of mind$_o$, I will argue, is the ability to control our experiences in acting and thereby knowing immediately that we are willing. [This obviously builds on agency features (C) and (D) from Part 2.] I then consider five developmental accounts of how children come to understand the *representing* function of mind, and conclude in favour of nativism, specifically a nativism that assumes an intimate relationship between the concept of mental representation and the language system. I then argue that innate conceptions of the representing function of mind can only be utilised by those who have first-person experience of agency, and defend this view against some familiar objections. Next I propose that early—at least, pre-verbal—understanding of other persons does not require any "theoretical" (*qua* propositional-attitude-utilising) insights into the representing function of mind—*possessing mind$_o$ is sufficient*. Finally I argue for gradualist rather than stage-wise accounts of children's grasp of belief, and suggest that if this development appears to have a stage-wise character then this *may* be due—it is an empirical question—to the executive (mental-agency-exercising) demands made by the diagnostic tests for "possessing a theory of mind".

Second, following directly from the previous claim I will review the evidence for the view that what appears to be a stage-like transition in understanding mental states between 3 and 4 years of age is in fact a transition in the child's executive control over his or her mental states. I begin this task by returning to the distinction I made in Part 2 between executive-performance and executive-competence errors and illustrate what the latter means in terms of Piaget's account of the transition towards so-called "concrete-operational" thinking at around 7 years of age. I interpret Piaget's theory of this transition to be one in terms of executive competence, and I contrast the Piagetian account of the transition with one that assumes a form of theory-change between 6 and 7 years. I suggest that the 3–4 transition has a similar, executive-competence character to that of the 6–7 transition. My conclusion in favour of the executive account of that transition will, however, be a tentative one—not because I think it may well turn out to be false but because we are in the early days of data collection.

Finally, I turn to psychopathology in order to set up one of the major empirical claims of the book—early impairments in mentalising, will lead to the impairment of mentalising abilities. The most serious competitor to this account is a modular theory which implies that one can understand the mental states of others without adequate experience of one's own agency. I will already have argued against this position on fairly a priori grounds, but at this point I will consider it in the context of the syndrome of autism. What is at issue is this. The modular view must predict that it is possible for individuals to suffer from a disorder in which they lack a theory of mind and (loosely speaking) *nothing else*, or at least that any additional symptoms they have are grounded in lacking a theory of mind. This is, more or less, the modular view of autism. The present claim, by contrast, is that the dependency of an adequate conception of mind on agency (thus on adequate mind$_o$) makes it likely that individuals who have difficulty mentalising (in understanding mental representation, in communicating, and so forth) will have experienced impaired executive functioning. In autism there is indeed a co-existence of executive and mentalising difficulties. I sketch how the claim that early executive dysfunctions cause later mentalising difficulties might be tested. Finally, I discuss parallels between autism and schizophrenia within a piagetian framework and with further brief reference to mind$_s$ and mind$_o$.

3.1: MENTAL UNITY

In this section I will follow up the implications for mental unity of the claim (made at the start of Part 2 and again in the opening paragraph of Part 3) that possessing a network of abilities for acting on objects that is supportive of externality entails that such a network is not merely practical ("exhausted in action") but that it is "theoretical". The view to be defended is that there is a link between the possession of this theory-like, reflective capacity and the possession of mental unity, a view I take to be justified by the fact that the ability to cognise objects as unitary items requires the subject to unify his or her experiences—to *synthesise* them—and that being a mind, as opposed to merely possessing "within one's body" a set of practical abilities for reaching, locating, and so forth, requires such mental unity.

This view is nothing if not unoriginal. It is Kant's famous doctrine of "the transcendental unity of apperception". Following Patricia Kitcher's recent discussion of Kant's psychological doctrines in her book *Kant's transcendental psychology* (1990), I am treating this as a piece of theoretical psychology rather than as a thesis about the logic of concepts such as "object" and "mind": it is a thesis about what is psychologically rather than logically necessary for being a mind, a thesis about how information-processing has to be carried forward. I will, however, be going some way beyond Kitcher towards the claim that agency—as described in Part 2—is necessary to the achievement of this unity.

The best route to take towards Kant's views on mental unity is one that begins with David Hume's sceptical views about mental unity. And if readers are in search of some "unity" in this book they might like to think of Kant as a champion of the doctrine of mental holism—a kind of functional role theorist—described early in Part 1, and Hume as its most illustrious opponent, as a prefiguration of Fodor.

Hume famously claimed that when he turned his inner eye on his mental life he encountered no unitary mind; rather he perceived an agglomeration of distinct impressions and concluded that the mind is therefore nothing more than a "bundle" of impressions. Hume (1739/1962, p.634) regarded mental states atomistically: "All perceptions are distinct. They are, therefore, distinguishable, and separable, and may be conceived as separately existent, and may exist separately without any contradiction or absurdity." But Hume despaired over ever giving an account of how these atomistic states are causally related to one another because he regarded causal connections as something that we *posit* on the basis of what we perceive—as something not independent of the positing mind. For if "the mind never perceives any real connection among distinct existences" (Hume, 1739/1962, p.636) what account can we give of these connections between atomic states? He admitted indeed that his account of personal identity was inconsistent.

But Hume was himself already *assuming* mental unity when he developed his account of causality (on which, as we have just seen, his account of personal identity foundered). Hume argued that the reason we take A to be the cause of B is that A-experiences and B-experiences are constantly conjoined and that our reflection on these conjunctions leads the mind naturally to posit a kind of causal necessity. But this is to assume that A and B are experienced *by the same mind*: if I see A and *you* see B then no expectations can be built up about what must follow from what in either of us.

As Kitcher (1990, pp.98–99) points out, Kant knew Hume's writings, and his account of mental unity can be regarded as an attempt to correct Hume's error. In other words, he tried to establish that, unless there were mental unity, the kind of causal judgements Hume described could not be made: "The doctrine of apperception is about the primary attribute of thinkers that is necessary for cognition" (Kitcher, 1990, p.94) Or in the terms used earlier, the network of abilities that underlies our capacity to represent objects as external to the self *presupposes* that this network exists within a unitary mind, a claim that is naturally related to the doctrine of mental holism and to meeting the Generality Constraint.

Kant did more than simply state this, however. He tried to give a psychological account of *how* the mind must "synthesise" its elements if it is to represent anything. (I am taking "represent" here to mean "represent as external to the self" and as having "conceptual content".) If it is a condition for successful representation that cognitive states should "represent something only in so far as they belong with all others to one consciousness, and therefore must be at least capable of being so connected" (Kant, translated by Kitcher, 1990, pp.108–109) what kind of information-processing is required? To answer this question I will be closely following Kitcher's reading of Kant.

To aid the description of how synthesis is supposed to work, Kitcher (1990, pp.117–123) calls mental states that result from synthesis "synthetic products" and the ingredients used in this production "synthetic progenitors". Furthermore, because cognition is continuous, any synthetic product is a potential synthetic progenitor, while every synthetic progenitor must itself have been a synthetic product. As she puts it (1990, p.119), "cognitive states belong to one consciousness just in case they are connectable by synthesis with a set of states already connected by synthesis, and all such states are connected with each other". Or in Kant's own words, "As *my* cognitive states (even if I am not conscious of them as such) they must conform to the condition under which alone they *can* stand together in one universal self-consciousness, because otherwise they would not without exception belong to me" (Kant, translated by Kitcher, 1990, p.119; original italics).

Kant saw this as a solution to Hume's problem—the problem, recall, that any account of how cognitive acts are possible (such as causality judgements) must *presuppose* mental unity. He tried to achieve it by putting a condition on mental unity. One reason why Hume's account foundered, recall, was that its author had no principled way of constraining mental states to belong to one mind (the "I see A, you see B" example given earlier). What does Kant say about this? What happens, in Kitcher's example, if Harry screams "Smoke!" (this expresses his cognitive state) and then this functions as a cognitive progenitor of a mental state of *mine*? We then appear to have the unfortunate consequence that minds are interweaving. Kitcher argues that Kant had an "implicit restriction" on this which was that the flow of synthesis within a mind must take place without any intervening "transmission through outer sense" (1990, p.121). Thus, two cognitive states CS_1 and CS_2 can only be progenitors of a resulting state CSR if the nature of CSR is dependent entirely on CS_1 and CS_2 without the mediation of a third state (CS_3) which is an outer sensation. This implies that the mental state caused by my hearing "Smoke!" has a different functional role (different causal liaisons) in Harry's mind than in mine and therefore is synthesised within my mind as mine rather than his. Kant can say this because, as Kitcher points out (and as I noted earlier) he had what would today be called a "functionalist" or, indeed, "functional role" view of mental states (see Part 1.1).

Of course the pressing question in all this is how synthesis is supposed to relate to self-hood. It may be tempting to think of the self as being that which is "responsible" for acts of synthesis; for Kant did sometimes write in terms of "I" being that which performs the acts of uniting, combining, and so forth. But this would be to assume what we need to explain. We certainly do not want to regard the self as something over and above the process of synthesis. And, given what has already been said, it might seem to be even more tempting to say that "the agent" is that which performs the synthesis. "But," as Kitcher (1990, p.122, my italics) rightly says, "acts or processes of synthesis could not be performed by agents. *They are unconscious activities within agents that enable them to have cognitive capacities required for agency."*

But although it is surely incorrect to place the agent outside the synthetic process (i.e. saying that an agent is whatever-it-is that whips up mental unity out of sensory inputs, memories, and so forth), it is equally unwise to say that the agent is the "emergent property" of an automatic and passive process of synthesis. Making agency the effect of synthesis is just as bad as making agency its cause: either way, agency is a ghost outside the machine—the executive ghost in the first place and the emergent ghost in the second.

We can avoid these alternatives, while integrating what has been said in this section with the claims of Part 2, in the following way. In Part 2 the argument was that only agents can experience objects as mind-independent entities ("externality"); whereas the Kantian argument is that such objective experience is only possible for subjects who can synthesise their mental states. So we have, then, two necessities for objective experience—agency and mental synthesis. Given this, we are faced with the question of whether these two necessities are mutually dependent or independently operating. Well, to say that they are independently operating hardly seems possible because it amounts to the claim that agency is something distinct from the process by which our disparate experiences are integrated: now agency is a ghost *in* the machine. The better option is to say that these necessities—agency and synthesis—are two faces of one process, the process through which experiences are integrated within one mind through the exercise of agency.

Consider reversibility. What happens here is that the subject integrates his or her perceptual inputs as he or she controls them, with the basic assumption being that there could be no mental synthesis without mental control of the kind exemplified in reversibility—and no control without synthesis. Unless we regard the subject's nervous system as integrating the inputs that action generates it is impossible to see how he or she could achieve transitions from one action to the next.

There is another consideration to be raised in favour of the view that synthesis and mental unity must interdepend. In 2.6 I laboured the point (in answer to 'Objection 3') that, because actions take place in space, they are "structured", in contrast to reactions to unusual events in space. Thus, a subject who knows what it is to act "on my left" must also know what it is to act "on my right" or "above me"; so that being a creature that is able to act in this way is to be a creature that has a structured knowledge of places in relation to itself. If this were not so, then the notion of "choosing" to act here or here or there—and surely there is no action without a range of possibilities to choose between—would have no foothold. If this is so, we can say that successful action requires the agent to synthesise its experience of places within a unified experiential field: having structured knowledge of space must require that the subject's experiences of places be synthesised within (what a psychologist might call) one central processor. Conversely, as I argued in 2.4 after Schopenhauer and Brewer, to perceive a place in this "unified experiential field" is to perceive that place as having implications for action: one cannot see a place as being there$_1$ rather than there$_2$ without knowing what it would be to act there$_1$ rather than there$_2$.

What I have just sketched hardly adds up to a proper account of the relation between agency and synthesis. However, if we do not at least accept the mutual dependence of agency and synthesis then, as I said, we come perilously close to regarding agency as a ghost in the synthetic machine.

It may appear that in this section we have moved a very long way indeed from the concerns of Piaget himself. But in fact we are not a million miles from his assimilation-accommodation theory of learning, because this discussion of the intimate relation between synthesis and agency carries an echo of the mutual dependence of these two Piagetian processes. Assimilation is the synthetic process whereby an action scheme (e.g. tracking) makes a datum part of itself (e.g. a person is successfully tracked); while this cannot be achieved without some *active* modification—accommodation—of the scheme (all motions cannot be tracked in exactly the same way). Accordingly, we might see assimilation as the intention to integrate a datum within the developing mind whereas accommodation is what the organism has to do to make this attempt successful.

But whether or not the reader finds this a satisfying parallel, we are now in a position to name the first sense in which we can be said to have a "mind"—mind as a synthetic unity (mind$_s$). This is mind as the functionalist conceives of it—as an entity constituted in terms of causal relations between perceptual inputs, behavioural outputs, and intra-mental states. What I have said in this section entails that mind$_s$ is (i) something that develops as externality develops, (ii) something that depends on agency, and (iii) something that will tend to be inadequate insofar as agency is inadequate.

3.2: BODILY AWARENESS, SELF-HOOD, AND OWNERSHIP

In this section we move towards a conception of mind richer than mind$_s$—one that is more or less co-extensive with the term "self"—and discuss the role of agency in its development. What is at stake here is the subject's ability to *ascribe experiences to himself or herself*, to take experiences as being his or her own. This was not necessary for mind$_s$, because the enjoyment of objective experience need not depend on any reflective conception of oneself as the *owner* of these experiences[56].

Where the framework was Kantian in the previous section, in this section it will be derived broadly from Schopenhauer—or at least from Schopenhauer as mediated through commentators such as Janaway (1989), Hamlyn (1980), and via the work of O'Shaughnessy (1980). Given the heavy use I have made of O'Shaughnessy in setting up action features (C) and (D) and the guest-appearances Schopenhauer has already made, some of the subsequent material will have a familiar ring to it.

The refractoriness thesis, whether derived from arguments about reversibility or from felt resistance (Baldwin, 1995), was sufficient to establish, I argued, that agency is required for us to know ourselves to be subjects of objective experience. But, of course, subjects do not know themselves *merely as existing in relation to the objects of their experiences*; they also have a reflective or "second order" awareness of themselves as possessors of mental lives, as mental entities abstracted away from, as it were, whatever they are experiencing at the time. It is notoriously difficult to say anything coherent about this form of awareness because it rests on the paradox that, in being self-aware, we, as subjects, take ourselves to be the objects of our reflections. How can we do this without losing our status as *subjects*? I am not about to resolve this paradox, and its resolution is a purely philosophical task. What I can do, however, is say something about the role of agency in the development of the belief we all share—our "theory" in the Part 2 sense—that we are in this paradoxical position. I will do so under the following headings:

(i)   The relation between bodily awareness and volition;
(ii) The sense in which selfhood can be experienced "immediately";
(iii) The relation between being a willing and a knowing self.

At the end of this I will, I hope, have carved out a sense of "mind" in which ownership rather than synthesis is the central quality.

Before doing this I should say why Schopenhauer is needed at this point. First, much of Schopenhauer's philosophical writing was both an extended commentary on Kant's *Critique of pure reason* and an attempt to answer Kantian questions (principally about what it takes to have objective knowledge) in such a way that "the will" played the central role. Willing and agency are not the same notion; but their relation is obviously an intimate one. Second, Schopenhauer was one of most forceful opponents of a purely representational theory of the mind, in contrast to Kant who, as we have seen, prefigured the present-day functionalist representational theories. In willing, Schopenhauer argued, we experience a form of knowledge that is not representational.

3.2(i) Bodily awareness and volition

We have just seen that the notion of self-awareness is paradoxical. How can the subject of experience also be its object? "Self-aware" is almost a solecism. But we *are* (what we like to call) self-aware, and this difficult-to-express conception is likely to be based on certain distinctive modes of experience. The thought I need to develop now is that one of the processes that grounds our self-awareness, and which is therefore a condition for successful mental development, is bodily awareness; and the idea to be developed is that as the child becomes aware of his or her body he or she becomes aware of a "mental" entity that is objective, and that this awareness is a necessary but not sufficient condition for self-awareness.

James Mark Baldwin (1906, vol.1, p.88) argued that bodily awareness functions as a bridge for children between their developing subjectivity and their developing objective knowledge, in the sense that a body is at once "inner" and "outer"—not external to the self and yet an object to be observed by the self and others. [This led him—like Andrew Melzoff (1990)—to give the imitation of others' actions a central role in our developing conception of mentality, see Russell (1978, section 1.2).] But if the body is not external to us then in what sense can it be *internal*? Some would insist, against this, that our body is essentially external to our mental life, that it is an object of our willing and apprehending which just happens, unlike the bodies of others, to be highly responsive to our acts of volition (as well as being viewed from a unique perspective, of course). On this view, what happens when I act is that I launch an act of will which causes a movement in my otherwise passive body: the body is the outer effect of an inner cause.

It is fair to say that the agenda for contemporary philosophical accounts of action has been set by those who have *rejected* views of this kind. Wittgenstein famously asked "What is left over if I subtract the

fact that my arm goes up from the fact that I raise my arm?" (1953, §
621), intending to dramatise the absurdity of answers such as "my
intending to raise my arm" and thus the absurdity of the picture of a
purely mental, willing entity trapped, as it were, inside the body, able,
if it pulls the right levers, to cause the body to move as it intends it to
move. It is similarly absurd to think that acts of will are purely mental
configurations (e.g. willing to move my arm in just *this* way) that map
onto purely physical configurations (my arm actually moving in just *this*
way). Against such views, O'Shaughnessy writes of a bodily movement's
being an act of trying to do something "coming to fruition" (1980, p.214)
rather than being its cause; acts of will do not cause movements, one
might say, any more than seeds "cause" plants. There is one process
rather than two discontinuous processes. But the philosopher, above all
others, who opposed the earlier ("mind wills→body obeys") picture was
Schopenhauer, a philosopher who probably had a strong influence on
Wittgenstein's views about action (Janaway, 1989, Ch.13).

If the earlier view can be said to be fairly close to the common-sense
understanding of volition then Schopenhauer's view, at first blush,
seems downright offensive to it. His essential claim is that "The act of
will and the act of the body are not two distinct objectively known states,
connected by the bond of causality—they do not stand in the relation of
cause and effect; rather they are one and the same, only given in two
completely different ways: once quite immediately and once in an
intuition for the understanding [meaning, roughly, as a representation
caused by perceptual experience]."(Schopenhauer, 1844/1966; p.143;
trans. Janaway, 1989, p.209). As Christopher Janaway (1989, Ch.8)
points out, Schopenhauer was presenting a "two aspect" theory of action,
in the sense that there is *one* event which can be viewed in two different
ways—as an act of will and as a bodily movement. (Compare the position
that personal-level accounts of visually guided action are "autonomous"
in relation to sub-personal accounts, discussed towards the end of 2.6.)
And so if "every true, genuine, immediate act of the will is also at once
and directly a manifest act of the body" then a very distinctive view of
the status of the body is implied. "My body is the *objectivity* of my will"
(Schopenhauer, 1844/1966, pp.102–103).

The obvious difficulty with this position is that it seems to have no
resources for explaining how acts of will can *fail* to become bodily
actions. For Schopenhauer, unlike O'Shaughnessy, is not only rejecting
the traditional causal picture (O'Shaughnessy, by contrast, has no
difficulty explaining how an act of will can fail to come to bodily fruition)
but *equating* willing and bodily movement. And to continue the contrast
between their closely related views, O'Shaughnessy has a theory of
action that is Schopenhauerian in spirit (see Janaway, 1989, Ch.8),

while being one that avoids this implausibility, by distinguishing between acts of will, which *can* be identified with bodily action, and "strivings" or "tryings" which cannot. Although trying to do something is non-contingently related to doing it (contrast the contingent relation between being happy and smiling) the two are not identical. But what is the common ground between Schopenhauer and O'Shaughnessy? The latter writes (1980, pp.349–350, original italics):

> Schopenhauer said: 'I cannot really imagine this will without this body.' If this wonderful remark is right—and we shall see that it is—then the psychological phenomena that occur when one engages in intentional physical action must at the very least depend on *the supposed reality* of the body. But more: we shall see that the psychological phenomena that occur in any physical action, and under howsoever psychological description, depend in general on *the actual existence of the body*.

This has strong implications for bodily awareness. It is not merely that being a subject of willing entails possessing a body—not simply that one is logically dependent on the other. For we can add to this that, if a subject is a subject of willing, then the experience of being embodied is *integral to the experience* the subject has when he or she is willing (see Janaway, 1989, p.228).

If this were *not* so, it is difficult to imagine how self-awareness would be possible. Imagine that, *per impossibile*, a bodiless entity—perhaps a supercomputer—developed subjectivity: it came to know itself to be the subject of objective experiences. To become thereafter self-aware this subject would have to achieve the paradoxical feat of making itself an object of its own reflection, a feat that we embodied creatures do indeed achieve. But how could this feat be achieved by a bodiless entity? We have a body that functions for us as the objective manifestation of our willing self; but this imagined subject does not. Without a body that relates to our will in the ways just discussed, how could self-reflective judgements find an object?

Finally, I need to say a little about two notions that seem to play almost identical roles in self-awareness and bodily awareness—control and ownership. (By "ownership" I intend what is sometimes called "self-ascription".) In the first case, having finite capacities for controlling the flow of perceptual inputs would appear to be a necessary condition for coming to reflect on certain experiences as "mine". (I have already said enough on this topic under the heading of reversibility.) In the second place, having finite capacities for controlling one's body would appear to be the main criterion on which one takes this body to be "mine". Of course, sensations occur in our bodies, and so one might think that the kind of experience I have when I, say, see my arm and feel an itch at a particular spot is sufficient for me to take that limb to be mine. But if this kind of experience were the *only* kind of bodily experience a creature ever had, it is difficult to see why it would ever judge a limb to be its own. The limb would be no more than a *conduit of sensations*.

A little more needs to said about ownership. In particular we need to think about whether what is being discussed here is something that is part of the phenomenology of experience or whether it is a conception that we gain as a result of *reflecting* on our experience. It is the former—a phenomenological fact. As we act, we have the immediate experience of controlling our body, or at least the experience of trying to do things that usually come off but which may not; and in doing this the question of whether it is our body or somebody else's that is being controlled *does not arise*: control and ownership are indissociable. Of course, we can, to some degree, control the limbs of other people (perhaps by telling them what to do and by manhandling them) and we can control objects if they are of the right shape and size; but in controlling our own body we experience the responsibility for what happens next in an immediate form, a form that I use the term "ownership" to describe.

When we add to this the fact that changes in perceptual inputs are normally (i.e. when not purely attentional) caused by bodily movements, the control and ownership involved in self- and bodily awareness reveal themselves as being still more closely related. I will have more to say about ownership after the next two sub-sections. But for now the conclusion is this: no self-awareness without a body of which one is in control and which one accordingly takes to be one's own.

3.2(ii) The "immediate" experience of willing

In this sub-section I shall be harking back to two of the four features of agency introduced in Part 2, namely, (C) that we know the nature of our actions without self-observation, and (D) that we have privileged, incorrigible knowledge of what we are trying to do. I shall argue that these, together with more controversial facts about our non-representational knowledge of our agency, broadly entail that a conception of agency—of the agency of others as well as of ourselves—must be grounded in *first-person experience*. This conclusion has clear relevance to the question of how we develop a conception of other minds. Let us turn again to Schopenhauer's thoughts about this question.

It was Schopenhauer who insisted that when we act we have knowledge of so doing that is not representational knowledge—unlike all other forms of knowledge. In this sense it is "immediate"—not mediated by representations. But even Schopenhauer did not believe that acting has *no* representational content; and this led him to claim that there are two things involved in agency. First, there is the immediate experience of willing (which, as we have seen, he identified with action and with the movements made in acting). Second, there are what he called the *motives* out of which we act—and these are representational, at least in part. He recognised, in other words, that any theory of action must accommodate *why* we do what we do, not simply the experience of doing it; and accounting for the whys and the wherefores means referring to beliefs, desires, and dispositions, of the causes of which we may have no knowledge.

But how can a line be drawn between the component of action which is known immediately and that which is known representationally? We cannot just point to features (C) and (D) here, because knowing our actions without observation and incorrigibly is not the same as this knowledge lacking representational content, as I said in Part 2. For although it makes sense to say that we know non-representationally that we are, say, in pain, it makes little sense to say that we know in a non-representational way what action we are engaged in, because much of what we do is goal-directed, and having a goal requires having a representation of present and future states of affairs. Moreover, we normally act for reasons, meaning that we must normally have succeeded in representing these reasons to ourselves.

David Hamlyn has tried to clarify Schopenhauer's position in the following way. He writes (1980, p.85) that "What I think that Schopenhauer has in mind in all this, although he does not really succeed in saying it clearly, is that it is the *fact* of willing that is known immediately, but not *what* we will. Thus in performing some bodily action, in which alone the will can be known by us, we are conscious directly and immediately *that* we do it." However, "to *know what* one is doing one has to place the action in a context of beliefs and desires—that being what knowledge of one's motives, and indeed the very existence of the motive, come to" (Hamlyn, 1980, p.137).

In the next section I will have a little more so say about these two components of action—the volitional and the representational—but for now I think we can conclude that there is a good deal of plausibility in the view that we know immediately that we are willing *something*— bracketing off the descriptions under which we place that something. I think it is important to recognise, however, that although knowing what one is doing involves representational knowledge of our beliefs and desires, this knowledge is still knowledge *without observation*, as we saw under feature (C). Knowledge about ourselves can be at once representational and knowledge that is not gleaned from what is available to perception or to any other kind of observation. In knowing *that* one is acting wilfully, however, there is no place for a representation.

To put it mildly, Schopenhauer had a very bold theory of the relation between self-knowledge and non-representational knowledge of our agency. He said that because this knowledge is non-representational it gives us access, behind the veil of appearances, to our essential nature—access to how we are in ourselves—and he constructed a metaphysical system based on the view that "the will" is the reality that underlies all phenomena represented by us. But I don't think we need to go quite so far to extract something relevant to the more humble enterprise of developmental psychology.

As a number of contemporary philosophers of action have insisted, the kind of knowledge available to the agent suggests the metaphors of experiencing from the "inside"[57] and thereby encountering oneself as "centre of responsibility" in Charles Taylor's phrase (1964, p.57). This is certainly in the spirit of the Schopenhauerian view, because these metaphors gain their meaning from the fact that there is something essential to agency that *cannot be known from the outside*. Any representational form of knowledge, by contrast, is potentially public; what Schopenhauer called "motives" can obviously be made public. Broadly speaking, everything that is representational about actions (what is being intended, believed, the actor's dispositions, and so forth) is often as available to the observer as it is to the agent. But this public knowledge is only half the story: to know what agency consists in is not merely to understand how motives function; it is also to have first-person, immediate, from-the-inside, experience of being responsible for what we do. I shall build on this conclusion later.

3.2(iii) Integrating the willing and the knowing subject

In this final sub-section, as in the previous one, we shall be concerned with the relation between the non-representational (or "immediate") and the representational features of agency. The first, of course, refers to the exercise of the will; but this time the second refers to knowledge not just of our motives but of the external world.

We can begin by asking: If Schopenhauer is broadly correct that (i) the body is not merely that which responds to our will, but is its physical manifestation and condition (its "objectivity" as he called it) and (ii) that our experience *that* we are willing is unmediated by representations, then what is implied about the subject's capacity for reflective or "second-order" awareness of himself or herself? It obviously seems to imply that a subject's primary mode of self-awareness is that of a willing, striving, embodied creature. But Schopenhauer did not attempt to deny that the subject is also somebody with knowledge about the world—why would a subject act if he or she apprehended nothing? Accordingly, he had a *parallel* view of the self—as an epistomological or "knowing" entity. He did not equate this form of self-hood with the body—for obvious reasons—but took it to be a kind of pure cognitive processor, an "extensionless point" at the terminus of this processing. He also took the willing aspect of the self to be the primary one—adopting a very broad view of the will that included everything from instincts to rational decision-making. However, the difficult and controversial issue is not one about primacy; indeed the idea that the willing subject is—developmentally at least—primary seems a rather plausible view if the central thesis in Part 2 is correct. The difficult issue is about the relation between these two aspects—the volitional and the epistemic.

Let us step back a little to approach this question. In Part 2, I tried to establish the following things about the relation between agency and our apprehension of the environment. I argued, following Brewer (1992) and others, that agency is necessary if a subject is to have an "egocentric" or "self-locating" space (a space organised around his or her own body), and generally sided with those who take the view that a creature could not perceive its environment *as* its environment without having the capacities and dispositions of an agent. I then argued that the experience of the environment as being refractory is only available to agents and that this means that only agents can come to know themselves as subjects whose experiences are caused by objective, mind-independent phenomena: it is impossible that there should be a subject of perceptual experience who is incapable of willing. This allows us to conclude that a subject of objective experience must have a willing as well as a knowing aspect.

But, as I have been saying throughout this section, it is important to distinguish between being a "subject" and possessing "self-awareness". We do not merely have the "first-order" experience of being subjects of objective experiences; we also achieve the paradoxical feat of making our subjectivity the object of our own apprehension. Accordingly, if this subject of experience is both a willer and a knower, what is implied about the possibility of the subject having reflective awareness of himself or herself? I think the only thing that can be said with confidence here is that the relation between the willing and the knowing components must be a relation, if not of identity, then at least of complete integration. Why? Self-awareness necessarily implies the possibility of having first-person thoughts—often called "I-thoughts" (Evans, 1982, Ch.7)—and so, as Janaway (1989, pp.300–301) points out, the "I" in "I will" and the "I" in "I perceive/know/believe etc." must be taken by the subject to refer to the same entity. Here we part company with Schopenhauer, because he was encumbered by the view that the willing and the knowing selves were distinct, although he had to admit that these two selves "flow together into the consciousness of one 'I' " (Schopenhauer, 1844/1966; p.243) pronouncing this to be "the miracle *par excellence*". But the distinctiveness of the willing and the knowing components is just what we should *not* be insisting on. In the following passage Christopher Janaway (1989, p.301, original italics) expresses this integration between the two components in the following terms:

> That which strives to alter the world must be conscious of itself as being that which, perceptually or otherwise, has knowledge of it. This is because the point of acting is to change something about the world that *I* perceive, or about *my* relation to it, while the capacity to perceive essentially informs, through beliefs and desires, the way I actively modify myself in response to what is perceived. A self which both wills and apprehends the world cannot be, in its own conception of itself, something composite. The unity of apperception extends out, if you like, to include the subject's bodily strivings.

Now recall what was established in the previous two sub-sections—(i) the dependency of self-awareness on being embodied and (ii) our immediate knowledge of ourselves as centres of responsibility for our actions. We can now add to these: (iii) the complete integration between willing and knowing.

Remember that the goal—in this section—is a view of mentality that places *ownership* rather than synthetic unity at the centre of the picture. These are the rudiments of this view:

(i) My immediate experience of myself as the owner of a body makes it possible for me to take myself to be responsible for the experiences that the actions of my body generate.

(ii) I encounter myself non-representationally and "from the inside" as that which is responsible for changes in my experience. Experience of responsibility helps to make these experiences my own.

(iii) There is no "purely knowing" self distinct from a "purely willing" self. Accordingly, there can be no conception of that which "I know" or "I believe" or "I perceive", no conception that these mental states are my own, unless I am also somebody who wills.

To sum up this section, there are two senses in which we can be said to have a mind, as distinct from and as logically prior to entertaining "theories" about minds. In the first place, a mind is something that must possess the synthetic unity to support objective experiences—mind$_s$. If we are to know anything, our perceptual inputs must be assimilated into a unitary system within which each mental state coheres with every other. It may help to think of this as a fact about the "central systems" as opposed to the "input systems" (Fodor, 1983). For no matter how much we discover about the modularity of the input systems and about the modular organisation of skills and knowledge in the brain, a mind must possess this unity. I said that *if*, as was argued in Part 2, a conception of the external world is only available to agents then it must be the case that *mind$_s$ is similarly exclusive to agents.*

To possess a mind in my second sense is more or less equivalent to being self-aware. In this sense, we have a mind because we take experiences to be our own and take ourselves to be finitely responsible for what we experience; while there must be the background possibility of having "I-thoughts"—something that was not necessary for mind$_s$. What is a stake here is ownership, and so I will label this "mind$_o$". Agency enters the picture in three ways here, as we have just seen: via bodily awareness, via the non-representational nature of responsibility, via the dependency of the apprehending self on a willing self.

You may ask why am I bothering with taxonomy? Would not another psychologist produce a different taxonomy from different motives; and what is there to choose between them? To answer the first question, one has no choice but to attempt some taxonomy if one wants to say anything coherent about the child's "pre-theoretical" mind—as I said at the start of Part 3. Theories of what characterises the pre-theoretical mind will surely constrain psychological views of how a "theory of mind" develops; and this cannot be done without prejudice to what one thinks the *content* of these theories is. (It will emerge through the remainder of Part 3 how this "constraining" works in the present case.) In answer to the second question, the fact that different psychologists may produce different taxonomies does not mean that it's all just up for grabs. Indeed it seems to me that any account of what it takes to have a mind that ignores the unity of experience, the self-ascription of experiences to this unitary self and the central contribution of agency to both is just false.

3.3: AGENCY AND THE ACQUISITION OF A "THEORY OF MIND"

My main task in this long section will be to show how the possession of mind$_o$ bears on the acquisition of a theory of mind, as that term is currently used. This will require me to highlight the role of the first-person, non-representational experience of agency within this development.

I need to take two preliminary steps. First it is necessary to place *desire* within the picture, because desire has both a representational and a non-representational aspect: it bridges, in other words, Schopenhauer's two domains of agency. Second, I need to take a bird's-eye view of the various accounts of how theories of the *representational* aspect of theory of mind develop. I do not have to be strongly committed to any one of them; but it will be useful to have some theory in play of how the child develops a representational conception of mind before discussing the relation between agency and theory of mind. I conclude that a broadly nativist theory is the best option. But before I do these two things I must say what the phrase "theory of mind" means.

To say a child "has a theory of mind" is normally taken to mean that he or she takes thinking to consist in having mental representations towards which different kinds of orientation (e.g. belief that, hope that, fear that) can be adopted. It means subscribing to the folk psychology of thought, in fact. A little more technically, the child appreciates how the following three are related: (a) the subject, (b) the propositional attitudes that the subject has to his or her mental contents and (c) the propositional contents being entertained. For example: (a) Harriet, (b) believes/hopes/disbelieves that (c) her car-keys are on the bedroom floor. The content of the proposition ("her car-keys are on the bedroom floor") is only in the running for truth: it is inherently neither true nor false. But knowing the kind of propositional attitude that relates an agent to the content will enable us to predict what the agent will *do* and explain why she did what she did. If the attitude is that of belief, we can predict what Harriet will do before leaving her flat because belief means being *committed to the truth of some proposition*; and we can later explain why she is looking under the bed.

The term "theory of mind" is normally intended to cover both first-person and third-person understanding of mind—both the child's ability to reflect, for example, on what he or she believed earlier (Gopnik & Astington, 1988) or on how a trick object (e.g. a stone "egg") presently appears to him or her (Flavell, Flavell, & Green, 1983) and the child's ability to predict and explain others' behaviour on the basis of what they believe and desire. But the latter (third-person) kind of question has turned out to be the primary one, partly because of what the famous "false belief" experiment (Wimmer & Perner, 1983) seems to demonstrate. In this, pre-school children are exposed to a situation (in a story or by acting out with experimenters) in which a protagonist leaves something at place A and then departs. During her absence the object is moved from place A to place B (with a suitable cover-story), after which the protagonist returns. The child is then asked whether the protagonist will look for the object at place A or at place B. To answer "place A" (which is what 4-year-olds, but not 3-year-olds, generally do) is taken to show that the child is in possession of the "theory" that beliefs—mental representations to whose truth we are committed—determine action. Action is not generated "directly" by real situations, but through a mental medium.

Now in this sense—in the third-person sense—having a theory of mind could equally well be called having a theory of agency. This is somewhat ironic because the debates in this area centre around questions about the child's understanding of the mind as a *representing* device—ignoring the kind of questions we have been tackling. But in fact, many of the questions posed within the theory of mind area concern what Schopenhauer called "motives"—the representational face *of agency*: we ask how children come to appreciate that people act out of *desires* and beliefs.

3.3(i) Desires and dispositions

The explanatory framework I have just described is sometimes referred to as belief-desire psychology, with a popular position being that pre-school children are "desire theorists" before they are "belief-desire theorists" (Wellman, 1991). Indeed the assumption is often made that the central developmental questions concern the transition between the two kinds of theory. But I need to emphasise that the role of desire within theory of mind development is at least as difficult to understand as that of belief because its status is ambiguous, insofar as it has both a representational and a non-representational face.

It is certainly possible to treat desire as a propositional attitude, as a description of the subject's mental orientation towards a representation. Thus, when we say "Harriet hopes that the car will start" our meaning would also have been carried, though awkwardly, by "... desires that ...". But desire is not like belief because it does not *have* to take a propositional content: "I want/need/desire a cheeseburger", for example. We do not, in contrast, make statements such as "I think a cheeseburger", to which the obvious response would be: "You think a cheeseburger *what?*"

There is, then, a class of verbs whose members are broadly affective and volitional, and each of which can be used in either propositional or non-propositional (object-governing) senses. In this class we find such verbs as "desire", "want", and "fear" and outside of it we find such verbs as "think", "believe", and "hope"; the latter set can only be used propositionally. Linguistically, then, it is very easy to draw a line between them, because we just note whether sentences containing them make sense when the verb does not govern a proposition. One cannot, to give another example, just "hope the car ": the phrase cries out for a that-clause.

However, what it is that marks these verbs out *psychologically* is by no means obvious. It is not merely that they have an affective tone, because "hope" is also an affective verb: a person who entertains hopes must also be capable of entertaining desires. Of course it may turn out that these verbs have no common element. But one can at least say that they share the property of implying a *non-cognitive* relation between a subject and an object, by which I mean that, in contrast to verbs like "think", "hope", and so forth, the ascription of *reasons* to the subject may have no role to play. There are many objects and events that we naturally desire, want, and fear; and the question does not arise as to *why* this should be so. Accordingly, if somebody seriously wanted an answer to the question of why we want food or sex or bodily comfort then we would begin to wonder whether he or she knew what these verbs mean; for we do not desire certain objects and outcomes for reasons, because fulfilling these desires is a not a means to some further end. Moreover, this question-asker could also be said to lack any notion of *disposition*—in this case a grasp of the fact that creatures are naturally disposed— naturally *designed*—to want certain kinds of object and outcome. Finally, all these non-cognitive verbs fan out from desire; for it is necessary that something is being desired in every case (e.g. to fear X implies we desire its absence, whereas to desire X may not mean that we fear X's absence). In parallel to this, the cognitive class of attitude verbs fans out from belief, in the sense that hoping, expecting, and so forth, all imply that something is believed, whereas believing something implies no hopes or expectations.

How does all this bear on questions about theory of mind development? Remember that we refer to what the child is acquiring as a grasp of "belief-*desire* psychology", because we can neither explain nor predict an agent's behaviour if we are only in possession of facts about his or her purely cognitive orientation to some possible state of affairs. If we are in the business of behavioural prediction, it is no use knowing what somebody believes, expects, and so forth if we don't also know what he or she *wants*. We are not in a position to predict what Harriet will do unless we assume that she wants to drive her car. (She may instead want an excuse to stay home.) Next, as we have just seen, for a child to grasp this relation between believing, desiring, and doing, he or she will need some understanding of disposition, because to understand that others are subject to desire must be to understand something about what kinds of thing they are naturally disposed to desire; while understanding *this* is to grasp something about other agents that is sub-cognitive, something about their essential needs rather than something about their epistemic and rational natures.

There is a paradox looming: our long-term and short-term dispositions fuel our desires and thus our actions, but they are something over which we have no control. Dispositions give us desires and desires are a core component of volition and volition implies "voluntary" which implies "free"; and yet dispositions are what cause us to desire things—*willy nilly*. Well this paradox is not one I am not about to resolve! It is the "problem of free will" itself: that we can will X and that only free agents can will anything, but what we will, is not determined by our will.

Accordingly the first conclusion of this sub-section is that for a child to acquire a theory of mind (in the sense close to "theory of agency") he or she must know what it means to have a disposition. Understanding why people do what they do does not only require us to understand others' representational capacities and their role in so-called practical syllogisms: it requires understanding something about causes rather than reasons, what *drives* us towards this or that, whether we like it or not.

The second conclusion is one that emerges not only from this sub-section but also from much of Part 1. It is that, although desires can take goals and be directed towards situations, they are rooted in something entirely non-representational. To be disposed to want a certain outcome is to be caused to have certain desires, and the causation of these desires cannot be understood as a representation of anything. To be thirsty is not to be in a representational state, and neither is having a taste for cheeseburgers or having left-wing sympathies. Although thoughts about cheeseburgers and basic human rights are representations, the mental *orientation* to them is not just another kind of representation.

Given this, it is wrong to equate "acquiring a theory of mind" with "acquiring a theory of mental representation" and equally mistaken to treat the former as a subset of the latter. To understand what it means for a propositional content to represent a possible state of affairs is necessary and central to a theory of mind; but there is much of a non-representational character that has also to be grasped. We have just discussed the causal aspect—the determination of the agent's mental states by his or her motives. The other, unambiguously non-representational aspect of agency—whose three features were listed at the end of the previous section—will be given a full treatment when we have surveyed the landscape of options for how the *representational* face of theory of mind might develop.

3.3(ii) Developmental theories of the representing mind:
Surveying the options

In this sub-section I will consider five views of theory of mind development, taking this to be synonymous with the representational aspect of the theory. I will not identify them explicitly with particular theorists because I am painting with a very broad brush and cannot do justice to their complexities; better to leave the attribution tacit than to saddle people with over-simple views. I will touch only lightly on their empirical strengths and weaknesses, concentrating instead on their conceptual claims. The first four are very close to accounts that can be found in the literature.

The question I will test these theories against is: How do children come to apply mental state predicates—such as "thinks that X"—to themselves and to others? I leave open, for the time being, the question of whether such predicate-application could be achieved outside a public language, coming round to it at the end.

- Reflection+analogy[58]. On this view, when children reflect on their own mental lives they find themselves (i) being committed to the truth of certain outcomes, (ii) erecting imaginary objects and states of affairs for their own amusement, (iii) anticipating that events will turn out a certain way, (iv) having an unshakeable certainty that something is so. Accordingly, when children hear adults talking about (i) "thinking" (*qua* believing) (ii) "pretending" (iii) "expecting", and (iv) "knowing", the meaning of these verbs is transparent to them. And of course children are well placed to think of other people as engaging in these mental acts simply because they know others to be people like themselves. The assumption is that having the reflective capacity to pick out these varieties of mental act from their own case is sufficient for children to understand their occurrences in others and thus to acquire the labels for them. Children only have to recruit their skills in reasoning by analogy, projecting from self to other.

Views of this kind are vulnerable on two fronts. In the first place, we find the assumption that the meanings of natural language expressions, such as "think", are grounded in the private experience of turning the attention inwards and encountering the mental act of thinking, with the content of this mental event giving the word its meaning. If the inner eye did not encounter these *sui generis* mental events then terms such as "think" would have no meaning. However, those who are convinced by Wittgenstein's so-called "private language argument" (actually: *anti* private language argument) would reject this view. The private language argument seems to establish that the meanings of linguistic expressions cannot be fixed by reference to the "private" experiences of the speakers of the language, because if this were so there would be no possibility of incorrect (and therefore of *correct*) application of the term: whatever seems to be the correct application of the term will *be* the correct application. Relatedly, it would make intersubjective agreement about the meaning of words impossible to achieve: instead there would be a private "meaning" in the mind of each member of the speech community. Whether a term has been used correctly, Wittgenstein claimed, is determined by public practices not by reflection on one's mental life. If this argument is correct then it just cannot be the case the children acquire the meaning of mental state predicates by reflecting on what it is like to undergo certain experiences.

This Wittgensteinian position provides one of the motivations behind the so-called "theory-theory" view of mental state terms[59]. On this view, mental predicates do not capture natural mental kinds—the cutting of the mental world at its joints—but capture instead a form of conceptualisation in which humans have to engage in the interests of a successful social life. Furthermore, it is worth mentioning that the position is thoroughly compatible with the mental holism discussed in Part 1.1; while the reflection+analogy view is compatible with the LOT doctrine insofar as it implies a "realist" view of mental kinds.

The second kind of objection focuses on how individuals are picked out as the "arguments" of mental state predicates; how, that is, the child is able to ascribe "thinks" to "I" and to "mummy" or indeed to anybody else. Remember, that what is distinctive about the reflection+analogy view is the claim that children *first* ascribe the predicate to themselves and *then* learn, by a process of analogy, to ascribe it to other people—all the time assuming that initially they are able to ascribe the predicate to themselves *and to themselves alone*. But is it *possible* that individuals should be able to ascribe a mental state predicate only to themselves? There are reasons for thinking it is not. As P.F. Strawson (1959)[60] has argued, to ascribe a predicate to oneself entails the ability to ascribe it to others: the "I" in "I think" would be empty if "I" being the thinker were the only conceivable option. We must see this as an instance of the Generality Constraint, in which ascribing a single ability to a subject implies crediting him or her with a network of other, generalisable abilities: ascribing the predicate to "I" entails the ability to apply it to others. Moreover—and here there is common cause again with the private language argument—we need to focus on the assumption that ascribing a mental state to oneself means one's undergoing a purely private experience. "If," Strawson writes (1959, p.100), "in identifying the things to which states of consciousness are to be ascribed, private experiences are all one has to go on then, just for the very reason as that for which there is, from one's own point of view, no question of telling that private experience is one's own, there is no question of telling that a private experience is another's. All private experiences, all states of consciousness will be mine, i.e. no one's". In other words, there are no possible grounds on which "pre-analogy" children can think "I am thinking" if introspection is all they have to go on; for they are not in a position to classify that experience as their own if there can be no thoughts about other experiencers. And even if these children did, by some miracle, acquire a conception of thinking from reflection on their own private experiences alone how, could a conception grounded in this way *ever be applied to others*?

Just a word about what "ascribing to oneself" means. That there must be the possibility of ascribing thoughts to other subjects does not imply that one could *wrongly* identify oneself as a thinker. The fact that first-person ascription implies a capacity for third-person ascription does not mean that one, as it were, might have the mental experience *first* and then hunt round for a subject of it, alighting perhaps on oneself: "There is thinking going on somewhere. Ah, it's me."

So there is both immunity from error in the self-ascription of mental predicates and a background capacity for ascribing these predicates to others as well as to the self. The reflection+analogy view makes the error of claiming that there can be the former without the latter.

- *Hypothesis-testing*[61] This view is an essentially empiricist option. It is that children do not possess innate conceptions of what it means to represent mentally. Rather, being faced with the problem of explaining why people behave in the way they do, children utilise their general capacities for hypothesis construction and testing and arrive at the theory that is *the* theory of mind. On this position, our mental-theoretical insights are something that each developing human *arrives at independently*, rather in the way in which different research teams will produce similar theories because they are testing ideas against the same Nature.

Like scientists, children begin with theories that are too simple (e.g. that people will always take the action that best fulfils their desires) and then, having gleaned new evidence (about, say, where people mistakenly search for things), they construct more complex theories (e.g. people take the action that *would* fulfil their desires *if* their beliefs were true). Indeed, proponents of this view sometimes take the parallel between the child and the scientist quite literally. Gopnik and Wellman, for example, write (1992, p.156): "Nevertheless, recent evidence suggests that during the period of three to four years many children are in a state of transition between two theories, similar, say, to the fifty years between the publication of *De Revolutionibus* and Kepler's discovery of elliptical orbits." Specifically, 3-year-old children are supposed to have constructed for themselves the false theory that mind mirrors the current state of reality, variously dubbed a "cognitive connection" *theory* (Flavell, 1988), a "situation" *theory* (Perner, 1991), a "Gibsonian" *theory* (so much the worse for James Gibson!) (Astington & Gopnik, 1991), and a "copy" *theory* (Wellman, 1991). What leads them to abandon this kind of theory is that it fails to fit the data[62].

There are two major problems with the hypothesis-testing view. Each shows why the analogy between the developing child and the scientist is a bad one.

First, no matter how much one may like to think of science as a social affair determined by tacit conventions and informal frameworks, original research is a matter of testing conjectures against Nature rather than against the conceptual system in which the scientist is operating. Of course, novice scientists have to acquire a body of knowledge from others, but original research involves asking a question that only Nature can answer. This is not the situation in which children find themselves. There is no *logical* bar against the claim that children of 4 abandon an earlier theory because it cannot explain the data; but the very people whose behaviour the old theory failed to explain *are in possession* of the superior theory. There *is* a regnant theory. The theory of mind theory, in other words, is "in the conceptual system". Well, if this theory is in the conceptual system then why say that it is constructed by each child *de novo*? Young children *may* perform this feat, but we do not have to assume they do any more than we have to assume that every clothed person is a tailor.

A related worry concerns both what it means to be "following a theory" and the process of abandoning one theory for another. In the first place, it is absurd to say that a creature is "following" a theory, or has "adopted" a theory, if that creature's information-processing system is actually *causing* it to behave in accordance with what we, as observers, like to call a theory. (Recall the remarks made in 2.6 in answer to Objection 3.) Otherwise we could explain, say, the behaviour of homing pigeons in terms of their theories about the azimuth of the sun and about geomagnetic forces. In other words, a theory—in the sense that is in play for the holders of this view—is something that is adopted *for a reason*, something that the holder could in principle *justify*. Moreover, the impressive, across-the-board consistency with which 3-year-old children fail theory-of-mind tasks does not necessarily imply that they are in the grip of a false theory. Failure of this kind could equally be due to the fact—if it is a fact—that all the tasks make similar processing demands. I will have much more to say about this latter possibility in later sections.

I now turn to the second problem with the child–scientist analogy. Why did scientists in the, say, Middle Ages have less adequate scientific theories than ours? Certainly not because their brains were less evolved: not because their relatively inadequate information-processing systems made them incapable of framing better hypotheses. It was because it is in the nature of scientific theories to evolve over time. Now we can ask the parallel question: Why do children of 4 have better theories than children of 3? In this case it seems entirely possible that the younger children were, unlike medieval scientists, *simply incapable of entertaining* the more complex theory. In short, the hypothesis-testing view only makes sense on the assumption that children's capacities for information-processing do not develop.

- *The meta-representational insight*[63] On this view, the (4-year-old) child's ability to understand the core components of belief-desire psychology is symptomatic of a broader understanding—the development of the meta-representational insight. This is an insight into what it means for one item (a thought, a sentence, a drawing, a photograph, a scale model, a mental image, a memory-trace) to stand in a representing relation to something in the world, a relation captured by Frege's famous distinction between "reference" and "sense". Reference is the object or situation to which the thought is directed while "sense" captures the way in which the mind represents that object or situation. The planet Venus, in Frege's example, has been for some people the referent of two senses—the "Morning Star" and the "Evening Star". Integral to an understanding of the reference–sense relation is the knowledge that representations can (a) misrepresent their referent and (b) be interpreted in different ways. Accordingly, those who adopt this view regard the grasp of mental representation as a *special case* of adequately representing the representing relationship, hence the term *meta*-representation.

This theory makes very clear predictions about the nature of the cognitive transition between 3 and 4 years of age. It claims, for example, that *any* task requiring the meta-representational insight will be failed by 3-year-old children, not only tasks that have a mentalistic content. Let us first consider tasks that do have a mentalistic content . In their "false belief" experiment, which I mentioned just now, Heinz Wimmer and Josef Perner (1983) told children a story about a boy who puts some chocolate away at place A and departs. During his absence, his mother moves the chocolate from place A to place B; the child returns wanting some chocolate. Children can then (after some control questions) be asked questions about where this protagonist now thinks the chocolate is located and about where he will look for it (these two questions are normally answered in the same way). Broadly speaking, children under 4 years of age say that he will look at place B (where the chocolate is now located unbeknown to the protagonist), whereas older children will say correctly that he will look at place A. The standard account of this difference is that the younger child does not understand what it means to have a false belief—a mental representation that the agent takes as corresponding to reality but which does not, in fact, thus correspond. The present theory must predict that a similar pattern of failure will be found when the medium of representation is not mental.

This prediction is moderately well confirmed by 3-year-old's failure on the "false photograph" devised by Deborah Zaitchik (1990). In this, the experimenter takes a Polaroid photograph of something (e.g. a cat on the mat), after which the situation is changed (the cat departs and a dog sits down) while the photograph is still developing. The child is then asked what the photograph will show when it is developed. Younger children say "a dog on the mat" (the time-2 state). I say that Zaitchik's study confirms this hypothesis only "moderately well" because the false photograph task is, in fact, a little harder than the false-belief task in which a change of situation at time-2 renders the *belief* of a protagonist false: the false belief and the false photograph tasks do not correlate.

Better evidence is provided in recent experiment by Lindsay Parkin and Josef Perner (in press) in which the medium was again non-mental but the fact of *mis*representation was unmistakable. The authors argued that the photograph in Zaitchik's experiment did not actually misrepresent a situation: it was simply out-of-date. A signpost pointing in the wrong direction, by contrast, is indeed a non-mental medium that nevertheless misrepresents. Parkin and Perner found that false belief performance correlated well with a task in which children had to say what a misleading signpost showed. Despite their knowing that a princess was in her castle and not in the wood, 3-year-olds said a pictured princess on a signpost pointing to the wood showed her in the *castle*.

There are, however, other ways of explaining this parallel which do not require reference to meta-representation, as we shall see. Moreover, the claim that under-4s have no conception of the relationship between photographs or models and the physical states they represent is highly controversial[64]; and the claim that they have no grasp of the representing function of language is both controversial and implausible[65].

This theory makes, therefore, clear though controversial predictions. But a theory can do this while being conceptually flawed. I believe there is indeed a conceptual flaw in the claim that understanding mental representation is a special case of understanding representation *per se*. It is a very simple flaw: to say this is to ignore the fact that mental contents (at least those in play within the theory of mind arena) can only be construed as the objects of propositional attitudes. For example, the protagonist's mental representation in the false belief task ("at A") must be understood as a representation *to whose truth the protagonist is committed*; and if a child does not understand this he or she has no conception of belief at all and certainly no resources for predicting what the protagonist will do on the basis of the representation. And so it is certainly wrong to equate the way in which (say) a signpost may misrepresent and the way in which a subject's thought may misrepresent; for there can be no commitment to truth nor indeed anything attitudinal in the signpost case. Additionally, the fact that representations can be interpreted in different ways would seem to capture the very respect in which non-mental representation and mental ones *diverge*. The mental representation that is the object of my propositional attitude (e.g. I believe {there's fish for supper}) is not "up for interpretation": its content is *exhausted* by my mental orientation to it. Indeed this may even be true of mental images, which some claim cannot be re-interpreted by the subjects[66].

I need to be a little more explicit about the difficulties with the meta-representational insight view. My argument is that the following two views are difficult to hold in tandem:

(1)   Between the ages of 3 and 4 years children gain a grasp of what it means for something to stand in a representing relationship to something else, with mental representation being a special case of this.

(2)   The fundamental respect in which mental representations differ from non-mental ones is that the former involve propositional attitudes—that understanding belief requires understanding what it is for an agent to be committed to the truth of his or her representation, in the present case.

If you subscribe to (2) then it is unnatural to subscribe to the view that a grasp of mental representation is a special case of grasping representation *per se*; for it implies that a child could have a perfectly good grasp of what it means for a sign or picture to misrepresent and no idea at all of how false beliefs lead to false behaviour. So what of the correlations that exist between performance on tasks such as Parkin and Perner's signpost task and performance on the false belief task? There are a number of accounts that could be given. One is that children come to understand what it means for a sign to mislead on the analogy with a person misleading—by being mistaken or by lying. Alternatively (the alternative for which I shall argue later) children who fail one task tend to fail the other because in both cases failure means the child's telling the experimenter *what he or she knows* and ignoring questions about what somebody will do or about what something shows.

There is a further reason why understanding mental representation cannot be construed as a special case of understanding representation *per se*—one discussed towards the end of the previous subsection. It is that understanding how beliefs function in the mental economy cannot be achieved without understanding how something that is *non*-representational functions in the mental economy. Beliefs are representations to whose truth the agent is committed and on the basis of which he or she will act; but to understand this is to understand how they relate to desires and dispositions. This fact drives a wedge between what is needed for acquiring a theory of mental representation and what is needed for acquiring a theory of representation *per se*.

This kind of difficulty makes theories that emphase the *sui generis* nature of mental representation more attractive; and this is a mark of our third theory.

- *Hard-wiring*[67]. This is a nativist view which uses the word "theory" in a way far removed from its usage in the hypothesis-testing view. In this sense of "theory", the visual system may be said to have theories of such things as contour and size invariance, or the language acquisition device to have theories about left- versus right-branching sentence structures and binding principles. In other words "theory" here means something very close to "system for parsing perceptual inputs to yield an interpretation". Unlike the "theory" referred to in the hypothesis-testing position this theory is modular: it is a *sui-generis*, informationally encapsulated input system (on which see Fodor, 1983).

The assumption behind this view is a highly plausible one, namely that understanding the representing function of mind is something too important to be left to the vagaries of learning and too under-determined by the evidence for it be plausible that general learning principles would so easily light on it. We do not have to learn how to see or learn how to hear; these things are hard-wired so we do not have to waste time acquiring them. Much the same goes for our theory of mind (see Fodor,

1987, pp.132–133). We parse behavioural inputs in such as way as to yield the interpretation "subject→attitude→content".

Although—as I shall argue in the next section—the hard-wiring view may explain rather less than it appears to explain, it does not appear to be as vulnerable to conceptual objections as were the previous three positions. It does, however, require commitment to the LOT doctrine.

The problem is this. The hard-wiring theorist wants to hold on to the view that the theory of mind operates independently from other processing systems. Supporters of this position claim that this theory matures during the second half of the second year of life, although they are forced to posit "pre-cursors" to theory of mind in order to accommodate earlier cases of "mentalising", such as joint-attention between about 8 and 12 months, as we shall see. In any event, they must reject the claim that understanding the subject→attitude→content triad is an essentially *linguistic* achievement, because if it were then it would cease to be modular in their sense. The question then becomes: What kind of evidence *forces* us to explain the behaviour of preverbal children in terms of this triad, in terms of a subject's attitudes to mental contents? What kind of non-verbal behaviour, that is, would compel us to conclude that this child has a grasp of mental orientations to *propositional* contents?

Alan Leslie (1987) has argued that a toddler's being able to comprehend the pretend actions of another person (e.g. mummy pretending a banana is a telephone) is such evidence. On this view, if the toddler is to make sense of what his or her mother is doing he or she must be thinking: mummy→pretend→*"that the banana is a telephone"*. I think a case can be made, however, for denying that this behaviour can *only* become intelligible to the toddler through his or her achieving such an imputation. Here is one way of doing so.

We start from the assumption that a toddler's own experience of pretending enables him or her to pick out pantomimed acts when seeing them performed by others. The experience of pantomiming (e.g. "drinking" from a wooden brick or "driving" the brick round a corner) enables the toddler to perceive a certain class of actions as being the kind of actions he or she performs when amusing himself or herself. This is not identical to the reflection+analogy view because it is not the view that the child acquires a *concept* of a certain kind of propositional attitude by reflecting on his or her own mental episodes and then projecting this on to other people. The child is not exercising a concept here because one need assume no grasp of how the pretending attitude is related to other kinds of propositional attitude, such as believing or knowing. The child does know however that it is possible to pantomime—to act something out when the usual object (a real telephone in this case) is absent. (I have much more to say about non-conceptual projection of this kind in my Coda.)

Second, somebody who is a pretender will inevitably have the ability to perceive how different kinds of objects afford different kinds of pretence, and this perception is very likely to extend beyond the acts that the pretender him or herself has performed in the past or intends to perform in the future. In other words, although it may not yet have occurred to the toddler to pretend that a banana is a telephone, he or she will probably know what is going on when seeing the pantomime of telephoning being applied to a banana. The toddler has to know three things: (a) what it is to pantomime, (b) what it is to telephone, and (c) that the other person is a pantomiming agent. It is not at all clear that knowing these three requires the toddler to impute the propositional representation "that the banana is a telephone" (governed by a pretending attitude) to another person. It is not at all clear, in fact, that the toddler has to regard his or her mother as having anything in particular in mind. It *does* of course require that the toddler regards the other person as an agent, but, as I shall be arguing at length, ascriptions of agency to others fall well short of ascriptions of thoughts to others: the notion of agency is more primitive than the notion of thinker. (Obviously, this claim needs a proper defence; and I admit that my scepticism about Leslie's views is only plausible if the claim is correct.)

The problem with hard-wiring views of this kind is that they depend on the assumption that there are forms of non-verbal behaviour—pretending is the prime example—that can only become intelligible to observers if the observer imputes propositions (i.e. *that* {something is the case}) to another individual. So it would seem that a strong and principled case has to be made for this view if it is not to invite the kind of debunking attempt made in the previous paragraph. The only way in which the supporter of this kind of hard-wiring view can be quite invulnerable to such debunking attempts is by subscribing to the LOT doctrine, because on that doctrine all perceptions of agency in others have to be tricked out in a propositional form. But if one is unconvinced by the LOT doctrine—as I argued in Part 1 that we should be—then this commitment will be too much to ask.

So there is at least a question mark over hard-wiring views that take the theory as an encapsulated module, and therefore as something independent of competence in natural language.

- *Linguistic hard-wiring.* Here one accepts the case for nativism while adding the claim that "thought" is an essentially linguistic notion, thereby producing the view that the innate theory is indissociable from the linguistic system. This is not to deny that preverbal children and some animals know that others are—or behave towards others in accordance with their being—intenders, attenders, agents, and experiencers of emotional states; but this falls far short of any conception of others as *thinkers*; far short of a grasp of the "subject→attitude→content" triad. This is not just to say *ex cathedra* "animals can't have beliefs"; but it is to say "animals can only manifest beliefs through using symbols" (see Russell, 1992, pp.507–509).

What inspires this view of thought? Each of the previous four views was based on broadly philosophical assumptions—on Descartes' view of consciousness, on one reading of what Adam Morton (1980, p.10) called the "theory-theory" view of mental types, on a reading Frege's sense–reference distinction, on Fodor's Platonic view of concepts, and this fifth view is no exception. It is traceable to Donald Davidson's (1975; Russell, 1984c, on Davidson and psychology) Frege-inspired account of linguistic meaning and specifically to his claim "that a creature cannot have thoughts unless it is the interpreter of the speech of another" with "a thought [being] defined by a system of belief" (1975, p.9). In a nutshell, Davidson's theory of meaning led him to propose that only a language user can have the concept of belief. To this he added the second premiss that only a behaver who has the concept of belief can have beliefs[68] and from these two premisses the conclusion follows that only a language user can *have* beliefs (Russell, 1982a, for discussion of this view in the context of animal and human learning).

The first premiss is of most relevance to us—the premiss *that only a language user can have the concept of belief*. Indeed I can say what I need to say while rejecting the second premiss (that only individuals with the concept of belief can *have* beliefs).

In order for a child to understand the speech (or sign language) of another he or she must be in possession of a theory about the conditions under which sentences are true. The child must, in other words, be able to fill in the blank in the following: "An utterance of sentence *s* by a speaker at place *x* at time *t* is true if and only if ...". But of course a sentence's *being* true and the speaker's *holding* it to be true are not the same thing, because the speaker may have a false belief about the truth of his or her uttered sentence. This is where, according to Davidson, we find the necessity for a concept of belief entering the picture. Without a concept of belief to—in Davidson's fine metaphor—"take up the slack" between them, no distinction could be made by the child between held truth and objective truth. And so the conclusion is that only language understanders can have the concept of belief.

But it can be objected that all that has been established here is that language users *must* have the concept of belief, that interpreting the speech of another requires this concept to be in play: it does not demonstrate that *only* those who interpret the language of another could have that concept (see Bishop, 1980). Let us accept (for the time being) that in terms of the strict logic of Davidson's argument this is correct; indeed holders of the straight (modular and language-independent) hard-wiring view could say the argument shows that having an innate belief-desire psychology is necessary for the child to understand the role of belief in language. But the nagging problem with *this* view, as we have seen, is that it has to give a satisfactory account of what a "concept of belief" would be like (something that takes up the slack, remember, between held belief and truth) in a creature whose only conception of the "held beliefs" of others is one expressed in terms of their nonverbal behaviour, in terms of what people do (rather than say) when exposed to different kinds of information. But if this is to be a concept of *belief* (rather than some grasp of how information, perception, and action are linked) then it must involve a conception of others as being committed to the truth of mentally represented propositions; and one can only make sense of this possibility by positing LOT, as I have just argued. And so somebody who is not happy with the LOT doctrine will tend to find the Davidsonian view sympathetic.

The linguistic hard-wiring view is the one I find the most sympathetic, but in what follows I am not going to be strongly committed to the "linguistic" part of it; in fact some of my views are compatible with those of Leslie. I will, in fact, assume for the sake of the subsequent discussion that nativism about the representational aspects of theory of mind is a sensible option and then discuss the developmental relation between this and agency. Predictably, I will try to show that there can be no conception of mind in subjects who have innate conceptions of mental representation but who are not agents. Agency is something that has to be experienced "first hand"; it does not reduce to a hard-wired theory.

3.3(iii) No "theory" without the experience of agency
In the view of many, opting for a nativist account of theory of mind development is essentially the end of the story, in the sense that this is supposed to make the explanatory framework complete, and so the empirical task can become that of specifying the nature of these innate mechanisms.

This has come to mean advancing on two fronts, namely, "fractionating" the theory of mind mechanism or "ToMM" (Leslie & Thaiss's, 1992, term) and describing mechanisms that are developmental "pre-cursors" to ToMM. Essential to this research programme are the dual assumptions that persons who suffer from autism lack ToMM (or at least that there is delay or deviance in its development) and that the mechanism matures in normal children some time after 18 months of age. Thus, in the first place, Leslie and Thaiss (1992) have argued that because autistic subjects generally perform well on Zaitchik's (1990, see earlier) false photograph task while failing the false belief task, their capacity for "decoupling" first-order from second- order representations is intact, although their mechanism for computing propositional attitudes is not. These mechanisms are, in turn, distinguished from "the selection processor", which enables the subject, in tasks like false belief and false photograph, to select the appropriate sources of information from the narrative[69]; this is immature in normal 3-year-olds, they argue. In the second place (in search of precursors to ToMM), Simon Baron-Cohen (1995) has noted that whereas normally-developing children begin sharing visual attention with others at around 9 months (this continues to develop until about 18 months: Butterworth & Jarrett, 1991), children with autism do not, broadly speaking. He concludes from these facts that persons with autism have deficits in—maybe even "lack"—a pre-cursor mechanism called The Shared Attention Mechanism or "SAM".

How is agency located within such a framework? One may look for a disorder in which one of the defining symptoms is a failure of executive control and then name the mechanism that the sufferers lack. Accordingly, Baron-Cohen, Cross, Crowson, and Robertson (in press) propose that people who suffer from Tourettes' Syndome[70] lack "The Intention Editor": they do things that they do not intend to do—or at least would not normally want to do. Alternatively, one may reason from first principles about the computational architecture a child will need if he or she is to understand agency and postulate distinct mechanisms that must mature and interact in given ways. Thus, Leslie (in press) has proposed the 'Theory of Body Mechanism' (ToBy) which parses events involving the *mechanical* properties of agents; and he makes some interesting claims about how this must relate to ToMM$_1$ (parsing agents' relations to actions) and ToMM$_2$ (parsing agents' relations to attitudes).

It is worth noting, in passing, that both Leslie and Baron-Cohen see themselves as doing a kind of theoretical neuropsychology. They both assume that their proposed mechanisms will sooner or later be tied to brain loci and circuitry.

I will set to one side the question of whether using nouns ("The X Mechanism") rather than verbs ("doing X") to describe mental functions actually buys the theorist anything very substantial, and say why *even if we knew for certain that the brain were peopled with these innate modules* (ToMM, SAM, and ToBy , not to mention their pal EDD[71]) we would still fall well short of an account of how children develop a theory of mind.

I will proceed in two stages. First, an account of theory of mind development must cover both its *syntax* and its *semantics*; and the hard-wiring accounts just described cover only the former. Second, although an ability to parse mental categories via innate mechanisms might exist in systems that are not agents, such systems would not be manifesting *mental* knowledge, *given the dependency of subjectivity and self-awareness on agency.*

I turn first, then, to the distinction between syntax and semantics, beginning, reasonably enough, with the distinction as it is drawn by students of language acquisition. Furthermore, let us assume—to parallel my assumption at the end of the previous subsection—that language acquisition requires innate knowledge of grammatical categories (nouns, verbs, etc.) and of permissible sentential structures. The immediate question then becomes whether *semantics* is required if the child is to map his or her innate knowledge onto the language to which he or she is exposed. Steven Pinker (1987) has argued that this is *not* possible without semantic cues: that the child will never be able to map his or her innate knowledge of, say, the noun category onto words such as "tree" and "boy" unless he or she employs semantic rules-of-thumb such as "most nouns refer to things and many refer to agents". Without this "semantic bootstrapping", as Pinker calls it, the bridge could never be built between innate formal knowledge and a particular language. Proponents of *"syntactic* bootstrapping" (Lasnik, 1988), on the other hand, argue that semantic generalisations of this kind are not necessary—because noting regularities in the distribution of words within sentences (e.g. that words like "tree" and "boy" are often preceded by closed-class words like "the") is sufficient for the child to learn which words are nouns in English.

Syntactic bootstrapping may seem implausible at first blush, but it is certainly not impossible. Indeed, might not a disorder exist in which people can parse sentences but in which their semantic system makes no contact with their syntactic skills (passing over the awkward question of how we would find evidence for their syntactic successes)? They have "the concept of an object", "the concept of an agent", and so forth but have no idea that "tree" refers to a kind of object and "boy" refers to a kind of agent: they are just "nouns". Victims of this disorder would obviously be unable to frame verbal thoughts and to understand speech. Their syntactic capacity would be *empty*.

Now imagine a kind of syntactic bootstrapping theory that is supposed to explain how children come to understand agency. The term "syntactic" is justified in the sense that the subject is supposed to be parsing the formal structure of agency episodes without accessing what it *means* to be an agent, with "what it means to be an agent" being what I discussed at length in the early sections of Part 2 under the four features; namely, monitoring, self-determination, non-observational knowledge, and incorrigibility. This "meaning" is a *first-person* meaning, an *experience* of being in control and of knowing immediately that one is willing.

In this syntactic theory, there is "hard-wiring for the direct perception of intention and goal directedness" (Leslie & Happé, 1989, p.210; and see also Premack, 1990). What constitutes the inputs to this system are invariant behavioural structures, such as the facial expressions indicative of startle and the bodily configurations indicative of reaching. This enables the child to parse the former as "reaction" and the latter as "action". What we may see the child as doing is, to modify one of Fodor's metaphors, putting one kind of input into a "reaction box" and another in an "action box"; rather as the language-learner in syntactic bootstrapping puts "tree" straight into a "noun box" and "run" straight into a "verb box" without semantic clues.

Remember, there is no quarrel being picked here with the view that such innate syntactic systems for parsing agency might exist. Indeed it is implausible that infants should have to *learn* to parse the behaviour of others as being intentional or otherwise. My point is that a *purely* syntactic ability in this domain is *empty*—a claim I will now spell out.

Imagine "The Mentaliser", a purely syntactic engine for parsing mental kinds and a close relative of "The Receiver" introduced in Part 2. Like The Receiver, The Mentaliser has no capacity for monitoring and reversing its actions and so it is not an agent—in the present terms. It sees somebody yawning and puts this input into its "non-intentional box", sees somebody putting a banana to her head and talking into it and puts the input into its "pretend box", sees somebody leaving his house, turning on his heels to go back indoors and re-emerging with an umbrella and computes the propositional contents of his belief and desire attitudes. In short, The Mentaliser is a prodigious parser of mental categories which never experiences agency for itself.

On the present view, The Mentaliser can have no conception of other minds, a denial that follows naturally from the main line of argument in Part 2. I suggested there that the refractoriness thesis (whether expressed in the reversibility or the felt-resistance form) establishes that experiencing oneself as an agent is necessary for knowing oneself to be the subject of objective experience—is necessary, in the present terms, for subjectivity. And so, because The Mentaliser is not an agent it cannot possess subjectivity; and if it does not possess subjectivity then it makes little sense to say that it is a mind.

But could there not be minds without subjectivity? Is it not mere stipulation to say minds must "possess subjectivity"? In a sense it is, but it is a stipulation that all those interested in the development of human mentality would surely need to make. Moreover, I have made some attempt to be precise about what subjectivity amounts to in my discussion of mind$_0$ in Section 3.2(iii), arguing that there are three conditions for this—(i) being embodied, (ii) having immediate knowledge of oneself as the centre of responsibility for actions, and (iii) experiencing complete integration between what is willed and what is known. The Mentaliser fulfils only the first of these conditions. Indeed if I am right in arguing (3.1) that agency is necessary for experiences to be synthesised within one mind (mind$_s$) then the Mentaliser will not even meet this, more basic, condition for mentality.

But the point could be pressed that minds may be known entirely "from the outside", insisting that there are two distinct capacities—(1) being a mind (to which subjectivity may indeed be integral) and (2) knowing other minds (to which the possession of subjectivity is irrelevant). What could one reply to this?

Two things can be said: (a) that a conception of other minds depends on a conception of others as agents (and we can add "with dispositions" to this, as argued earlier) and (b) that conceiving of others as agents is only possible if one experiences one's own agency. The first of these claims is the less controversial by far. It is not merely that, as I said earlier, theory of mind experiments (at least those of the false belief variety) could equally well be called "theory of agency" experiments. It is also the case that one can hardly be said to have a grasp of the quintessentially mental state of belief without being able to regard beliefs as representations on the basis of which believers act. Moreover, there are quite obvious conceptual links between regarding others as rational and regarding them as agents; because to ascribe rationality to another person requires us to see them as "capable of assessing positions, of following out reasons, and possibly of being critical. All these things presuppose our not being merely passive in relation to putative objects of knowledge" (Hamlyn, 1990, p.148).

The second point (no conception of others as agents without first-person experience of agency) has to be correct if the account of agency for which I have been arguing throughout this book is correct. In Part 2, I argued, following O'Shaughnessy, that agency is known both non-observationally and incorrigibly, and earlier in Part 3 presented Schopenhauer's claim that knowledge of our actions is immediate, non-representational knowledge. These two claims overlap and together imply that the fact of being an agent is a *first-person fact*: it is not a fact about what happens to the body in acting, not a fact about what is on public view. This is captured by Thomas Nagel when he writes (1979, pp.189–190) of "a clash between the view of action from the inside and *any* view of it from the outside. Any external view of an act as something that happens ... seems to omit the doing of it."

Let us now return to our syntax–semantics distinction. If it is true that agency can only be known from the inside, then we have a clear view of what it means to say that parsing behavioural facts omits the semantics of agency and is, accordingly, empty. The Mentaliser's ability to code the syntax of agency—in terms of "colourless movements" (J.B. Watson's term)—would not count as a grasp of agency, because this depends on the experience of trying to achieve goals and of being in control of one's body and thus—the point I have been stressing—of one's immediate mental life. Similarly, a creature that never felt pain might be able to parse the syntax of pain from grimaces and suchlike; but its conception of pain would be empty.

There must indeed be question mark over whether The Mentaliser would even be able to entertain first-person thoughts. Even if we granted The Mentaliser a mind$_s$—dropping the condition that this requires agency—it is still only an apprehending rather than a willing subject; only the point at which inputs terminate. But if the position that I sketched after Janaway (1989) is correct—if, that is, self-hood requires the *co-reference* of "I" in "I will" and "I perceive/think/know ..."—then The Mentaliser will be incapable of entertaining first-person thoughts even if it did, *per impossibile*, develop a form of subjectivity.

We have, then, a substantial conclusion: *no creature can acquire a theory of mind unless it is an agent.* This is obviously a conceptual claim; but it is one that naturally inspires the hypothesis that inadequate agency in early childhood will tend to result in inadequate conceptions of mental states. This will be discussed in the context of the evidence in a later section. But next, I need to say something about the transition from a pre-theoretical to a theoretical grasp of mentality.

3.3(iv) A pre-theoretical understanding of mentality
Let us put to the side for now the question of when children gain a truly theoretical conception of mind (as described at the start of 3.3) and consider instead what a *pre*-theoretical understanding of mind would be like. I have just argued that experiencing agency is *necessary* to developing a theory of mind; but what is it *sufficient* for?

Some developmental psychologists torture themselves on the horns of the following non-dilemma: if children are not little mentalists then they must surely be little Behaviourists whose understanding of others' actions consists solely in their ability to code the relations between environmental stimuli and the responses made to them. The escape from this imaginary problem usually takes one of two forms. Subscribers to modular nativism posit, as we have seen, various kinds of "pre-cursors to ToMM"; while those who bridle at this mechanistic way of thinking tend to argue (i) that affective relatedness to other persons is so fundamental a fact about human life as to transcend the cognitive domain, (ii) that infants are naturally resonant to the mental and emotional states of others and so (iii) the "problem of other minds" is not something that they require a dry, behavioural calculus to solve[72].

However, the alternative to saying that children have a full grasp of the subject→attitude→content triad is not saying that they conceive of others non-mentalistically; because there is no impediment to the view that they perceive agency in others—that they regard some observations of others as observations of their agency[73]—and to regard others as agents is to regard them as mental kinds, at least in some minimal sense. (Behaviorism is, in fact, a highly sophisticated option available only to those with sufficient imagination to slough off their human nature.)

What I need to do is to silence the alarm bells ringing in some minds at hearing the phrase "perceive agency in others". For if this means ascribing a mental category to others on the basis of first-person experience, is this not identical to the reflection+analogy position which I rejected earlier on the grounds that a child could never be in the position to ascribe a mental predicate to him or herself and to him or herself alone? It cannot be the case, I argued, that mental knowledge is first-person knowledge about oneself projected onto others by analogy to become third-person knowledge about others. To answer: there is all the difference in the world between (i) picking oneself out as the referent for a predicate {– "am an agent"} on the basis of observations of one's own agency and (ii) *experiencing* one's agency. Indeed, how could one ever "ascribe agency predicates to the self" *if the fact of agency is a non-representational fact?* Predicate ascription is not at issue.

The richness of the pre-theoretical child's perception of others' agency must be decided empirically; and many kinds of data will be relevant. For example, recent experiments by Andrew Meltzoff (1990) on 14-month-olds' ability to perceive when they are being imitated raises questions about how toddlers see the exercise of their own agency mirrored in the behaviour of others (see Campbell, 1995, for a discussion of what Meltzoff's findings tell us about development of the self). Specifically, his data are consistent with infants of this age being able to adopt a third-person perspective towards their actions, knowing what their actions look like when performed by another person. This not only implies self-awareness as the actions are being performed, but also that they are capable of projecting their agency onto others. But I will have nothing more to say about this, because the only point I need to press is that there is no impediment to the view that agency cannot be perceived in others unless one experiences the elements of agency first-hand—self-determination, goal-directedness and the non-observational, relatively incorrigible knowledge that it affords—all of which I spelt out in Part 2. None of these elements involves the ascription of predicates to the self and therefore the Cartesian problem of how one can ascribe a predicate to oneself before ascribing it to others does not arise.

We still need to get clearer, though, about how the present view differs from the reflection+analogy theory and how it resembles it. It differs in the following respect. On the present view, the pre-theoretical child possesses a $mind_0$ and accordingly possesses a mental life at whose core is the experience of action-based responsibility for what he or she perceives. Recall the earlier claim that possessing a $mind_0$ is equivalent to a primitive form of self-awareness. As I expressed it then (p.180), "in this sense, we have a mind because we take experiences to be our own and take ourselves to be finitely responsible for what we experience; while there must be the background possibility of having 'I'-thoughts—something that was not necessary for $mind_s$. What is at stake here is ownership[...] Agency enters the picture in three ways here ...: via bodily awareness, via the non-representational nature of responsibility, via the dependency of the apprehending self on a willing self."

What this implies is that, in order to have this experience, *the child does not have to exercise a network of concepts*. The child exercises no concepts, say, of pretending or of believing or of intending or of knowing, because he or she has no grasp of how these are related one to another. The child possesses, on this view, nothing that one might call "the concept of an agent" because one does not require the concept of agency to experience one's agency, the concept of control to experience oneself as controlling one's perceptual inputs, the concept of bodily awareness to possess bodily awareness, and so forth. One can, however, regard the pre-theoretical child as having first-person thoughts—thoughts about, say, what he or she wants and about how the world appears to him or her[74]. The claim I am making, then, is that although having these experiences—constitutive of $mind_0$—does not require the possession of concepts[75] it is sufficient for the pre-theoretical child to know that some observations of others are observations of agents, with questions about the richness of this awareness of others' agency having to yield to empirical answers. As I said earlier, to see another as an agent is to see the other as a mental kind, in at least some minimal sense. What I am taking to be an entirely empirical question—a question that cannot be answered *imaginatively*, in the style of fin de siècle theorists such as

James Mark Baldwin—is how rich is this awareness of others' mentality in fact.

Now note the *difference* between this position and that of the reflection+analogy theorist. Such a theorist has to say that there is no such thing as a "pre-theoretical child" because the child is not acquiring a theory as he or she develops mastery of concepts such as "intending", "thinking", and so forth. Rather, what is happening is that the child is using his or her reflective capacities to carve the mental world at its joints, a dissection that is more or less isomorphic to that which exists in the system of verbal concepts.

What this view shares with the reflection+analogy view is the claim that the pre-theoretical child can be assumed to have a mental life—he or she has a mind$_o$—*far richer than that which he or she is able to ascribe to others*. This is in stark contrast to the views of the theory-theorists in developmental psychology, taking this term to refer to those who believe that studying developing theories of mind holds the key to understanding how a representational mental life develops. They will claim that the child's access to his or her own mental life and mental powers is only a special case of the child's cognitive access to theoretical notions *transcending* the first and the third person. Thus Leslie and Happé (1989, p.210) write in a discussion of pretence that "solitary pretence comes out simply as the special case in which the agent of PRETEND is self". On the present view, by contrast, the child will only understand what it means for another to pretend if the child is him or herself a pretender. I will not debate the issue of whether being a pretender is *sufficient* for a perception of another as a pretender. I take the view that innate input systems for parsing agency events is necessary; but the issue is far from being decided.

So the essential claim here is that we can regard the pre-theoretical child as having a mind$_o$ and thus as being able, at the very least, to regard certain experiences as his or her own insofar as they are determined by his or her actions. What elements of this are projectible to others? Although this is an empirical question, something needs to be said about the necessity for the pre-theoretical child's perceiving others as *apprehenders* as well as agents. The child will experience the complete integration of himself or herself as apprehender and as a willer, while taking some observations of others to be observations of their agency; and this is consistent with the claim that the child is also perceiving others as apprehenders. But does this not imply an ability to see others as "representers"? Yes, but in a sense that falls short of grasping of the "subject→attitude→content" triad. To see others as acting on the basis of information to which they are exposed and as being able to change at will what information is available to them is to see others as enjoyers of particular experiences; it is not, as Perner (1991) is surely right to insist, even to see them as representing an object or a situation as being a certain way. To see others as having certain kinds of information available to them and as apprehending this information does not require one to regard them as having attitudes to contents. Ascription of agency would seem to require, then, some minimal conception of others' perspectives; indeed this is suggested by the intimate linkage between perspective-changing, the appearance–reality distinction, and agency discussed at length in Part 2.

It may help the reader to anchor these claims with some terminology—something that can be easily done by borrowing from Tomasello, Kruger, and Ratner (1993), whose position is rather similar to the present one. What I am calling the pre-theoretical child is, for these authors, an "intentional agent" who can understand the simple perspectives of others, as contrasted with "mental agents" who can understand others' beliefs. Where I part company with Tomasello et al., however, is in their assumption that the transition from intentional agency to mental agency takes place between 3 and 4 years of age. This is because (a) there is a case to be made for a *gradualist* view of this development and (b) because the experiments that purport to show such a shift between 3 and 4 years may be revealing instead a shift in agency itself. The second of these two claims will be thoroughly defended in the next section and the first will be defended now.

3.3(v) The case for "gradual dawning"[76]

In *On certainty* Wittgenstein wrote: "When we begin to believe anything, what we believe is not a single proposition, it is a whole system of propositions. (Light dawns gradually over the whole.)" (1969, §141). Beliefs are acquired, in other words, holistically, and, as he goes on to say in §144,

> The child learns to believe a host of things. I.e. it learns to act according to these beliefs. Bit by bit there forms a system of what is believed, and in that system some things stand unshakeably fast and some are more or less liable to shift. What stands fast does so, not because it is intrinsically obvious or convincing; it is rather held fast by what lies around it.

My unshakeable convictions, for example, that other people are sentient and that the earth existed many years before I was born are unshakeable not because I one day encountered them as glittering truths or because a mentor told me it was so: they are unshakeable by virtue of their roles within my belief system.

Wittgenstein was writing about *what* a child comes to believe with certainty. But could not this way of thinking be extended to the child's acquisition of certainty that people, including him or herself, have beliefs on which they generally act? (This extension of the Wittgensteinian thought is not, of course, something I am attempting merely as an *exercise*: it is consistent not only with the views expressed in the previous section but also with the holism about mental content that was being discussed in Part 1.)

Let us look at little closer at the metaphor of light dawning gradually over the whole. A town in daylight is the terminus of development—"belief-desire psychology"—at which all normally endowed humans will eventually arrive. Although the sun rises continuously, different features of the town will be illuminated at different times. A park will soon emerge from darkness while an alleyway between high buildings is illuminated much later; as, analogously, the ability to ascribe beliefs in some contexts will arrive earlier than the ability to ascribe them in others. And just as the fact of different parts of the town becoming illuminated at different times is no evidence against the sun's rise being continuous, so the appearance of discontinuities in the child's grasp of belief is no evidence against the view that the real situation is one of gradual development; these discontinuities could be artifactual products of our testing procedure. We might take the metaphor a little further and say that the height of buildings to the east of a plot of land corresponds to the processing demands placed on the child in a certain context; passing false belief tasks makes greater processing demands than passing true belief tasks, for example.

My aim now is to spell out how this metaphor applies to the broad facts of development. In fact the spelling out will be nothing more than a re-statement of the views of Andrew Woodfield (1993)—and a rather crude re-statement in fact which omits the lessons Woodfield draws from recent work on contexualist semantics[77].

My target is the assumption fundamental to much developmental work on theory of mind that there is a canonical test or set of tests for a subject's having the concept of belief. Let us imagine, with Woodfield, a dialogue between a mother of a child who has just turned 3 and a Socratic philosopher who holds that words have determinate meanings to be unearthed by enquiry and reflection (in contrast to Wittgensteinians who hold that utterances get their meanings from their role in particular "language games"). This Socratic philosopher's view is that what it takes to understand belief can be given a more or less precise, context-neutral definition; it should not be relativised to contexts.

Mother says that her daughter Susie has some understanding of belief because she consistently gives the correct answer to true belief questions. (When asked where Johnny thinks the chocolate is after Johnny sees it being placed in the green cupboard she points to the green cupboard.) The philosopher then points out to the mother that really this task fails to tap the essence of the belief concept and goes on to demonstrate Susie's failure on the false belief version (as in Wimmer & Perner, 1983). What happens next? Perhaps the mother accepts that her judgement was superficial and defers to the philosopher. But what if the mother was herself a philosopher? Indeed what if she was of a Wittgensteinian turn of mind? In this case she would deny that passing the true belief tasks is possible "without really understanding beliefs" (Wellman, 1991, p.23) and would insist that Susie does indeed have some grasp of belief, a grasp that is manifest *when the standards for what is to count as understanding belief are pitched low*. This can count as a low-grade understanding of belief because understanding belief admits of degrees and because the standards of what is to count as a grasp of belief can vary from low to high. The philosopher-mother will insist that she is not just being stubborn; it is, rather, that mothers who give way are really abandoning a low standard for a high standard when there is no reason for thinking that the higher standard *is the canonical standard*. It is better to stick to your guns. Like Crimmins (1992, pp.92–98; cited in Woodfield, 1993) she will say that having the concept of X is a matter of having the normal idea of X and that the conversational context fixes what is the normal idea: truth conditions vary with the tacitly adopted standards for normality.

The contextualist option is, then, open to us. Woodfield's next step is to say why it is actually a *preferable* one to the Socratic option and to its psychological manifestation as the view that the false belief task and its cognates constitute a set of acid tests for grasping the concept of belief.

First, all those who take the view that belief-desire psychology begins at around age 4 argue that the child develops a series of inadequate theories before this time. As we have seen, Wellman (1991), for example, proposes that children are Simple Desire Theorists at about 2, Copy Theorists at around 3, and full-blown Belief-Desire theorists at about 4, whereas Perner (1991) says that under 4s are Situation Theorists, with similar views being proposed by Gopnik and others. In fact, if you are going to say that acquiring the adult concept of belief is a matter of acquiring the full theory at a particular time then you have no choice but to do this, because the alternative is to say that before that time their judgements were determined by nothing! This is because, if you are wedded to the idea that "theories" inevitably underlie whatever consistency there is in children's judgements then you must postulate *proto-theories* as the precursors of the One True Theory to explain whatever consistency there is before this time.

The argument Woodfield fields against the proto-theory view and in favour of the contextualist-cum-gradual-dawning view is roughly this. If you are going to proliferate proto-theories then there had better be a strong motivation for doing so—given the pressures on any theorist to be parsimonious. Why postulate, as it were, a number of suns rising and falling over different parts of the city when one can explain the same patterns of light and shade by postulating one city and one sun? Accordingly, Woodfield claims that, when we look closely at the way in which one proto-theory is supposed to give way to another, their much-vaunted advantage in explaining the consistency of under-4s' behaviour melts away. Specifically, psychologists who postulate pre-cursor theories are faced with the following problems. If they admit that there can be graded understanding of the proto-theories (as does Wellman for one) then one child may subscribe to the Copy Theory, say, not at all, weakly, and strongly. There will also be overlaps, in which a child, say, has weak commitments to, say, both the Simple Desire Theory and to the Copy Theory, and at the same time. There is furthermore a question over whether a child can understand a theory without subscribing to it. For example do 3-year-olds understand the Simple Desire Theory but reject it; or have they forgotten about it? And, might not children sometimes be 'between theories', producing a pattern of answers that is explicable by neither of the adjacent theories? Well, if the theory-theorist accepts all this then, in Woodfield's words "the developmental chart starts to look embarrassingly complicated" (1993, p.6), so complicated indeed that the process of acquiring the concept of belief does indeed look like a graded one.

In short, what confidence do we have that the theory-theorist is not simply imposing his or her own explanatory schema onto pre-school development to give the appearance of discrete transitions followed by plateaux? We would have such confidence if it could be shown that the attribution of theories to the child were *constrained*. But, as Woodfield says (1993, p.7) apropos Henry Wellman, "Wellman's toolbox contains only three types of explanatory theories he can impute to children. Why not four, or ten? It's all a matter of how fine-grained you are prepared to be when you define the protoconcepts that figure in these theories." And, on the subject of protoconcepts, the theorist will naturally balk at referring to children's "beliefs" at all and so must invent a new proto-entity. Indeed Josef Perner (Perner, Baker, & Hutton, 1994) has invented the term "prelief"; but, again, where do we stop? Why not, in Woodfield's example, invent the term "shwant" for children whose concept of "wanting X" is applied only to cases where the shwanter can see what he or she desires immediately in front of him or her?

One must, however, give some account of why children are very consistent in the way they fail mentalising tasks such as false belief at 3 and pass them at 4. First, why the consistency in passing? We have to be careful here. Nothing in Woodfield's argument shows us that it *cannot be true* that the 3–4 transition is a transition towards a fundamentally more adequate understanding of belief: contextualism about belief ascription is perfectly compatible with the view that sometimes children take giant steps. Four-year-olds may be able to think thoughts about beliefs which are impossible for younger children to think; but what Woodfield's argument shows is that nothing forces us to regard this ability as developing the canonical concept of belief. With regard to the consistency in failing, the fact that we have jettisoned the theory-theory account leaves us free to posit any number of explanations for the consistency. Woodfield floats one in terms of what one may call over-generalisation. The false belief task, he says (1993, p.8), "exemplifies an abstract structure which is somewhat similar to that which characterises the Standard [i.e. true] Belief task. They pass the latter because they have abstracted the pattern and learned to respond to it. They fail the false belief task because they categorise the situation as exemplifying the same pattern as the Standard Belief task." There are a number of ways one might test this claim. For example, one might try to find out whether children make similar overgeneralisation errors on tasks that have no mentalising content, or one might change the structure of the false belief task in such a way that no analogy is invited between this and the standard situation in order to see whether younger children now succeed.

As I said at the end of the previous sub-section, the account I shall now defend is one that takes the 3–4 transition to be a transition in the exercise of agency, or at least in one aspect of agency, namely, the ability to program and regulate one's behaviour, specifically to program and regulate the judgements one is asked to make about situations. This is generally referred to as "executive functioning".

3.4: "EXECUTIVE" VERSUS "THEORY-THEORY" ACCOUNTS OF DEVELOPMENTAL TRANSITIONS: THE 6–7 TRANSITION AND THE 3–4 TRANSITION

In this section I shall be presenting the case for the following view. A fundamental change in children's cognition does occur as they enter their fourth year of life, but this transition is not caused by the acquisition of any new theory—neither of representation in general

(Perner, 1991) nor of belief in particular (Gopnik & Wellman, 1992). It looks as if theory-change is taking place because the transition is marked by success at a wide range of "mentalising" tasks, and because, as I have just been discussing, the patterns of failure are very consistent. But many of these tasks have a similar *structure* and accordingly make similar processing demands on the children. My alternative proposal is, therefore, that under-4s fail tasks with this structure because they have inadequate strategic control over their mental processes, specifically over the items of information that must be held in mind when answering the relevant questions. This is an *executive* as opposed to a *theoretical* failure, something that reveals inadequate development in executive control.

Before entering into this debate however, we need to be as clear as possible about what an executive failure amounts to. Recall that when discussing search experiments in Part 2, I distinguished between an executive *performance* and an executive *competence* error. The same distinction can be applied here. In the case of an executive performance error we say that a child is failing, say, the false belief task because he or she knows what to do but just cannot do it at the time; the child is seduced by the wrong cues against his or her better knowledge. Recall the analogy I made in Part 2 between this kind of failure and Luria's (controversial) claim that frontal patients may say what is the right thing to do while doing the wrong thing.

An executive *competence* error is a more profound affair. On the sensorimotor level it means, as we discussed at length, that infants have failed to grasp how their physical actions affect their experiences. On the verbal-cognitive level it means, as we shall see, children's failure to *regulate their attention in such a way that they are able to think explicitly and at will about certain mental or abstract properties and processes— such as beliefs, properties of objects (e.g. "amount"), and logical relations.* The latter statement errs, I admit, on the side of the cryptic; and worse still, it makes the line between broadly executive and broadly representational accounts of development a rather subtle one. However, the line between any executive theory and all theory-theory accounts is clear enough, as is that between all executive-performance accounts and all representational accounts.

However, we need to view these distinctions in a less abstract style—my next task.

3.4(i) What is an executive error and an executive transition?
As we discussed briefly in Part 2, the term "executive"—as in "executive functions"—issues from theories of pre-frontal lobe function. Many accounts of the function of the pre-frontal cortices have appeared over

the past 50 or so years but all of them claim that one of the principal responsibilities of this area of the brain is the *control* of behaviour. They do this because, although frontal patients' IQs may be relatively unaffected, their capacity for, to borrow Shallice's terms, "programming, regulation, and verification of activity" (1988, p.330) is impaired; although sometimes the impairment is only subtle and occurs in ways difficult to measure with laboratory tests (Shallice & Burgess, 1991). Programming, regulation, and verification (or "monitoring") are clearly not co-extensive with agency, as I have been using the term, but it goes without saying that they capture some of its central manifestations.

Some theories of pre-frontal function emphasise the overseeing of lower-level programs and their top-down modulation under conditions of novelty and decision-making (Norman & Shallice, 1986), some emphasise the control of behaviour by representations (or "mental models") held in working-memory (Goldman-Rakic, 1987), some emphasise their role in keeping attention trained on the task, failure to achieve which results in "goal neglect" in spite of understanding what the task requires, and which indicates lower general intelligence or 'g' (Duncan, in press). And there are other options beside these.

However, all these theories imply roughly the same thing about the nature of an executive *error*. As Bruce Pennington (1994) argues, executive errors are those made when behaviour is controlled by salient features of the environment (salient, sometimes, by virtue of what has been done previously) rather than by an appropriate rule held in mind. So, in making an executive error, the subject manifests one or both of the following: (a) an inability to inhibit a *prepotent but wrong* action (including in this verbal judgements) and (b) the failure to modulate behaviour by a rule held in working memory, meaning, in this context, prospective memory, memory *for what will have to be done*. Obviously these two interdepend; but tasks can vary in the degree in which they encourage prepotent responses and in the degree to which they render difficult the on-line maintenance of rule.

Just a word in passing about the nature of rules that must be held in mind. We do not have to "hold in mind" the "rule" that we must open doors before we walk through them; however some of us do have to hold in mind rules such as "turn the coffee machine off before leaving your office in the evening". The former does not require prospective memory but the former does because nothing in the environment (the coffee machine has no light to show it's on) tells me what to do. Furthermore there are no immediate consequences of forgetting the rule, unlike, say, forgetting that on the one computer system one must type "logout" to quit and on another type "logoff"—the immediate consequence is that one fails to leave the system. In short, the rule must be fundamentally *arbitrary* in the sense of being "non-naturally" (Grice, 1957) related to our goals.

All so-called "frontal" tasks require the subject to control his or her behaviour by an essentially arbitrary rule. However not all of them encourage a prepotent response in any obvious sense. In the Tower of London[78] (ToL), for example, the requirement is to plan rather than to overcome prepotency; although the task does encourage the prepotent response of moving *directly* to the target peg. Moreover, in the Wisconsin Card Sorting Task[79] (WCST) there is no natural or environmental prepotency (e.g. a desired goal which must be avoided), only a prepotency engendered through prior learning (e.g. sorting by colour).

What I will do now, *en route* to explaining the difference between executive and theory-theory accounts of the 3–4 transition, is to suggest that the tension between these two kinds of developmental accounts (executive versus theory-theory) is *not specific* to the 3–4 transition. Indeed it can probably be applied to just about *any* major cognitive–developmental transition. I will first describe the tension between executive and theory-theory accounts of a transition that appears to take place between about 6 and 7 years of age.

It may seem odd to discuss a cognitive transition taking place in older children before discussing one that takes place in younger children; and so to that extent the architecture of this section is unusual. The main reason I am doing this is that I want the section on autism to follow on directly from my discussion of the 3–4 transition. A second reason is that doing it this way round illustrates how one can describe the difference between executive and theory-theory accounts *without referring to theory of mind development*: the distinction cuts across the content of what is being acquired.

The "6–7 transition" as an executive transition

About 20–25 years ago the developmental transition exercising the minds of psychologists was the 6-year to 7-year transition, the transition between what Piaget called "pre-operational" and "concrete operational" thinking. According to Piaget, the judgements of children between the ages of about 4 and about 6 were distorted by their natural tendency to become "centred" on unidimensional, salient features of the situation about which they had to make a judgement. Accordingly he claimed that what constituted concrete operational thinking was the ability to decentre one's attention from this salient variable and to regulate—Piaget called it "autoregulation"—one's attention in such a way that a judgement could be made that was based on the co-ordination of two superficially conflicting representations.

There are many examples of this process, but the most famous is the *conservation* experiment. In this, children are presented with situations in which an abstract property such as length, number, amount of substance, weight, or volume is perceptually transformed—where there is a transformation of a salient unidimensional feature—which, of course, does not affect the conservation of the underlying property. For example, children are shown two rows of six sweets arranged in one-to-one correspondence and they agree that both rows "have the same amount to eat" in them. After this, the experimenter spreads out one of the rows so that it extends further than the other one; although of course the density of the sweets in the transformed row is now less. Then, in response to a question about whether the rows still have the same amount to sweets to eat, children under 7 or so usually say that the transformed row now has more to eat. They may sometimes say "less" because it is less dense; but in any event they base their judgements on a single, unidimensional change and will often justify their answer by saying something like "because it's longer now". Non-conservation is an extremely robust phenomenon. The experimenter might try to draw the child's attention to the fact that, say, although the transformed row is longer it is also less dense and even encourage the child to count again that there are still six in each, but this usually results in children sticking to their guns.

In the present terms, Piaget's account of the transition between pre-operational and concrete operational thinking is an executive account. In the first place, the younger children fail because they are seduced by salient perceptual changes—by prepotency—and are accordingly forced to frame their judgements in terms of a single variable and ignore the conflicting (and regulating) variable. Piaget (e.g. 1950) saw the conservation test as a way of diagnosing the perceptual or "intuitive" character of young children's thought. By this he did not strictly mean that their thought was captured by appearances; this was Jerome Bruner's (1966) view. Rather he meant that, like perception, their thought was *irreversible* (Piaget's term). Once we have perceived something we cannot go back and unperceive it, and in having a perceptual experience we cannot reverse it and enjoy it again—*unless the experience was generated by a reversible action*. Preoperational children's thought does not have the character of action; and adequate thinking has, for Piaget, the character of internalised action.

This can be seen as an illustration of what Piaget meant by saying that thought is "internalised action". Just as motoric-cum-attentional reversibility was necessary for the infant to gain a conception of objects as the objective causes of his or her experiences, so achieving a reversibility of thought—regulating one's mental attention towards different dimensions in order to frame an adequate judgement—is necessary if the child is to appreciate the status of certain objective, invariant, and abstract properties. It must be said, however, that the two senses of "reversibility" are not structurally identical: one is not simply a more mental version of the other. For what is particular to the reversibility of thought is its requirement that the child hold two dimensions in mind at once, to which there is no clear analogue in the kind of reversibility discussed in Part 2. What is the conceptual link between the pre-operational child's irreversibility of thought and his or her inability to focus on more than one dimension at a time? One can put it this way. If subjects are to realise that the value of a single dimension does not by itself determine the value of the whole—the "amount"— then they must be able to represent that single dimension as part of a whole: they must be able, that is, to have "background" representations of other dimensions as they attend to just one of them.

Piaget painted a picture, then, of younger children's attention being, as it were, glued to a unidimensional change, whereas older children can direct their attention at will rather than having the world direct it for them. In fact there is more than an analogy with visual attention here because we have evidence from eye-movement studies that non-conservers and conservers look at the displays in predictably different ways (O'Bryan & Boersma, 1971); although Piaget's view was that the control of visual attention preceded—"prefigured"—the control of mental attention. In any event, what the nonconserver is supposed to lack is mental agency, not a concept.

What does it mean to deny that nonconservers "lack a concept"? It means that what the conservation experiment demonstrates is not the under-7s' global failure to think about abstract properties like number (and how could one prove this negative?); rather it shows that in this situation, when they are asked directly about whether an amount is conserved, they are unable to recruit what they know about these properties in the service of an answer. That is to say, young children do not believe that *as a general rule* spreading out their sweets actually gives them more to eat. (Do we ever see them doing this?) For this reason, it is possible to show that in situations where the child was not asked a *direct* question (e.g. Light, Buckingham, & Robins, 1979) or not asked a question at all (e.g. Russell, 1979b; and see later) conservation-based responses are more common.

What was the role of witnessing the transformation? Some have claimed that this was crucial, so that when the salience of the transformation was decreased more correct answers were forthcoming (McGarrigle & Donaldson, 1974); however this was almost certainly the artifactual result of the children simply ignoring the transformation and/or relying on a counting strategy (Moore & Frye, 1986). It is more likely, in fact, that focusing on the unidimensional change is caused by hearing abstract questions containing phrase like "same amount of X"; and indeed 5-year-old children's interpretations of such phrases is unidimensional (in terms of height or global shape) when they have *not* just been presented with a perceptual transformation (Russell, 1975). Further support for this view came from a study using a nonverbal test of length conservation (Russell, 1979b). Four-year-old nonconservers of length could justify their correct nonverbal response (pointing to the card on which the two pencils were the same size though reoriented, rather than to the comparison card) using conservation language, but when they were re-tested with the standard procedure in which the experimenter used the phrase "same size" they failed. The 4-year-olds could describe their own choices using phrases like "same size" and "both big" or "both little" but *when used by another person* these same phrases would direct their attention unidimensionally. Younger children, it seemed, can think about the abstract properties that are conserved, but cannot answer questions about them because hearing phrases of that kind causes their attention to become fixated on unidimensional attributes. Their response to such questioning highlights the fact that their judgements lack the requisite degree of reversibility; but it also highlights, I shall argue, the fact that their error is an executive competence error: they cannot think *"explicitly and at will"* about the abstract property.

What does it mean to say that nonconservation (and indeed any example of pre-operational thought) exemplifies an executive performance or an executive competence error? I have just said that it is a problem of executive *competence*. Conserving children may not have acquired a new concept, but they have acquired the ability to "think explicitly and at will" about abstract properties—with "explicitly" referring to the fact that they can frame judgements in terms of other people's references to "same amount of X", and "at will" to the fact that they can regulate their attention when invited to think about these properties. Indeed these children are now able to share their thoughts about number, length, volume etc. with other people in more situations because when others refer to things being "the same X" they will generally have the same thought as them.

If, by contrast, under-7s are making a *performance* error, if, that is, they really know the answer but something about the task structure seduces them towards saying the wrong thing, then it should be a simple matter to show them the error of their ways. It is not. One of the clearest demonstrations of this is the way in which a nonconserver will typically behave in a situation stage-managed to ensure that he or she is viewing the transformed materials from a symmetrically conflicting perspective to that of another nonconserver. The two of them are then told to agree an answer to a conservation question. In conservation of length[80] for example, one child views the materials from an angle that encourages her to say the pencil X is longer than pencil Y and her partner has to view them *vis-à-vis* her in order to encourage the opposite answer that pencil Y is longer now than pencil X (Russell, 1982b); while in conservation of liquid one child views a post-transformation beaker from the side (from where the amount looks more) and his partner views it from the top—from where it looks less (Russell, Mills, & Reiff-Musgrove, 1990). In our experiments, and in others we performed on spatial perspective-taking (Russell, 1981a), reasoning about class–subclass relations (Russell, 1981b) and appearance–reality judgements (Russell & Haworth, 1988), the children are not allowed out of the room until an answer had been agreed! We were, therefore, putting so*cial pressure* on these nonconserving children to agree an answer, and, if a conserving answer is available to them—if, that is, they are only making a *performance* error—then they should abandon their nonconserving judgement. Our findings were very consistent[81]: children in symmetrical conflict experiments are no more likely than are control children to give the correct answer. In other words, they agree to disagree, and will decide on all kinds of pragmatic bases whose incorrect answer is to be adopted (e.g. in terms of whose turn it is to answer). We sometimes found, indeed, that which child's answer is adopted is a function of separately assessed social dominance (e.g. in Russell 1982b, though not in Russell et al., 1990).

The 6–7 transition as a theory-change

I have made this long excursion into the nature of the 6–7 transition in order to show what it means to say that a developmental transition is one of executive *competence*. But what would a theory-theory account of the 6–7 transition look like? As it turns out, I am well-placed to say what this would look like because the account I proposed in the early 1980s would today be regarded as *echt* theory-theory—embarrassingly "well-placed" in the light of what I will go on to argue about the 3–4 transition. We can now consider the strengths and weaknesses of a theory-theory account of the same phenomenon.

In 1982 I published an article called "Propositional attitudes" in which I argued that not only must children come to understand the relationship between attitudes and contents, but they must come to appreciate that there are different ways of believing a content (Russell, 1982b). For example "I think that two and two equal four", "I think Italy will win the 1998 World Cup", "I think that Birmingham is a larger city than Bristol", and "I think that pistachio is the best flavour of ice-cream" are not in *this* sense expressions of the same propositional attitude. There are many distinctions possible but we should at least distinguish between attitudes that are broadly *subjective* and those that are broadly *objective*, with expressions of appearance-to-me, taste, opinion, and so forth being in the first category and logico-mathematical statements and statements of empirical fact being in the latter. Moreover, although any propositional attitude (as the term is properly used) can be applied to any content, there are important constraints on which contents can attract which "propositional attitudes" in the sense employed in that paper. I will now call the latter *mental orientations*, to prevent confusion.

Thus, given one content such as "... Bob Dylan is a genius" or "... p implies q, ~q therefore ~p", any attitude—believe-, hope-, fear-, expect-, guess-, have-an-inkling-that—can be applied to it. Some are more sensible than others but there are no logical constraints. However, in the case of what I am now calling *mental orientations* there *are* constraints. Something is wrong, for example, if one's mental orientation to "2+2=4" is subjective, or if one's mental orientation to "Fresh strawberries are good with yoghurt" is as towards that of hard fact. In short, what must develop is a theoretical grasp of the different kinds of mental orientations that different contents—indeed different kinds and domains of knowledge—naturally invite.

I argued that what constitutes being a preoperational child is the inability to draw these—in contemporary parlance—"theoretical" distinctions. Two things must develop: children must come to understand what it means to have a subjective versus an objective mental orientation to any content, and they must come to appreciate which kinds of content invite which kinds of mental orientation.

Why, then, do children fail conservation tasks? My hypothesis was that younger children's natural inclination is to take a *subjective* mental orientation towards some contents that adults regard as quintessentially objective—logico-mathematical contents in particular. This means that when younger children are asked, for example, whether X is the same size as Y they naturally interpret this as we would interpret a question such "Does X *look bigger to you* than Y": the question of whether something is "bigger" than something else is, to these children, a perspective-relative fact and so the criteria for being bigger change with point of view[82]. If this is so, it is no surprise that in the experiments in which we put social pressure on pairs of nonconservers to agree an answer from symmetrically conflicting perspectives "two wrongs don't make a right"; for them, there is nothing objective to disagree *about*. It is as if two adults had been asked to agree which is the better of two malt whiskeys; any agreed answer would still be subjective.

This account of the 6–7 transition certainly bears some resemblance to what I called earlier "the meta-representational insight" theory insofar as what is supposed to be acquired is an abstract, domain-general, autonomous theoretical grasp tied to no particular contents. Children are not, on this view, acquiring knowledge about substances, length, logic, and so forth, but about how judgements about them *should be regarded*, just as on the meta-representational insight view children are supposed to gain a grasp of the representing relation that spreads across types of representation (mental, pictorial, linguistic, and so forth).

In order to test this conjecture I did a series of experiments on children's abilities at drawing various kinds of abstract distinction presented in sentences without a context (e.g. Russell, 1983). The idea was that if this theoretical grasp really is abstract, domain-general, and autonomous we should find that success in understanding distinctions between objective and subjective sentences (e.g. "John read the book" versus "John enjoyed the book") should be possible at around 7 years of age but not before. (In the experiments, the basis of the distinction was explained to the children *after* they had made a response to each pair, and we then looked at how they responded on the subsequent pair.) It turned out that children between 5 and 6 years of age were indeed worse than chance on the objective–subjective discrimination whereas children between 7 and 8 years of age were better than chance. By contrast, they were better than chance at the lower age-level when they had to discriminate between non-intentional and intentional sentences (e.g. "John dropped the plate" versus "John sold the plate")—these are sentences about agency not about mental-representational states—and between sentences that differ in degree of generality (e.g. "Leopards have heads" is a more general statement than "Leopards have spots" in the sense that it is less successful at picking out a particular class of object).

However, there *was* a similarity between the pattern of performance on the objective–subjective distinction and performance on a fourth distinction between absolute and relative sentences (e.g. "George bought a glass dish" versus "George bought a strong dish"), which I explained in terms of the fact that objective–subjective and absolute–relative "both imply a division between mental and non-mental states of affairs" (Russell, 1983; p.266). This may not be true of the absolute–relative distinction in general but it was certainly true of my sentences, in which the relative sentences implied the "presence or implied presence of a mental act of *evaluation*" (1983, p.266) and in which some of the relative sentences were clearly mentalistic ("John was last to come" versus "John was happy to come").

In a previous study with a similar procedure (Russell, 1982c) I had also looked at the ability to discriminate between necessarily true and contingent statements (e.g. "The circle is round" versus "The circle is big") and found that 5–6 year olds were better than chance, and indeed were better than chance at discriminating contradictions from contingent statements (e.g. "The coin is paper"/"The coin is a 10p") without the usual *post hoc* instruction about the basis of the distinction. This throws into stronger relief the difficulty children of this age had with the subjective–objective and the absolute–relative distinctions.

In a later study on the same theme children played a true-or-false game in which they had to judge whether their partner had said something true or false (Russell, 1984a). In addition to the objectivity–subjectivity of the spoken sentences, their plausibility and empirical truth were varied, as were the absolute and *relative* ages and social dominance of the informants. We found that only children of 7 years and above were influenced by the objectivity–subjectivity of the sentences, with the subjective ones being believed more often and with the children being better at spotting if they were false. We also found that above 7 years, but not before, the younger and less dominant informants were believed more often than were the older and more dominant ones—possibly because they assumed such informants to be less able to dissemble.

Still later, I showed that it was around 7 years of age that children become capable of interpreting logically opaque—intensional (see note 30, Part 2)—sentences correctly (Russell, 1987b). This means that below this age they do not appreciate that a true sentence which begins with an attitude verb such as "John is thinking that a is s" can become false when the label "a" is changed to another, equally accurate label for the referent: the thinker may not know that this label applies to the referent. To take one of the examples from the study, if somebody has stolen my watch and if, unbeknown to me, this person has red hair then it cannot be said of JR "He is thinking: 'I must find the person with red hair who stole my watch' ": this is objectively true of the person but cannot be true of my *thought* about him. To grasp this fact is to grasp that truth about the content of a thought is fixed by the *mental* situation of the thinker not by the physical situation of the world. And this is another facet, clearly enough, of the subjective–objective distinction.

At the time, the charge of artificiality was sometimes levelled against these experiments; but their artificiality was, in fact, their *raison d'être*. The whole idea was to show that these distinctions are grasped in an abstract, domain-general, autonomous way—that is, purely as *sentences*. I thought indeed that I had shown that "at an age when children are coming to understand a cluster of logico-mathematical principles when presented concretely [i.e. they pass 'concrete operational tests'] they are also growing able to reflect on some basic features of the linguistic-conceptual system" (Russell, 1983, p.266) The idea was that both of these advances are essentially "theoretical".

Now for the crucial question: How and why did the children develop this new theoretical insight? Dyadic interaction experiments again turned out to be a rich source of data. In common with a number of workers in the USA (e.g. Miller & Brownwell, 1975; Silverman & Geiringer, 1973), I had found that when a nonconserver is paired with a conserver in a conflict experiment it is the judgement of the conserver that is adopted and that this occurs irrespective of separately assessed social dominance (Russell, 1982b). That is to say, the conserver can be a submissive child and yet "win the argument". Moreover, this seemed to be occurring not because the nonconserver was steam-rollered by the conserver's remorseless logic but simply by virtue of being exposed to the correct answer[83]. On the basis of this I conjectured that there is a period of development during which children spontaneously give a subjective answer to concrete operational questions while recognising the superiority of the objective one when they hear it. "Exposure to the correct judgement makes [the child] aware that *it is possible to make objective judgements about length relations*. The speculation is that changes in propositional attitude [i.e. different kinds of mental orientation] set the scene for, or canalise, changes in what actual propositions come to be expressed." (Russell, 1982b, p.83, original italics). In other words, once they can draw the relevant theoretical distinctions they also develop the right kind of theoretical *preferences*.

Standing back from all this, what are the strengths and the weaknesses of a theory-theory approach to the 6–7 transition? Both are fairly clear. The basic weakness is that the theory-theory approach is long on description and short on explanation. *Why*, that is, do younger children have a natural preference for the subjective orientation to questions about abstract properties? And this question becomes even more difficult to answer when we remember that they can also show the *opposite* preference—for objective orientations to mentalistic questions. For example, there is the phenomenon of "intellectual realism" in which under-7s answer in terms of perspective-neutral facts about a display when we ask them about how something looks from another's perspective (Light & Nix, 1983).

But still more pressing is the question of *why children abandon one "theory" for another at age 7*. The idea that children have to be exposed to the superior judgement and once exposed to it—*if* they are old enough—adopt it, does not inspire confidence. Commenting at the time on views like this, Peter Bryant (1982, p.250) wrote that such a theory's "main conceptual problem is that it does not explain its own limitations, for, if communication were all, it is difficult to see why intellectual development could not be polished off in one concentrated one-hour tutorial." What is it that constrains children to stick to their old ways of thinking at one age and welcome the superior judgement like an epiphany somewhat later? Bryant went on to say that Piaget's equilibration model of cognitive change, especially as developed in his later writings (e.g. Piaget, 1977), did at least contain ideas about developmental mechanisms—testable ideas. And this was from one of Piaget's foremost critics!

Indeed the point needs to be hammered home that criticisms of this kind could be levelled at *any* theory-theory account of development. They must explain (i) why some theories and not others come first, (ii) why they are abandoned, and (iii) why, if something as rationalistic as theory development is taking place, we cannot accelerate mental development just by giving 2-year-olds the good word.

In any event, I abandoned my theory-theory approach in the mid 1980s and gradually came round to the idea that Piagetian theory, far from being the descriptive exercise that many accuse it of being, was better placed than most theories to model the mechanisms underlying cognitive change. "Underlying" is important here; for the problem with the position I put forward was that it was all about surface manifestations: it told a story about what happened rather than about what in the developing child made it happen.

But what of the *strengths* of the theory-theory approach? First, adequate description of what develops is at least as important in psychology as the explanation of how something develops. For what if subsequent research had shown there to be strong and reliable correlations between the ability to draw the kind of abstract distinctions I described earlier and performance on conservation and other concrete operational tasks? By itself this would not explain how development happens but it would tell us something significant about the breadth and character of the 6–7 transition; while the implications for ego-development and moral development would be irresistible (on which see Russell, 1984b). Second, might it not turn out that an account of development at the theory-theory level is actually *explanatorily* stronger than one in terms of processing mechanisms? The theory-theorist can say that yes there certainly are broad, processing-constraints on development (e.g. constraints on attention-shifting and strategic control) but these *under-determine the nature of the changes*. Positing constraints on the timing of transitions, far from being an explanation of change at a deeper level, is doing no more than saying why changes do not happen sooner: they merely show us *which brakes have to be released*. We want to know why the changes take the form they do; we want to know, that is, about the *content* of the changes, and perhaps the essentially rationalist, theory-theory approach is well placed to do this?

In any event, *we* are now well-placed, I hope, to appreciate the conflict between an executive and a theory-theory approach to the 3–4 transition; we can now step back a few years and apply the same distinction. The story I will tell, however, does not really parallel the one I have just told because theory-theory accounts of the 3–4 transition are in a far healthier state than my theory-theory account of the 6–7 transition ever was. It will also be an unfinished story because it impossible to decide, given the present state of the data, between executive and theory-theory accounts. But we can at least give the executive account a run for its money.

3.4(ii) Executive processes in the 3–4 transition

I will begin with false belief, focusing first on understanding the relation between false belief and behaviour (the false belief experiment) and then on the ability to implant false beliefs into the minds other people (strategic deception experiments). In the first place, I will argue that an executive account of why 3-year-olds generally fail the false belief task is plausible, although it falls well short of being compelling, and in the second that there is strong evidence that younger children's difficulty with strategic deception tasks resides in the executive demands of the task rather than in the mentalising demands—although the evidence is not actually decisive. I then compare the structure of the false belief and strategic deception tasks with that of the other kinds of mentalising tasks that 3-year-olds generally fail, and argue, on this basis, that if the younger children fail mentalising tasks because of executive difficulties then these difficulties are ones of executive *competence* not of executive performance. That is to say, this group of tasks taps the development of the ability to think "explicitly at will" about mental kinds, which must be distinguished from, on the one hand, the development of a new theoretical insight and, on the other, from a mere performance error caused by the tasks' masking an ability to think explicitly and at will about mental kinds which remains unchanged between 3 and 4.

The false belief experiment

This experiment was originally conducted with Austrian children; it contained a narrative about a boy called "Maxi" going shopping with his mother and returning home, and it was acted out with a model kitchen in which chocolate was transferred from one cupboard to another

(Wimmer & Perner, 1983). But it can be run in a number of ways so long as the following narrative structure is maintained:

- A protagonist sees a desired object (e.g. a sweetmeat or a coin) placed at location A, after which he or she departs.
- While the protagonist is away the object is transferred to another place (B), after a suitable cover story, and usually by another protagonist rather than by the experimenter.
- The child sees the protagonist return and is told that he or she now wants the object.

The test question is either about where the protagonist will look for the object or where he or she thinks the object is now located. The control questions—questions to ensure the child has understood and remembered the narrative—are the following: about where the object was to start with, about where it is now, and about whether the protagonist knows[84] whether the object has been moved in his or her absence or about whether he or she saw the object moved. Broadly speaking, 3-year-old children are worse than chance at this task—they say the protagonist will go to B (where the object really is)—whereas 4-year-olds are generally better than chance at it—saying the protagonist will go to A.

Theory-theory accounts of failure tend to say that the younger children lack any grasp of the fact that what people do is determined by how they mentally represent reality not by the present configuration of reality. They cannot appreciate that the protagonist will go to A because what he or she has experienced (placement at A) commits him or her to the truth of the proposition "object at A". The fact that successful children will often *justify* their answers whereas unsuccessful children who have been told what the protagonist actually did (went to A) can give no reason for his or her behaviour (Wimmer & Weichbold, 1994) would seem to bolster this kind of account.

What is the "executive" alternative to this view? Putting to one side the distinction between competence and performance errors, we can focus on the two related features of executive errors which I mentioned earlier: (i) failure to guide one's behaviour by a rule held in prospective memory and (ii) failure to inhibit a prepotent but incorrect response. In the first place, the rule is "answer in terms of the protagonist's state of ignorance" and in the second place it is the tendency to refer to the target object. If the representation of the rule is labile and weak, the prepotency effect does not have to be very strong for an error to result; whereas if the subject is very susceptible to prepotency effects then even a strong representation of the rule will be over-written. What is happening, therefore, is that the younger children cannot frame their thoughts in a sufficiently "top-down" manner: what they think is determined by what strikes them at salient not by the demands of the question[85]. The parallel between this view and Piaget's account of nonconservation is, I hope, obvious.

There are two kinds of data that would undermine theory-theory accounts and support an executive account:

(1) Evidence that when the executive requirements of the false belief task are stripped away (or at least reduced) 3-year-old children *succeed*.

(2) Evidence that there is a similar pattern of *failure* when 3- and 4-year-old children are given tasks that make the same kinds of executive demands as the false belief task but which do not require children to understand the relation between a representation (mental or otherwise) and that which it represents.

Turning to (1), how might one strip away the executive requirements of the false belief task? Perhaps the simplest thought is this. When young children see a desired object being hidden and are then asked a question about where someone will look for it their natural inclination is to tell you that *they* know where it is. They see it as their brief to tell you where the item is. In order to explore this possibility we ran seven kinds of false belief task in addition to the standard object-hiding version (Curtis, Lewin, & Russell, 1991). In each of these seven narratives the children heard about changes in *state* rather than about changes in location—about changes in object properties (weight, shape, colour, temperature), changes in a machine's state (e.g. working to not working), about changes in biological state (e.g. thirst to satiation), and in emotional state (e.g. happy to unhappy). There were two examples of each kind of story. What was constant, however, was the fact that there was a protagonist who was ignorant of the change from one state to the other. The data were very clear. The pattern of failure on the standard relocation tasks was very similar to that on the state-change tasks: 3-year-olds generally worse than chance and 4-year-olds generally better than chance. Indeed at age 3 performance on five of the seven state-change tasks had correlations significant at $P < 0.001$ with performance on the re-location task (the exceptions being the weight and drive-state tasks).

This tells us that the younger children's problem is definitely not with inhibiting a prepotent reference to an *object*. If their problem is with inhibition at all, then it must be with inhibiting the framing of an answer *in terms of their own current state of knowledge*. When, for example, they are asked in our experiment whether John's mum thinks that John is now happy or sad, the child says "sad" because he or she knows, even if mum does not, that John, having gone off happily with his favourite chocolate-bar, is now crying because he dropped the chocolate in the road. What is involved in this narrative is a protagonist's knowledge about another's mental state, not his or her knowledge of where an object is located.

So if their problem is with—we might call it—"failing to suppress the salience of their own knowledge" then we need a form of false belief task in which, when the protagonist returns, it is impossible for the child to refer explicitly to a new state of affairs. In this experiment[86], our rationale was that if the object ceases to exist after the protagonist has departed, then, because there is no knowledge of where the object is *really* located to seduce the subject away from the correct strategy, success should be general, *if* the children's problem is indeed with disengaging their attention from what they know to be the case. We used a procedure very similar to the original Maxi narrative of Wimmer and Perner (1983) plus the introduction of a third character—a brother—who ate the chocolate after it had been put in the first cupboard. In reality, it was the experimenter who ate the chocolate. Note here that when the subject is asked where Maxi will look for the chocolate or where he thinks it now is, there is no option of saying "nowhere" or "silly question". There was a degree of improvement in the performance of the 3-year-olds in this situation (better than on standard task with a "search" question though not better with a "think" question), but where there was an improvement this only constituted a change from being worse than chance to being on chance—just over 50% of the children were still failing.

There was, however, something about the way in which a minority of the children failed that made us think there were indeed problems with suppressing the salience of their own knowledge. When asked where Maxi thought the chocolate was now located some of them said "in your tummy" or "in your mouth"; indeed a few said that Maxi would *look* "in your mouth" or even "in your tummy"! This result was similar to what Wimmer and Perner found in one of their follow-up experiments. They too had told a story about the chocolate being eaten—their experiment had a similar rationale to ours—but instead of taking the chocolate out of existence they had moved it behind the scenes away from the mini-stage on which the vignette was being acted out. What happened was that quite a number of the younger children pointed to the *behind-the-scenes* object when asked where Maxi would look for it.

Accordingly, the latter result might be taken to suggest that when there is no new situation of the object to which to refer directly—one cannot point to the non-existence of an object—the children do not know what to do. They bend over backwards, as it were, to refer to a new situation, no matter how implausible; and this can be taken as evidence that they try to refer to the new situation (about which they are ignorant of course) at all costs. Accordingly, my next experiment was one in which the children were *ignorant* of the new situation of the object, with the thought being that if they did not know what is the new situation, there would be *no* knowledge from which to disengage—and thus success. In this case there were four "B" (hiding) locations rather than only one and the children closed their eyes during the transfer of the object from the original location to one of the new ones. Thus, when the protagonist returned and they were asked where he would look for his coin (or where he thought it was) they themselves were ignorant of the new location. However, this ignorance did not prevent them from guessing which of the four boxes contained the coin after the transfer and thus from pointing randomly to one of the four boxes in answer to the question. They were worse than chance.

Next, I reasoned that if the children did not have to refer to any location and did not therefore have to manifest any knowledge about the new situation then the salience of their own knowledge (or beliefs and guesses) could not seduce them into giving the wrong answer. All I did here was to change the question to "Will [the protagonist] go to the right place or the wrong place?", having first established that they knew what *was* the right place and the wrong place to look for the object. However what normally happened when they were asked this question was that they would point to one of the locations, and so, not surprisingly, their performance was no better than on the standard task.

My final attempt to strip away the executive components of the false belief task involved a change of tack. This time I decided to remove the requirement to make any *prediction* based on false belief and instead gave the children a task in which they had to work out the *true* location of the object on the basis of a protagonist's false belief about where it was. Like Fodor (1992), although from a different theoretical perspective, I thought that what makes the false belief task difficult is that the children have to make a unique prediction about an outcome, and that this requirement encourages them to lapse into error. Fodor argued that this was because younger children possess the "computational resources" generally to make judgements in terms of the rule that "agents act to satisfy their desires", but lack the resources to do this in terms of their more complex (innate) rule "agents act in ways which *would* satisfy their desires *if* their beliefs were true". Their need to make a prediction forces them to lapse back to the easier rule. [Note that although the executive approach does not mention innate rules it can be construed as an attempt to spell out what these "computational requirements" are. They are requirements to suppress the salience of one's current knowledge state (prepotency) while framing a judgement in terms of a question held in working memory.]

This time the child knew that there was an object (some chocolate) in one of two boxes—a red box and a blue box—but did not know in which; and he or she knew that the experimenter had put it there. A puppet then came on the scene and said "I think the chocolate is in the red box" and departed. The experimenter then told the child that although the puppet "thinks the chocolate is in the red box, *what he thinks is wrong*" and then invited the child to work out where the chocolate actually was. This was extremely easy for 3-year-olds. Twenty-five out of 30 gave the correct answer as contrasted with a comparison task in which the children knew where chocolate was, the puppet said that he thought it was in the *other* box, and the children were asked to predict where the puppet would look for it: only 5 out of 30 passed in this case.

There is however a fatal ambiguity in this result. Although it is entirely *consistent* with the hypothesis that children fail the standard task because they are overwhelmed by what they currently know, their successes can easily be explained without reference to their understanding of false belief. All they have to do, a sceptic would argue, is to extract from the experimenter's statement "what the puppet thinks is wrong" the fact that it is wrong that the chocolate is in the red box. They can ignore the phrase about thinking and simply reason "p or q, ~p, therefore q". And so long as positive results can be debunked in this way, with due acknowledgement to Lloyd Morgan's Canon, the evidence for executive failures underlying the younger child's failure can be dismissed.

It has to be said, then, that my attempt to unmask 3-year-olds' understanding of false belief by stripping away the executive requirements of the standard task was a pretty thorough failure. There was only one positive result and that could easily be debunked. But even if the attempt had *succeeded*, the best one could then do would be to line up behind some published studies (Lewis & Osborne, 1990; Mitchell & Lacohée, 1991; Siegal & Beattie, 1991)[87] which showed that 3-year-olds can be encouraged to perform at better than chance levels on false belief tasks when relatively minor modifications are made to the test questions and to the procedure. One might wish to explain these three findings in terms of "boosting the salience" of the working memory element at the expense of the salience of the child's own knowledge state; but that is little more than *post-hoc*ery, given that "salience"—like other supposed seducers towards failure in developmental tasks such as "lack of human sense" (Donaldson, 1978)—must be defined before the experiment is run, not appealed to after the data are in.

In any event, I will set aside the question of whether the average 3-year-old knows what it means for someone to hold a false belief (returning to it when we reconsider the distinction between executive-competence and executive-performance errors) and turn to the second research strategy. This was the strategy, recall, of asking whether 3-year-olds show a similar pattern of *failure* to that shown with the false belief task when they are given a task that has the same executive structure as the false belief task but does not require the subject *to understand the relation between a representation and that which it represents.*

Our general strategy here was somewhat similar to that employed by other sceptics about the false belief task being a test of false belief. Doug Frye and his colleagues (Frye, Zalazo, & Palfai, in press) argue that the reason the false belief task and its cognates are difficult is that they require a form of conditional reasoning that 3-year-olds generally cannot achieve. Accordingly, they presented 3- and 4-year-olds with tasks that had no mentalistic elements but an inferential structure similar to the false belief task, and found that the patterns of successes and failures were similar to those shown with false belief performance. (Of course this kind of result is a rather bad one for the present account if these tasks can be said to encourage no prepotent response[88]. I will tackle that question later.)

The strategy was suggested by Chris Moore, and it led to a collaborative study (Moore et al., in press). The idea was to use a task with a narrative structure similar to that of the false belief task but with a mental content that was non-representational—in contrast to the Frye et al. strategy. The mental content of the task was not representational because *desires* formed its topic rather than beliefs. We called it the "conflicting desire task". Recall [3.3(i)] that to desire an object is to be related to an object in the world not to be related to a representation of the world as being a certain way. For this reason, as we saw, verbs such as "think" and "believe" *must* govern propositions (we cannot, recall, "believe a cheeseburger") whereas verbs such as "want" and "need" *need not* govern propositions. It is otiose to say that "John wants water" actually means that "John wants it to be the case that he drinks water" (he does not want something to *be the case*: he wants to satisfy his thirst); whereas putting a "that-clause" after verbs such as "think", "hope", is certainly not otiose: it is necessary. Putting issues of linguistic usage to one side, it is generally accepted by proponents of the theory-theory approach that children of 3 or even 2 years of age understand what it is to desire something simply because desires do not have to represent the world as being a certain way (Perner, 1991; Wellman, 1991).

To understand the rationale of the conflicting desire task, it is necessary to reconsider the executive requirements of the false belief task. If we give children the benefit of the doubt and assume that, like us, they know what it is to have a false belief—if we take this to be our "null hypothesis" (Pinker, 1984, p.7)—then we should say that when they are asked a question such as "Where will Maxi look for his chocolate?", they are holding in mind two representations that "compete" for dominance—(a) of the *fact* that Maxi wrongly believes and (b) of the *fact* they themselves believe. Although they have to frame their answer in terms of (a), (b) is more potent, given that truth is generally more potent than falsity. But imagine that the question were about what the protagonist wants or needs instead of about what he believes. In this case the competing representations in the child's mind are not of facts or situations (they are not "representations *of representations* of reality"): they are representations of needs for objects (a) the protagonist's need for object A and (b) the child's own need for object B. On the plausible assumption that one's own needs are more potent than other people's, we can then assume that children who are asked a question about what the protagonist needs *are being faced with just the same kind of executive challenge as they are faced with in the false belief task*. They must suppress the salience of their own needs and frame their answer in terms of the other people's needs.

It would appear from a previous study that very young children do not have problems with tasks in which their own desire differs from that of another person. Wellman (1991, p.218) told 2-year-olds that Jane can spend the afternoon at the pool or playing with the dog, after which they were asked which of the two activities they themselves would prefer. Having then been told that Jane wanted to do the *opposite*, they were asked where Jane would go—to the pool or to the dog's kennel. These very young children tended to say Jane would do what Jane herself preferred not what they themselves preferred. There are, however, two respects in which this falls short of being the kind of conflicting desire task that we require. In the first place, we cannot be confident that the children had genuine preferences for one activity or the other—they may simply have plumped for one over the other—and in the second place the narrative structure was far simpler than that of the false belief task.

To deal with the first problem Moore and Sapp took steps to establish a *genuine* preference in the children for one object over another by employing a contrast between a large attractive animal sticker against a small plain one which a cover-story had established to be the *protagonist's* preference (see Moore et al., in press, Experiment 1). In this case, nearly twice as many 3-year-olds said that the protagonist would chose the object that they themselves preferred. In a comparison condition where the children had no particular preference, however, all of them gave the correct answer.

To deal with the second problem, of requiring a narrative structure similar to that of the false belief task, we (Jarrold, Russell, Lumb, & McCallum, see Moore et al., in press, Expt.2) made the parallel shown in Table 1.

In our conflicting desire analogue to the false belief task, 3-year-olds played a game against a puppet in which each tried to be first to complete a simple jigsaw of a frog. Each player had his or her own jigsaw and they obtained the jigsaw pieces by turning over cards from a pack. For example, drawing a white card meant that no new piece was won, drawing a red card meant winning the head section, and drawing a blue card meant winning the frog's eyes.

At time t_1 (see Table 1), both the child and the puppet had headless frogs: they both needed a red card. At time t_2, the child turned over a red card and thereby won a head for his or her frog, with the result that he or she now needed a blue card for the eyes, while the puppet continued to need a red card. At time t_3 the child was then asked (in addition to control questions to ensure he or she had understood what was going on) whether the puppet wanted the red or the blue card. (Remember that they themselves needed the blue card while the puppet needed the red one.) Of 20 3-year-olds, 13 wrongly said that the puppet needed the blue card, which is similar to the proportion of same-age, control children who failed our comparison false belief task (10 failed out of 18).

TABLE 1

The structural parallel between the "false belief" and the "conflicting desire" tasks

	False belief	Conflicting desire
t_1		
	Both child and protagonist believe the same thing.	Both child and protagonist need the same thing.
t_2		
	Child comes to believe something different, while protagonist's belief is unchanged.	Child comes to need something different, while protagonist's need is unchanged.
t_3		
	Child is asked about protagonist's belief (which conflicts with his or her own new belief).	Child is asked about protagonist's need (which conflicts with his or her own revised need).

These are just two experiments, and obviously a lot more needs to be done; but the data are entirely consistent with the view that what leads younger children into error in the false belief task is not their weak grasp of false beliefs, but their difficulty with suppressing the salience of their own mental states[89]. This is what Piaget called *egocentrism*.

We will consider how well this view generalises to other forms of mentalising task after we have looked at the kind of strategic deception experiments that can be performed with 3- and 4-year-olds.

Strategic deception experiments

True deception requires the implanting of a false belief into the mind of another person. Accordingly, those who hold that the 3–4 transition is a transition towards either a theory of mental representation or of meta-representation in general must also hold that true deception does not occur before the age of 4 years.

I am not going to debate the question of whether naturalistic studies (e.g. Dunn, 1991) or experimental studies (Chandler, Fritz, & Hala, 1989; Hala, Chandler, & Fritz, 1991; Sodian, 1991; Sodian, Taylor, Harris, & Perner, 1991) have supported or undermined this claim. Instead I will examine the tension that exists between deception as a mentalistic achievement and as an executive achievement.

That tension is very clearly present in the experiment often regarded as the first theory of mind experiment ; in fact the phrase was coined by David Premack. Woodruff and Premack (1979) presented four chimpanzees with the following problem. When an animal was inside its cage it could see two boxes out of reach; one of these boxes contained food; and there were trainers present who could bring the food to the animal. There were two trainers—a friendly trainer, and a mask-wearing, villainous-looking trainer who would do such things as swat the animal with a rolled-up newspaper when they met in the corridor. On each trial the chimp saw food placed in one of the boxes, shortly after which one of the two trainers would arrive on the scene. The animals learned that if they indicated the baited box in the presence of the good trainer he would fetch the food for them. If, however, they did this in the presence of the bad trainer he would take the food away. What they ended up doing was pointing to the *empty* container in the presence of the bad trainer. One could say that they learned to "deceive" him.

It would, however, be rash to say that this was a case of "implanting a false belief" into the trainer's mind. Why? Principally because the animals had *learned* (over a period of about nine months) to point to the empty box, an achievement that can be explained perfectly well without reference to mental representation: they learned to make the responses that gained them the reward. This is by no means to trivialise the learning; for the animals did not merely withhold a response but learned, in indicating the empty box, an "original" act. Moreover, the chimpanzees were able to do something that not only rats (Holland, 1979) but also very young children (Diamond, 1991) often fail to do—inhibit an inappropriate action directly towards a goal.

But even if the animals had pointed to the empty box after experiencing the loss of the food to the bad trainer on only *one* occasion we could still be sceptical about whether they were manifesting any mental insight. For while it is entirely possible that they were computing "do *A* to make *T* represent my belief as {food at place B}", it is also entirely possible that they were simply luring the trainer away from the food—that they were directly manipulating his *behaviour*. To do this they would certainly require some understanding of others as agents, but nothing that we would need to dignify by the phrase "a theory of mind". And more to the present point, any situation in which the subject indicates the place where a goal is *absent* in order to win a reward requires, by the definition given earlier, executive skill. For we can see both the inhibition of the prepotent response (pointing to the baited box) and the retention of a rule in working memory (indicating the empty box gets me the food). Indeed any kind of deceptive behaviour has this dual nature, insofar as telling the truth is what we are naturally inclined to do and while doing which act we must keep a procedure activated in working memory.

This then is the tension between an executive and a theory-theory account of performance on strategic deception tasks. However, before launching research into why young children fail such tasks we have to devise a procedure in which the deceptive act is *not reinforced*.

Recall that *learned* "deception" is not really deception at all. To deceive somebody is to draw an inference: it is to reason "if I do *this* then he will do or think *that*". It is a prospective act, not something that one has learned to be profitable from noting the consequences of past actions (Dennett, 1978b). As long as the deceptive act is something that has brought rewards in the past it is possible to debunk its deceptive—its *mentalistic*—status. For this reason, I devised a task that measured strategic deception in children (and potentially in animals) in which subjects were never reinforced for performing the deceptive action before the first test trial; for they had instead to draw the inference on a single trial that indicating the place where the goal object was *not* would misdirect the opponent and win them the reward.

This was called the "windows task" for reasons that will soon become apparent (Russell, Mauthner, Sharpe, & Tidswell, 1991). Child and opponent (a second experimenter) sat face-to-face with two boxes between them. When they both had their eyes closed, the experimenter, who sat next to the child, put a chocolate in one of the two boxes and shut the lid. The child's task was to point to either of the two boxes in order to "tell" the opponent where to look for the chocolate; and this obviously meant having to guess. If the opponent went to the baited box then the opponent kept the chocolate; if he went to the empty box then the child was given the chocolate. What the child learned, therefore, trial-by-trial was that it was in her interests to make the opponent go to the empty box, while being ignorant of which of the two boxes *was* the empty one. Accordingly, the subject was not being reinforced for pointing to the empty box because the response she made was not a response to a box that she knew to be empty. This continued for 15 trials and the child's understanding of the consequences of pointing was checked.

In the test phase, the boxes were exchanged for ones in each of which a window had been cut, facing the child. This meant, of course, that the child could see which box contained the chocolate and which one was empty while the opponent could not. Initially, I was interested in what the child would do on this first trial. She had never been reinforced for pointing to the empty box, but would she realise that she now had the opportunity to mislead the opponent? Essentially, we found that 3-year-olds would point, incorrectly, to the baited box, whereas 4-year-olds would point to the empty box. A similar split was observed between the behaviour of two groups of mentally handicapped subjects with mental ages of around 4–5 years: those without autism behaved like normal 4-year-olds whereas those who also had received a diagnosis of autism behaved like normal 3-year-olds.

So far, these data are just what would be predicted by the theory-theory view. The under-4s are failing to deceive strategically because, lacking a conception of false belief, they are unable to implant false beliefs into the minds of others. I discuss autism in the final section, but for now I will say that the data are also consistent with a popular view of the core deficit in autism—deviance or delay in the ability to "mentalise" (Baron-Cohen, Leslie, & Frith, 1985; Leslie, 1987). Indeed there was an empirical as well as a conceptual parallel between success on the windows task and success on the kind of mentalising tasks that 3-year-olds fail: there was significant statistical relationship between passing the windows task and passing the false belief task in these subjects.

There was another feature of the data, however, that was not so easy to explain in terms of a mentalising deficit. When the subjects had made their initial response on the first windows trial they were given a further

19 trials in the expectation that sooner or later they would learn—as Woodruff and Premack's chimps learned—to point to the box that they could see was empty. It turned out, however, that many of them never pointed to the empty box at all throughout the 20 trials. Eleven of the 17 3-year-olds pointed to the baited box on every trial and 7 of the 11 autistic subjects did so; whereas none of the 4-year-old children and none of the mentally handicapped children without autism (all but one had a diagnosis of Down's Syndrome) did so.

Why should a difficulty with mentalising cause subjects to perseverate in this way? No answer immediately suggests itself [90]. However, perseveratively making an incorrect response in the face of evidence that it is incorrect would appear to reveal a quintessentially executive problem; it is, as we have seen, what "frontal" patients sometimes do when performing on such tasks as the WCST. Pinpointing the exact problem is no easy matter, but we are clearly witnessing the control of a subject's behaviour by the environment rather than by a rule held in mind—a rule that is not only arbitrary but counter-intuitive insofar as it tells the subject to do the exact opposite of "what comes naturally".

Well, if executive difficulties can explain the perseveration why should they not also explain the *first* response on the windows trial? (I will postpone discussion of the data from autistic subjects until the next section.) That is to say, on the first trial they were not pointing to the baited box because they had no conception of what it would be to misinform their opponent; rather, they were pointing to the baited box because they could not, as it were, disengage their attention from this object. How could one pit the predictions of an executive account such as this against those of a theory-theory account?

The way we tried to answer this question was by adopting the second of the two strategies introduced earlier—by stripping away the mentalising requirements of the windows task in order to see whether the younger children's difficulties remained. (The first strategy, recall, was that of stripping away the executive requirements. This could have been achieved by studying the *comprehension* rather than the execution of a deceptive act.) Thus, we removed the need for misinforming the opponent simply by removing the opponent; so it was now the experimenter (sitting next to the child) who opened the boxes. In this case, of course, the executive demands are just the same because the subject must indicate the location without the chocolate—tell the experimenter to open the empty box. The experimenter, in contrast to the opponent, cannot be misinformed: he *knows* where the chocolate is because he can see it. For this reason, he cannot be strategically deceived about its location.

In our next two experiments, therefore, we compared performance on the windows task with and without an opponent in pre-school children (Russell, Jarrold, & Potel, 1994) and in mentally handicapped subjects who either had or had not received a diagnosis of autism (Hughes & Russell, 1993). The essential outcome was that removing the opponent had no significant effect. The 3-year-old and the autistic subjects were still more likely to point to the baited box on the first windows trial and were more likely to perseverate for all 20 trials; and there were no significant differences between conditions. (By the way, having the child tell the opponent or experimenter which box to open by referring to its colour rather than by pointing to it also had no effect on the data.) In a subsequent experiment with pre-schoolers (Russell et al., 1994; Expt. 2) we also removed the windows—the subjects simply being *told* which of the two boxes contained the chocolate. This too had no effect, which tells us that it is not simply the *sight* of the desired object that prevents disengagement from it: it is knowledge of the chocolate's location that causes disengagement problems.

This is, however, very far from being the end of the story because mere removal of the opponent does not necessarily remove all the mentalising elements from the original task. That is to say, in the no-opponent condition the subject still has to *misdirect* the experimenter sitting next to her, even if she no longer has to *misinform* an opponent without knowledge; indeed the experimenter could easily be construed as a competitor for resources. For this reason we cannot confidently conclude that subjects fail the windows task because of its executive rather than because of its mentalising requirements until we see the same pattern of data not only without an opponent but without an *experimenter*— when the task is entirely automated[91].

There is a further difficulty with the conclusion. It is that one could accept that young children's difficulty with the windows task has nothing to do with mentalising, while denying that their difficulty is an essentially executive one. For example, one could focus on the fact that the task requires the drawing of a primitive inference: it requires the child to apply a conditional rule—'*if* X is at B *then* point to A; *if* X is at A *then* point to B'. Perhaps this would be the position favoured by Frye et al. (in press) who, as we saw earlier, argue that younger children fail the false belief task because it requires them to make a conditional inference. The present position, by contrast, is that the difficulty is not with understanding any conditional rule but with holding it in working memory while the world calls out the prepotent response of indicating the desired object.

One way of testing these two accounts against each other is by reducing the degree to which the world evokes the prepotent response.

To understand how this can be done we must bear in mind that the chocolate visible (or known to exist) in one of the boxes has a dual nature: it is both the goal object and a signifier of the location to be avoided. Accordingly, we need to change the task so that the signifying role remains but the chocolate is absent. If performance improves—if, that is, the children perform better when the conditional element remains but the prepotency is diminished—then we will have shown that the children's problem is with prepotency.

How could this be done? A chimpanzee study again provided the inspiration. Sarah Boysen (1993) had shown that chimpanzees fail a kind of strategic sharing task. Two plates of sweets are placed between two chimps, with one plate containing (say) five sweets and the other plate containing only one. The animal being tested has to indicate one of the two plates, and whichever one is indicated is given to its partner. Obviously, the correct strategy here—at least if you want the larger amount—is to indicate the plate with only one sweet on it. However, despite the animals' impressive intellectual achievements in other areas (which included learning Arabic numerals—see later), they were unable to behave in their own interests: they pointed to the larger amount and consequently lost it to the partner. Drawing a parallel between this and the windows task is irresistible.

What Boysen did next was, in effect, to reduce the prepotency of the incorrect response by exploiting the fact that the animals knew Arabic numerals. Thus, in the next phase of the experiment, each plate contained a card showing a numeral representing the different amounts—1 or 5. In this case, the animals did behave strategically, pointing to the plate showing the numeral 1, obtaining five sweets in exchange, and demonstrating thereby that the conditional nature of the task presented no challenges.

In order to find out whether presenting 3-year-old children with representations of chocolates rather than with the real thing made the windows task any easier, we gave them two kinds of task with two kinds of materials (Russell, Jarrold, Davis, & Halligan, submitted). One task was a strategic sharing task similar to Boysen's and the other was the windows task; half the children saw chocolates (one versus five or nothing versus one) and half of them saw brown circles drawn on card representing chocolates (one versus five or nothing versus one). Overall, the strategic deception task was more difficult than the strategic sharing task and, overall (i.e. pooling the data from the two tasks) the children were more successful when they were presented with the representations of chocolates rather than with the real thing. However they were no more successful with the representations on each task. There was a clear trend in that direction, especially on the windows task;

indeed about half as many children (6 versus 10) perseverated on every trial with the brown circles than with the chocolate buttons. But the difference was not statistically reliable, and the windows task still presented significant difficulties when symbolic rather than real chocolates were used.

A rather more successful attempt to reduce the executive demands of the windows task was made by Suzanne Hala (Hala, Russell, & Maberly, submitted). She asked whether children's inability to inhibit reference to the baited box was due to the fact that they have to make a highly natural response—one normally made in an unreflective way. For we would expect that the more natural and spontaneous a response is the more difficult it will be to inhibit. Pointing to what you want is certainly very natural, and even when children are told to say the colour of the box rather than point to it they generally point in addition to speaking (Russell et al., 1994). Hala found that when, instead of pointing, 3-year-olds are told to orient a cardboard pointing-hand to their chosen box or to place a cardboard star on it—both highly non-natural responses—they are much more successful. However, the children were still generally incorrect on the first five or so trials; so what the introduction of the non-natural response was doing was helping them to pull back from perseveration rather than helping them make the appropriate response initially.

The conservative conclusion from these studies, therefore, is that *both* prepotency and conditional rule use have their roles to play here. Moreover, the contrast between the two positions is rather less stark than I have drawn it, insofar as both processes involve the *selection of appropriate strategies given a state of reality*. Success on conditional learning tasks in monkeys (e.g. "if blue rotate handle, if red pull handle"; Halsband & Passingham, 1985) is associated with the premotor area (Brodmann's area 8), an area that "selects things in the outside world" (Passingham, 1993, p.123), and conditional reasoning can be regarded as a form of planning, and planning is a quintessentially executive process. [A recent imagining study by Fletcher and colleagues (Fletcher et al., 1994) found that this area is active when adults listen to stories with a mentalistic content.] But genuine disputes cannot be resolved by stretching one's terminology! *Is* it the case, in other words, that younger children fail some tasks with a mentalistic content because they cannot suppress the salience of what they currently know and currently experience?

One conclusion, at least, seems safe. It is that we can be lured into thinking we have discovered a major transition in children's ability to deceive strategically between 3 and 4 years when what we have really discovered is a transition in their executive functioning—broadly conceived. Every piece of data that reveals such "luring" speaks against the claim that there is a 3–4 transition in mentalising.

So far, however, we have only looked at two kinds of 3–4 transition tasks—false belief and strategic deception. And even if there were industrial-strength evidence that a very specific executive process (suppress a prepotent response and choose or answer on the basis of a rule held in mind) can explain why younger children fail them, they are only two tasks. So can this account explain 3-year-olds' failures on *all* varieties of 3–4 mentalising tasks? The short answer is "no". This negative answer will lead me to argue that when 3-year-olds fail such tasks they do not make simple *performance* errors, and that, like older children who fail concrete operational tasks, their difficulty is one of executive *competence*.

The 3–4 transition as one of executive competence

I will not review all the 3–4 mentalising tasks because my intention is to show that the kind of executive account I have been presenting has a *limited* application. It will, therefore, be enough to show that it fails to explain performance on just one or two such tasks. But first, are there tasks to which it does apply apart from false belief and strategic deception?

It certainly applies to the so-called "Smarties" task in which the subject has to ascribe a false belief about the contents of a Smarties tube (having just found out that it contains a pencil not sweets) to another child (Perner, Leekam, & Wimmer, 1987). And it applies equally well to a similar task in which subjects have to acknowledge that they had a false belief about the contents of a box at an earlier time (Gopnik & Astington, 1988). In both these cases, the wrong answer is a report of one's own current knowledge.

Another kind of task to which an executive account can be extended is the kind of appearance–reality task devised by John Flavell (Flavell et al., 1983), in which children are presented with either trick objects (e.g. an "egg" made of stone) or objects whose properties are apparently altered (e.g. a white card behind a blue light-filter). In the trick object task, the 3-year-old's predominant error when asked what the object *looks like*, is to say "a stone", while in the property change task they are likely to say that the card is blue when asked what colour it is "really and truly". In short, they are "realists" when they should be "phenomenists" and "phenomenists" when they should be "realists". The explanation that Flavell originally gave for this result is fully in the spirit of the present account. When a subject is asked a question about what something looks like or what it is really, Flavell argues, he or she has to hold in mind two competing representations. What happens in the case of younger children is that the representation that is the more "cognitively salient", which is "the most upfront in consciousness" (Flavell et al., 1983, p.99), wins out. The younger child lacks the ability to *frame* his or her answer and is instead *caused* to produce an answer on the basis of the more potent information. A potential weakness of this account is that one should be able to say a priori which of the two representations will be the more cognitively salient; but it is certainly plausible to say that the real nature of a trick object and the apparent nature of a perceptually transformed object is what is likely to grab the attention.

The picture looks a good deal more complicated, however, when we consider tasks in which children have to ascribe knowledge or ignorance to other people on the basis of their perceptual experiences. The present account would predict that 3-year-olds will ascribe their own knowledge state to others irrespective of what the other person has seen or heard. Certainly children often do this; indeed the false belief task control question with which they normally have the most difficulty is the so-called "ignorance" question ("Does [the protagonist] know that the coin is now at B?") because it leads them to ascribe their own knowledge to the ignorant protagonist[92]. But when 3-year-olds are questioned about whether other people know the contents of a box, given various conditions of their own knowledge and of the other's perceptual access (Wimmer, Hogrefe, & Perner, 1988), the dominant error is *not* the egocentric one of ascribing what they currently know or do not know to the other person. Indeed they often deny that the other child knows something (what is in a box) which they themselves know and when the other child shares their perspective. Some studies have suggested that Wimmer et al.'s procedure underestimates 3-year-olds' abilities (Pillow, 1989; Pratt & Bryant, 1990), but it may well be that these studies, in turn, *over*estimated them (Povinelli & deBlois, 1992, Discussion).

In any event, the following data cannot be explained in terms of executive difficulties—at least as we have described them so far. Yet again, the procedure is derived from one originally used with non-human primates (Povinelli, Nelson, & Boysen, 1990). Daniel Povinelli and Sandra de Blois (1992) presented 3- and 4-year-old children with four possible hiding places of a desired object, with the situation having been stage-managed to ensure that the children knew which one of two experimenters had hidden the object (one of them had left the room during the hiding). When, in the test phase, each of the experimenters pointed to different locations, the question was whether the children would take the advice of the informed rather than of the uninformed experimenter. The 4-year-olds generally did and the 3-year-olds generally did not.

We now move to a similar situation in which the child has to take the advice of the appropriate person about the location of an object. This time, however, the clue the subject has to use is the degree of certainty that the person expresses rather than whether or not the person was a witness to the hiding. In a series of experiments, Chris Moore and his colleagues (Moore, Bryant, & Furrow, 1989; Moore & Davidge, 1989; Moore, Pure, & Furrow, 1990) asked whether children could interpret mental and modal expressions of certainty. In a nutshell, what 4-year-olds can do and 3-year-olds cannot is to appreciate that a statement of the kind "I'm sure that ..." or "It must be ..." or "I know that ..." [it is in box A not box B] is a better guide to reality than ones like "I think that..." or "It might be..." or "I guess that..." [it is in box B not box A]. In practice the child is faced with two closed boxes while one puppet makes one kind of assertion and another puppet makes the other kind; after which the child is asked to say which box contains the object. Furthermore, success on these kinds of task correlates well with success on the standard false belief task, on the own past false belief task, and on the appearance–reality task (Moore et al., 1990). The four tasks seem to be tapping the same kind of ability.

Clearly, in the Povinelli and in the Moore procedures there is no knowledge and no "cognitively salient" representation from which the child must disengage. And this is not the only area of difficulty for the executive account. It is also fails to explain why 4-year-olds are generally good at justifying their own information-based behaviour and 3-year-olds are not (Povinelli & deBlois, 1992, Expt 1). Moreover, if 3-year-olds really have a secure grasp of the fact that agents' search is generated by their sometimes-false beliefs—an understanding that is masked by their tendency to given the prepotent response—then why is it that they can generally give no reasons why the protagonist in the false belief task went to the original location rather than to the one to which they predicted he would go (Wimmer & Weichbold, 1994)?

The data force us, therefore, to reject the view that failure on *all* 3–4 mentalising tasks is caused by failing to inhibit the prepotent response of answering in terms of one's own current knowledge state while holding the information on which to frame the answer in working memory. This does not mean, however, that an executive account of the 3–4 transition has to be abandoned. What we should do, I will argue, is to view the executive transition as one of executive *competence*, as a transition of a similar status to that taking place between 6 and 7 years of age. In other words, the situation is not that children's understanding of mental states remains *unchanged* between 3 and 4 years of age, while they continue to make performance errors on certain kinds of task. Rather, a general advance in executive functioning enables children to reflect on mental states in a way that had previously been impossible to achieve. On this view, what one may call the "classic" mentalising tasks such as false belief, strategic deception, and appearance–reality reveal an executive transition while not directly measuring the grasp of a mental concept. Tasks of the kind used by Povinelli and by Moore, on the other hand, do not tap executive development in the sense in which that term is being used here[93] and do not test for the presence of a mental concept; but they do reveal the ability to attend to and reflect on mental states and orientations that general executive development makes available.

Before passing on, I should say something about how, on this view, one should regard the difference between the 3–4 and the 6–7 transitions. I have described them both as transitions of "executive competence".

Although the two transitions share an executive character, on the present view, the tasks that measure them differ radically in terms of content, with the content of the 3–4 transition tasks being less abstract than the contents of the 6–7 transition tasks. With regard to the executive requirements, in both kinds of task children have to juggle two competing representations and suppress the salience of one of them, and in both cases the ability to do this affords new modes of reflection. In the earlier transition they have to choose one representation over another; but in the later one they have to *co-ordinate* two representations by way of framing a judgement *about an abstract property*. In the false belief experiment they have to frame their answers in terms of the protagonist's belief rather in terms of their own belief; in the conservation task they do not frame their answer in terms of one dimension or another, but have, rather, to un-glue their attention from whichever is the more salient dimension and frame their answers in terms of the abstract notions such as amount or space or time[94].

We need, furthermore, to re-consider the difference between an executive performance and an executive competence error. An executive performance error is what subjects make against their better judgement—like Luria's frontal patients who knew they were sorting by the wrong category could not help but continue. There is no reason to believe that the executive transition is of this nature. One can identify prepotency (salience of one's own knowledge) as a factor that can lead 3-year-olds into error and thus as something that may be luring them towards a performance error, but, as we have just seen, some 3–4 mentalising tasks are not failed for this reason. Moreover, the experiment of Wimmer and Weichbold (1994), just mentioned, showed that when, in the false belief task, 3-year-olds are shown where Maxi goes (to the *original* location) they are unable to explain *why*. If these

3-year-olds were making a performance error, if, that is, the "Where will Maxi go?" question caused them to refer the new location despite their having a secure understanding of how false beliefs lead to false search, they should have been able to explain why Maxi went wrong.

So what does it mean to say that the 3–4 transition may be one of executive *competence*? Earlier I defined a child's (as opposed to an infant's) executive competence error as one in which there is a failure "to regulate his or her attention in such a way that he or she is able to think explicitly and at will about certain mental or abstract properties or processes" and later tried to show how this could be applied to the 6–7 transition. It can be applied to the 3–4 transition in the following way. The younger child has some conception of belief but lacks the kind of top-down control over his or her mental processes necessary for answering questions about mental representation; the child's mental-reflective capacities are swamped by the salience of his or her own knowledge. Endogenous changes around the age of 4 years[95] make this control possible, and children become able to reflect on what they know rather than being determined by it, able to reflect on the mental states of others and on their different propositional attitudes to contents, and generally adopt a supervisory and regulatory relation to what they and others know, believe, and experience. What develops, on this view, is not a new theory but the capacity to render explicit the distinction between themselves as "mental agents", their propositional attitudes, and the contents of their thoughts. Endogenous executive changes make possible a reflective orientation to these contents.

How might such a theory be tested? There are two main ways. The first is correlational. Here, one would look at the relationship between performance on tasks that tap mental insights but do not measure executive processes and tasks that measure executive processes but do not require mentalising. I think "mental insights" and "executive processes" could be interpreted broadly here. Obviously Moore's mental verb assessment task comes within the former category but so do tasks that assess meta-cognition, moral judgement, responsibility, and self-awareness. "Executive processes" might, as I argued before, be stretched to encompass all those tasks that require the organisation of behaviour relative to environmental contingencies—in which case conditional learning would not be excluded.

The second way of testing the theory is clinically. That is to say, one would ask whether children with early impairments in executive functioning also have impairments in mentalising—broadly construed. If they did not, then this would be fatal evidence against the theory. However an easier first step would be to ask whether mentalising and executive difficulties at least *co-exist* in clinical populations, because the existence of mentalising difficulties in the absence of executive difficulties would likewise be fatal. They certainly co-exist in autism.

Accordingly, in the final section of this book I will discuss the co-existence of executive and mentalising difficulties in autism, arguing that this is highly consistent with the central thesis of Part 3 that adequate executive development is necessary for adequate ego development—mind$_0$—which is in turn necessary for an adequate grasp of the "subject→attitude→content" triad. I need to begin, however, by describing the dominant and far more popular view that the core deficit in autism is an innate dysfunction of the theory of mind mechanism (ToMM)—the modular system I discussed earlier. The present position is best understood against the background of this.

3.5: AUTISM, EXECUTIVE DYSFUNCTIONS, AND "MIND BLINDNESS"

There is no shortage of evidence for the view that the core component of autism is a delay or deviance in the development of a mechanism dedicated to computing the "subject→attitude→content" relation for both the self and others—the ToMM (Leslie & Thaiss, 1992). In children with autism, we find an absence or poverty of pretence (Baron-Cohen, 1987), impaired performance on the false belief task (Baron-Cohen, Leslie & Frith, 1985) coupled with mental-age-normal performance on tasks that require a grasp of *pictorial* representation (Leslie & Thaiss, 1992) and difficulties with a wide range of other mentalising tasks (see papers in Baron-Cohen, Tager-Flusberg, & Cohen, 1993).

It is important to bear in mind that these experiments are not simply telling us that autism is associated with difficulty in understanding why people act, speak, and react as they do: they are not just telling us what we already know[96]. They show us that people who suffer from autism are not just broadly impaired in the personal-affective area: they are impaired *specifically* in their understanding of mental representation. If this is so, then many of their everyday social and communicative abnormalities can be explained rather elegantly (Frith & Happé, 1994; Happé, 1993).

But although the case has been thoroughly made that autism is associated with mentalising problems, there are at least two major impediments to the view that the disorder is caused by the lack or dysfunction of a *sui generis* module. The first impediment is conceptual, and will be familiar from what has gone before; the second is entirely empirical.

First, on the ToMM-deficit view no principled distinction is drawn between self-awareness and other-awareness. The theory spreads across both the self and the other, with the result that self-awareness is construed as a special case of successfully computing the relation between *any* agent, *any* attitude, and *any* content. What is wrong with this? Much of Part 3 has been taken up with saying what is wrong with it. Principally, it ignores the fact that self-awareness is bound up—in ways I discussed at length—with a form of immediate knowledge that one is willing, and that this is a kind of knowledge we cannot have about others. In the context of autism it implies that autistic persons' *pre-theoretical* mental life ($mind_0$) is unimpaired, and that deviance and impoverishment are revealed only when the subject→attitude→content triad has to be computed; this is a matter to which I will return. Recall what I said earlier (pp.197–199) about the ToMM being "all syntax and no semantics" (the case of The Mentaliser). In contrast with this, the present view is "all semantics and no syntax", locating the autistic person's difficulty at the level of first-person, pre-theoretical experience—$mind_0$ or even $mind_s$ [see (3.5(ii) later].

The empirical difficulty with the ToMM-deficit hypothesis is that it implies that all other cognitive and social difficulties experienced in autism are derivatives of the lack of the ToMM—or lack of one of its components. Now, nobody expects the hypothesis to explain every single feature of autism (unusual gait, speech pitch and prosody; lack of fear of animals; high pain threshold ...); and indeed in that sense there is never going to be a general *psychological* theory of autism. (I mean as distinct from a neuro-physiological model which pin-points the dysfunctional brain circuits responsible for the constellation of autistic symptoms: Bachevalier, 1994). However, one *can* reasonably expect the theory to account for autistic persons' pervasive and dramatic impairments in agency. What I am referring to here is the fact that autism is invariably associated with an excessive desire for sameness and routine, accompanied by so-called "catastrophic" reactions to change and by a lack of spontaneity. Broadly speaking, the inability to cope with novelty is at least as strongly associated with autism as is the "mind-blindness" referred to on the ToMM-deficit view[97]; and coping with novelty is surely one of the hallmarks of successful agency given that novel situations force the subject to improvise, instead of relying on routine schemas. [Recall the previous discussion of the "supervisory attentional system" which Norman and Shallice claimed to be the core component of the executive system, one of whose principal functions is coping with novelty.]

Advocates of the ToMM deficit view have responded to the challenge of explaining agency impairments in two main ways. Baron-Cohen

(1989) has argued that the inability to predict and explain the behaviour of other people will generate anxiety which will in turn lead the individual to impose predictability and order on his or her social life. But why should the anxiety caused by the unpredictablity of others' behaviour be mitigated by being predictable oneself? There is no way of ensuring that others will not invade one's ordered world. At best, such a view can only explain social withdrawal, which many autistic persons do not, in fact, demonstrate[98]. Moreover, there is no evidence that the performance of routines by autistic persons *is* anxiety-reducing; indeed the parents of autistic children tend to report that stereotypies are more likely to be produced when the child has nothing to occupy him or her and when he or she is alone rather than with other people and/or anxious (Turner, 1995).

The second way of explaining the coexistence of executive and mentalising difficulties is owing to Christopher and Uta Frith (1991) who argue that successful mentalising and successful agency are grounded in the ability to "meta-represent". I must confront this claim because its implicit assumption that representational achievements must ground executive achievements makes it the opposite of the present position. I will discuss it right at the end of Part 3. We turn first, however, to the experimental evidence for executive dysfunctions in autism—as opposed to the everyday observations of executive difficulties.

3.5(i) Executive dysfunctions in autism
Persons with autism perform poorly on the two classic "frontal" tasks—the Tower of London or ToL[99] (a planning task) and the Wisconsin Card Sorting Task or WCST (a set-shifting task)[100]. Among the first people to show this were Sally Ozonoff and her colleagues in Denver[101] (Ozonoff, Pennington, & Rogers, 1991; Ozonoff, Rogers, & Pennington, 1991). More importantly, they showed that performance on executive tasks was a better discriminator between high-functioning (i.e. near normal IQ) autistic and control groups than was performance on theory of mind tasks. One exception was the "second order" false belief task (e.g. "What does Sally think that John is thinking ..."); but it is equally possible to regard this as an executive task, on a par with the ToL, in which a number of representations have to be held on-line in working memory[102]. (Many normal subjects will fail a *fourth*-order false belief task; but surely not because they have a weak grasp of the nature of belief.) More recently, Bennetto, Pennington, and Rogers (in press) reported that subjects with autism show similar memory deficits to frontal patients, performing poorly on tests of temporal ordering, source memory, and free recall, while showing adequate recognition

memory, short-term span, and cued recall. Broadly speaking, the memory tasks on which frontal patients fail are the ones that require active, strategic process and those on which they succeed require the *undergoing* of processes such as feelings of familiarity (trace strength) and being susceptible to the right cue (having strong cue–target associations). However, the question of whether autistic persons have *working* memory deficits is a more controversial one which I shall discuss later.

The existence of this kind of data led Pennington (1994) to argue that autism is essentially a disorder of the prefrontal cortices, in line with Damasio and Maurer's (1978) earlier neurological model of the disorder. I shall assess this view in the next sub-section, but for now it is worth pointing out that some of the more powerful neurological models of autism have failed to implicate the prefrontal brain specifically. Jocelyne Bachevalier (1994) has recently presented a neurological model of autism based partly on animal work, in which the medial temporal lobe (especially structures involving the amygdala) is principally implicated. There are certainly striking parallels between autism in humans and the Klüver-Bucy syndrome in monkeys caused by bilateral removal of the temporal lobes. Hoon and Reiss (1992) report the case of a boy with congenital damage to the mesial-temporal lobe who met 7 of the 16 DSM-3-R criteria for autism (e.g. no symbolic play, "lived in a world of his own"). More controversially, Eric Courchesne and his colleges (Courchesne, Akshoomoff, & Townsend, 1992) have implicated the neocerebellum, arguing that it plays a crucial role in the directing of attention[103].

In ignorance of the work of the Denver team, I stumbled towards the view that subjects with autism have deficits similar to those of frontal patients by studying their performance on the windows task. The perseverative, "stuck-in-set" (Sandson & Albert, 1984) behaviour of the subjects with mental ages as high as 5 on the test trials was certainly reminiscent of the behaviour of frontal patients (Russell et al., 1991).

Moreover, like the 3-year-old normal children described earlier (Russell et al., 1994), children with a diagnosis of autism but with mental ages of around 5–6 continue to fail the windows task (pointing to the baited box on the first trial and on most or all of the subsequent trials) when there is no opponent present (Hughes & Russell, 1993)—another fact that clearly suggests executive rather than mentalising difficulties. In fact, we found that 21 of our 42 autistic subjects with mental ages of around 5 years perseverated on all 20 trials; whereas none of the mentally handicapped children did so. Moreover, the qualitative differences between the behaviour of autistic children and children with mental handicap but without autism was very striking. The mentally handicapped children often began with the wrong strategy but they gradually benefited from negative feedback [note the similarity to the Hala et al. data (p.237) on 3-year-olds making a non-natural response]; but the autistic children almost never showed this pattern. More recently Wareham (1994) tested a small sample of 6-year-old children of *normal* intelligence but with a diagnosis of Asperger Syndrome[104] on the windows task and found, in addition to general difficulty with the task, one subject who could articulate the rule perfectly and yet perseveratively pointed to the baited box on every trial. This confirms Ozonoff, Rogers, and Pennington's (1991) finding that people who suffer from Asperger Syndrome do indeed have executive problems.

However, as I said when discussing the performance of normal children, failing the windows task without an opponent is nevertheless failing to *misdirect* another person if not actually to misinform them; so there may be residual "mentalising" demands. Moreover, the task can easily be construed by the subject as one in which he or she has to compete with the experimenter for resources, and competition is a social activity. This led us to ask how autistic and comparison (normal and mentally handicapped) subjects would perform on a task that made somewhat similar demands to the windows task (without an opponent) but in which the experimenter did not have to be misdirected and there was no competition for resources between subject and experimenter. The task would have to require both the inhibition of a direct response to a goal and the use of an indirect act (a arbitrary rule to be retained in working memory) which would result in the goal being attained.

A visit to London's Science Museum by my (then) graduate student Claire Hughes provided the inspiration for such a task. In the task she subsequently designed, a goal could only be attained if a seemingly irrelevant action was performed first; and if this act was not performed a direct reach made the object disappear. The goal was a marble resting on hollow plinth inside a box, visible through an aperture in the box. Reaching for the marble through the aperture broke a light beam, thereby causing a trap-door to open at the top of the plinth and the marble to vanish. The only way the marble could be retrieved was by first throwing a switch on the side of the box and then reaching. We had, therefore, the ingredients for a classic executive task—(a) the inhibition of a prepotent response[105] (the direct reach) and (b) the retention of an arbitrary rule in working memory (throw a switch before reaching).

The difficulties our autistic subjects experienced with this task were severe. Fixing the criterion for "success" as a run of three switch-and-reach sequences within 15 trials, we found that only half of our autistic subjects with mental ages approaching 5 years succeeded, and that success was only universal in the sub-group (containing 10 subjects) with mental ages of around 11 years. By contrast, 92% of the mentally handicapped subjects attained criterion, with success being unrelated to mental age. It was, moreover, a trivially easy task for our normally developing control group whose members were aged between 3 and 4 years (Hughes & Russell, 1993). In fact we found in a later study that children as young as two can attain criterion on the task (Russell, Lee, & Drake, 1993). Thus, we can conclude that when the two ingredients of prepotency and an arbitrary rule are clearly present, the failure of autistic subjects is dramatic.

Moreover, given what I said earlier about parallels between the 3–4 and the 6–7 transitions, one would have to predict that, *if* concrete operational tasks such as conservation are essentially executive tasks then autistic subjects should be impaired on them. This prediction has been fulfilled. Yirmiya, Sigman, Kasari, and Mundy (1992) found that 28% of a group of *nonretarded* autistic subjects between 9 and 14 years could not conserve at all. On the present hypothesis, this is because the subjects had difficulty inhibiting the prepotent response of framing their answer in term of salient unidimensional changes.

However, as I noted previously, there are *some* executive tasks, notably the ToL, that contain no obvious element of prepotency. And in others, such as the WCST, the prepotency in the task arises from prior learning (e.g. to sort by colour) rather than directly from the environment. We felt it was important, therefore, to confirm the Ozonoff, Pennington, and Rogers (1991) finding that persons with autism are indeed impaired on these two tasks. Further to this, Hughes administered a computerised version of the ToL in which it was somewhat easier for the subject to maintain the arbitrary rule in mind (some items must not be placed above others and only one item can be manipulated at a time) because the computer would disallow all illegal moves. In addition to this she administered a further computerised task called the ID/ED ('intradimensional/extradimensional') shift, which is similar to the WCST insofar as it required set-shifting (shift attention from thick, black item in background to thin, white item in foreground). The autistic subjects were clearly impaired relative to mentally handicapped and to normal subjects on both of these tasks (Hughes, Russell, & Robbins, 1994). The fact that there is no obviously prepotent response on the ToL and no incorrect strategy from which they had to disengage suggests that autism is associated with a deficit in planning *per se*. Although note that this is *on-line* planning (in contrast to planning for the future) in which a number of representations have to be retained and ordered in working memory. More recently, in fact, our attention has been directed towards possible working memory deficits.

There are a number of reasons for looking at working memory in autism. First, all executive tasks have a working memory component, and indeed Patricia Goldman-Rakic's (1987) influential theory of prefrontal functioning holds that "representational memory" is *the* core component of executive tasks. [A recent factor-analytic study of a large population of normal adults' performance on a range of "frontal" tasks provided some support for this view (Diagneault, Braün, & Whitaker, 1992).] Second, Alan Baddeley and Graham Hitch's (1974; Baddeley, 1986) well-known model of working memory distinguishes between those aspects of working memory that make demands on the "central executive" and those that do not; and this affords the prediction that if persons with autism do indeed have executive deficits then they should be impaired on tasks that recruit central functioning and be unimpaired on those that do not. By the "central executive" Baddeley intends a system of limited capacity that organises current mental operations (e.g. subtracting one set of digits from another, monitoring the input for a relevant cue). Because this system has a fixed capacity it requires subsidiary or "slave" systems to hold data off-line while these central operations are being performed (e.g. keeping a tally of the results of previous calculations while performing the current one). Accordingly, if all that is required is the retention of data (as required, for example, in simple serial recall of words) then the central executive is being minimally taxed. However, if the subject has to perform mental operations (such as comprehension, spotting the odd-one-out, or counting) while at the same time holding data off-line in a rehearsal "loop", then the capacity of the whole system can be measured.

Chris Jarrold and I (Russell, Jarrold & Henry, in press) showed, first of all, that the most studied subsidiary working memory system (the so-called "articulatory loop") is unimpaired[106] in autistic children. This is to be expected if the central executive is not being taxed by such tasks. However we found, to our surprise, that when executive working memory tests are admininistered which require the storage of data together with the simultaneous performance of mental operations they are *also* unimpaired. However it must be noted that, in the latter tasks, although there was no impairment relative to mentally handicapped controls there *was* impairment relative to normal subjects. This fact may explain why Bennetto et al. found, in the memory study mentioned earlier, that high-functioning autistic subjects *were* impaired on executive working memory tasks[107]: their autistic subjects were compared with subjects of near-normal intelligence rather than with mentally handicapped subjects. It is possible that many forms of impairment are associated with executive working memory problems—as well as with peripheral ones[108].

What these data suggest is that executive *capacity* is not impaired in persons with autism, in the sense that their space for, and the efficiency of, on-line computation—it is difficult to disentangle these (Case, Kurland, & Goldberg, 1982; Towse & Hitch, 1995)—may be no worse than that of other mentally handicapped subjects. So why are they so clearly impaired on the ToL? This may well be because the ToL tests not only the efficiency of working memory but also the *selection of strategies*; the subject must select his or her *own* strategies. For although there is a shortest route to the solution, there are many possible routes; and so ToL is an "open-ended" task to this extent. However the kind of executive working memory task used by us and by Bennetto et al. required nothing from the subject beyond the performance of a simple, "closed" operation—counting dots on cards, finding the odd-one-out of three, doing a simple sum. This explanation could be tested by giving autistic subjects a form of storage-plus-procedure working memory task in which the procedure is open-ended (e.g. generating numbers randomly or saying any word that starts with the letter 'G')[109]. Baddeley (1986) has shown, in fact, that such random generation tasks are particularly effective at taking up central executive space. Indeed, he takes this to be indirect evidence for the Norman and Shallice (1986) supervisory-attentional-system model of the central executive (Baddeley, 1986, Ch.10) insofar as their model gives this system responsibility for generating novel acts[110].

The basic idea, then, is that tasks which require the generation of strategies (as does the ToL) utilise more "mental energy" in persons with autism. For this reason their difficulty cannot really be called one of working memory, which properly refers to the capacity and efficiency of the on-line memory system. Let us turn finally, then, to the role of strategy generation.

A prime responsibility of the executive system is to *generate relevant behaviour*. When this generative system is dysfunctional, one would expect the environment, or past learning (e.g. on the WCST), or routine schemas, or current drive states to determine what the organism does next—by default. On a higher level, the generative system causes ideas to come to mind; it accounts, by definition, for creativity. But on the most basic level, it is what accounts for the self-determination of perceptual inputs discussed at length in Part 2.

Certainly, taking a "failure of generativity" perspective on autism makes many of the everyday features of the disorder look more intelligible. On this view, the reason for the absence or paucity of pretend play in autism is not, as Leslie (1987) argues, that autistic children have an impaired ability to decouple the primary (veridical) representation of an object and act in terms of its secondary (imagined) nature: their difficulty is not "meta-representational" at all. Rather, they do not play because they cannot generate ideas for play. It has to be said, though, that it is difficult to decide empirically between these two views (the meta-representational and the generative) because much depends on how broadly one interprets the term "meta-representation"—as we shall see later. One might begin by extracting the claim from the generative view that autistic children should be able to comprehend symbolic acts, and get into pretend mode with encouragement, even if they do not produce these acts. Experiments that show this (Jarrold, Smith, Boucher, & Harris, 1994; Kavanaugh & Harris, 1994) are, however, difficult to interpret because one cannot be sure whether the subjects are showing that they know pretence when they see it or are simply complying with the rules of conduct that the experimenter has imposed. But, that said, the conceptual distinction between understanding what it is to imagine and the ability to generate imaginative acts is clear enough.

What other everyday features of autism can "lack of generativity" explain? It is common for persons with autism with sufficient general intelligence to reflect on their disorder to say that what makes holding conversations difficult for them is that they can think of nothing to say (Turner, 1995). Furthermore, an individual who wants to say or do *something* but lacks the ability to generate his or her own ideas would be expected to select one domain and stick within it and thus be provided both with strict "rules of engagement" plus a smidgen of novelty. This would explain the "restricted range of interests" that is a central diagnostic feature of the disorder. The world of video-recorders, for example, is a highly predictable world with modest degrees of variability around, say, programming procedures and fascia design.

Why should generativity problems lead to the frequent obsessive desire for routine that is another central feature of autism? Why, for example, should problems with producing novel behaviour off the cuff lead a child to insist that bath-time must be 6pm and never 8pm? What is happening here, perhaps, is that the individual is minimising the likelihood of encountering an unpredictable event because when such events occur there will be a demand for appropriate "off the cuff" action.

It must be said, however, that there are clear impediments to claiming that the core executive deficit in autism, or in any disorder, is with "generativity"; and these problems will remain even if generativity (rather than, say, prepotency and set-shifting or set-maintenance[111]) were found to be autistic subjects' core difficulties in the standard executive tasks. Not only are generativity accounts difficult to discriminate, as I said just now, from those expressed in terms of meta-representational deficits (imaginative fecundity is at least as representational a matter as an executive one) but they rest on a notion that at present—some would say "ultimately"—is mysterious. What is generativity? At its worst, explaining a subject's failure on a task that requires the generation of ideas and behaviour in terms of "a failure of generativity" is reminiscent of the doctor in Molière's play who explained the action of a sleeping draught in terms of its "dormative properties". In other words, saying that a certain population has difficulty generating plans and ideas is only a starting-point. Do we invent the "Plans and Ideas Generating System" (or PIGS) to explain this and then speculate about its exact locus in the pre-frontal cortex? What we clearly do *not* want to posit is a homunculus just bursting with ideas and pulling all the right executive levers. At the very *least*, we have to say something sensible about how lack of generativity relates to other kinds of deficits existing in autism. I will have a little more to say about this towards the end of the next sub-section, but here is one speculative move that can be made in that direction—a broadly empiricist one. Its starting assumption is that one of the main determinants of the ability to generate ideas is that individuals should *experience* the world in the right kind of way; a way that ensures that their minds have a quantum of raw-material from which the imagination can weave its products. Generally speaking, they should have a "wide" attentional net which admits more data than that required for the fulfilment of immediate goals.

Although it is simplistic, this "not-getting-more-out-than-you-put-in" idea does make some rather clear predictions. First, it entails that creative individuals will find it more difficult than matched controls to filter out task-irrelevant information. Data bearing on this claim are not plentiful. We do know, however, that high creatives performing a counting task, while not being more distracted by irrelevant information than are low creatures, do recall more of the irrelevant material (words and semantic categories) after the sorting is complete (Russell, 1976). High creatives were also found to be more likely to use irrelevant words earlier presented in a memory task in the later solution of anagrams (Mendlesohn & Griswold, 1964). With regard to autism, it predicts supra-normal abilities for focusing on what is relevant in a situation—a kind of mental tunnel vision. I will discuss the evidence for this and how it relates to the "pure" executive accounts of the disorder in the next sub-section.

We have obviously moved quite a long way from a pure executive view of autism during the last passage. But we can do this without losing sight of the distinction between a disorder whose core component is the lack of a theoretical grasp of the subject–attitude–content triad and one whose core component is self-determination—whether manifested in over-riding the present external or mental environment or in generating one's own mental environment.

3.5(ii) How do mentalising difficulties relate to executive difficulties in autism?

I hope my account of the relation between executive and mentalising difficulties will come as no surprise to the reader. It is as follows:

If agency plays the role in the development of self awareness—or "ego development"—that I have claimed it does, then human beings with congenital impairments in agency will undergo deviant ego-development; and if ego-development is impaired so too will be the acquisition of a theory of mind. My concern here is with what I called "mind$_0$"— the individual's immediate knowledge of being a centre of responsibility for his or her action-generated experiences, of having the power to determine what is experienced and thus of being the "owner" of a mental life. If there is an early impairment in the ability to determine what one does and how one's attention is directed then there will develop an inadequate sense of oneself—given that, at this primitive, pre-theoretical level, first-person experience is an experience of the flowing together of apprehension and *willing*—see 3.2(iii).

What I need to stress right now is that this is supposed to be an entirely empirical, causal claim which the conceptual arguments of sections 3.1 and 3.2 are intended to make intelligible. Looking at what Schopenhauer and others have said about the relation between agency and the self may inspire all kinds of hypotheses about psychopathology, but it can hardly be said to demonstrate their *truth*. That is, if what I said earlier is correct, an account of agency expressed purely in terms of third-person experience is conceptually flawed, but it does not foreclose the hypothesis that persons with autism have an innate impairment in ToMM. Moreover, it allows many other kinds of accounts of the forms of the *pre*-theoretical impairment that may be present in autism. One such theory is owing to Peter Hobson (1989; 1993) who claims that what is lacking in autism is not a ToMM but the natural proclivity to feel and express relatedness to other people. This differs from the present view insofar as what I am arguing is that interpersonal-cum-affective impairments in autism may be derivatives of an impaired sense of self. I am not saying, however, that it is an easy matter to argue for this derivation. It is not immediately obvious, for example, why an impaired first-person sense should result in a lack of empathy (Yirmiya et al., 1992)[112].

I should also stress that what I am proposing is not supposed to be a "theory of autism". (As I said earlier, autism is a *sui generis* disorder that may well not yield to any general psychological account.) It is, rather, an hypothesis about *why we find in autism both mentalising and executive dysfunctions*.

It is also important to bear in mind that it is an essentially developmental hypothesis; and it is similar to Hobson's position in this respect. The idea is that *early* inadequate experiences of agency will *cause* inadequate ego development. Causal theories are bold but vulnerable, and it would be well now to face up to some areas of vulnerability.

Let us consider the first "area of vulnerability". What I have variously called "ego-development", "sense of self", and "self-awareness" are supposed to provide the bridge between early impaired agency and later mentalising impairments. But how does one test for these impairments *without also testing for mentalising ability*? This is also a challenge faced by Hobson's proposed form of pre-theoretical-deficit account; and so one may be advised to take a cue from him. Hobson's strategy is to focus on a well-documented difficulty that autistic persons have in expressing the division between themselves and others in everyday life, and then to mount experimental tests to explore its nature. Accordingly, he notes that persons with autism often fail to select the appropriate personal pronoun, referring, for example, to themselves in the third rather than the first person as well as sometimes producing the opposite error of referring to another person in the *first* person. He mentions the case of an autistic boy who walked up to his teacher when she had returned to school after an illness and said "I'm better now" (Hobson, 1993, p.97). Hobson and his colleagues investigated the nature and frequency of such errors using a task in which photographs of the self and others had to be identified. I will not describe the complete pattern of data but, generally speaking, autistic subjects who could comprehend personal pronouns proficiently were less likely than controls to use them when shown photographs of themselves and of others—especially second-person pronouns (Lee, Hobson, & Chiat, 1993). I am not saying that this is cast-iron evidence for impaired ego-development; but it does at least answer the point that ego-development cannot be studied without also studying the imputation of mental states to self and others.

Here is a second way in which one might study self-awareness without studying theory of mind at the same time. In further work on memory in autism (I described previous work a few pages back) Jarrold and I came across a form of memory impairment consistent with an impairment in self-awareness. In order to find out whether children with autism are impaired on the kind of memory tasks on which frontal patients tend to be impaired, we gave groups of autistic, mentally handicapped, and normally developing children two tests of temporal encoding and two tests of source memory. In the former, the subjects either had to arrange pictures in the order in which they had been presented or say which of two items had been presented more recently. We found them to be unimpaired. In the latter, they either had to say how they knew the contents of a box (did you see or were you told?) or they had to say which of four agents was responsible for placing a card into a grid[113]. The children with autism were unimpaired on the first task[114] and dramatically impaired on the second.

What happened in the latter task was this. The experimenter and the child each had a play-person doll to manipulate, making up the four "agents". Each of them had six cards which he or she placed onto an array of pictures corresponding to the 24 cards. At test, the subjects had to say for each of the 24 cards which agent had been responsible for the placement. The children with autism were not only very poor at doing this with all four agents but, in exact contrast to the comparison children, they were worse at remembering which cards they themselves had placed on the grid than they were at remembering which cards the experimenter and their own doll had placed on the grid[115]. In other words what the children with autism did themselves seemed to have been less memorable—less salient?— than what they had seen another person do. Perhaps this is because people who suffer from autism are inefficient *monitors* of the actions that they take[116], and action-monitoring, recall, was the first of our four features of agency. (I will discuss action-monitoring in schizophrenia shortly.)

A second "area of vulnerability" in this developmental-causal account is more clearly exposed. Here, an objector could say that one really has no justification for saying that there *is* a causal relation between executive and mentalising impairments—in either direction. Let us imagine that in the pre-frontal brain there are two centres, one broadly responsible for computing mental representations and one broadly responsible for the executive control of behaviour and attention[117] and that these are adjacent. It is not surprising, the argument runs, that the two kinds of disorder co-exist in autism: they co-exist because of anatomy not because of early psychological events.

This objection can be answered in the following ways. First, accounts of this co-existence presented at the neuroanatomical level should not *automatically* be preferred over developmental-causal accounts simply on the grounds that the former are more parsimonious and make no reference to psychological constructs. This is because the two accounts make different empirical claims. The present account makes the (admittedly difficult to test) prediction that very early damage to the executive centres will bring about difficulties with "mentalising". We are not, however, in a position to assess this claim at present. We know a little about the executive and social consequences of early head injury [see the special issue of the journal *Developmental Neuropsychology*, 7(2), 1991] and about the kinds of executive disorder experienced by children with attention-deficit hyperactivity disorder (ADHD) and phenylketonuria (PKU) (Smith, Kates, & Vriezen, 1993, for a review) but our knowledge of the neuro-physiology of these cases and of the exact nature of the cognitive dysfunctions is very sparse. If it were found, however, that children who begin life with executive dysfunctions *but with otherwise normal interpersonal functioning* acquire mentalising problems, we would have reason to prefer the present view over the neuro-anatomical account.

But what if it turned out that developmentally-later dysfunctions in mentalising were correlated with neurological dysfunctions in the neighbouring, mental-representation-computing centre? Supporters of the neuro-anatomical view might then claim victory and say that the causal link has been shown to be purely anatomical rather than developmental. But if they did, their position would have been reduced to the absurd view that an explanation of developmental change is only genuinely psychological if we are confident that the change was *not* accompanied by neural change.

The second way of dealing with the objection (that the executive–mentalising relation must yield to an entirely anatomical explanation) would be by saying that, although neurophysiology can help to explain why psychological change takes the form it does, a purely psychological theory may help us understand why the brain is structured the way it is. Thus, one could say that it is no mere geographical accident that the neural substrate for the executive control of mental representations and the neural substrate for mentalising[118] are next to each other; in contrast, say, to the fact that the olfactory bulb sits right under the prefrontal cortex. In other words, I think it is right to run with a psychological account as far as one can without worrying that it can be undermined at any moment by evidence from neuro-anatomy.

Finally, what is being offered here, as I said earlier, is a general account of the relation between executive and mentalising difficulties— not a theory of autism—and so it must also be assessed in terms of its success at explaining mental disorders other than autism. In schizophrenia, for example, we find both executive dysfunctions (Shallice, Burgess, & Frith, 1991) and disordered mental *judgements* if not disordered mental *concepts*—not the absence of a theory of mind so much as the misapplication of that theory—a theory of mind gone haywire. The conjecture must be that schizophrenia, like autism, is essentially an executive disorder; but, unlike autism, is a disorder in which the executive system breaks down many years after the individual has developed a conception of mentality. Superficially this proposal is similar to that of Frith and Frith (1991); although there are also fundamental disagreements—to be covered in the next section.

Recall that one of the central features of agency is action-monitoring (feature A in Part 2). One may say that this is the most fundamental feature of agency because it enables the organism to draw the most primitive of appearance–reality distinctions—a distinction between those changes in experience caused by events in the world and those caused by actions. Through acting in relation to objects we change the way objects appear to us without changing their nature or state. In monitoring the launch of an action by efference copying and by making predictions about the phenomenal changes our actions can cause, we gain a conception of subjective versus objective changes in experience.

The fundamental claim in Frith's (1992) theory is that the action-monitoring system has broken down in patients with acute schizophrenia (see also Feinberg, 1978). Thus, patients who, say, turn on a lamp but do not monitor the motor command to perform this action will find themselves doing something that does not appear to be under their control. They will lack the kind of experience described in action feature C—that of knowing without observation what they are doing. Accordingly, the patients will lose a sense of responsibility for what they do; they will be responsible for their actions in fact—they will arise from their own motives—but they will not experience themselves as a centre of responsibility. (Mind$_o$, remember, involves the experience of being in control of one's actions not just being in control *in fact*.) According to the present account, an early deficit in action-monitoring will result in a radically impoverished sense of self-hood and consequently result in a weak grasp of mental concepts. [In fact, we know nothing about action-monitoring in autism, in contrast to action-monitoring in schizophrenia (Frith & Done, 1989); though note my earlier (p.254) report of autistic subjects' difficulty with recalling their own actions in the Russell and Jarrold study]. According to Frith, if this deficit arises later in life (the onset of schizophrenia is often in the early 20s) the consequences will not be an insecure sense of self-hood but the belief that other agents are controlling one's behaviour—a so-called "delusion of alien control". We might regard this as an essentially rational mind being forced to construct a false theory from bad evidence.

Another important symptom of schizophrenia is the presence of auditory hallucinations, and Frith also explains these in terms of dysfunctional action-monitoring. In this case we are dealing with the mental action of thinking a thought framed in subvocal speech. If the launch of such mental actions is not monitored, the consequence will be that thoughts will appear in the mind as spoken sentences. An apparent problem with this view would appear to be the fact that these voices are often heard in the third person. Frith (1992) explains this, however, by saying that these are un-monitored thoughts ascribed to others.

What I wish to do now is to point up the *limitations* of this kind of executive view of schizophrenic symptoms and show how these limitations *parallel* those encountered in *purely* executive accounts of autistic symptoms, by which I mean an account that aims to explain all aspects of autistic experience in executive terms.

Although schizophrenics often hear voices and have delusions of alien control, other disorders of perception and cognition are at least equally as common. Putting it in the most general form, patients experience difficulty with the meaning and relevance of their experiences. "Relevance" here means both the context that the flow of past events imposes on present experience—a context formed by memories of regularities and previous outcomes—and the global structure of what is being immediately experienced. In both cases, a patient may fail to see the wider picture, focusing on, and perhaps over-interpreting, something inconsequential. For example, in the first case, significance may be read into the fact that the therapist is wearing a red tie today or, in the second, the patient will find himself or herself experiencing not a garden but one single bud. It is not uncommon for writers on schizophrenia to refer to the experience of schizophrenics as "fragmented"—an agglomeration of parts without a whole. In the light of this, David Hemsley (1993; also see Patterson, 1987) has constructed a theory of schizophrenia that explains symptoms such as delusional beliefs and the intrusion of ideas in terms of difficulties with constructing the right kind of moment-to-moment expectancies and "response biases" on the basis of stored regularities and context. It elegantly explains, for example, why schizophrenics perform as they do on the forms of simple conditioning tasks originally given to rats, in which a failure to learn a new association is caused by the prior learning that a stimulus did not predict reinforcement—that it was irrelevant. They are poor at learning what *is* irrelevant and therefore their learning of new contingencies is not impaired.

Problems with relevance are difficult to explain in terms of failed action-monitoring. But Hemsley's model *in turn* lacks a convincing account of auditory hallucinations and delusions of alien control. Frith is surely right to criticise formulations of the kind that hallucinations occur because of "the lack of structure which ... characterises [schizophrenics'] sensory experience" (Gray et al., 1990) as having a cognitive basis "too vague to be useful" (Frith, 1992, p.30).

So perhaps the safest conclusion to make is that there may be no psychological theory that can explain delusions and hallucinations, on the one hand, and problems with relevance and global meaning, on the other. Schizophrenia may form a complex of disorders (i.e. with no psychological or "information-processing" core), some of which may be explicable in terms of disordered agency and some of which will not.

This situation parallels that in autism. Like schizophrenics, persons with autism have profound problems with relevance, with meaning, and with global perception. It is plausible to explain some relevance problems as derivative of mentalising problems (Happé, 1993) insofar as the relevance is social and communicative. (What confers relevance on what others do is usually their background beliefs and intentions.) So one might take relevance to be rooted in executive impairments by this indirect root, on the assumption that executive dysfunctions caused mentalising dysfunctions. But not all relevance problems are of this nature because they concern meaningfulness in general rather than specifically social meaning. I will give just one example (for others see Frith & Happé, 1994). Persons with autism are very good at repeating back nonsensical speech and unlikely to repair a mistake in a spoken passage (Aurnhammer-Frith, 1969), as if they were processing language not for its meaning—in which phrases and words are relevant to one another—but merely for its sound. They are processing bottom-up. This seduction towards the local and atomistic and away from the global extends to perceptual tasks such as the embedded figures tests in which the subject is told to find a figure or shape embedded within a larger figure or shape. What makes this task difficult for normal subjects is their natural tendency to see things as a whole. Autistic subjects often do exceptionally well on it (Shah & Frith, 1993), making the parallel with schizophrenic cognition irresistible.

Uta Frith (1989) calls the kind of difficulties I have just described difficulties of "central coherence", and, mirroring Hemsley and Gray et al.'s attempt to explain schizophrenics' (possibly executively derived) delusions and hallucinations in terms of dysfunctions of processing relevance and globality, she has, with Francesca Happé, tried to characterise executive errors in autism in terms of central coherence (Frith & Happé, 1994). Their argument is that when a prepotent response has to be inhibited there are two things involved—inhibition and the "recognition of a context-appropriate response", and that what makes a prepotent response incorrect is the "change in context", and that therefore "autistic people may have no problem in inhibiting action where context is appropriate" (Frith & Happé, 1994, p.127). I think it is fair to say, however, that even if we set aside the fact that there is more to executive dysfunctioning than overcoming prepotency, there is here a kind of over-stretching of explanatory terms similar to that of which C. Frith complained in the parallel move made by Gray et al. (1990).

What is "context"? As I said, in describing executive errors the rule that must be held in mind in competition with the prepotent response must be an *arbitrary* rule (all true rules are). If one neglects this, then the task ceases to be an executive task. If, that is, the response the child has to make bears a *natural* relation to the attainment of the goal, then we are simply testing means–end behaviour rather than executive functioning. Take the example of the Hughes and Russell (1993) "box task". If the child had to perform the meaningful and *context-appropriate* action of opening a flap in the box before reaching in, rather than the arbitrary action of throwing a switch, then *this would cease to be a test of executive functioning*: opening a flap before reaching in is itself a kind of prepotent action. Calling this action meaningful or "context appropriate" and concluding that the box task is really testing central coherence is stretching the notion of context to its breaking point: it is not context that tells us, for example, to stand up before we start walking or to open the door before we enter a room.

But how should we regard the relation between poor central cohesion and executive dysfunctioning?

The conservative conclusion—the one I have been pushing—is that a general psychological account of autism and schizophrenia will never be forthcoming. Psychology—with its information-processing models—may help us to understand certain causal relations between symptoms, and psychologists may be able to point to two or three core psychological deficits, but the *sui generis* cluster of symptoms may lack a common psychological cause and core. This clearly means yielding some ground to the kind of objector, mentioned earlier, who says that neuro-anatomy rather than psychological causation explains why symptoms co-exist.

A far less conservative conclusion—perhaps it is a downright fanciful one—returns us to the speculative remarks I made at the end of the previous sub-section about the relation between so-called "generativity" (*qua* imaginative fecundity) and the processing of irrelevant information. This would allow us to claim that central coherence problems are in part responsible for the difficulties persons with autism experience when they have to generate novel actions and ideas: this might provide a *psychological* account of why central coherence and executive difficulties co-exist. The argument would be that, because the attentional window of autistic persons is very small, they assimilate relatively little information that has no direct bearing on their own immediate purposes and assimilate little information that emanates from their background experience (the "wood" in which they see the "tree"). An individual who experiences the world in an over-focused and over-functional manner is not only unlikely to be skilled at switching set but will be unimaginative, because, on the proposal sketched before, this individual will lack the material on which his or her imagination must work.

One must be careful in saying this, however, not to characterise the central coherence view as the view that autistic individuals are too efficient at discarding irrelevant information; indeed this is almost the *opposite* of U. Frith's proposal. U. Frith's position, remember, is that persons with autism cannot pick up global, background *relevance*. To resolve this apparent paradox, we need a term that encompasses both irrelevant information and information *that is relevant but only as scene-setting*—"non-focal" information perhaps. In any event, if such information is not processed it will not be synthesised within the mind$_s$; and this will ensure that the mind$_s$'s owner will lack the raw material for generating plans, hypotheses, strategies, and ideas.

It might seem as if I am drifting rather close to a ToMM-deficit position here, given that proponents of the central cohesion view tend to hold both views in tandem (e.g. Frith, 1989; Happé, 1993)[119]. But notwithstanding this, I think a line should be drawn very clearly between approaches to autism that emphasise executive dysfunctions and central coherence and those that emphasise dysfunctions of the ToMM. For what the first two share is a concern with first-person, pre-theoretical experience—with lack of control over one's action-generated experiences in the first and with a kind of mental tunnel-vision in the second. They are surely both well placed to explain mentalising problems as derivatives of these two kinds of disordered experience. And, more generally, they both draw our attention to disorders of the mind itself as opposed to disorders of the individual's ability to compute the right theoretical accounts of the representations and attitudes that cause behaviour. Indeed it may not be stretching things too far to say that while the executive account concerns itself with mind$_o$—with the subject's sense of him or herself as a centre of responsibility for generating experiences—the central cohesion account (and its close relatives in the field of schizophrenia) concern themselves with mind$_s$—with the synthesising of experiences into a whole, with, that is, mental unity. Both appear to be disordered in autism and schizophrenia.

I argued earlier (in 3.1) that mind$_s$ as well as mind$_o$ is grounded in agency. However, this grounding is at such an abstract level in the first case that one would be ill-advised to say that "when you get down deep enough" central cohesion too is a product of agency, because it is difficult to see what kind of evidence would bear on such a claim. Moreover, there can be no successful agency emanating from minds without synthesised *contents*: there cannot be intentions without some coherent idea about what to do.

3.5(iii) Agency without meta-representation

My final task is to defend the view that an executive account of how minds fail to function (and, by extension, develop) does not have to be underwritten by a *representational* account of the executive deficits. That is to say, if one has identified an executive deficit (and, by extension, a form of executive development) this can be the end of the story: one does not necessarily then have to explain this in turn as a representational failure—because executive accounts are (or at least can be) the bedrock. This is not to say that dysfunctions with an executive flavour can *never* yield to an explanation that does not make reference to the executive; indeed in the previous section I floated just such an account. Recall that the suggestion was made that impoverished "generativity" may result from a kind of over-focused experience of which central coherence difficulties are a symptom. My point is that referring to a dysfunction *in a process that makes adequate agency possible*—such as action-monitoring—can be sufficient in itself: it does not require filling out by a story about representational deficits. If, by contrast, generativity is taken to mean something close to imaginative fecundity (e.g. producing ideas for pretend play), it is not a process that makes adequate agency possible: agents can be very unimaginative.

I will make this point by returning to C. Frith's (1992) account of the relation between the symptomatologies of schizophrenia and of autism. Frith's proposal that the volitional disorders in these two areas are grounded in disorders of "meta-representation" can be questioned on conceptual grounds, I shall argue.

Frith and Frith (1991) raised the possibility that there are "hidden affinities" between the difficulties with communication and mind-reading in autism and the volitional impairments in schizophrenia. This is common ground with the thesis of Part 3. But where I have been arguing that these affinities centre on action, Frith and Frith claim that they are centred on representation. This is the Friths' proposal in synopsis:

(1) Successful action requires monitoring (agency feature A described in Part 2).
(2) The ability to engage in this—what Frith (1992) calls "self-monitoring"— depends on the construction of "second-order" representations of goals. It depends more generally on a capacity for meta-representation as the term is used by Leslie (1987) in his theory of pretend play.
(3) The core deficit in autism is an inability to meta-represent[120].
(4) Consequently, the hidden affinity between the two disorders is that they are both disorders of meta-representation.

Two kinds of claims can be distinguished in Frith's position. The first is about affinities between *symptoms*, and a second—the one I shall criticise—concerns affinities in the causation of the disorder. In the first place, Frith argues that the symptoms of both disorders can be interpreted in terms of taking second-order representations to be first-order ones. Schizophrenic patients who launch second-order representations of the thoughts of other people and do not monitor themselves as doing this will take these representations to be first-order—literal representations of reality—and thus have the paranoid delusion that people are *actually* saying about them what they imagined others were saying. The autistic person, on the other hand, will fail, for example, to interpret a figurative, second-order statement (in which the speakers' background intentions have to be considered) as such and take it to be something said literally and in earnest—as a first-order report. I have no quarrel to raise with this.

We now come to Frith's causal claim about the grounding of executive disorders in failures of meta-representation. My objection is to the second stage of the argument—(2). In saying this, Frith distinguishes between two kinds of intentions—"stimulus intentions" and "willed intentions". Stimulus intentions are triggered by environmental events while willed intentions are endogenous. As we discussed earlier [3.2(ii)], acting intentionally has two components—a representational component (motives, a goal) and a non-representational or "immediate" component (the experience of agency, of controlling one's body or one's attention). I suggest that what Frith does in (2) is to invert the order of precedence of these two while regarding the possession of a goal in excessively high-level terms. In the first place, action-monitoring is a primitive sub-personal mechanism which can be described apart from an organism's goals; indeed Frith (1992, p.76) gives the same characterisation of it as I gave in Part 2 with reference to Von Holst and Mittelstaedt's experiments on efference-copying in the fruit fly (see Gallistel, 1980). Action-monitoring *may*, in humans, involve the monitoring of very high-level intentions towards imaginatively rich goals, but essentially it involves the sub-personal processes of copying a motor command and matching the copy against the outcome, and of predicting the phenomenal result of an action—processes that do not even require that the organism should have a represented goal, let alone a second-order representation of a goal. As I said when discussing feature A—notwithstanding the term "monitoring"—there is no homuncular inner-eye recording the launch and outcome of an action directed towards an outcome: it is sub-personal. And there is nothing second-order about it.

We must now consider the question of whether having a goal requires the individual to have a second-order representation. When Leslie

(1987) originally introduced the notion of meta-representation (borrowed from Pylyshyn, 1984) to characterise the cognitive achievements of pretend play it had a relatively clear meaning. Meta-representation involved placing a veridical representation in mental quotation marks and thus affording the unconstrained manipulation of the resultant representation: you can do anything you like with a meta-representation of a banana. Does *this* sound like representing a goal? As we discussed in the context of the connectionist modelling of object permanence, there are quite strict conditions on whether behaviour is goal-directed or not, but none of them would seem to include that the goal have a second-order status, in Leslie's sense.

Supporters of the Frith view would probably reply that, although this is so, the theory is concerned only with those cases in which individuals not only behave in a goal-directed fashion but in a fashion that suggests that they know they have a goal. Clearly, there is a distinction to be drawn between cases where we have goals and cases where we have them and we know we do; but if the theory is supposed to apply only to the latter cases then it has rather little to say about agency. It simply tells us that individuals with meta-representational impairments do not know they have goals and that this affects their ability to act on them in some circumstances; it tells us nothing about impairments in agency at a more basic level—the kind of impairments with which the present account is concerned, and indeed the kind of impairments with which Frith himself seems to be concerned. For example, Frith takes the following kind of data as evidence for his view that schizophrenics have action-monitoring impairments. In two studies (Frith & Done, 1989; Malenka, Angel, Hampton, & Berger, 1982), patients were given a task in which they had to follow a target on computer screen. Normal subjects were able to correct erroneous actions before witnessing their outcomes, because they had recorded the launched action; but the schizophrenic and alcoholic subjects (in the Malenka et al. study) did not do this. This suggests an impairment in action-monitoring right enough, but does it suggest that this was rooted in the schizophrenics' and alcoholics' lack of knowledge that they had a goal?

Let us look further at how Frith draws the distinction between forms of goal-directed behaviour that are meta-representational and those that are not. He distinguishes (Frith, 1992; pp.122–123) between "stimulus elicited" (e.g. stopping at a red light) and goal-directed behaviour. In his view, referring to well-known work on the 3–4 transition in mentalising, he argues that younger children "do not know they have a goal". How would we test for this? He gives the example of a reversal experiment in which children initially learn that a sweet is always to be found in the red box, after which the correct box becomes the adjacent blue one. The child who knows he or she had a goal will manage the reversal effectively, says Frith, whereas the child whose behaviour is merely stimulus-elicited will perseverate with the wrong response. Analogising this to the windows task, one would say that on this view 3-year-olds and autistic subjects perseverate because they do not know they have the goal of getting a chocolate. That is to say, the perseverators are such because they cannot represent themselves as having that particular goal.

This is unpersuasive even as a high-level description of what is going on, essentially because the link between meta-knowledge of having a goal and disengaging from a prepotent response is not being explained. A subject could surely have very rich meta-knowledge about the outcome he or she wants and yet be unable, for whatever reason, to disengage from the wrong strategy and engage the correct one. That is to say, there is no conceptual link between knowing what you want and knowing how to stop doing the wrong thing to get it. Furthermore, the parallel Frith goes on to draw between the control of behaviour by the meta-knowledge of goals and Norman and Shallice's supervisory attentional system does nothing to explain the link. Meta-knowledge of a goal will not of itself cause disengagement from old habits, and we are surely better advised to look for an executive account of how this disengagement is achieved (in humans and other animals). But what would "an executive account" of succeeding (and failing) to disengage from old habits look like? To anticipate work I will describe very shortly, it might be an account that makes use of Jordan's "forward model" discussed towards the end of Part 1 (Jordan, 1990; Jordan & Rumelhart, 1992; see Fig. 1, p.54). We need a system that can predict the outcome of taking a certain action, a prediction that is made on the basis of past outcomes. Doing this *before the next action is taken* would not only prevent the subject from becoming locked into a cycle of ineffective acts but would enable early reversal; just as the failure of such a system would be expected to cause perseveration. We do not need to reach for higher-order concepts such as "awareness of goals" here.

One of the implicit themes of this book has been that notions like "awareness" sometimes have little explanatory role to play in cognitive-development psychology because what children are aware of is, in part, a function of how they can control their mental and physical actions. Terms like "awareness" and "knowledge" usually describe *explicanda*, and so citing their absence in younger children may sometimes explain rather little about why they think the way they do.

At this point, it would bolster my argument if some existence-proof that the intentional behaviour which Frith believes cannot be explained without recourse to the concept of "second-order representations" can indeed be computationally modelled without it. For this reason I will describe some recent computational modelling of schizophrenic cognition by Gordon Brown and his colleagues (Brown et al., 1994). This utilises Jordan's forward model and holds some promise of being such an existence-proof. I say "promise" here because the actual simulation of hallucinations and alien control has yet to be run. The authors did, however, "lesion" the forward model by disrupting the time-course of the flow of information; manipulating, specifically, the rate at which the forward model sent its predictions of the next world-state to the controller sub-network, leaving the latter unaltered (Brown et al., 1994, pp.79–82). This enabled them to mimic Parkinsonian difficulties with movement amplitude, and, by disrupting the output of the schema-selector, enabled them to to mimic difficulties with selecting willed intentions—see later.

The goal of Brown et al.'s work was to model some of the "positive" symptoms (e.g. the hallucinations and delusions of control) in acute schizophrenia as well as the "negative" symptoms of the chronic phase (e.g. lack of spontaneity and stereotyped thinking [cf autism]) in addition to the motor initiation problems of Parkinson's patients. (They did this while staying close to what we know about the functions of fronto-striatal system; but the neuro-psychology is not directly relevant to the present issue.) I will only mention what they have to say about the positive symptoms of schizophrenia.

Brown et al. accept that Frith's account of the positive symptoms is broadly correct: that there is a severing of the link between the generator of intentions and the monitor that compares the outputs of this generator with the real-world changes caused by actions[121]. But their basic aim was to model the process of generating and monitoring intentions within a neural network, using the Jordan forward model. It may be recalled that a forward model takes as its input a plan of action (a "willed intention" in Frith's terms), specified normally by a motor command, plus a representation of the current state of the world, and gives as its output a (perhaps approximate) prediction of the way the environment will be perceived when the action has been taken (see Fig. 1, p.54). Recall also that this process of prediction should not be confused with the more primitive process of efference-copying: the forward model does not merely make a copy of a motor command. The authors then proceeded in the following way:

(1) Identify willed intentions with the plan units of Jordan's sequential connectionist network (Fig. 1, p.54).

(2) Specify the way in which new plans are selected by assuming that the predicted altered state of the world will *disinhibit* certain plans. That is to say, those which have that world-state as their condition for firing will fire.

(3) Select among those plans that are disinhibited in terms of higher-level goals. (Brown et al. intend this as a simulation of the Norman and Shallice "supervisory attentional system".)

(4) The source of high-level goals and their associated high-level action plans is taken to be the pre-frontal cortex while the functions of the forward model are supposed to be carried forward by the basal ganglia (see also Jackson & Houghton, 1992).

The question we have to ask now is this: Is second-order representation being smuggled into this model? Let us consider (1) and (2). First, is calling a unit a "plan unit" a kind of cheating, in the sense that one is stipulating what needs to be explained? Is it possible, in other words, for a system to have a plan that is not represented by the system to itself *as* such? It seems to me that if "no" is the answer to this question then we could never ascribe any form of strategic, intentional behaviour to creatures that were not self-aware. More important, do we want to say that a plan only exists insofar as it is represented as being a plan? This would have the strange consequence that plans have no *sui generis* character: that they are nothing apart from the theories of them. (This is not to say that the plan must be encoded *symbolically*: the *sui generis* character resides in the relation between the units and other elements and processes in the network, not in the unit's "shape".) Thus, there is no reason why a modeller should not specify plan units that have this character autonomously (i.e. not in virtue of some higher-level representation) without being accused of smuggling in *explicanda*.

Having said this, the forward model itself does have a kind of recursive or higher-level function; but it has this only in the sense that it achieves a supra-modal representation of the relation between what happens in the world and the state of the motor system. *In this sense only*, the model is not a simple, first-order mapping of input to output. Recall that if action is to be successful—so that accommodation can keep pace with assimilation, if you like—the system must translate the error signal telling it about the real-world outcome of its action into instructions for altering the configuration of motor signals on the next occasion. But how can the transformation of errors specified by real-world co-ordinates be translated into the "action space" (encoded by what Jordan calls "the controller") that the network has at its disposal? This is the problem, recall, that the forward model was meant to solve. The forward model is a sub-network whose inputs are the *outputs* of the action units which encode—at least in Jordan's model—particular joint angles and shoulder positions. These are then passed upwards through the network via a layer of hidden units to the output units of the forward model, whose activity encodes the X–Y co-ordinates of the (say) end point of the arm in the world that will be caused by the activity of that pattern of action units. When this mapping from facts about the body to facts about perceptual-motor outcomes has been learned, the real-world consequences of particular actions will also have been learned. In error correction, the error signal is back-propagated through the net from the output units of the forward model to its input units which are, recall, the output units of the action units.

If we do not encounter second-order representations at this level do we encounter them when we move upwards to (2) towards the process of disinhibiting plans on the basis of these predictions? And do we encounter them when we move still further upwards to (3) and the selection between these triggered plans in terms of high-level goals? Like most computational models this one has a hierarchy of processes (high selects among low) and, like most, it involves the taking of outputs from one process and making them the inputs of another sub-process; but there is no meta-representation here. That is to say, in no sense is the system achieving what it achieves by virtue of copying a lower-level representation and then operating on that as "decoupled" from its real-world liaisons.

None of this is meant to imply that something like Leslie's "decoupler" mechanism cannot exist[122]; and one must even leave open the possibility that purely connectionist models may fail to implement it satisfactorily. I *am* saying, though, that intentional behaviour (that which is more than "stimulus intentions" in Frith's scheme) does not require second-order computations; which is all that is required to cast doubt on Frith's model.

As I said, the reason for spending so much time disputing Frith's position is that it implies a view of how agency relates to awareness that is the opposite of the one being presented here, not because I think it has nothing to tell us about disordered thought! Indeed, it is obvious that my own position is not only in debt to the Friths' work: it borrows their insight (about the volitional roots of disordered experience and the affinities between autism and schizophrenia) and then has the cheek to give it the opposite theoretical spin.

What is more, it could turn out that although Chris Frith is mistaken about the necessary dependency of executive processes on meta-representational ones, he could be entirely correct that autism is a disorder of meta-representation. Conversely, the case I have tried to build up in Part 2 and in the early sections of Part 3 in favour of the dependency of adequate ego-development on adequate agency may be completely wrong, and yet it could be *true* that the executive deficits are primary. In other words, broadly philosophical positions may inspire empirical claims in developmental psychology (on which process, see Russell, 1979a), but once the claims are made they are autonomous: they are entirely empirical. Let us examine predictions derived from the competing views.

There is a powerful way of testing causal theories in developmental psychology, which is to take children who have yet to reach the age at which a competence is normally manifested and test for the skills that a theory holds to be necessary for this competence. By this means, the theorist can predict that children who are impaired on the earlier, conditional skill will have difficulty acquiring the later competence. For example (see Bryant & Bradley, 1985), the theory that a form of phonological coding is necessary for successful reading will predict that pre-readers who have impaired phonological skills (such as rhyming) will be those who become poor readers a couple of years later. Using the same logic, a theory that says that early executive impairments cause later impairments in mentalising will predict that screening very young infants who are at risk from developing autism (i.e. having relatives with autism, Asperger Syndrome, or schizophrenia) will enable us to predict which children from that set will develop autism. The screening tests would range from those that are executive but with no social element, such as switching locus of visual attention from a central, competing stimulus to a peripheral stimulus (Atkinson, Hood, Wattam-Bell, & Braddick, 1992), to those that, although requiring attentional regulation, involve a social component—such as joint attention with another person. If the children who develop autism are those who are impaired on the latter (social) but *not* on the former (purely executive) skill it would be strong evidence *against* the executive view.

In conclusion, we have obviously travelled a very long way from the so-called "transcendental" arguments of the earlier sections of Parts 2 and 3—from debates about what must necessarily be experienced if mental development is to be successful. I have, however, remained well within the central thesis of this book in the last few pages—the thesis that one must experience one's own agency if one is to develop conceptions of the external world and of mentality.

It is also obvious, however, that one can ask questions about the role of agency in cognition and in mental development *without* grounding these questions in anything remotely philosophical. We can witness this, for example, in the recent growth of interest in the role of the central executive of working memory, where much of the theoretical impetus is derived from the experiments of Alan Baddeley and others and from models of frontal impairment. None of this work is philosophically motivated. Developmental psychologists—at least some of them— operate differently. Our instinct is to root questions in philosophy, because transcendental and developmental questions are so hard to disentangle.

NOTES

55. I used this (rather pretentious) phrase in Russell 1979a. The idea is that philosophy is done within an area where there is broad agreement about the facts—about what is to count as an example of an intentional act, for example. But ambitious philosophical theories can have implications for the problem cases about which there is little agreement (e.g. is a movement that the subject reports as one he or she intended to do but which was actually caused by electrical stimulation of the brain "an intention"?). It also happens the other way round. Witness the way in which the philosophical discussions of intention have been influenced by Freud's case studies, in which questions are raised about such matters as whether there can be unconscious intentions.

56. Kitcher (1990, pp.92–94) criticises Strawson's view that "Unity of consciousness to which a series of experiences belong implies, then, the *possibility* of self ascription." (Strawson, 1966, p.98). I am simply assuming that there can be mental unity without *actual* rather than possible self-ascription.

57. For example, Nagel (1979, pp.189–199) describes a "clash between the view of action from the inside and *any* view of it from the outside. Any external view of an act as something that happens [...] seems to omit the doing of it." I discuss this question more fully in 3.3(iii).

58. This view may seen to be co-extensive with the so-called "simulation" view the development of mental concepts, for example as put forward by Paul Harris (1991). In fact this is a much cruder and more radical theory than simulation theory. In my Coda chapter I make this point carefully.

59. The phrase "the theory theory" was coined in a book by Adam Morton in 1980. He writes: "The first stage towards the theory theory is found in some places in Wittgenstein, in Austin, and in Sellars. Putnam's and Fodor's functionalism represents an intermediate stage ..." (1980, p.10, footnote) and papers by Putnam, David Lewis, and D. M. Rosenthal are examples of explicit theory-theory views.

60. Strawson (1959, p.100, original italics) writes: "Now one thing is certain: that *if* the things one ascribes states of consciousness to, in ascribing them to others are thought of as a set of Cartesian egos to which only private experiences can, in correct logical grammar, be ascribed *then* this question [i.e. of how we can ascribe states of consciousness to others] is unanswerable and the problem insoluble. If, in identifying the things to which states of consciousness are to be ascribed, private experiences are to be all one has to go on, then, just for the very same reason as that which there is, from one's own point of view, no question of telling that a private

experience is one's own, there is also no question of telling that a private experience is another's. All private experiences, all states of consciousness will be mine, i.e. no one's. To put it briefly. One can ascribe states of consciousness to oneself only if one can ascribe them to others. One can ascribe them to others only if one can identify other subjects of experience. And one cannot identify others if one can identify them *only* as subjects of experience, possessors of states of consciousness."

This is the culmination of an argument, but it may be useful to look at the first step ("one can ascribe states of consciousness to oneself only if one can ascribe them to others"). This rests on what Strawson calls the "purely logical point" made a little earlier that "the idea of a predicate is correlative with that of a *range* of distinguishable individuals of which the predicate can be significantly, though not necessarily truly, affirmed." (op cit., original italics, p.99). This "purely logical point" is the point from which Evans (1982) derives the Generality Constraint, discussed here in Part 2.

61. This is fairly close to the views of Alison Gopnik (1993).
62. Gopnik (1993, p.10) writes: "Their theories allow prediction, and they change (eventually) as a result of falsifying evidence" .
63. This is fairly close to the views of Josef Perner (1991)—a crude version of them though.
64. The work of Judy DeLoache (e.g. DeLoache, Kolstad, & Anderson, 1991) for example suggests that children of three understand how a scale model or a photograph represents something as being a certain way. Josef Perner (1991) disputes this, saying that DeLoache's subjects could have been utilising a "situation theory" rather than a "meta-representational theory" to achieve their successes.
65. Perner and his student Martin Docherty are exploring the possibility that children under 4 years do not understand synonyms, taking this to be an acid test for whether they grasp the representing function of language. This is an interesting avenue to follow, but it appears that children do not understand homonyms until they are around 7 years (Cramer, 1983); and why should not homonym understanding be taken as an equally good acid test?
66. Daniel Reisberg (e.g. Chambers & Reisberg, 1985) has claimed that adults are unable to reverse mental images of ambiguous figures such as the duck–rabbit illusion. But see Peterson, Kihlstrom, Rose, and Glisky (1992) for conflicting data.
67. This is obviously very close to the position of Alan Leslie (1987).
68. It is very important not to confuse the view that only language users can have beliefs with the view for which I argued in answering "Objection 3" (Part 2.6)—that we must describe the achievement of externality (a non-verbal achievement) in the language of folk psychology, using such terms as "believe" and "know". It is one thing to say that a certain form of behaviour comes within the ambit of folk-psychological explanation and another to say that the category "belief" features in the mental life of the creature. But in any event, I am only concerned here with the view that only language users can have the *concept* of belief.
69. I would say that doing this is an executive achievement rather than something distinct from the executive system—as it is in Leslie's theory. But this is not crucial in this context.

70. Sufferers from this syndrome show motor and vocal tics and frequently have obsessive thoughts. To the extent that they perform actions that they do not intend to perform, their disorder is an executive one.

71. EDD is the "eye direction detector", on which see Baron-Cohen (1995).

72. This kind of thought is evident in the work of, for example, Colwyn Trevarthen (Trevarthen & Hubley, 1978), Vasu Reddy (1991), and Peter Hobson (1993).

73. I am grateful to Jennifer Hornsby for suggesting this way of putting it.

74. I am assuming that the child has what might be called a "sub-conceptual" understanding of the first person. The child has experiences and he or she knows they are his or her own (this much is constitutive of $mind_o$), but the child has no conception of him or herself as thinking something is the case. I take this latter to require a *concept* of the first person and to be something, given what I said before, that cannot exist without a concept of other persons.

75. It is tempting to draw a parallel here with issues raised in Part 2 about the possibility of "autonomous" non-conceptual content, meaning content in the absence of any concepts at all. I am arguing for a kind of autonomy of non-conceptual content in the social realm.

76. The application of the phrase "gradual dawning" in this context and of course its derivation from Wittgenstein is owing to the philosopher Peter Smith. It is from a paper he gave in Sheffield in the summer of 1993.

77. The idea behind this is that the sentences people utter when they ascribe understanding to another person (e.g. "He thinks that *p*") are semantically under-determined. Such sentences contain, as it were, empty slots which are filled out contextually. In this case, to borrow Woodfield's example, if I say "Tom knows who John Major is" and you say "Tom does not know who John Major is" we may not be contradicting each other: both sentences may be true. See Boer and Lycan (1986).

78. This is a task that tests planning ability—a derivative of the better-known Tower of Hanoi. In the Tower of London, the subject sees a target configuration of three balls of different colours on three sticks and is given a duplicate set of sticks and balls in which the balls are in a different configuration. The task is to transform the starting state into the goal state in as few moves as possible while not holding two balls at the same time. The task was developed by Ros McCarthy and Tim Shallice.

79. See note 18 in Part 1 for a description of this task.

80. Imagine looking down at two pencils of the same length; one has been pushed up so that its point is about an inch further up than the other. Another person sits *vis-à-vis* you so that to this person the pencil that is further down is, to him, further up. The idea of the experiment was that if two nonconservers are put into this situation and asked whether the pencils were the same size, they would realise that they could not both be right and therefore change the basis of their judgement.

81. Willem Doise (e.g. Doise, Mungy, & Perret-Clermont, 1975) and his group do, however, find that what they call "socio-cognitive conflict" is effective. But they treat symmetrical (both wrong) and symmetrical (one right and one wrong) interactions together as part of the same "socio-cognitive" process. The facilitation that they find is probably a function of one child benefiting from his or her partner's superior knowledge (asymmetrical) or spontaneous improvement (symmetrical) (see Russell, 1981b).

82. One should be careful to avoid saying that conservation tests present the child with illusions because in most kinds of conservation (e.g. length) one item does not actually look bigger than another—at least to an adult. They do, however, encourage children to base their judgement on one salient perceptual dimension, and perhaps one item does indeed look bigger to these children when they are asked the question.

83. A typical interaction was: Child A: "That one." Child B: "That one." Child A: "No that one." Child B: "No that one." Child A: "OK we'll say yours."

84. There is some debate over whether "Does [the protagonist] know the chocolate has moved?" is a control question or a test question. It is a mentalistic question and therefore similar to the test question to that extent. However, it is a control question to the extent that one has to check not merely whether the child knows that the protagonist has had no visual access to the transfer but whether the child knows that the protagonist has no *information* about the transfer. What one is asking is whether the child knows the protagonist is informed, and this does not require him or her to have a full-blown understanding of what "know" means (e.g. versus "guess" or versus "think").

85. There is some similarity between this account and the "simulation" account of Paul Harris (1991). The main difference between this view and simulation theory is that Harris rejects the idea that mental concepts are theoretical entities (overlapping somewhat with "reflection+analogy" view), whereas an executive theory is not inconsistent with the theory theory. I discuss simulation theory in my Coda chapter.

86. The studies I am referring to here are not published. However the reader will note that their results do not support the present line, so I am *not* referring to unpublished work that *supports* my views.

87. The Lewis and Osborne and the Siegal and Beattie studies showed that 3-year-olds' performance was better than chance when temporal markers (e.g. "before" and "after") were included. But there have been a number of failures to reproduce this result, e.g. Sullivan and Winner, 1993.

88. One of the tasks involved learning the conditional rule that if a light is on a marble will drop diagonally, but if it is off the marble will drop vertically. There is no prepotency here. In passing, the Frye, Zalazo, and Palfai (in press) hypothesis has the fatal weakness that it predicts that a *true* belief task should be as hard as a false belief task.

89. Clements and Perner (1994) have shown that there is a transitional period in false belief performance during which 3-year-olds will look at the correct, empty location but wrongly say that the protagonist will visit the location with the object. What one could say about this is that the child is able to disengage his or her visual attention from the object before he or she is able to disengage his or her mental attention. In support of this distinction one could cite work critical of "spotlight" theories of visual attention (e.g. Driver & Baylis, 1989)—theories that make an analogy between eye-movements and visual attention.

90. Right at the end of Part 3 we will be discussing an attempt to explain perseveration in terms of meta-representational difficulties—that of Chris Frith.

91. We are currently working on this.

92. A study by my graduate student Al Lumb has shown that if children are not corrected for giving the wrong answer to the ignorance question (i.e. "Does [the protagonist] know the chocolate has moved?")—this is a control against parroting the right answer—they are almost certain to give the correct answer to the false belief question. Whether or not the ignorance question is testing the child's grasp of a propositional attitude (see note 84) these data raise the possibility that the false belief test is not specifically testing false belief but is testing the child's understanding of informational access.

93. However if one takes a very broad view of "executive", such as that taken by John Duncan (in press), then one *could* say that this task tests an executive capacity. However, I think it is well to restrict the definition for developmental purposes.

94. This does not necessarily imply that Piaget was correct in thinking that the child actually "constructs" a concept of amount by co-ordinating dimensions. It may be that ideas about conservation are more primitive than this and that the ability to shift mental attention between dimensions allows children to *manifest* knowledge that is already present in a primitive form—as argued by Jerome Bruner (1966) for example.

95. There is a growth spurt in frontal lobe development lasting from 4 years to about 7 years (Luria, 1973), and there is a growth spurt in fissuration at around age 6 which is associated with increased motor skill (Rourke, Baker, Fisk, & Stang, 1983). In other words, although it would be nice to be able to refer to a one growth spurt at about age 4 and another at age 7 it is not really possible to do so.

96. Researchers normally refer to a triad of impairments—in verbal and nonverbal communication, in social functioning, and in imagination. This was believed before theory of mind research got underway.

97. High-functioning adults with autism may regress sharply—handflapping, for example—when faced with an unexpected occurrence such as their car breaking down.

98. Some children with autism are certainly not socially withdrawn. This is known as the "odd" category—the others being the "aloof" and the "passive" (see Frith, 1989).

99. See note 78.

100. See note 18 in Part 1 for a description of the task. It is worth pointing out, however, that more recent evidence suggests that lesions in non-frontal areas of the brain can also affect performance on the WCST. Corcoran and Upton (1993) showed that patients with seizures and sclerosis of the hippocampus are impaired on it.

101. The Ozonoff et al. study was the first to compare performance on executive and theory of mind tasks, not the first to look at autistic performance on "frontal tasks". The very first work on executive functions in autism was done by Steel, Gorman, and Flexman (1984) and there have been important studies since by Rumsey and Hamburger (1988), Prior and Hoffman (1990), and by Szatmari et al. (1989). My aim is not to review the literature; I will be painting with broad brush in this section.

102. Tager-Flusberg and Sullivan (1994) showed that when the second-order false belief task does not contain an embedded question of the form "What does John think that Jane thinks?", subjects with autism who have passed the first-order false belief task are not specifically impaired. In their test,

the subjects did not have to hold embedded information in mind when the question was asked.

103. As I said in note 101 my aim is not to review the literature here, but nevertheless the work of DeLong (1978) and of Ornitz (1985) should be mentioned in this context.

104. The question is whether there are two distinct populations—high functioning persons with autism and persons with Asperger Syndrome. It may well be that the latter is simply a mild form of autism, although with some distinctive features such as clumsiness plus more obsessive interests, special areas of knowledge, and general "eccentricity" than the Kanner-type autistic individual—together with a desire to lead a normal social life.

105. It is very important to bear in mind that "prepotent" is not being defined with circularity. It is not being defined simply as "the kind of impulsive error that young children and persons with autism are naturally inclined to make". Here is an illustration. Bruce Hood (unpublished data, Department of Experimental Psychology, Cambridge) has devised a test of search after invisible displacement called "the tubes task". In the crucial condition, a ball is dropped into an opaque tube which curves diagonally down into a catch-tray. *Directly beneath* the mouth of the tube is another catch-tray that is not, of course, connected to the tube. Hood found that normally developing children below the age of about 3 years will, when the ball is dropped into the mouth of the tube, search in the catch-tray that is not connected to the tube *but is directly beneath* the tube's mouth. This has all the appearance of an impulsive error, though one that children often make trial after trial. The error is also made by tamarin monkeys (Hood, personal communication). This is then an impulsive error but it is not a prepotent error because it is not evoked by (a) perception or knowledge of a current state of reality nor by (b) past learning of an arbitrary rule (as on the WCST, for example). Chris Jarrold and I found that children with autism are not impaired on the tubes task (report submitted to Wellcome Trust, March, 1995).

106. The word-length effect is supposed to show that what limits short-term memory for words is not the number of words in the list but how long they take to articulate. For example, a subject may have a span of 6 single-syllable words but a span of 3 or 4 three-syllable words.

107. There may be two other reasons why our data were different from those of Bennetto et al. First, one of the tasks on which they found subjects with autism to be impaired was one where they had to fill in the missing word at the end of a series of sentences and then recall the words. They may have had difficulty with this task because of their problems with meaning and relevance. Second, in their version of the so-called Case counting task in which items on a card have to be counted and then the totals recalled Bennetto et al. did not control for the time it took to count the stimuli. Towse and Hitch (1995) have reported that counting time may be all-important on this task.

108. It is also worth making the point that in at least one population—that of children with cerebral palsy (White, Craft, Hala, & Park, 1994)—there is very slow overt speech rate along with normal short-term span. This suggest either that overt and covert speech rates are not related or that rehearsal efficiency is not what is being tested in these span experiments.

109. The obvious problem here is that children with autism are very bad at being random (for data: Turner, 1995), so even if they managed some degree of randomness this would be expected to use up more mental energy than the same degree would require in the control children.

110. There is an inevitable equivocation in the Baddeley model between the central executive as a generator of strategies and as a performer of these strategies.

111. It is worth mentioning that some workers on executive dysfunctions have stressed the maintenance of schemas—Duncan (in press), Oaksford and Malloch (1994).

112. Although it does not take much imagination to relate the two. If an individual has severely impaired self-awareness consequent on early executive impairments, then he or she would be expected to lack an adequate third-person perspective on what it is like for him or herself to be (say) in pain, and this would be expected to involve awareness of his or her own pain-behaviour. Lacking this, it would be difficult to identify pain-behaviour in others. It may be identified "cold-bloodedly" as the expression of discomfort, but there would be no idea of "what it would be like for me".

113. Strictly speaking this is not really a test of source memory, which normally refers to what *kind* of source a true memory had, as in the first source task. The four different agents were not the source of information: they did something rather than informed the subject of something.

114. Note that we are again finding different results from those of Bennetto et al. This may have been due to the fact that their subjects were high-functioning and consequently were compared with a control population that was essentially normal. (On some tasks our subjects were impaired against normally developing children but not against mentally handicapped children.) See note 107 for two further reasons.

115. There was another intriguing result. On the first trial the subjects were not warned that they had to recall who had placed which cards on the grid. On the second trial, however, they knew that this question was coming up. The normally developing and the mentally handicapped children did significantly better on the second trial, as one would expect. The children with autism, however, did significantly *worse* on the second trial. So far, we have been unable to explain this.

116. Chris Jarrold and I looked into this question by running three new conditions: (a) child places all the cards from four different locations, (b) experimenter places all the cards from four different locations, (c) there is no agent but the child watches the "card" move from four locations on a computer screen. If the problem is with self-monitoring then children with autism should be unimpaired on these tasks because no self–other discrimination has to be made. With certain caveats, they *are* unimpaired. (JR 1/11/95).

117. The theory of mind module in the orbito-frontal region and the executive module in the dorsolateral region let us say. See Baron-Cohen (1995) for some ideas about the loci of ToMM and related "modules". But recall the findings of Fletcher et al. (submitted) from an imaging study which shows that the area in the normal adult brain that "lights up" when

comprehending theory of mind stories is Brodmann's area 8 or pre-motor cortex. This area is associated with conditional learning in the monkey (Halsband & Passingham, 1985).

118. I have to admit finding the concept of a *locus* for theory of mind unintelligible—in much the same way as a locus for "consciousness" is unintelligible.

119. However Franky Happé (1994) has recently reported data suggesting that central cohesion and theory of mind are not closely related, in the sense that performance on the blocks design task is not related to performance on theory of mind tasks in children with autism.

120. This is rather an odd view in the light of the fact that the good performance of autistic subjects on the false photograph task and on tasks requiring an understanding of map-like representations has lead Leslie (Leslie & Thaiss, 1992) to claim that it is not meta-representation *per se* that is impaired in autism but something closer to a grasp of the attitudes.

121. Frith equates this with the hippocampus. However, recent work has suggested that the cerebellum is the monitor for efference copying (e.g. Stein & Glickstein, 1993). This claim marries intriguingly with Eric Courchesne's ideas (previously mentioned; see Courchesne et al., 1992) about autistic deficits being rooted in the cerebellum.

122. I understand that "decoupling" is a term used in symbolic AI.

Coda: Looking back and going forward

LOOKING BACK

We have climbed a long way, and it would be a good idea to look back over the ground covered. When we have done this we will make out a route that can be taken from here—a middle way between a simulation[123] account of the development of mental concepts and a theory-theory account of their development.

My aims in Part 1 were broadly negative and motivated by the view that certain fundamental processes in mental development cannot be understood within the terms of two popular meta-theories of mental representation—the language of thought doctrine (LOT) and mental models theory. There were two reasons for this. First, each theory has its particular difficulty: the LOT doctrine (at least Fodor's version) cannot accommodate the holism of the mental, while there is no way to express the ambitious version of mental models theory (i.e. Johnson-Laird's version rather than McGinn's version) without encountering the homunculus problem. Second, theories of this kind cannot explain how children come to the view that there is a physical world out there and that people have minds, because such processes cannot be explained in purely representational terms. This is because the exercise of a subject's agency must contribute to these acquisitions. I promised that a broadly piagetian theory has the resources to do this, but only said what *kind* of theory the piagetian theory was, leaving a proper account of it to Parts 2 and 3. In this respect, Part 1 was promissory.

There was some ambivalence towards connectionism in Part 1. On the one hand connectionism naturally avoids the twin pitfalls of atomism and a homuncular view of mental representation; but at the same time it expresses a thoroughly "bottom-up" view of cognition: data comes in, flows upwards through the net a number of times until (perhaps via back-propagation or some other means) the target mapping is achieved. Connectionism scores with learning, but seems to lack the resources for explaining how structured thoughts are applied to the world. Relatedly, in buying out of mental symbols it finds itself owing an account of the systematicity and productivity of verbal thought. Connectionism has, however, made some progress in modelling agency, albeit some very simple manifestations of it. Because the rest of the book would be focused on the contribution of agency to knowledge of the physical and mental world, I described some examples of this work. Connectionist models give plausible accounts of how information has to flow through the system in order that, for example, goal-directed actions can be corrected (e.g. Jordan's forward model) and attention can be directed successfully (e.g. Houghton's competitive queuing model). This is where—given our interests—connectionism scores; it scores in describing how intentions (perhaps coded on "plan-units") and information about the present state of the world and predictions about future states have to interact in successful action.

By the end of Part 1 we had reached the following point. The ground had been cleared for a general theory of the development of physical and mental knowledge which placed agency at the centre. In constructing the positive thesis, however, there had to be a starting-point different from that of the representational theories. I expressed this difference in terms of theories that are "inside out" versus theories that are "outside in". In the former case, the concern is with how representations have to be configured if they are to guide behaviour adequately; in the latter case one views an active organism in a world of objects and asks how that organism has to interact with these objects if it is to gain a conception of them and of itself. What such a theory needs, first and foremost, is a clear view of agency and how agency contributes to this development. In Part 2, I tried to provide this.

In Part 1, I had defined "agency" provisionally as "the ability to alter one's perceptual inputs at will". At the beginning of Part 2, I described four features of agency, with two of them being descriptive of the mode of information-processing that agents achieve and two being descriptive of the kind of knowledge available only to agents. The latter two had more relevance to the concerns of Part 3 (about mental knowledge), but

I made much of the second of the first two: *reversibility*. In some respects, the central claim of the book is that a conception of objects as being the causes of one's experience must come about through the exercise of reversibility, meaning the ability to control the order in which one has experiences and thus the ability to distinguish between sequences of experience that are world-caused and those that are self-caused. I argued that reversibility enables the agent to experience the physical world as refractory—as resisting the will—and that only by this route can a subject become aware of how his or her experiences are constrained to be. Only freedom can show up limitation.

I then tried to be explicit about the implications of this thesis for the development of self–world dualism, with reference to the case of The Receiver—a robot that responds to inputs but never monitors the launch of its movements, and which cannot alter its perceptual inputs at will. The Receiver, I argued, is merely "a point at which perceptual inputs converge" and so to that extent it lacks the experiential raw material from which to develop a sense of self: it cannot gain a conception of itself as the subject of objective experiences. In the first place, it cannot experience refractoriness and therefore can never regard objects as the causes of its experiences. The second reason why The Receiver could gain no conception of itself as a subject of experiences was more difficult to express. To put it broadly, because it intends nothing it never experiences mental events that are generated "in its own world". It may be able to distinguish between different kinds of optic flow, but this distinction does not amount to a distinction between inner and outer —and thus between subjective and objective.

In the next section of Part 2, I asked what this kind of view implies about how we develop the conception that objects not only cause our experiences but that they exist in a space that we and they co-inhabit. To have a conception of the external world—I called this "externality"— requires having some grasp of where one is located relative to objects. In describing how agency contributes to this knowledge I had to answer the opposing view that a system like the Receiver could *infer* its position in space on the basis of its sensory input alone. Here I argued that a system that is no more than the point at which sensory inputs converge could never grasp the way in which its current experience is *contingent on* where it is presently located: "inferences from *this* experience to *my* location are only possible for creatures that already possess some conception of themselves as spatially located within an objective world" (p.98). I then had to say what agency contributes *positively* to the sense of oneself as an item in the world. Here, I followed Brewer's path—a path first taken by Schopenhauer. The thought was that any subject whose experience locates it egocentrically in relation to objects must be something that is a subject of willing. Schopenhauer argued that the contents of the subject's perceptions guide its actions in space; they "advise" it, as it were, about how to act. One cannot experience a datum as being at a certain place relative to oneself (e.g. as being up or down) without knowing something about the implications that this percept has for action. I suggested that the following three things are not mentally distinct: (1) a place's location relative to us; (2) what we can do in relation to that place; (3) our purposes. These three form a unity.

The next task was to discuss what is required for subjects not merely to have thoughts about *places* relative to themselves, but to have thoughts about *objects* that are spatially related to their body. I argued that what is required for this concept is that subjects have "structured" knowledge about how their actions (e.g. eye-movements) can affect their experiences of objects, in tension with knowledge (following the reversibility thesis) of how their experiences of objects are constrained to be, relative to these actions. It follows from this that to know that an object exists when it is not currently being perceived (e.g. it is occluded by another object) is fundamentally a matter of knowing *what can be done to render the object perceptible*—that knowing about an external datum is conceptually linked to knowing how one's experience (or re-experiencing) of an object can be affected by what one does.

I began subsequently to discuss empirical issues in infant development, and did so by describing the tension between the piagetian view of object permanence, just described, and the view that object permanence is a matter of maintaining a representation of a currently occluded object during its absence. I called the latter "representation permanence". On the first view, object permanence is equivalent to "externality" and must accordingly be assessed in terms of action; whereas on the latter view it can be assessed in terms of how infants react to unusual (i.e. permanence-violating) events. The argument here was that it is possible for a creature to be able to maintain a representation of an object when the object is currently invisible without that creature having anything that one could call a "concept" of an object. Next, I tried to spell out what this thesis implies about the role of agency in object permanence by answering three objections.

First, I said that to allow that a representation has "content"— this must be ascribed to the object-representations of infants in dishabituation experiments—can be done without allowing that *concepts* are being exercised. Second, I admitted that objectivity cannot emerge from the exercise of agency *alone*, but argued that this does not undermine the current thesis; it merely shows up the difference between "Piagetian" and "piagetian". In this context the piagetian differs from the Piagetian insofar as the former allows that there are innate capacities for coding allocentric relations in space: these relations are not—*pace* the Piagetian—constructed in action. In the third place, I argued that (a) successful action requires a form of structured spatial knowledge that appropriate reaction does not, and that, accordingly, only the former can tell us what a creature knows about the spatial relation between itself and an object, and (b) that when we talk about externality we should not talk about "representations that *cause* behaviour", for we are at the "personal" rather than the "sub-personal" level, and that level is explanatorily autonomous.

During the subsequent review of the development of search in infancy a distinction was drawn between "executive performance" and "executive competence" errors. In the former case, there is knowledge existing alongside an inability to control one's behaviour; in the latter there is the failure to appreciate how actions determine changes in perceptual input. The piagetian view is that infants' difficulties with search tasks are executive-competence difficulties. This implies that as the ability to initiate, inhibit, and order actions develops, infants enjoy progressively richer experiences of the refractory nature of the input and their knowledge of the mind-independence of objects becomes more secure in the process.

In the final section of Part 2, I discussed the computational modelling of the development of externality. For saying that externality must be regarded as a personal-level ability is not to say that computational models of how the brain supports externality cannot be produced. (To say so would be like denying that there can be theories of the neural mechanisms supporting folk psychology; sub-personal mechanism must obviously support what happens at the personal level.) I argued that the development of externality (what piagetians intend by "object permanence") is best done in a connectionist style, and here I reprised some of the conclusions of Part 1.

At the beginning of Part 3, I distinguished between the development of mind itself (I usually referred to this as the "pre-theoretical mind") and the development of the child's theories of the mind's nature, with the implication being that current work in theory of mind development has led us to neglect this distinction. My principal aim here was to describe the contribution of agency to the development of the pre-theoretical mind and then to draw out the implications of this for empirical work on theory of mind development in children and for mentalising difficulties in autism.

The first step was to build on some of the conclusions of Part 2 and argue that possessing externality implies the possession of a certain form of unified or synthetic mentality ($mind_s$). To enjoy objective experience requires a form of mental unity. It is possible, however, to possess a mind$_s$ without any reflective conception of oneself as the owner of these experiences (mind$_o$), so the next task was to discuss the contribution of agency to this more reflective or "second order" form of mentality. What is at issue here is the subject's ability not merely to regard his or her experiences as being of something objective and mind-independent but the subject's capacity for taking experiences as belonging to his or her self. The topic had become, therefore, a pre-theoretical form of self-awareness, with the obvious challenge being to say how a self-awareness can exist that *is* pre-theoretical—one that does not depend on the exercise of mental concepts.

This form of mind$_o$ has three ingredients, I argued. First, there is bodily awareness. The experience of being embodied is integral to the experience of willing. Schopenhauer referred to the body as "the objectivity of my will"; and, in possessing a body that one takes as one's own because one controls it (not because it is the conduit of sensations) the paradoxical feat is achieved of making what is subjective a possible object of reflection. Second, there is the "immediate" experience of willing. Here I built directly on material from Part 2. To know *that* one is willing and acting is to have a form of knowledge unmediated by representations. This was again what Schopenhauer argued; and it is a claim that underlay the latter two features of agency set out in Part 2 (knowing what we are doing without observation and knowing our "tryings" incorrigibly). In addition to being immediate, this kind of knowledge is "inner" (recall the discussion of The Receiver's lack of such knowledge). Third, the possessor of a mind$_o$ is able to entertain first-person thoughts (or "I-thoughts") and one condition for this is that he or she experience a complete integration of what he or she wills with what he or she knows: "That which strives to alter the world must be conscious of itself as being that which, perceptually or otherwise, has knowledge of it" (Janaway, 1989; p.301). I took it that the existence of these three established the dependency of having a pre-theoretical form of self-awareness (mind$_o$) on agency.

With the notion of mind$_o$ in place, I turned to the theoretical from the pre-theoretical mind—to what it takes to have a "theory of mind". Following nearly everybody who has written about this topic, I took "theory of mind" to refer to the subject's grasp of how an agent, his or her propositional attitudes, and his or her propositional contents are related. After a brief discussion of the role of understanding desire, the aim of which was to show how something of a *non-representational character* has to be grasped in acquiring this theory, I concluded that "acquiring a theory of mind" cannot be equated with "acquiring a theory of representation".

We next considered theories of how it is possible for an individual to acquire a grasp of the *representational* aspects of a theory of mind—a grasp of what it means to "think that *p*". Five options were surveyed. The first three, I argued, had conceptual flaws. The "reflection+analogy" view was flawed to the extent that Cartesian theories of mental content are flawed; the "hypothesis-testing" view was based on a bad analogy between theory-construction in science and the process of mental development; the "meta-representational insight" was based on the view—just rejected—that grasping mental representation is a special case of grasping any kind of representing relationship. The other two theories were nativist. I argued that nativism was a good option, but said that a view that regards knowledge of the representing function of mind as closely tied to linguistic knowledge is a better alternative than one that regards it as existing in a distinct mental module. The problem with the latter view—some, of course, would say that this is not a problem at all—is that it depends on accepting the LOT doctrine.

In the next couple of sub-sections I discussed how a theoretical grasp of mentality depends on a pre-theoretical experience of it—on $mind_o$. In doing this I drew a parallel between the semantics and the syntax of language, with pre-theoretical paralleling being the former. I introduced The Mentaliser—a relative of The Receiver—which was a system capable of parsing others' behaviour into the correct folk-psychological categories, but which was not an agent. The Mentaliser, I argued, was all syntax and no semantics, and, what's more, it had a "theory of mind" without actually possessing a mind of its own—an empty theory.

I then tackled an issue that will be taken up again shortly. I looked at the extent to which a creature whose experience of mind is pre-theoretical and grounded in agency—$mind_o$—can perceive mentality in other people on the basis of its own experience of agency. The fact is that very young children do possess something that we can call "social understanding"; but we do not wish to be committed to the view that the existence of early social understanding is necessarily evidence for the child possessing a theory of mind. And I suggested that to call these "pre-cursors to theory of mind" is a fudge.

The challenge to be faced was this. Throughout Part 3 we have been concerned with how mentality is grounded in *first person* experience; questions about social interaction were pushed to the side. But children are obviously social creatures, and one does not wish to be saddled with the absurd view (given what was said earlier in favour of a language-based grasp of mental categories) that they possess social understanding only insofar as they use and comprehend language. In other words, how far can this agency-grounded awareness of mentality be ascribed to others? To say that the child is applying to others what he or she knows about him or herself is to say something that sounds awfully like the reflection+analogy view which was rejected earlier. How I tried to deal with this was by arguing that the child's being an agent can enable him or her to appreciate that some observations of others are observations of their agency. I then went a little further and suggested that, insofar as possessing $mind_0$ is not a matter of possessing a network of *concepts*, there is no impediment to the view that the child perceives elements of $mind_0$ in other people by virtue of experiencing his or her own agency, and said that what elements these are is a matter to be decided empirically.

It has to be said, however, that at the point at which I began to discuss empirical issues [roughly before 3.3(v)] I had left a major conceptual issue unresolved—just how Cartesian can we allow ourselves to be about the ascription of $mind_0$ to others, and just how much must we borrow from the theory-theory approach to avoid the Cartesian option? I will take some steps towards resolving the dilemma in the second half of this final chapter.

Having borrowed others' arguments for the claim that a theory of mind may develop as a gradual, holistic dawning rather than in discontinuous stages, I looked at the evidence for such stage-wise changes in Section 3.4. In order to gain a better perspective on the 3–4 transition, I looked at a later, apparently stage-wise, change at about 7 years—what Piaget called the transition between pre-operational and concrete operational thought. This was done in order to illustrate the difference between theory-theory and executive accounts of stage-wise change where the transition is not one whose content is mental-theoretical, taking Piaget's account of concrete operational thought to be executive and the views I expressed about 15 years ago as theory-theory in nature. In discussing both transitions I argued that what may appear to be a case of the child's acquiring new concepts may instead be a case of the child gaining control over the process of framing judgements when he or she is asked to frame them.

We returned at this point to the distinction between "executive-performance" and "executive-competence" errors. The former kind of error, recall, is one that a subject makes in spite of what he or she knows (e.g. Diamond's account of infants' commission of the A-not-B error). An executive-competence error, on the other hand, is one that the subject makes because he or she does not understand the relation between his or her agency and his or her experiences (this was the piagetian account of why infants take about 18 months to search successfully for objects). With regard to the 3–4 transition in theory of mind development, an executive-performance account of why 3-year-olds fail such tasks as "false belief" is that the structure of the tasks simply masks an understanding that remains *unchanged* from 3 years to 4 years and beyond. An executive-competence account, by contrast, says that, although young children are led into error because of inadequate executive control over competing representations, *when such control is acquired* (I gestured vaguely to endogenous changes at this point) they gain a firmer grasp of the relation between themselves, their propositional attitudes, and their mental contents. That is to say, as they gain control over their own minds they come to a clearer view of what it means for mind to represent. The obvious difference between this and the theory-theory view is that it does *not* say that a concept of belief is acquired at age 4; rather, the concept develops gradually, and what looks like a discontinuous stage-wise development of mental concepts is in fact a discontinuity in the development of executive functioning. I used the "windows task" as an existence-proof that a kind of failure that looks as if it diagnoses a failure to manipulate another's mental state is almost certainly diagnosing a failure to control one's own.

In the concluding section I discussed autism. It is clear that the present thesis is very well-placed to explain why we find in this disorder a combination of executive and mentalising difficulties. The essential claim was that this combination of deficits can be explained by saying that persons with autism have a disorder of the pre-theoretical mind— $mind_0$ or perhaps even $mind_s$—and that this is why they have a weak grasp of the representing function of mind.

The final issue to be tackled concerned the relation between disorders of agency and disorders of meta-representation. C. Frith's writings on the cognitive neuropsychology of schizophrenia contain a clear expression of the view that even a feature of agency as primitive as action-monitoring requires meta-representation; and Frith's view had to be confronted insofar as it is the symmetrical opposite of the present thesis. I argued that we do not have to call on what Leslie and others call "meta-representation" in order to explain a process as primitive as action-monitoring. I illustrated this point through Gordon Brown's computational model of Frith's theory, a theory that is supposed to explain why hallucinations and delusions of alien control exist in schizophrenia. I noted that this model did not make use of meta-representational devices; a malfunctioning of the "forward model" was sufficient.

GOING FORWARD

To press on with my unremarkable metaphor, having a clearer view of the ground that has been covered usually brings the dubious advantage of also seeing of how far one has still to climb—and of the ravines and pitfalls ahead. To reach higher ground, I have to discern the narrow path between two approaches to the acquisition of a theory of mind—between simulation theory and the theory theory (see note 123).

But, setting mountaineering metaphors to one side, what simulation theory gives us is a treatment of the first-person conditions for theory of mind development; what the theory theory gives us is a treatment of the role of concept-use in that development. But what neither gives us is any perspective on how agency, on the one hand, and language acquisition, on the other, grounds a theory of mind.

Common ground with simulation theory

I have already discussed—in 3.3(ii)—something that is essentially a caricature of simulation theory—the "reflection+analogy" view. Recall that this view was rejected because it assumed that children, in reflecting on their own experiences, "cut the mental world at its joints", thereby becoming able to apply mental concepts to themselves which they then project onto others. On this view, the experience of pretending, of desiring, of believing, and so forth are sufficient—together with an inner eye that can swivel back onto these mental occurrences—to put these concepts in a state fit to be applied, as predicates, first to the self and then to others. I borrowed arguments from Wittgenstein and from Strawson to the effect that the application of mental predicates just cannot be a solitary enterprise. In the first place, the possession of a private language is being assumed; while in the second place the unintelligible claim is made that a creature should be in a position to apply a predicate to itself and to itself alone before being in a position to ascribe it to another. I will proceed on the assumption that these arguments are indeed decisive against the reflection+analogy view (although see note 124).

Why did I not just be done with it and call the reflection+analogy view "simulation theory"? Because there are different varieties of simulation theory and none them are as brazen as this. Harris (1991), for one, while suggesting a role for self-reflection and analogy, is more concerned with giving an empirical account (similar to the executive account) of what makes mental simulation difficult for young children than with saying how mental concepts are grounded. And none of the philosophers who support simulation theory would endorse the reflection+analogy view as I have stated it. In fact, philosophers who endorse simulation theory generally do not make developmental issues their central concern, asking what the process of ascribing thoughts to others amounts to rather than how mental concepts are grounded. Let us look very briefly at some of their views.

Gordon's (1986) position is distinct from the reflection+analogy view insofar as he claims that in performing mental simulation all that is required is that there be "contagion" between the mental states of the subject and others together with a capacity for imaginative projection by the subject which does not require the employment of concepts. Goldman (1989) and Heal[124] (in press), on the other hand, although clearly simulation theorists, say that there can be no imaginative projection without the use of concepts. Writing about what is required for ascribing fear of an object to another Heal says, "What is required is that I take it that the other undergoes in reality what I am aware of undergoing in imagination. And I cannot do this without having the concepts of 'state of myself', 'similarity' and 'state of the other'." (Heal, in press; p.42). I accept that concepts are required for mental simulation and so, however central the role of simulation in everyday mind-reading turns out to be, the Wittgenstein-Strawson line cannot be defused simply by saying that we project thoughts onto others without the exercise of concepts. If imaginative projection is the name of the game then the players must be armed with *some* concepts of mentality.

Perhaps it is now a little easier to make out the narrow path that has to be trodden. I need to articulate the view that children's exercise of agency is one of the things that enables them to perceive others as agents, and that elements of $mind_0$ may be perceived in others' behaviour on the basis of their own experienced agency. Children, in this picture, are not simulating a mental state (e.g. fear of an object) in others, but are perceiving others as mental kinds similar to themselves; and children naturally recruit what they themselves experiences to do this. But this view must be neither (1) the reflection+analogy view, nor (2) the view that mental simulation can be achieved without concepts, nor (3) the view that all mental concepts are grounded in an innate or constructed theory and that alone (which would make first-person mental knowledge theory-relative and do scant justice to the way in which first-person experience grounds a concept of mind).

The first thing to say at this point—although for the third time in the book—is that perceiving another person as the possessor of a $mind_0$ is a pre-theoretical achievement, and this is to say that the child, in doing this, has no general view of mental categories (e.g. of the distinctions between varieties of propositional attitude) and certainly does not know that beliefs and desires lead to intentions. No concepts are being handled. Let us look again at the three elements of $mind_0$ and consider how the experience of mind$_0$ may lead to the perception of elements of it in others.

1. Children's bodies are the "objectivity" of their will. Accordingly, when they see other behaving bodies they see them as being controlled in much the same way in which they control their own body; and so when they see another body behaving they *see* another will in operation. For this to succeed children do not imaginatively project onto others what they are intending on the model of what they themselves would intend in similar circumstances. *This would only be necessary if there were a duality between the will and bodily action* and this is exactly what—after Schopenhauer, Wittgenstein, O'Shaughnessy and others—I have been arguing *against*.

2. The pre-theoretical child's knowledge that he or she is willing is not representational knowledge—it is "immediate". Although there can be immediate—in the sense of non-inferential— knowledge that *does* involve the exercise of concepts, insofar as the pre-theoretical child's knowledge is both immediate and *non-representational*, it does *not* involve the exercise of concepts; indeed it is not strictly "knowledge" at all. But obviously children do not experience *another's* willing in this immediate fashion, and so it is reasonable to say that whenever they perceive another as trying to achieve some end, they must be exercising concepts such as "other agent", "trying", and "goal". Certainly, for children to see another person as intending to bring about X, they will require some minimal grasp of the relevant concepts; but *this* kind of ascription is not what is at issue here. What is at issue is the way children encounter themselves non-representationally when they act. They encounter themselves " 'from the inside' as that which is responsible for changes in [their] experience" (p.179). And they perceive others as embodied wills, as we have just seen. If we put these two things together (embodied will and inner-located responsibility) we have a picture of the pre-theoretical child as perceiving the actions of another body as being not merely an objectified will, but as the embodiment of a centre of responsibility for what is being done. It is not merely that in doing this children perceive a will in action: they perceive these wilful actions as being *centred*, as it were, on a point. If children could not achieve something like this, it is difficult to see how they could go on to attribute first-person thoughts to others. Such thoughts are attributed not to bodies that act wilfully, but to centres in which these wilful acts are generated. It would interesting to speculate

about the *phenomenology* of a social experience of this kind, but there would be little point to it in the present context.

It is not, however, pointless to say that unless an ability were in place for perceiving others as centres of responsibility (the facts about whose mentality are not exhausted by facts about how their bodies purposefully move) one would never be in a position to explain others' behaviour by reference to mental *categories*. Only if one is able to entertain the possibility that another creature has a "centred" mental life—in the sense just described—will one be able to use that creature as an argument for the mental predicates that one knows innately or in the use of which one gradually acquires expertise. Consider, in illustration, Thomas Nagel's (1974) famous thought-experiment in which he asked "What is it like to be a bat?". We can certainly try to imagine what it could be like to be such a creature despite the vast differences between that animal's sensory systems and our own. Why? Is it because we possess a folk psychology within the ambit of which we may be relaxed enough to include other creatures? Or is it because we find it natural to ascribe subjectivity to something that is responsible in some degree for what it experiences—putting to one side questions about whether it has *concepts* of anything mental.

3. The third element of $mind_0$ referred to pre-theoretical children's experience of the complete integration of what they will with that which they apprehend—what they bring about and what they perceive and know. There is, indeed, not merely an integration between what children will and what they apprehend, but a complete apprehension of themselves *qua* willers and themselves *qua* apprehenders. We need this because one cannot construct a picture of the pre-theoretical mind in which there are subjects whose consciousness of themselves as affecting the world through willing is distinct from their consciousness of themselves as knowing and perceiving things. Let us now add this fact to the picture of $mind_0$ that is now beginning to emerge. Pre-theoretical children are in a position to perceive an objectified will and locate a centre of responsibility in another body; so what this third condition bears on is their ability to see another as making informational contact with the world.

If children experience the complete integration of their volitions and their apprehendings, and if they perceive the other as something wilful and centred, then—I believe we can plausibly say—they perceive others on the basis of this as being capable of generating varieties of experience and of becoming exposed thereby to different sources of information, given that agents act on the basis of what they perceive and of what they are informed about. What I am saying is that, insofar as children experience a complete integration between their willing and apprehending selves, and insofar as they perceive other bodies as centres of willing, they will also perceive other bodies as being subject to the pick-up of information. This is not, I should stress, an *argument*: it is a conjecture.

What is being claimed is that the pre-theoretical child perceives other people as creatures who can be informed or not informed about the way the world is, and that their ability to do this depends on their ability to perceive them as agents like themselves. To perceive agency in another must also be to perceive the other as capable of picking up information.

Notice that I am talking here about "information" rather than knowledge, because having some grasp of what another "knows" implies the ability to distinguish knowing from other propositional attitudes (such as believing or guessing); and that is just the kind of capacity that one cannot ascribe to the possessor of a pre-theoretical mind$_0$. But to see that another is informed about something does not require that the subject grasp that another is *related* to his or her mental contents in any way. For example, the child does not need to exercise mental concepts—does not need to know about the network of other concepts within which "knowing" is embedded—to appreciate that another person can be informed about what the child him or herself is informed about (e.g. because they are watching it together) or not informed about (e.g. because the other person is out of the room). I am saying that this ability to perceive others as subject to the pick-up of information requires that the child see others as centres of volition, given the indissociable linkage between these two.

This, then, is as far as the present thesis can move towards simulation theory. There is, I have been arguing, something grounded in first-person experience that is projected onto others—experiencing agency first-hand makes it possible for us to perceive others in a certain way—but there is no implication from this that ascribing beliefs to others is something that can be achieved without possessing a network of structured concepts, and no implication that mental *concepts* are grounded in first-person experience. What is grounded in first-person experience is the ability to perceive others as embodied, "centred" wills which can be informed and uninformed about the way the world is. These are not theory-relative achievements.

It is not impossible that a reader might, at this point, start to think something like the following: "Why are you worrying about the extent to which so-called pre-theoretical children can project what they know immediately of their own mentality onto others? Maybe very little projection occurs until mental concepts are in place. The early sociability of children may amount to little more than innate behavioural routines that we have evolved to maintain the bond between children and caretakers, and they may not require to the child to see the other as a mental kind at all. You may be right that the sort of projection you refer to fills out the 'semantics' of the theory of mind just as its conceptual structure fills out its 'syntax'; but why say there is semantics *before*—logically and developmentally—the syntax. Why worry about what children can or cannot project onto others from their own case without mental concepts?".

This is the answer. It may be recalled that in Part 1.1, I rounded off the discussion of LOT by quoting remarks of Jane Heal critical of a view of mentality that regards minds as nothing more than systems in which representations interact in such as way as to control behaviour in the light of inputs. On this view, mentality is a kind of third-person explanatory hypothesis allowing us to predict and understand what any putatively mental system is up to. "This invites the reposte," Heal wrote, "'why should I approach any objects in the natural world with this conceptual baggage'?" (Heal, 1993-94, p.335). In other words, some ability to perceive others as mental kinds must be in place before we can set about explaining what they are up to in terms of such as categories as "intention" and "belief"; we must see others as possessing whatever-it-is that legitimises their being treated as arguments for mental predicates. As we saw in the discussion of Heal's positive views, what is of central importance here is being—and the ability to regard another as being—an effective subject and "unified locus of cognitive virtues"; and I am saying that unless the child is a unified, effective subject, he or she can never come to regard others as being effective subjects or as loci at which mental concepts can be exercised. This is not something that we have to regard as part-and-parcel of the exercise of mental concepts, I am suggesting: it is something that is not only logically prior but developmentally prior to any application of mental predicates to others.

It goes without saying that determining the exact nature of this pre-theoretical perception of others as unified, effective subjects is an empirical affair. What I have been doing here is trying to articulate the kind of thing that this social perception can be said to be.

Common ground with the theory-theory

Throughout this book there have been endorsements of a broadly Wittgensteinian view of mental content; and one cannot make these and reject the theory-theory view of mental content at the same time. Indeed the theory-theory view has *not* been rejected—only the view that this theory develops at about 4 years of age. I have been assuming that when a child comes to the view that there are such entities as beliefs, desires, hopes, expectations, and so forth, he or she is indeed utilising a theory. What this boils down to is the claim that "a belief"—taking this as the paradigmatic mental concept—is not a natural kind in the sense in which, say, "a gene" is a natural kind. The notion of belief exists to be used in making ourselves intelligible to ourselves; and there is no contradiction between saying (a) a belief is a theoretical rather than real entity and (b) the theory of belief is innate. The theory is a natural or "biological" entity, but the terms out of which the theory is constructed are not. (There could be innate theories about goblins or golden mountains.) At least that is what I will take endorsement of the theory-theory view of mental content as amounting to.

In 3.3(ii) I argued in favour of nativism about the theory of mind, a form of nativism that tied its possession to linguistic competence. Then in 3.3(v) I argued for a gradualist view of its development. I will wind up the book with an attempt at bringing these two claims together.

First of all, as I said earlier, linguistic competence and a theory of mind are conceptually interdependent, and this fact makes it unlikely that a theory of mind could exist as a *sui generis* and innate module. (I made no attempt to derive a hypothesis about human biology from this fact about concepts; my intention was merely to say what looks plausible given the conceptual claim.) What can be said about this conceptual interdependence? I mentioned Donald Davidson's views when presenting the case for a form of linguistic nativism about theory of mind, and the following is a slightly different way of expressing what I said then. Davidson (1975) wrote of the "autonomy" of meaning, referring to the fact that one can know what an utterance means without knowing about the intentions or beliefs that prompted it. Among English-speakers, for example, an utterance of "It is raining" by a speaker x at time t is true if and only if it is raining near the speaker at that time. Once the meaning of a sentence is understood, an utterance of it can be used to serve a host of extra-linguistic purposes, such as saying "It is raining" with a disbelieving sneer. Davidson takes this fact to imply that linguistic meaning cannot be defined and analysed in terms of speakers' extra-linguistic cognitive states: meaning is autonomous in *this* sense.

But broadly, we speak sentences that we hold to be true, and trying to say what is true is not an extra-linguistic purpose in the sense that, say, trying to amuse or to intimidate another person is an extra-linguistic purpose. How might a grasp of the autonomy of meaning relate to a grasp of what it means to hold something to be true? Certainly, somebody could never belong to a speech community unless he or she were armed with two kinds of knowledge—about the autonomy of meaning and about what it takes to hold an utterance to be true. It is the latter that is our concern.

In the first place, if knowing that the meaning of a sentence is something with an existence distinct from whatever intentions and beliefs the speaker of the sentence has, then it has to be the case that understanding the autonomy of meaning must require some understanding of human psychology. For how could the autonomy be grasped without some knowledge of that in relation to which it is autonomous? And in the second place—and more important for our purposes—*how could a conception of holding true exist in a creature that knew nothing about the autonomy of meaning*? Holding true is what we do of sentences with a *sui generis* meaning: it cannot be analysed extra-linguistically.

What one can conclude from this is that a concept of belief cannot exist in a creature that understands nothing about how a string of symbols can have autonomous meaning. And to put things this way can help us to understand why a concept of belief had to evolve in us. It had to evolve in order that we could "take up the slack" (Davidson's metaphor) between being true and holding true. It evolved because one can hold something to be true when it is not true—because we can hold utterances to be true and be wrong about it. If this "slack" could not be "taken up" then there would be such a loose relation between our sentences and our psychology that communication would involve something less than the communication of *thoughts*.

This has two implications for the developmental psychology of mental concepts. First, as I argued in Part 3, it makes the hypothesis that theory of mind is independent of and developmentally prior to linguistic competence an hypothesis that can only be stated coherently if one also assumes the truth of the LOT doctrine. In the second place, it makes a gradualist view of theory of mind development look more inviting than the view that a concept of belief only appears after an intellectual revolution around age 4. Let us consider this gradualism.

On this loosely Davidsonian view, it makes little sense to say that children pass through a period in which they are successful language-users but in which they have no concept of belief at all. This is because making statements and understanding the statements of others is not something that can be achieved with just a grasp of the autonomy of meaning and a grasp of that *alone*. This does not mean that as soon as a child uses language, he or she has a fully fledged concept of false belief. Indeed it is not absurd to say that children begin their linguistic life with the false belief that all beliefs are true; but if they did, they would still have *some* understanding of belief. They would be armed with the distinction between holding true and being true, and they would have a potential for entertaining the possibility that beliefs can be false while not actually entertaining it. There is nothing wrong with saying that this could exist without a concept of lying and without any clear understanding of what it means to act on the basis of outdated and therefore false information.

It now falls to me to say something about what this gradual emergence of a theory of mind—in the sense of a conception of the "agent→attitude→propositional content" triad—would look like in a very young language-user. Where would we look for its emergence? We could look at the very young children's use of negation, in particular at their tendency to begin their negating career by placing the negative term outside the sentence. Consider the following dialogue between a child of 2 years 3 months and her mother. She is helping her mother cut up zucchini (courgettes) for supper (Jaeger, 1988, reported in Van Valin, 1991, pp.18–19).

> Child: Me like zucchini.
> Mother: OK, you can have some.
> Child: No! Me like zucchini. (With negative headshake)
> Mother: Oh, you mean you don't like zucchini.
> Child: Yeah.
> Mother: Can you say "I don't like zucchini"?
> Child: No me like zucchini.
> Mother: OK, you don't have to have any.

Now it does not take a great deal of imagination to credit this small girl with some grasp of the relation between herself, her attitudes (in a loose sense) and a proposition. The relation is this: "I" → " reject the truth of the proposition" → "I like zucchini". Perhaps I should add that this NEG+Sentence pattern is in the running for being a cross-linguistic universal in early acquisition; and because he takes it to be a pattern that does not occur in adult speech in any human language[125] Chomsky uses it as an illustration of the fact that children do not model their grammar on what they hear (Van Valin, 1991, p.19).

A child of 2;3 is clearly going to fail the false belief task and all cognate tasks; indeed, he or she will not even get to first base with the control questions and so the issue of whether he or she "has a concept of false belief" *cannot even arise*, on the standard view. But interchanges like this suggest that very young children have an embryonic grasp of the agent→attitude→content triad and have a more-than-embryonic grasp of the distinction between a sentence's meaning something irrespective of the speaker's purposes (Davidson's "autonomy of meaning") and a speaker who can hold the sentence true *or false*.

Denial is as important a process in mental development as any. When we see young children refusing to eat eggs or to put their shoes on or some toys away we are seeing the emerging will plain; while the psycho-linguist can regard these same children as taking up strong attitudes to propositions as they mentally hold up a sentence and frame it with a "No!". Within the topic of negation, in fact, we see both the major and a rather minor theme of this book flowing together—the major theme of the dependency of self-awareness on a refractory world, and the minor theme of the gradual and language-grounded emergence of theory of mind.

NOTES

123. There has been a long debate between simulation theory and the theory-theory about which I have been silent in this book. An excellent series of papers can be found in a special issue of the journal *Mind and Language*, 7, (1/2), 1992. Some would claim that the difference between simulation theory and theory-theory dissolves when examined closely; but see Heal (1994) for arguments against that view.

124. Heal tackles the question of whether there is at least some minimal degree of theoretical understanding that must be present if simulation is to work. She rejects, as we have seen, Gordon's view that "mere contagion style" simulation will get us to "thoughts about thoughts", and she also draws a clear distinction between simulation of mental contents (i.e. the particular mental episodes that another is undergoing) and the simulation of mental types, such as simulating the varieties of propositional attitudes on the basis of first-person experience. It is the latter that we are interested in here. Mental contents, she argues, can be simulated "demonstratively", that is, by one's putting on a performance of what it would be like to believe that *p*, for example. But can we say that mental types may be simulated demonstratively? She writes (in press, p.41): "I do not see any obvious or immediate *a priori* argument that anything more than the minimal theoretical assumption is necessary. It is not, for example, obvious that the differences between varieties of propositional attitude cannot be handled demonstratively just as the contents are. But there may be *a priori* arguments against this view and also empirical evidence which bears on how our abilities actually develop." I will go on to argue that the acquisition of language may ground this "minimal theoretical assumption".

125. Apparently this is not correct. Van Valin (1991, footnote 8) points out that there is a Papuan language called Barai which has the NEG+Sentence pattern.

References

Acredolo, L. P., Adams, D., & Goodwyn, S. W. (1984). The role of self-produced movement and visual tracking in infant spatial orientation. *Journal of Experimental Child Psychology, 38*, 312–327.

Allport, A. (1987). Selection for action: Some behavioural and neurophysiological considerations of attention and action. In H. Neurer & A. F. Sanders (Eds.), *Perspectives on perception and action*. Hillsdale, NJ: Lawrence Erlbaum Associates Inc.

Anscombe, G. E. M. (1957). *Intention*. Oxford: Basil Blackwell.

Astington, J. W., & Gopnik, A. (1991). Theoretical explanations of children's understanding of the mind. *British Journal of Developmental Psychology, 9*, 7–31.

Atkinson, J., Hood, B., Wattam-Bell, J., & Braddick, O. J. (1992). Changes in infants' ability to switch attention in the first three months of life. *Perception, 21*, 643–653.

Aurnhammer-Frith, U. (1969). Emphasis and meaning in recall in normal and autistic children. *Language and Speech, 12*, 29–38.

Bachevalier, J. (1994). Medial temporal lobe structures and autism: A review of clinical and experimental findings. *Neuropsychologia, 32*, 627–648.

Baddeley, A. (1986). *Working memory*. Cambridge: Cambridge University Press.

Baddeley, A., & Hitch, G. J. (1974). Working memory. In G. Bower (Ed.), *Recent advances in learning and motivation. Vol. VIII*. New York: Academic Press.

Baillargeon, R. (1986). Representing the existence of and the location of hidden objects: Object permanence in six- and eight-month-old infants. *Cognition, 23*, 21–41.

Baillargeon, R. (1987). Object permanence in 3.5- to 4.5-month old infants. *Developmental Psychology, 23*, 655–664.

Baillargeon, R., DeVos, J., & Graber, M. (1989). Location memory in 8-month-old infants in non-search AB task: Further evidence. *Cognitive Development, 4*, 345–367.

Baillargeon, R., & Graber, M. (1987). Where's the rabbit? 5.5-month-old infants representation of the height of a hidden object. *Cognitive Development, 2*, 375–392.

Baillargeon, R., Graber, M., DeVos, J., & Black, J. (1990). Why do infants fail to search for hidden objects? *Cognition, 36*, 255–284.

Baldwin, J. M. (1906). *Thought and things (3 volumes)*. London: Swann & Sonnenschein.

Baldwin, T. (1995). Objectivity, causality and agency. In J. Bermúdez, A. J. Marcel, & N. Eilan (Eds.), *The self and the body*. Cambridge, MA: MIT Press (Bradford Books).

Baron-Cohen, S. (1987). Autism and symbolic play. *British Journal of Developmental Psychology, 5*, 139–148.

Baron-Cohen, S. (1989). Do autistic children have obsessions and compulsions? *British Journal of Clinical Psychology, 9*, 193–200.

Baron-Cohen, S. (1995). *Mindblindness*. Cambridge, MA: MIT Press (Bradford Books).

Baron-Cohen, S., Cross, P., Crowson, M., & Robertson, M. (in press). Can children with Gilles de la Tourette Syndrome edit their intentions? *Psychological Medicine*.

Baron-Cohen, S., Leslie, A. M., & Frith, U. (1985). Does the autistic child have a 'theory of mind'? *Cognition, 21*, 37–46.

Baron-Cohen, S., Tager-Flusberg, H., & Cohen, D. J. (1993). *Understanding other minds: Perspectives from autism*. Oxford: Oxford University Press.

Bates, E., & Elman, J. (1993). Connectionism and the study of change. In M. Johnson (Ed.), *Brain development and cognition*. Oxford: Basil Blackwell.

Bennetto, L., Pennington, B. F., & Rogers, S. J. (in press). Intact and impaired memory functions in autism. *Child Development*.

Bermúdez, J. (1994). Peacock's argument against the autonomy of nonceptual representational content. *Mind and Language, 9*, 402–418.

Bermúdez, J. (1995). Ecological perception and the notion of a non-conceptual point of view. In J. Bermúdez, A. J. Marcel, & N. Eilan (Eds.), *The body and the self*. Cambridge, MA: MIT Press.

Bermúdez, J. (submitted). *Autonomous nonconceptual content: Reply to Peacocke*.

Bishop, J. (1980). More thought on thought and talk. *Mind, 89*, 1–16.

Bjork, E. L., & Cummings, E. M. (1984). Infant search error: Stage of concept development or stage of memory development? *Memory and Cognition, 12*, 1–19.

Block, N. (1987). Functional role and truth conditions. *Proceedings of the Aristotelian Society, 61*, 157–181.

Bloom, L. (1973). *One word at a time: The use of single-word utterances before syntax*. Cambridge, MA: MIT Press.

Boer, S., & Lycan, W. (1986). *Knowing who*. Cambridge, MA: MIT Press.

Bower, T. G. R. (1966). The visual world of infants. *Scientific American, 215*(6), 80–92.

Bower, T. G. R. (1967). The development of object permanence: Some studies of existence constancy. *Perception and Psychophysics, 2*, 411–418.

Bower, T. G. R. (1974). *Development in infancy*. San Francisco: Freeman.

Boysen, S. T. (1993). Counting in chimpanzees: Nonhuman principles and emergent properties of number. In S. T. Boysen & E. J. Capaldi (Eds.), *The development of numerical competence*. Hillsdale, NJ: Lawrence Erlbaum Associates Inc.

Braine, M. D. S. (1992). What sort of innate structure is needed to 'bootstrap' into syntax? *Cognition, 45*, 77–100.

Brewer, B. (1992). Self-location and agency. *Mind, 101*, 17–34.

Brewer, B. (1993). The integration of spatial vision and action. In N. Eilan, R. McCarthy, & B. Brewer (Eds.), *Spatial representation: Problems in philosophy and psychology*. Oxford: Basil Blackwell.

Brewer, B., & Pears, J. (1993). Introduction: Frames of reference. In N. Eilan, R. McCarthy, & B. Brewer (Eds.), *Spatial representation: Problems in philosophy and psychology*. Oxford: Basil Blackwell.

Brooks, R. A. (1991). Intelligence without representation. *Artificial Intelligence, 47*, 139–159.

Brown, G. D. A., Britain, A. A., Elevevåg, B., & Mitchell, I. J. (1994). A computational approach to fronto-striatal dysfunction in schizophrenia and Parkinson's disease. In M. Oaksford & G. D. A. Brown (Eds.), *Neurodyamics and psychology*. London: Academic Press.

Bruner, J. S. (1959). A psychologist's viewpoint. Review of Inhelder and Piaget's 'The growth of logical thinking from childhood to adolescence'. *British Journal of Psychology, 50*, 363–370.

Bruner, J. S. (1966). *Studies in cognitive growth*. London: Wiley.

Bryant, P. E. (1982). The role of conflict and agreement between intellectual strategies in children's ideas about measurement. *British Journal of Psychology, 73*, 243–251.

Bryant, P. E., & Bradley, L. (1985). *Children's reading problems*. Oxford: Basil Blackwell.

Butterworth, G., & Jarrett, N. (1991). What minds have in common is space: Spatial mechanisms serving joint visual attention in infancy. *British Journal of Developmental Psychology, 9*, 55–71.

Byrne, R., & Johnson-Laird, P. N. (1989). Spatial reasoning. *Journal of Memory and Language, 28*, 564–575.

Campbell, J. (1984). Possession of concepts. *Proceedings of the Aristotelian Society, 85*, 149–170.

Campbell, J. (1993). The role of physical objects in spatial thinking. In N. Eilan, R. McCarthy, & B. Brewer (Eds.), *Spatial representation: Problems in philosophy and psychology*. Oxford: Basil Blackwell.

Campbell, J. (1995). The body image and self-consciousness. In J. Bermúdez, A. J. Marcel, & N. Eilan (Eds.), *The body and the self*. Cambridge, MA: MIT Press.

Case, R. (1985). *Intellectual development: Birth to adulthood*. New York: Academic Press.

Case, R., Kurland, M., & Goldberg, J. (1982). Operational efficiency and the growth of short-term memory span. *Journal of Experimental Child Psychology, 33*, 386–404.

Chambers, D., & Reisberg, D. (1985). Can mental images be ambiguous? *Journal of Experimental Psychology: Human Perception and Performance, 11*, 317–328.

Chandler, M. J., Fritz, A. S., & Hala, S. M. (1989). Small-scale deceit: Deception as a marker of two-three-, and four-year-olds' 'theory of mind'. *Child Development, 60*, 1263–1277.

Chomsky, N. (1980). *Rules and representations.* Oxford: Basil Blackwell.

Chrisley, R. L. (1993). Connectionism, cognitive maps and the development of causality. *Artificial Intelligence Review, 7,* 329–354.

Clark, A. (1989). *Microcognition.* Cambridge, MA: MIT Press (Bradford Books).

Clark, A. (1993). Minimal rationalism. *Mind, 102,* 587–610.

Clark A. (1995). Language of thought (2). In S. Guttenplan (Ed.), *A companion to the philosophy of mind.* Oxford: Blackwell.

Clements, W. A., & Perner, J. (1994). Implicit understanding of belief. *Cognitive Development, 9,* 377–395.

Cohen, J. D., & Servan-Schreiber, D. (1992). Context, cortex and dopamine: A connectionist approach to behaviour and biology in schizophrenia. *Psychological Review, 99,* 45–77.

Corcoran, R., & Upton, D. (1993). A role for the hippocampus in card-sorting? *Cortex, 29,* 293–304.

Courchesne, E., Akshoomoff, N. A., & Townsend, J. (1992). Recent advances in autism. In H. Naruse & E. M. Ornitz (Eds.), *Neurobiology of autism.* New York: Elsevier Science Publishers.

Crane, T. (1990). The language of thought: No syntax without semantics. *Mind and Language, 5,* 187–212.

Crane, T. (1992). The non-conceptual content of experience. In T. Crane (Ed.), *The contents of experience.* Cambridge: Cambridge University Press.

Craik, K. (1943). *The nature of explanation.* Cambridge: Cambridge University Press.

Cramer, P. (1983). Homonym understanding and conservation. *Journal of Experimental Child Psychology, 36,* 179–195.

Crimmins, M. (1992). *Talk about beliefs.* Cambridge, MA: MIT Press.

Cummins, R. (1989). *Meaning and mental representation.* Cambridge, MA: MIT Press (Bradford Books).

Curtis, E., Lewin, D., & Russell, J. (1991). *False beliefs tasks without an object.* Unpublished MS. Cambridge University.

Damasio, A. R., & Maurer, R. G. (1978). A neurological model for childhood autism. *Archives of Neurology, 35,* 777–786.

Davidson, D. (1975). Thought and talk. In S. Guttenplan (Ed.), *Mind and language.* Oxford: Clarendon Press.

Dehaene, S., & Changeaux, J-P. (1991). The Wisconsin Card Sorting Test: Theoretical analysis and modelling in a neural network. *Cerebral Cortex, 1,* 62–79

DeLoache, J. S., Kolstad, V., & Anderson, K. N. (1991). Physical similarity and young children's understanding of scale models. *Child Development, 62,* 111–126.

DeLong, G. R. (1978). A neuropsychologic interpretation of infantile autism. In M. Rutter & E. Shopler (Eds.), *Autism: A reappraisal of concepts and treatment.* New York: Plenum Press.

Dennett, D. (1969). *Content and consciousness.* London: Routledge & Kegan Paul.

Dennett, D. (1978a). *Why you can't make a computer that feels pain.* Reprinted in Dennett, D. (1981). *Brainstorms.* Brighton, UK: Harvester Press.

Dennett, D. (1978b). Beliefs about beliefs (commentary on Premack and Woodruff). *Behavioural and Brain Sciences, 4,* 568–569.

Diagneault, S., Braün, C. M. J., & Whitaker, H. A. (1992). An empirical test of two opposing models of prefrontal function. *Brain and Cognition, 19,* 48–71.

Diamond, A. (1991). Neuropsychological insights into the meaning of object concept development. In S. Carey & R. Gelman (Eds.), *The epigenesis of mind.* Hillsdale, NJ: Lawrence Erlbaum Associates Inc.

Diamond, A., Cruttenden, L., & Neiderman, D. (1994). A-not-B with multiple wells: 1. Why are multiple wells sometimes easier than two wells? 2. Memory or memory+inhibition? *Developmental Psychology, 30,* 192–205.

Diamond, A., & Goldman-Rakic, P. S. (1986). Comparative development in human infants and rhesus monkeys of cognitive functions that depend upon the prefrontal cortex. *Neuroscience Abstracts (Part I), 11,* 724–747.

Dickinson, A. (1988). Intentionality in animal conditioning. In L. Weiskrantz (Ed.), *Thought without language.* Oxford: Clarendon Press.

Dickinson, A., & Balleine, B. (1993). Actions and responses. In N. Eilan, R. McCarthy, & B. Brewer (Eds.), *Spatial representation: Problems in philosophy and psychology.* Oxford: Basil Blackwell.

Doise, W., Mugny, G., & Perret-Clermont (1975). Social interaction and the development of cognitive operations. *European Journal of Social Psychology, 5,* 367–383.

Donaldson, M. (1978). *Children's minds.* Glasgow: Fontana.

Drew, E. A. (1975). An experimenal investigation of Luria's theory of the effects of frontal lobe lesions in man. *Neuropsychologia, 13,* 421–429.

Driver, J. S., & Baylis, G. C. (1989). Movement and visual attention: The spotlight metaphor breaks down. *Journal of Experimental Psychology: Human Perception and Performance, 15,* 448–456.

Dummett, M. (1975). What is a theory of meaning? In S. Guttenplan (Ed.), *Mind and language.* Oxford: Oxford University Press.

Duncan, J. (in press). Attention, intelligence and the frontal lobes. In M. S. Gazzaniga (Ed.), *The cognitive neurosciences.* Cambridge, MA: MIT Press.

Dunn, J. (1991). Understanding others: Evidence from naturalistic studies of children. In A. Whiten (Ed.), *Natural theories of mind.* Oxford: Basil Blackwell.

Elman, J. L. (1990). Finding structure in time. *Cognitive Science, 14,* 179–211.

Elman, J. L. (1993). Learning and development in neural networks: The importance of starting small. *Cognition, 48,* 71–99.

Evans, G. (1982). *The varieties of reference* (J. McDowell, Ed.). Oxford: Oxford University Press.

Evans, G. (1985). Things without the mind. In his *Collected papers.* Oxford: Clarendon Press.

Feinberg, I. (1978). Efference copy and corollary discharge: Implications for thinking and its disorders. *Schizophrenia Bulletin, 4,* 636–640.

Fikes, R. E., & Nilsson, N. J. (1971). STRIPS: A new approach to the application of theorem-proving to problem solving. *Artificial Intelligence, 27,* 189–208.

Flavell, J. H. (1988). The development of children's knowledge about the mind: From cognitive connections to mental representations. In J. W. Astington, P. L. Harris, & D. R. Olson (Eds.), *Developing theories of mind.* Cambridge: Cambridge University Press.

Flavell, J. H., Flavell, E. R., & Green, F. L. (1983). Development of the appearance–reality distinction. *Cognitive Psychology, 15,* 95–120.

Fletcher, P., Happé, F., Baker, S., Dolan, R., Frackowiak, R., & Frith, C. (submitted). *Other minds in the brain: A functional imaging study of "theory of mind" in story comprehension.*

Fodor, J. A. (1976). *The language of thought.* Brighton, UK: Harvester Press.

Fodor, J A. (1980). Methodological solipsism. *The Behavioural and Brain Sciences, 3,* 63–109.

Fodor, J. A. (1983). *The modularity of mind.* Cambridge, MA: MIT Press (Bradford Books).

Fodor, J. A. (1987). *Psychosemantics.* Cambridge, MA: MIT Press (Bradford Books).

Fodor, J. A. (1992). A theory of the child's theory of mind. *Cognition, 44,* 283–296.

Fodor, J. A., & Lepore, E. (1991). Why meaning (probably) isn't conceptual role. *Mind and Language, 6,* 328–343.

Fodor, J. A., & Lepore, E. (1992). *Holism: A shopper's guide.* Oxford: Basil Blackwell.

Fodor, J. A., & Pylyshyn, Z. (1988). Connectionism and cognitive architecture: A critical analysis. *Cognition, 28,* 3–71.

Frith, C. D. (1992). *The cognitive psychology of schizophrenia.* Hove, UK: Lawrence Erlbaum Associates Ltd.

Frith, C. D., & Done, D. J. (1989). Experiences of alien control in schizophrenia reflect a disorder in the central monitoring of action. *Psychological Medicine, 19,* 358–363.

Frith, C. D., & Frith, U. (1991). Elective affinities between schizophrenia and childhood autism: In P. Bebbington (Ed.), *Social psychiatry: Theory, methodology, and practice.* New Brunswick, NJ: Transactions Press.

Frith, U. (1989). *Autism: Explaining the enigma.* Oxford: Basil Blackwell.

Frith, U., & Happé, F. G. E. (1994). Autism: Beyond "theory of mind". *Cognition, 50,* 115–132.

Frye, D., Zelazo, P. D., & Palfai, T. (in press). The cognitive basis of theory of mind. *Cognitive Development.*

Gallistel, C. R. (1980). *The organisation of action: A new synthesis.* Hillsdale, NJ: Lawrence Erlbaum Associates Inc.

Galloti, K. M., Baron, J., & Sabini, J. P. (1986). Individual differences in syllogistic reasoning: Deduction rules or mental models? *Journal of Experimental Psychology, General, 115,* 16–25.

Gibson, J. J. (1979). *The ecological approach to visual perception.* Boston: Houghton Mifflin.

Gibson, E. J. (1987). Introductory essay: What does infant perception tell us about theories of perception? *Journal of Experimental Psychology, 13,* 515–531.

Goldman, A. (1989). Interpretation psychologised. *Mind and Language, 4,* 161–185.

Goldman-Rakic, P. S. (1987). Circuitry of the primate prefrontal cortex and regulation of behaviour. In F. Plum (Ed.), *Handbook of physiology: The nervous system.* Oxford: Oxford University Press.

Gopnik, A. (1993). How we know our minds: The illusion of first-person knowledge of intentionality. *Behavioural and Brain Sciences, 16,* 1–14.

Gopnik, A., & Astington, J. W. (1988). Children's understanding of representational change and its relation to the understanding of false belief and the appearance–reality distinction. *Child Development, 59,* 26–37.

Gopnik, A., & Meltzoff, A. N. (1987). The development of categorisation in the second year of life and its relation to other cognitive and linguistic developments. *Child Development, 58*, 1523–1531.

Gopnik, A., & Wellman, H. M. (1992). Why the child's theory of mind really is a theory. *Mind and Language, 7*, 145–171.

Gordon, R. M. (1986). Folk psychology as simulation. *Mind and Language, 1*, 158–171.

Gould, J. R. (1984). Natural history of honey bee learning. In P. Marler & H. S. Terrace (Eds.), *The biology of learning*. Berlin: Springer-Verlag.

Gray, J., Feldon, J., Rawlins, J., Hemsley, D., & Smith, A. (1990). The neuropsychology of schizophrenia. *Behavioural and Brain Science, 14*, 1–84.

Grice, H. P. (1957). Meaning. *Philosophical Review, 66*, 377–388.

Hala, S. M., Chander, M. J., & Fritz, A. S. (1991). Fledgling theories of mind: Deception as a marker of three-year-olds' understanding of false belief. *Child Development, 62*, 83–97.

Hala, S. M., Russell, J., & Maberley, L. (Submitted). *Social versus executive factors in performance on the windows task.*

Halford, G. S. (1982). *The development of thought* Hillsdale, NJ: Lawrence Erlbaum Associates Inc.

Halford, G. S. (1993). *Children's understanding: The development of mental models*. Hillsdale, NJ: Lawrence Erlbaum Associates Inc.

Halford, G. S., & Wilson, W. H. (1980). A category theory approach to cognitive development. *Cognitive Psychology, 12*, 356–411.

Halsband, U., & Passingham, R. E. (1985). Premotor cortex and the conditions for movement in monkeys (*Macacca mulatta*). *Behavioural Brain Research, 18*, 269–276.

Hamlyn, D. W. (1978). *Experience and the growth of understanding*. London: Routledge & Kegan Paul.

Hamlyn, D. W. (1980). *Schopenhauer*. London: Routledge & Kegan Paul.

Hamlyn, D. W. (1990). *In and out of the black box*. Oxford: Basil Blackwell.

Hampshire, S. (1959). *Thought and action*. London: Chatto & Windus.

Happé, F. G. E.(1993). Communicative competence and theory of mind: A test of relevance theory. *Cognition, 48*, 101–119.

Happé, F. G. E. (1994). Wechsler IQ profile and theory of mind in autism: A research note. *Journal of Child Psychology and Psychiatry, 35*, 1461–1471.

Harman, G. E. (1982). Conceptual role semantics. *Notre Dame Journal of Formal Logic, 23*, 242–256.

Harris, P. L. (1973). Perseverative errors in search by young infants. *Child Development, 44*, 28–33.

Harris, P. L. (1974). Perseverative search at a visibly empty place by young infants. *Journal of Experimental Child Psychology, 18*, 535–542.

Harris, P. L. (1991). The work of the imagination. In A. Whiten (Ed.), *Natural theories of mind*. Oxford: Basil Blackwell.

Heal, J. (1993–94). Semantic holism: Still a good buy. *Proceedings of the Aristotelian Society, XCIV*, 323–339.

Heal, J. (1994). Objectivity, simulation and the unity of consciousness. *Proceedings of the British Academy, 83*, 129–144.

Heal, J. (in press). How to think about thinking. In M. Davies & T. Stone (Eds.), *Mental simulation: Philosophical and psychological essays*. Oxford: Blackwell.

Hemsley, D. R. (1993). A simple (or simplistic?) cognitive model for schizophrenia. *Behavioural Research and Therapy, 31*, 633–645.

Hinton, G. E. (1986). Learning distributed representations of concepts. *Proceedings of the Eighth Annual Conference of the Cognitive Science Society.* Hillsdale, NJ: Lawrence Erlbaum Associates Inc.

Hinton, G. E. (1992). How neural networks learn from experience. *Scientific American, 267,* 104–110.

Hobson, R. P. (1989). Beyond cognition: A theory of autism. In G. Dawson (Ed.), *Autism, nature diagnosis and treatment.* New York: Guilford Press.

Hobson, R. P. (1993). *Autism and the development of mind.* Hove, UK: Lawrence Erlbaum Associates Ltd.

Hodges, J. R., & McCarthy, R. A. (1993). Autobiographical amnesia resulting from bilateral paramedian thalamic infarction. *Brain, 116,* 921–940.

Holland, P. C. (1979). Differential effects of omission contingencies on various components of Pavlovian appetitive responding in rats. *Journal of Experimental Psychology: Animal Behaviour Processes, 5,* 178–183.

Hood, B., & Willats, P. (1986). Reaching in the dark to an object's remembered position. *British Journal of Developmental Psychology, 4,* 57–65.

Hoon, A. H., & Reiss, A. L. (1992). The mesial-temporal lobe and autism: Case report and review. *Developmental Medicine and Child Neurology, 32,* 252–259.

Hopkins, J. (1987). Synthesis in the imagination. In J. Russell (Ed.), *Philosophical perspectives on developmental psychology.* Oxford: Basil Blackwell.

Hornsby, J. (1985). Physicalism, events, and part–whole relations. In E. Lepore & B. McLaughlin (Eds.), *Actions and events.* Oxford: Clarendon Press.

Horobin, K., & Acredolo, L. (1986). The role of attentiveness, mobility history, and separation of hiding sites on stage IV search behaviour. *Journal of Experimental Child Psychology, 41,* 114–127.

Houghton, G. (1990). The problem of serial order: A neural network model of sequence learning and recall. In R. Dale, C. Mellish, & M. Zock (Eds.), *Current research in natural language generation.* London: Academic Press.

Houghton, G. (1994). Inhibitory control of neurodynamics: Opponent mechanisms in sequencing and selective attention. In M. Oaksford & G. D. A. Brown (Eds.), *Neurodynamics and psychology.* London: Academic Press.

Houghton, G., & Tipper, S. P. (in press). A model of inhibitory mechanisms in selective attention. In D. Dagenbach & T. Carr (Eds.), *Inhibitory mechanisms in attention, memory and language.* London: Academic Press.

Hughes, C., & Russell, J. (1993). Autistic children's difficulty with mental disengagement from an object: Its implications for theories of autism. *Developmental Psychology, 29,* 498–510.

Hughes, C., Russell, J., & Robbins, T. W. (1994). Evidence for executive dysfunction in autism. *Neuropsychologia, 32,* 477–492.

Hume, D. (1739/1962). *A treatise on human nature.* (A. Selby-Bigge, Ed.), Oxford: Oxford University Press.

Jackson, S., & Houghton, G. (1992). *Basal ganglia function in the control of visuospatial attention: A neuronal network model.* Technical Report, 92–6. Institute of Cognitive and Decision Sciences, University of Oregon.

Janaway, C. (1983). The subject and the objective order. *Proceedings of the Aristotelian Society, 84,* 147–165.

Janaway, C. (1989). *Self and world in Schopenhauer's philosophy.* Oxford: Clarendon Press.

Jarrold, C., Smith, P., Boucher, J., & Harris, P. L. (1994). Comprehension of pretence in children with autism. *Journal of Autism and Developmental Disorders, 24,* 433–455.

Johnson-Laird, P. N. (1983). *Mental models.* Cambridge: Cambridge University Press.

Johnson-Laird, P. N. (1988). The development of reasoning ability. In G. Butterworth & P. Bryant (Eds.), *Causes of development.* Hemel Hempstead, UK: Harvester Wheatsheaf.

Johnson-Laird, P. N., & Bara, B. (1984). Syllogistic inference. *Cognition, 16,* 1–61.

Jordan, M. I. (1990). Motor learning and the degrees of freedom problem. In M. Jeannerod (Ed.), *Attention and performance XIII: Motor representation and control.* Hillsdale, NJ: Lawrence Elbaum Associates Inc.

Jordan, M. I., & Rumelhart, D. E. (1992). Forward models: Supervised learning with a distal teacher. *Cognitive Science, 16,* 307–354.

Karmiloff-Smith, A. (1992). *Beyond modularity.* Cambridge, MA: MIT Press.

Karmiloff-Smith, A. (1993). NeoPiagetians: A theoretical misnomer? *Newsletter of the Society for Research in Child Development,* Spring.

Kavanaugh, R. D., & Harris, P. L. (1994). Imagining the outcome of pretend transformations: Assessing the competence of normal and autistic children. *Developmental Psychology, 30,* 847–854.

Keeton, W. T. (1981). Navigation. In D. J. McFarland (Ed.), *Oxford companion to animal behaviour.* Oxford: Oxford University Press.

Keil, F. (1987). Conceptual development and category structure. In U. Neisser (Ed.), *Concepts and conceptual development.* Cambridge: Cambridge University Press.

Kellman, P. J., & Spelke, E. S. (1983). Perception of partly occluded objects in infancy. *Cognitive Psychology, 15,* 483–524.

Kermoian, R., & Campos, J. J. (1988). Locomotor experience: a facilitator of spatial cognitive development. *Child Development, 59,* 908–917.

Khalidi, M. A. (1993). Review of Fodor and Lepore: "Holism: A Shopper's Guide". *Mind, 102,* 650–654.

Kitcher, P. (1990). *Kant's transcendental psychology.* Oxford: Oxford University Press.

Lasnik, H. (1988). On certain substitutes for negative data. In W. Demopoulos & R. May (Eds.), *Learnability and linguistic theory.* Dordrecht, Netherlands: Reidel.

Lee, A., Hobson, R. P., & Chiat, S. (1993). I, you, me and autism: An experimental study. *Journal of Autism and Developmental Disorders, 24,* 155–176.

Leslie, A. M. (1987). Pretence and representation: The origins of 'theory of mind'. *Psychological Review, 94,* 412–426.

Leslie, A. M. (1988). Some implications of pretense for mechanisms underlying the child's theory of mind. In J. Astington, P. L. Harris, & D. R. Olson (Eds.), *Developing theories of mind.* Cambridge: Cambridge University Press.

Leslie, A. M. (in press). ToMM, ToBy, and Agency: Core architecture and domain specificity. In A. Hirshfeld & R. Gelman (Eds.), *Domain specificity in cognition and culture.* Cambridge: Cambridge University Press.

Leslie, A. M., & Happé, F. (1989). Autism and ostensive communication: The relevance of metarepresentation. *Development and Psychopathology, 1,* 205–212.

Leslie, A. M., & Keeble, S. (1987). Do six-month-olds perceive causality? *Cognition, 25,* 265–288.

Leslie, A. M., & Thaiss, L. (1992). Domain specificity in conceptual development: Neuropsychological evidence from autism. *Cognition, 43,* 225–251.

Lewis, C., & Osborne, A. (1990). Three-year-old's problems with false belief: Conceptual deficit or linguistic artefact. *Child Development, 61,* 1514–1519.

Light, P.H., Buckingham, N., & Robins, A. H. (1979). The conservation task in an interactional setting. *British Journal of Educational Psychology, 49,* 304–310.

Light, P. H., & Nix, C. (1983). "Own view" versus "good view" in a perspective-taking task. *Child Development, 65,* 480–483.

Lockman, J. J. (1984). The development of detour ability during infancy. *Child Development, 55,* 482–491.

Luria, A. R. (1966). *Higher cortical functions in man.* London: Tavistock.

Luria, A. R. (1973). *The working brain: An introduction to neuropsychology.* New York: Basic Books.

Malenka, R. C., Angel, R. W., Hampton, B., & Berger, P. A. (1982). Impaired central error-correcting behaviour in schizophrenia. *Archives of General Psychiatry, 39,* 101–107.

Mandler, J. (1988). How to build a better baby: On the development of an accessible representational system. *Cognitive Development, 3,* 113–136.

Mareschal, D. (1991). *Cascade-correlation and the Genetron: Possible implementations of equilibration.* Technical Report 91–10–17. McGill Cognitive Science Centre, Montreal.

Marr, D. (1982). *Vision.* San Francisco: Freeman.

McClelland, J. L. (1989). Parallel distributed processing: Implications for cognition and development. In R. G. M. Morris (Ed.), *Parallel distributed processing.* Oxford: Clarendon Press.

McClelland, J. L. (1992). *The interaction of nature and nurture in development: A parallel distributed processing perspective.* Techical Report PDP.CNS.92.6. Department of Psychology. Carnegie Mellon University, Pittsburgh, PA, USA.

McCloskey, M. (1983). Naive theories of motion. In D. Gentner & A. L. Stevens (Eds.), *Mental models.* Hillsdale, NJ: Lawrence Erlbaum Associates Inc.

McCune-Nicolich, L. (1981). Towards symbolic function: Structure of early use of pretend games and potential parallels with language. *Child Development, 52,* 785–797.

McGarrigle, J., & Donaldson, M. (1974). Conservation accidents. *Cognition, 3,* 341–350.

McGinn, C. (1989). *Mental content.* Oxford: Basil Blackwell.

Meins, S. E., & Russell, J. (in press). Security and search: The role of executive capacity in early development. *British Journal of Developmental Psychology.*

Meltzoff, A. (1990). Foundations for a developing conception of the self. In D. Cicchetti & M. Beeghly (Eds.), *The self in transition.* Chicago and London: Chicago University Press.

Mendlesohn, G. A., & Griswold, B. B. (1964). Differential use of incidental stimuli in problem solving as function of creativity. *Journal of Abnormal and Social Psychology, 68,* 431–436

Miller, S. A., & Brownell, C. A. (1975). Peers, persuasion and Piaget: Dyadic interaction between conservers and nonconservers. *Child Development, 46,* 992–997.

Mitchell, P. M., & Lacohée, H. (1991). Children's early understanding of false belief. *Cognition, 39*, 107–127.

Moore, C., Bryant, D., & Furrow, D. (1989). Mental terms and the development of certainty. *Child Development, 60*, 167–171.

Moore, C., & Davidge, J. (1989). The development of mental terms: Pragmatics or semantics. *Journal of Child Language, 61*, 722–730.

Moore, C., & Frye, D. (1986). The effect of experimenter's intention on the child's understanding of conservation. *Cognition, 22*, 283–299.

Moore, C., Jarrold, C., Russell, J., Lumb, A., Sapp, F., & MacCallum, F. (in press). Conflicting desire and the child's theory of mind. *Cognitive Development.*

Moore, C., Pure, K., & Furrow, D. (1990). Children's understanding of the modal expression of certainty and uncertainty and its relation to the development of a representational theory of mind. *Child Development, 61*, 722–730.

Mollon, J. D. (1982). Colour vision and colour blindness. In H. B. Barlow & J. D. Mollon (Eds.), *The senses.* Cambridge: Cambridge University Press.

Morton, A. (1980). *Frames of mind.* Oxford: Clarendon Press.

Munakata, Y., McClelland, J. L., Johnson, M. H., & Siegler, R. S. (1994). *Now you see it, now you don't: A gradualist framework for understanding infants' successes and failures in object permanence tasks.* Technical Report PDP.CNS.94.2. May, 1994. Carnegie Mellon University, Pittsburgh PA, USA.

Nadel, L. (1990). Varieties of spatial cognition. In A. Diamond (Ed.), *The development and neural basis of higher cognitive functions.* New York: New York Academy of Sciences.

Nagel, T. (1974). "What is it like to be a bat?" *Philosophical Review, 83*, 435–451.

Nagel, T. (1979). Subjective and objective. In *Mortal questions.* Cambridge: Cambridge University Press.

Neisser, U. (1991). Two perceptually-given aspects of the self and their development. *Developmental Review, 11*, 197–209.

Nelson, K. (1975). The nominal shift in semantic-syntactic development. *Cognitive Psychology, 7*, 461–479.

Newport, E. (1991). Contrasting conceptions of the critical period for language. In S. Carey & R. Gelman (Eds.), *The epigenesis of mind.* Hillsdale, NJ: Lawrence Erlbaum Associates Inc.

Norman, D. A., & Shallice, T. (1986). Attention to action: Willed and automatic control of behaviour. In R. J. Davidson, G. E. Schwartz, & D. Shapiro (Eds.), *Consciousness and self-regulation: Advances in research.* (Vol.4). New York: Plenum Press.

Oaksford, M., & Malloch, M. I. (1994). Dynamic schemata: Evidence from cognitive neuropsychology. In M. Oaksford & G. D. A. Brown (Eds.), *Neurodynamics and psychology.* London: Academic Press.

O'Bryan, K. G., & Boersma, F. J. (1971). Eye movements, perceptual activity, and conservation. *Journal of Experimental Child Psychology, 12*, 157–169.

O'Keefe, J. (1993). Kant and the sea horse. In N.Eilan, R. McCarthy, & B. Brewer (Eds.), *Spatial representation: Problems in philosophy and psychology.* Oxford: Basil Blackwell.

O'Keefe, J., & Nadel, L. (1978). *The hippocampus as a cognitive map.* Oxford: Clarendon Press.

Olson, D. R. (1993). The development of representations: The origins of mental life. *Canadian Psychology, 34*, 1–14.

Ornitz, E. M. (1985). The functional neuroanatomy of infantile autism. *International Journal of Neuroscience, 19,* 85–124.

O'Shaughnessy, B. (1980). *The will.* (Volume II). Cambridge: Cambridge University Press.

Ozonoff, S., Pennington, B. F., & Rogers, S. J. (1991). Executive function deficits in high-functioning autistic individuals: Relationships to theory of mind. *Journal of Child Psychology and Psychiatry, 32,* 1081–1105.

Ozonoff, S., Rogers, S. J., & Pennington, B. F. (1991). Asperger's syndome: Evidence of an empirical distinction from high-functioning autism. *Journal of Experimental Child Psychology and Psychiatry, 32,* 1107–1122.

Papert, S. (1963). Intelligence chez l'enfant at chez le robot. In L. Apostel, J. Grize, S. Papert, & J. Piaget. La filiation des structures. *Etudes D'Epistemologie Genetique, 22,* 92–130.

Parkin, L. J., & Perner, J. (in press). Wrong directions in children's theory of mind: What it means to understand belief as a representation. *Cognition.*

Parmelee, A. H., Wenner, W. H., & Schulz, H. R. (1964). Infant sleep patterns from birth to 16 weeks of age. *Journal of Pediatrics, 65,* 576–582.

Passingham, R. (1993). *The frontal lobes and voluntary action.* Oxford: Oxford University Press.

Patterson, T. (1987). Studies towards the sub-cortical pathogenesis of schizophrenia. *Schizophrenia Bulletin, 13,* 555–576.

Peacocke, C. (1983). *Sense and content.* Oxford: Clarendon Press.

Peacocke, C. (1992). *A study of concepts.* Cambridge, MA: MIT Press.

Peacocke, C. (1993). Intuitive mechanics, psychological reality and the idea of a material object. In N. Eilan, R. McCarthy, & B. Brewer (Eds.), *Spatial representation: Problems in philosophy and psychology.* Oxford: Basil Blackwell.

Peacocke, C. (1994). Non-conceptual content: Kinds, rationales and relations. *Mind and Language, 9,* 419–430.

Pennington, B. F. (1994). The working memory function of the prefrontal cortices: Implications for development and individual differences in cognition. In M. Haith (Ed.), *Future oriented processes in development.* Chicago: Universtiy of Chicago Press.

Perner, J. (1991). *Understanding the representational mind.* Cambridge, MA: MIT Press (Bradford Books).

Perner, J., Baker, S., & Hutton, D. (1994). Prelief: The conceptual origin of belief and pretence. In C. Lewis & P. Mitchell (Eds.), *Origins of an understanding of mind.* Hove, UK: Lawrence Erlbaum Associates Ltd.

Perner, J., Leekam, S., & Wimmer, H. (1987). Three-year-olds' difficulty with false belief: The case for a conceptual deficit. *British Journal of Developmental Psychology, 5,* 125–137.

Peterson, M. A., Kihlstrom, J. F., Rose, P. M., & Glisky, M. L. (1992). Mental images can be ambiguous: Reconstruals and reference-frame reversals. *Memory and Cognition, 20,* 107–128.

Piaget, J. (1950). *The psychology of intelligence.* London: Routledge & Kegan Paul.

Piaget, J. (1955). *The child's construction of reality.* London: Routledge & Kegan Paul.

Piaget, J. (1972). Language and thought from a genetic point of view. In P. Adams (Ed.), *Language in thinking.* Harmondsworth, UK: Penguin Books.

Piaget, J. (1977). *The development of thought: Equilibration of cognitive structures.* Oxford: Blackwell.

Pillow, B. H. (1989). Early understanding of perception as a source of knowledge. *Journal of Experimental Child Psychology, 47*, 116–129.

Pinker, S. (1984). *Language learnability and language development.* Cambridge, MA: Harvard University Press.

Pinker, S. (1987). The bootstrapping problem in language acquisition. In B. MacWhinney (Ed.), *Mechanisms of language acquisition.* Hillsdale, NJ: Lawrence Erlbaum Associates Inc.

Povinelli, D. J., & deBlois, S. (1992). Young children's (*Homo sapiens*) understanding of knowledge formation in themselves and others. *Journal of Comparative Psychology, 106*, 228–238.

Povinelli, D. J., Nelson, K. E., & Boysen, S. T. (1990). Inferences about guessing and knowing by chimpanzees (*Pan troglodytes*). *Journal of Comparative Psychology, 104*, 203–210.

Pratt, C., & Bryant, P. E. (1990). Young children understand that looking leads to knowing (so long as they are looking into a single barrel). *Child Development, 61*, 973–982.

Premack, D. (1990). The infant's theory of self-propelled objects. *Cognition, 36*, 1–16.

Prior, M., & Hoffman, W. (1990). Brief report: Neurological testing of autistic children through an exploration of frontal lobe tests. *Journal of Autism and Developmental Disorders, 20*, 581–590.

Pylyshyn, Z. (1984). *Computation and cognition: Toward a foundation for cognitive science.* Cambridge, MA: MIT Press.

Quine, W. V. (1953). Two dogmas of empiricism. In his collection *From a logical point of view.* Cambridge, MA: Harper.

Reason, J. T. (1979). On actions not as planned. In G. Underwood & R. Stevens (Eds.), *Aspects of consciousness. Volume 1.* London: Academic Press.

Reddy, V. (1991). Playing with other's expectations: Teasing and mucking about in the first year. In A. Whiten (Ed.), *Natural theories of mind.* Oxford: Blackwell.

Rescorla, R. A., & Wagner, A. R. (1972). A theory of Pavlovian conditioning: Variations in the effectiveness of reinforcement and non-reinforcement. In A. H. Black & W. F. Prokasy (Eds.), *Classical conditioning II: Current research and theory.* New York: Appleton-Century Crofts.

Rips, L. J. (1986). Mental muddles. In M. Brand & R. M. Harnish (Eds.), *Problems in the representation of knowledge and belief.* Tucson: University of Arizona Press.

Rourke, B. P., Baker, D., Fisk, J. L., & Stang, J. D. (1983). *Child neuropsychology: An introduction to research, theory and clinical practice.* New York: Guilford Press.

Rumelhart, D. E., & Norman, D. (1982). Simulating a skilled typist: A study of skilled motor performance. *Cognitive Science, 6*, 1–36.

Rumsey, J. M., & Hamburger, S. D. (1988). Neuropsychological findings in high-functioning men with infantile autism, residual state. *Journal of Clinical and Experimental Neuropsychology, 10*, 201–221.

Russell, J. (1975). The interpretation of conservation instructions by five-year-old children. *Journal of Child Psychology and Psychiatry, 16*, 233–244.

Russell, J. (1976). The utilization of irrelevant information by high and low creatives. *Psychologial Reports, 39*, 105–107.

Russell, J. (1978). *The acquisition of knowledge.* London: Macmillan.

Russell, J. (1979a). The status of genetic epistemology. *Journal for the Theory of Social Behaviour, 9,* 53–70.

Russell, J. (1979b). Verbal and non-verbal judgements of length invariance. *British Journal of Psychology, 70,* 313–317.

Russell, J. (1981a). Why 'socio-cognitive conflict' may be impossible: The status of egocentric errors in the dyadic performance of a spatial task. *Educational Psychology, 1,* 159–169.

Russell, J. (1981b). Dyadic interaction in a logical reasoning problem. *Child Development, 52,* 1322–1325.

Russell, J. (1982a). Action from knowledge and conditioned behaviour. Part three: The human case. *Behaviorism, 9,* 107–125.

Russell, J. (1982b). Propositional attitudes. In M. Beveridge (Ed.), *Children thinking through language.* London: Edward Arnold.

Russell, J. (1982c). The child's appreciation of the necessary truth and the necessary falseness of propositions. *British Journal of Psychology, 73,* 253–266.

Russell, J. (1983). Children's ability to distinguish between types of proposition. *British Journal of Developmental Psychology, 1,* 259–268.

Russell, J. (1984a). Should I believe you or what you say? Children's belief of children's statements. *Developmental Psychology, 20,* 261–270.

Russell, J. (1984b). The subject–object division in language acquisition and ego development. *New Ideas in Psychology, 2,* 64–82.

Russell, J. (1984c). *Explaining mental life: Some philosophical issues in psychology.* London: Macmillan.

Russell, J. (1987a). Rule-following, mental models and the developmental view. In M. Chapman & R. A. Dixon (Eds.), *Meaning and the growth of understanding: Wittgenstein's significance for developmental psychology.* New York: Springer-Verlag.

Russell, J. (1987b). "Can we say ... ?" Children's understanding of intensionality. *Cognition, 25,* 289–308.

Russell, J. (1988). Cognisance and cognitive science. Part one: The Generality Constraint. *Philosophical Psychology, 1,* 235–258.

Russell, J. (1989). Cognisance and cognitive science. Part two: Towards an empirical psychology of cognisance. *Philosophical Psychology, 2,* 165–201.

Russell, J. (1992). The theory theory: "So good they named it twice?". *Cognitive Development, 7.* 485–519.

Russell, J. (1996). Development and evolution of the symbolic function: The role of working memory. In P. Mellars & K. Gibson (Eds.), *Modelling the early human mind.* Cambridge: McDonald Institute for Archeological Research.

Russell, J., & Haworth, H. M. (1988). Appearance versus reality in dyadic interaction: Evidence for a lingering phenomenism. *International Journal of Behavioural Development, 11,* 155–170.

Russell, J., Jarrold, C., & Henry, L. (in press). Working memory in children with autism and in mentally handicapped children. *Journal of Child Psychology and Psychiatry.*

Russell, J., Jarrold, C., Halligan, S., & Davis, S. (submitted). *Executive and representational factors in children's strategic behaviour.*

Russell, J., Jarrold, C., & Potel, D. (1994). What makes strategic deception difficult—the deception or the strategy? *British Journal of Developmental Psychology, 12,* 301–314.

Russell, J., Lee, S., & Drake, A. (1993). *Detour reaching in toddlers.* Unpublished MS. Department of Experimental Psychology, Cambridge.

Russell, J., Mauthner, N., Sharpe, S., & Tidswell, T. (1991). The 'windows task' as a measure of strategic deception in preschoolers and autistic subjects. *British Journal of Developmental Psychology, 9,* 331–349.

Russell, J., Mills, I., & Reiff-Musgrove, P. (1990). The role of symmetrical and asymmetrical social conflict in cognitive change. *Journal of Experimental Child Psychology, 49,* 58–78.

Sandson, J., & Albert, M. L. (1984). Varieties of perseveration. *Neuropsychologia, 22,* 715–732.

Searle, J. (1984). *Minds, brains and science.* Cambridge, MA: Harvard University Press.

Schopenhauer, A. (1844/1966). *Die Welt als Wille und Vorstellung I.* [Page references to the translation as *The world and will and representation. Vol. 1.,* trs. E. Payne.] New York: Dover Press.

Shah, A., & Frith, U. (1993). Why do autistic individuals show superior performance on the Block Design Task? *Journal of Child Psychology and Psychiatry, 24,* 1351–1364.

Shallice, T. (1988). *From neuropsychology to mental structure.* Cambridge: Cambridge University Press.

Shallice, T., & Burgess, P. (1991). Deficits in strategy application following frontal lobe damage in man. *Brain, 114,* 727–741.

Shallice, T., Burgess, P., & Frith, C. D. (1991). Can the neuropsychological case-study approach be applied to schizophrenia? *Psychological Medicine, 21,* 661–673.

Siegal, M., & Beattie, K. (1991). Where to look first for children's knowledge of false beliefs. *Cognition, 38,* 1–12.

Siegler, R. (1989). Mechanisms of cognitive development. *Annual Review of Psychology, 40,* 353–379.

Silverman, I. W., & Geiringer, E. (1973). Dyadic interaction and conservation induction. A test of Piaget's equilibration model. *Child Development, 44,* 815–820.

Slater, A., & Morison, V. (1985). Shape constancy and slant perception at birth. *Perception, 14,* 337–344.

Smith, M. L., Kates, M. H., & Vriezen, E. R. (1993). The development of frontal-lobe functions. In S. J. Segalowitz & I. Rapin (Ed.), *Handbook of Neuropsychology, Vol. 7.* New York: Elsevier Science Publishers.

Smolensky, P. (1988). On the proper treatment of connectionism. *Behavioural and Brain Sciences, 11,* 1–74.

Sodian, B. (1991). The development of deception in young children. *British Journal of Developmental Psychology, 9,* 173–188.

Sodian, B., Taylor, C., Harris, P. L., & Perner, J. (1991). Early deception and children's theory of mind: False trails and genuine markers. *Child Development, 62,* 468–483.

Solomon, R. L., & Corbit, J. D. (1974). An opponent process theory of motivation I: Temporal dynamics of affect. *Psychologial Review, 81,* 119–145.

Spelke, E. S. (1991). Physical knowledge in infancy: Reflections on Piaget's theory. In S. Carey & R. Gelman (Eds.), *The epigenesis of mind.* Hillsdale, NJ: Lawrence Erlbaum Associates Inc.

Spelke, E. S., & de Walle, G.(1993). Perceiving and reasoning about objects. In N. Eilan, R. McCarthy, & B. Brewer (Eds.), *Spatial representation*. Oxford: Basil Blackwell.

Steel, J. G. Gorman, R., & Flexman, J. E. (1984). Neuropsychiatric testing in an autistic idiot-savant: Evidence for nonverbal abstract capacity. *Journal of the Americal Academy of Child Psychiatry, 23*, 704–707.

Stein, J., & Glickstein, B. (1993). The role of the cerebellum in efference copying. *Physiological Review, 72*, 967–1017.

Stenning, K. (1991). Distinguishing conceptual and empirical issues about mental models. In Y. Rogers, A. Rutherford, and P. Bibby (Eds.), *Models in the mind*. San Diego, CA: Academic Press.

Stenning, K., & Oberlander, J. (1995). A cognitive theory of graphic and linguistic reasoning: Logic and implementation. *Cognitive Science, 19*, 97–140.

Strawson, P. F. (1959). *Individuals: An essay in descriptive metaphysics*. London: Methuen.

Strawson, P.F. (1966). *The bounds of sense*. London: Methuen.

Stich, S. P. (1983). *From folk psychology to cognitive science*. Cambridge, MA: MIT Press (Bradford Books).

Sullivan, K., & Winner, E. (1993). Three-year-olds' understanding of mental states: the influence of trickery. *Journal of Experimental Child Psychology, 56*, 135–148.

Suppes, P., & Zinnes, J. L. (1963). Basic measurement theory. In R. D. Luce, R. R. Bush, & E. Galanter (Eds.), *Handbook of mathematical psychology*. New York: John Wiley.

Sutton, R. S., & Barto, A. G. (1981). An adaptive network that constructs and uses an internal model of the world. *Cognition and Brain Theory, 4*, 217–246.

Szatmari, P., Barolucci, B., Bremner, R., Bond, S., & Rich, S. (1989). A follow-up study of high-functioning autistic children. *Journal of Autism and Developmental Disorders, 19*, 213–225.

Tager-Flusberg, H., & Sullivan, K. (1994). Predicting and explaining behaviour: A comparison of autistic, mentally retarded and normal children. *Journal of Child Psychology and Psychiatry, 35*, 1059–1076.

Taylor, C. (1964). *The explanation of behaviour*. London: Routledge & Kegan Paul.

Tipper, S.P. (1985). The negative priming effect: Inhibitory effects of ignored primes. *Quarterly Journal of Experimental Psychology, 35*A, 571–590.

Tomasello, M., & Farrar, M. J. (1986). Object permanence and relational words: A lexical training study. *Journal of Child Language, 13*, 495–505.

Tomasello, M., Kruger, A. C., & Ratner, H. H. (1993). Cultural learning. *Behavioural and Brain Sciences, 16*, 495–552.

Towse, J. N., & Hitch, G. J. (1995). Is there a relationship between task demand and storage space in tests of working memory? *Quarterly Journal of Experimental Psychology: Human Experimental Psychology 48*A, 108–124.

Trevarthen, C., & Hubley, P. (1978). Secondary intersubjectivity: Confidence, confiding and acts of meaning in the first year. In A. Lock (Ed.), *Action, gesture and symbol: The emergence of language*. London: Academic Press.

Turner, M. (1995). *Steretoyped behaviour in autism*. Unpublished PhD thesis, University of Cambridge, UK.

Van Valin, R. D. (1991). Functionalist linguistic theory and language acquisition. *First Language, 11*, 7–40.

Wareham, A. (1994). *Executive function and mental concepts in children with Asperger's syndrome*. Unpublished M.Phil thesis. University of Cambridge.

Wellman, H. (1991). *The child's theory of mind*. Cambridge, MA: MIT Press.

Wellman, H. M., Cross, D., & Bartsch, K. (1987). A meta-analysis of research on Stage 4 object permanence: The A-not-B error. *Monographs of the Society for Research in Child Development, 5*, (Whole number 3).

Werner, H., & Kaplan, B. (1963). *Symbol formation*. New York: John Wiley.

White, D. A., Craft, S., Hala, S., & Park, T. S. (1994). Working memory and articulation rate in children with spastic diplegic cerebral palsy. *Neuropsychology, 8*, 180–186.

Willats, P. (1984). Stages in the development of intentional search. *Developmental Psychology, 20*, 389–396.

Wimmer, H., Hogrefe, G., & Perner, J. (1988). Children's understanding of informational access as a source of knowledge. *Child Development, 59*, 386–396.

Wimmer, H., & Perner, J. (1983). Beliefs about beliefs: Representation and constraining function of wrong beliefs in young children's understanding of deception. *Cognition, 13*, 103–128.

Wimmer, H., & Weichbold, V. (1994). Children's theory of mind: Fodor's heuristics or understanding informational causation. *Cognition, 53*, 45–57.

Wittgenstein, L. (1953). *Philosophical investigations*. Oxford: Basil Blackwell.

Wittgenstein, L. (1969). *On certainty*. Oxford: Basil Blackwell.

Woodfield, A. (1993). *What do people mean when they say that a child understands beliefs*. Unpublished MS. Department of Philosophy, University of Bristol, UK.

Woodruff, G., & Premack, D. (1979). Intentional communication in the chimpanzee: The development of deception. *Cognition, 7*, 333–363.

Yirmiya, N., Sigman, M. D., Kasari, C., & Mundy, P. (1992). Empathy and cognition in high-functioning children with autism. *Child Development, 63*, 150–160.

Zaitchik, D. (1990). When representations conflict with reality: The pre-schooler's problem with false beliefs and 'false' photographs. *Cognition, 35*, 41–68.

Author index

Subject index